Discarded

University of Cincinnati
Blue Ash College Library

THE FREDERICK DOUGLASS ENCYCLOPEDIA

THE FREDERICK DOUGLASS ENCYCLOPEDIA

JULIUS E. THOMPSON, JAMES L. CONYERS, JR., AND NANCY J. DAWSON, EDITORS

GREENWOOD PRESS
An Imprint of ABC-CLIO, LLC

A B C ➤ C L I O

Santa Barbara, California • Denver, Colorado • Oxford, England

Copyright 2010 by James L. Conyers, Jr., Nancy J. Dawson, and the Estate of Julius E. Thompson

All rights reserved. No part of this publication may be reproduced, stored in a retrieval system, or transmitted, in any form or by any means, electronic, mechanical, photocopying, recording, or otherwise, except for the inclusion of brief quotations in a review, without prior permission in writing from the publisher.

Library of Congress Cataloging-in-Publication Data

The Frederick Douglass Encyclopedia / Julius E. Thompson, James L. Conyers, Jr.,
  and Nancy J. Dawson, editors.
    p. cm.
  Includes bibliographical references and index.
  ISBN 978–0–313–31988–4 (hard copy : alk. paper) — ISBN 978–0–313–38559–9 (ebook)
1. Douglass, Frederick, 1818-1895—Encyclopedias. I. Thompson, Julius Eric. II. Conyers, James L. III. Dawson, Nancy J., 1966–
E449.D75F76 2010
973.8092—dc22   2009038719

ISBN: 978–0–313–31988–4
EISBN: 978–0–313–38559–9

14 13 12 11 10   1 2 3 4 5

This book is also available on the World Wide Web as an eBook.
Visit www.abc-clio.com for details.

Greenwood Press
An Imprint of ABC-CLIO, LLC

ABC-CLIO, LLC
130 Cremona Drive, P.O. Box 1911
Santa Barbara, California 93116-1911

This book is printed on acid-free paper ∞

Manufactured in the United States of America

Contents

List of Entries — vii

Guide to Related Topics — ix

Preface — xiii

Chronology — xv

Encyclopedia — 1

Bibliography — 219

About the Editors and Contributors — 231

Index — 237

List of Entries

Abolitionists
Africa
African Aid Society (AAS)
African American Presses
African Methodist Episcopal (AME) Church
Allen, Richard (1760–1831)
American Colonization Society (ACS)
Anthony, Susan B. (1820–1906)
Artistic Representations
Bailey, Harriet (1792–1825)
Black Codes
Black Existentialism
British Antislavery Movement
Catholicism
Childhood
Christianity
Civil Rights Acts
Cleveland, Stephen Grover (1837–1908)
Compromise of 1850
Crummell, Alexander (1819–1898)
Davis, Jefferson (1808–1889)
Douglass, Annie (1849–1860)
Douglass, Frederick, Jr. (1842–1892)
Douglass, Helen Pitts (1838–1903)
Douglass, Lewis Henry (1840–1908)
Douglass Sprague, Rosetta (1839–1906)
Emancipation of the West Indies
Emancipation Proclamation
Emerson, Ralph Waldo (1803–1882)
England
European Lecture Circuit (1845–1847)
Fifteenth Amendment
Fifty-fourth Regiment of Massachusetts Volunteer Infantry
Freedman's Savings and Trust Company (Freedman's Bank)
Fugitive Slave Act
Garnet, Henry Highland (1815–1882)
Garrison, William Lloyd (1805–1879)
German Enlightenment
Grandfather Clause
Great Britain
Greeley, Horace (1811–1872)
Greener, Richard T. (1844–1922)
Grimke, Angelina Emily (1805–1879)
Grimke, Francis J. (1850–1937)
Harpers Ferry
Hughes, Langston (1902–1967)
Imperialism in the Caribbean
Industrial Education
Jim Crow Laws
Joint Committee of Fifteen
Kansas-Nebraska Act
Ku Klux Klan (KKK)
Liberator
Lincoln, Abraham (1809–1865)
Lincoln, Mary Todd (1818–1882)
Longfellow, Henry Wadsworth (1807–1882)

Louisiana

L'Ouverture, Toussaint François Dominique (1743–1803)

Lynchings, 1882–1895

Manifest Destiny

Maryland

Massachusetts

Massachusetts Anti-Slavery Society (MASS)

Methodism

Mississippi

Missouri Compromise of 1820

Murray-Douglass, Anna (1813–1882)

My Bondage and My Freedom

NAACP (National Association for the Advancement of Colored People)

Narrative of the Life of Frederick Douglass

National American Woman Suffrage Association (NAWSA)

National Anti-Slavery Standard

Native Americans

Nell, William Cooper (1816–1874)

New England

North Star

Notes on America

"Nuestra América"

Pennington, James William Charles (1807–1870)

Plessy vs. Ferguson

Recorder of Deeds

Republican Party

Rhetorical Techniques

Rochester, New York

Seneca Falls Convention

Sherman, William T. (1820–1891)

South Carolina

Sumner, Charles (1811–1874)

Talbot County, Maryland

Truth, Sojourner (1797–1883)

Tubman, Harriet (1820–1913)

Turner, Nat (1800–1831)

U.S. Senate

U.S. Supreme Court

Vesey, Denmark (1767–1822)

Washington, Booker T. (1856–1915)

Washington, D.C.

Webster, Daniel (1782–1852)

Wells-Barnett, Ida B. (1862–1931)

West Point

"What to the Slave is Your Fourth of July? (The Meaning of July Fourth for the Negro)"

Women's Suffrage

World's Columbian Exposition (Chicago, 1893)

Guide to Related Topics

Abolitionism and Civil Rights:
Abolitionists
Grimke, Angelina Emily
Massachusetts Anti-Slavery Society (MASS)
Nell, William Cooper
Sumner, Charles
Truth, Sojourner
Tubman, Harriet

Art:
Artistic Representations

Biography:
Childhood
Maryland
My Bondage and My Freedom
Narrative of the Life of Frederick Douglass

Civil/Human Rights:
NAACP (National Association for the Advancement of Colored People)
Nell, William Cooper

Civil War:
Abolitionists
Davis, Jefferson
Emancipation Proclamation
Fifty-fourth Regiment of Massachusetts Volunteer Infantry
Fugitive Slave Act
Harpers Ferry
Lincoln, Abraham
Sherman, William T.
South Carolina

Clergy/Ministers:
Allen, Richard
Garnet, Henry Highland
Grimke, Francis J.
Pennington, James William Charles
Tubman, Harriet
Turner, Nat
Vesey, Denmark

Education:
Industrial Education
Washington, Booker T.
West Point

Emancipation:
Emancipation Proclamation

Emigration:
American Colonization Society (ACS)
Crummell, Alexander

Family:
Bailey, Harriet
Douglass, Annie
Douglass, Frederick, Jr.
Douglass, Helen Pitts
Douglass, Lewis Henry
Douglass Sprague, Rosetta
Murray-Douglass, Anna

Geopolitics:
Africa
Emancipation of the West Indies
England
Great Britain
Imperialism in the Caribbean

Louisiana
L'Ouverture, Toussaint François Dominique
New England
"Nuestra América"
Rochester, New York
Washington, D.C.

Heritage:
Africa

Imperialism:
Emancipation of the West Indies
Imperialism in the Caribbean
L'Ouverture, Toussaint François Dominique
Manifest Destiny
"Nuestra América"
World's Columbian Exposition (Chicago, 1893)

Journalism:
African American Presses
Greeley, Horace
Wells-Barnett, Ida B.

Lectures:
England
European Lecture Circuit

Legislation/Case Law:
Black Codes
Civil Rights Acts
Compromise of 1850
Emancipation Proclamation
Fifteenth Amendment
Fugitive Slave Act
Grandfather Clause
Jim Crow Laws
Kansas-Nebraska Act
Missouri Compromise of 1820
Plessy vs. Ferguson

Literature:
My Bondage and My Freedom
Narrative of the Life of Frederick Douglass
Notes on America

Movements:
Abolitionists
African Aid Society (AAS)
American Colonization Society (ACS)
British Antislavery Movement
Massachusetts Anti-Slavery Society (MASS)
National American Woman Suffrage Association (NAWSA)

Newspapers/Journals:
Liberator
National Anti-Slavery Standard
North Star

Philosophy:
Black Existentialism
Emerson, Ralph Waldo
German Enlightenment
Greener, Richard T.
Vesey, Denmark

Poetry:
Emerson, Ralph Waldo
Hughes, Langston
Longfellow, Henry Wadsworth

Politics:
Joint Committee of Fifteen
Recorder of Deeds
Republican Party
Sumner, Charles
U.S. Senate
U.S. Supreme Court
Webster, Daniel
World's Columbian Exposition (Chicago, 1893)

Presidents/Wives:
Cleveland, Stephen Grover
Davis, Jefferson
Lincoln, Abraham
Lincoln, Mary Todd

Racism:
Black Codes
Jim Crow Laws

Ku Klux Klan (KKK)
Lynchings, 1882–1895

Reconstruction:
Anthony, Susan B.
Black Codes
Freedman's Savings and Trust Company (Freedman's Bank)
Grandfather Clause
Joint Committee of Fifteen
Ku Klux Klan (KKK)
Lynchings, 1882–1895

Religion:
African Aid Society
African Methodist Episcopal (AME) Church
Allen, Richard
Catholicism
Christianity
Methodism

Slavery:
Abolitionists
Compromise of 1850
Emancipation of the West Indies
Fugitive Slave Act
Kansas-Nebraska Act
L'Ouverture, Toussaint François Dominique
Mississippi
Missouri Compromise of 1820
Native Americans
Notes on America
U.S. Supreme Court

Speeches:
Rhetorical Techniques
"What to the Slave is Your Fourth of July? (The Meaning of July Fourth for the Negro)"

States:
Louisiana
Maryland
Massachusetts
Mississippi
Rochester, New York
South Carolina
Talbot County, Maryland
Washington, D.C.

Suffrage:
Anthony, Susan B.
National American Woman Suffrage Association (NAWSA)
Seneca Falls Convention
Tubman, Harriet
Women's Suffrage

Preface

This reference work, *The Frederick Douglass Encyclopedia*, seeks to place the achievements, contributions, and the lifelong body of work of the leading African American activist and abolitionist of the nineteenth century before contemporary students, scholars, and the general public. It is a work six years in the making and represents the efforts of over a hundred scholars committed to highlighting Douglass's career as well as the wide range of individuals, groups, and public issues with which he associated. This book presents a lifetime (1817–1895) of serious work and efforts in the human struggle to fight the injustices of American slavery, racism, and discrimination against women, free blacks, and Native Americans.

Clearly, when viewed against the background of the long difficult human journey from 1800 to 1899, Douglass continues to stand as a giant of his era. In the long memory of African Americans and Americans from this same period, only the contributions from **Harriet Tubman** (1820–1913), **Sojourner Truth** (1791–1883), and Frances Ellen Watkins Harper (1825–1911), might compare to Douglass's historical contributions to the advancement of African American people and to the reform of American society in the nineteenth century. The poet Robert Hayden (1913–1980) reminds us in the lines from his poem, "Frederick Douglass":

> When it is finally ours, this freedom, this liberty, this beautiful and terrible thing,
> needful to man as air...

Douglass is central to the collective struggle and story of the black freedom movement in the nineteenth century. It is the hope of the editors and contributors to this reference work that contemporary students will find this volume an especially useful tool in understanding Frederick Douglass's place in African American and American history. Douglass's status is secure as a prominent internationally-known human rights advocate based on his decades-long work advancing the human experience from one generation to the next. Indeed, his body of work challenges contemporary students and the lay public alike to reach out and promote freedom, justice, and equality in this twenty-first century. As William S. McFeely locates Douglass in *Frederick Douglass* (1991), we are reminded that Douglass was "an inspired leader in the struggle to transcend the limitations of bondage and race" placed on him by the confines of a cruel and terror-filled period in American history: the late period of African American slavery and the Emancipation Era which followed. Frederick Douglass continues to influence the modern black struggle for the triumph of freedom in yet another age and period of American history.

Further Reading

Hayden, Robert. "Frederick Douglass," in Robert Hayden, *Collected Poems*, Robert Hayden, Frederick Glaysher, ed. New York: Liveright Publishing Corp, 1985, 62. Also see Jerry W. Ward, Jr., ed., *Trouble the Water: 250 Years of African American Poetry*. New York: Penguin Books, 1997, 150.

Martin, Waldo E., Jr. *The Mind of Frederick Douglass*. Chapel Hill: University of North Carolina Press, 1984, 253–278.

McFeely, William S. *Frederick Douglass*. New York: W. W. Norton & Co., 1991, from the cover.

Quarles, Benjamin. *Frederick Douglass*. New York: Atheneum, 1968.

Chronology

1817	Born as Frederick Bailey on the Eastern Shore of Maryland; estimated birthday of Douglass as February 14th.
1826	Transported to Baltimore by his owner's son.
1836	On January 1, Bailey makes a resolution that he will be free by the end of the year. He plans an escape. But early in April he is jailed after his plan is discovered.
1838	Liberate himself to New Bedford, MA; changes his name to Frederick Douglass.
1839	Marries Anna Murray.
1841	Delivers a speech in Nantucket, Massachusetts, on antislavery.
1842	Makes his first appearance in print, agitating for freedom for an enslaved African American named George Latimer.
1845	Writes his autobiography, titled THE LIFE OF FREDERICK DOUGLASS, AN AMERICAN SLAVE WRITTEN BY HIMSELF.
1847	Establishes the newspaper the *North Star*.
1848	Advocates for women's rights.
1848	In September, delegates meet in Cleveland, Ohio, to select Douglass as President of the National Negro Convention.
1850	The Fugitive Slave Law is passed.
1850	Douglass supports John Brown.
1852	Delivers Fourth of July oration, "The Meaning of July Fourth for the Negro," at Corinthian Hall in Rochester, New York.
1853	Becomes the first African American to write a short story published by an African American.
1855	Becomes the first African nominated as a candidate by the Liberty Party for secretary of state.
1855	Publishes his second autobiography, MY BONDAGE AND MY FREEDOM.
1859	Moves to Canada and England to avoid being implicated as an accessory to the Harpers Ferry Raid.
1863	Serves as an advisor to President Abraham Lincoln in signing the Emancipation Proclamation.

1863	Recruited for the Massachusetts Fifty-fourth Regiment of the United States Army.
1865	Edits the newspaper the *New National Era*.
1871	Appointed as Assistant Secretary of the Santo Domingo Commission.
1872	Nominated as a vice presidential candidate by the Woman Suffrage Association-Equal Rights Party.
1874	Appointed president of Freedmen's Savings Bank.
1877	Appointed U.S. Marshal for the District of Columbia.
1881	Appointed by President Ulysses Grant as Recorder of Deeds.
1884	Married Helen Pitts.
1886	Traveled abroad to Europe and Africa.
1888	Becomes the first African American to be nominated as presidential candidate; he receives one vote.
1889	Appointed as Minister to Haiti.
1895	February 20th Douglass passes away in Washington, D.C.

A

Abolitionists

Frederick Douglass was the primary symbol and spokesman for this movement of nineteenth-century antislavery reformists from the late 1830s until the end of the Civil War.

> As a former slave and as the most prominent African American abolitionist, Douglass agitated on behalf of all those enslaved. By his example and through his antislavery speeches, his newspaper columns, and two autobiographies published before the war, he argued for the immediate end of slavery. He tied slavery in the South to racism in the North and insisted on slavery's abolishment as the means for all African Americans becoming full and equal citizens in the United States.

Douglass's initiation into abolitionism began in 1839, a few months after he escaped from slavery in **Maryland** and moved to New Bedford, **Massachusetts**. In New Bedford, he learned about the antislavery movement when he accepted a subscription to William Lloyd Garrison's *Liberator* and after hearing Garrison's address at an antislavery meeting. From Garrison, he learned that abolitionists associated the freedom of enslaved persons and anti-racism with the will of God.

Douglass's career as an abolitionist agitator began in the summer of 1841 when he attended an antislavery meeting in Nantucket, Massachusetts, and told the audience of his experiences in bondage. Garrison was impressed with Douglass and recognized that the fugitive slave would have a powerful impact on the abolitionist movement by contradicting the pro-slavery argument that African Americans were inherently unfit for freedom. Garrison hired Douglass as an antislavery agent for the **Massachusetts Anti-Slavery Society (MASS)** to tour Northern American states describing slavery's degradations.

From his experiences as an antislavery agent in the North, Douglass started connecting slavery to racial prejudice against African Americans. When traveling to different towns to speak, he experienced the humiliation of **Jim Crow** racism on trains and ferries and at hotels. He realized that the discrimination free blacks suffered in the North was because of their association, based on skin color, with the majority of Southern blacks living in bondage. The American color caste system defined the free blacks living in the North as an underclass by limiting or denying them economic and civil rights. The substandard condition in which most of them thus lived exemplified for pro-slavery supporters why Southern blacks should never be free.

In his antislavery speeches, Douglass argued that if the economic and civil conditions of African Americans in the North were improved, then it would undercut the pro-slavery argument that freed slaves would be a burden on American society. And, because of racial prejudice due to slavery, it was necessary to abolish bondage before Northern blacks would receive equal treatment. The fight to end slavery was linked to the broader issue of recognizing the equal humanity of all African Americans. Thus he began agitating against laws and customs that privileged whiteness. For example, he campaigned successfully against the 1841 proposed Rhode Island State Constitution which attempted to entrench white republicanism by stating that only white males should have suffrage rights.

From 1846 to 1848, Douglass was in **Great Britain** urging Britons to stop their support of American slavery. His speeches there embarrassed the South by focusing on the contradictions between America's espousal of liberty and Christianity and the conditions in which enslaved Southerners were forced to live. He urged British Christian denominations to stop supporting churches that buttressed the slaveholding South.

When Douglass returned to the United States, he established his own antislavery newspaper in **Rochester, New York**, the *North Star*, from which he articulated abolitionist strategy. British abolitionists had encouraged him to take more of a leadership role in the movement. He hoped his prominent position as editor would eliminate the prejudice of Americans who believed that African Americans lacked the intellectual capacity to manage a newspaper. He argued in his columns that the solution to ending slavery and racial prejudice was the passage of legislation entitling black men to civil, political, and social equality. Through the *North Star*, he influenced political discourse on antislavery, since prominent politicians like William Seward and Salmon P. Chase were subscribers. By publishing his paper, Douglass was striking out for independence from Garrison and the MASS to become a spokesman, as opposed to an agent, in the abolitionist movement.

Douglass's antislavery philosophy began to diverge from Garrison's. As an agent, Douglass had chafed under the racism of white abolitionists who expected him to defer to their leadership. What terminated their relationship, however, was the issue of whether politics was an appropriate means for ending slavery. Garrison had held that since the Constitution was an immoral, pro-slavery document, abolitionists should try to persuade Northerners to secede from the South and found a new country free from the taint of slavery. Since America as constituted was immoral, it was wrong for Christians to participate in politics by voting. Garrison opposed any form of political or armed resistance to achieve emancipation.

After moving to Rochester, Douglass began corresponding with antislavery philanthropist Gerrit Smith, who would influence Douglass gradually to accept the doctrine that the Constitution was antislavery. Historian David Blight describes Smith as Douglass's ideological father for the impact he had on Douglass's approach to abolitionism until the Civil War. Smith's constitutional position was based on lawyer Salmon P. Chase's controversial argument that the founding fathers had intended to do away with slavery, and that slavery, as a creation of federal law, could also be abolished by law. According to this doctrine, the duty of abolitionists was to restrict slavery, especially in the Western territories, until they could encourage state governments to emancipate their enslaved populations. This doctrine of nonextensionism became the basis of the **Republican Party**'s platform.

By the late 1840s, Douglass rejected the Garrisonian approach that the North should secede from the Union, a situation that would not have benefited the enslaved population of the South. In 1848, Douglass became a "voting abolitionist" and started agitating for a legal and political solution to ending slavery. After he turned against Garrison's disunionist doctrine, New England abolitionists regarded him as an apostate.

Though he was most in sympathy with the Liberty Party, an abolitionist party aligned with Smith, he endorsed the nonextensionist Free Soil Party in the 1848 election because it had broader appeal among the electorate. Though Douglass did not support the principle of "Free Soil," which favored keeping enslaved persons out of the Western territories, his endorsement of this party was an indication that he was prepared to support any political means for limiting slavery.

In the national debates of the 1850s over the extension of slavery, Douglass was the representative of voiceless and enslaved African Americans. He was the predominant spokesman for the case that the destiny of the nation was tied to African Americans achieving emancipation and civil rights. After the **U.S. Senate** passed the stricter **Fugitive Slave Act** in 1850, Douglass argued that slavery was a state of war. He also endorsed slaves' use of violence to rebel against the white South. Douglass himself used illegal means to defeat slavery when he turned his Rochester farm into an underground railroad station that helped fugitive slaves escape to Canada.

From 1851, Douglass expressed his more radical approach to abolitionism as editor of the new journal, *Frederick Douglass's Paper*. This paper endorsed Smith's National Liberty Party, which called for armed rebellion to fight slavery. Douglass had come to fully embrace the Smith-Chase doctrine that slavery was illegal and that the federal government had the power to abolish it anywhere.

To win support for the nonextensionist politics, Douglass began linking slave power—the disproportionate power that pro-slavery Southerners had in politics and the courts—to issues that restricted the rights of whites. Douglass recognized that the more often the majority of white Northerners believed slave power threatened their rights, the more they would perceive the struggle against the slaveholding South as irrepressible and thus be prepared for the ultimate confrontation over slavery. Douglass hoped these debates would force whites to think about the humanity of enslaved African Americans. From 1854, Douglass believed it was possible for a broad coalition of whites to work together with radical abolitionists in an umbrella political organization like the Republican Party to undermine slavery.

While he endorsed political parties with broad appeal for expediency, his evolving abolitionist philosophy became more radical. Douglass's friendship with Smith influenced his endorsement of what John Stauffer calls "Bible politics." Bible politics found expression in the Radical Abolition Party launched by Smith in 1855. Douglass, from his introduction to abolitionism, had regarded the antislavery struggle in millennialist terms whereby the forces of good and evil would struggle until the end of slavery and racial discrimination. The Radical Abolitionist Party was the first to argue that idea, based on slavery itself being a state of war against slaveholders. At the party's inaugural convention, Douglass asked for donations to purchase firearms so that **John Brown** and his sons could fight to keep Kansas free. In 1855, the Radical Abolition and National Liberty Parties nominated Douglass for the office of

Secretary of State of New York, making him the first African American nominated for political office.

The most controversial chapter of Douglass's antislavery career was the extent of his involvement in John Brown's attack on the federal arsenal at **Harpers Ferry**. Since 1847, Douglass had supported Brown's earlier proposals to build an armed force of fugitive slaves which would free enslaved Southerners. Brown wrote his constitution for the proposed state of fugitive slaves to be located in the Appalachian Mountains while staying in Douglass's Rochester home. Just before the attack on Harpers Ferry, Douglass met with Brown in Chambersville, Pennsylvania, where he brought Brown money and a comrade, Shields Green, a fugitive slave who would be killed in the raid. Douglass himself did not join in the attack because he believed it was too quixotic to succeed. However, he was implicated in the plot when Brown was arrested because Brown had in his possession a letter written by Douglass.

After the South seceded, Douglass agitated that the Civil War be turned into an abolitionist war, by which the fate of the nation would be linked to winning emancipation and full citizenship rights for African Americans. Through speeches and column-writing, and in two meetings with President **Abraham Lincoln**, Douglass urged that African Americans be allowed to serve in the Union Army and that they receive equal treatment to establish an example for a just compensation for blacks after the war. By the fall of 1864, when it appeared that the war would fulfill what, for Douglass, was its millennialist purpose of ridding the nation of the sin of slavery, he urged an abolitionist peace by which blacks would achieve citizenship rights, suffrage, and an end to all racial discrimination. His proposals were adopted by Radical Republicans who won passage for the Fourteenth and **Fifteenth Amendment**s, which were intended to guarantee civil rights and suffrage to protect black freedom.

Further Reading

Douglass, Frederick. *Life and Times of Frederick Douglass 1818–1895*. Hartford, Conn.: Park Publishing Co., 1888.

McFeely, William S. *Frederick Douglass*. New York: W. W. Norton & Co., 1991.

Stauffer, John. *The Black Hearts of Men: Radical Abolitionist and the Transformation of Race*. Cambridge, Mass: Harvard University Press, 2002.

—*Oleta Prinsloo*

Africa

In the long memory of African Americans, Africa is an iconic symbol of tradition and lost heritage. Their view of this ancient continent as an historic ancestral home creates ambivalence toward its significance in the lives and futures of African Americans. Black poets across the centuries frequently have reflected on the central need of Africa in black Americans' lives.

Such declarations by black poets point to the historical, cultural, and psychological needs for Africa in the lives of the African American people across time and space. Black poets remind African Americans of their common historical experiences and how the black community has had to contend with racism, imperialism, oppression, slavery, and segregation for centuries.

By the nineteenth century, some pro-African consciousness did exist among such black leaders as Martin Delany (1812–1885), Paul Cuffe (1759–1817), George Washington Williams (1849–1891), and Edward Blyden (1832–1912). Some among this group believed that blacks in America had to seriously consider a return to Africa as the best solution for the crisis facing them in nineteenth-century America, where a majority of blacks were held in bondage.

How did "the most famous black person in the world," Frederick Douglass, respond to the meaning of Africa for black people in nineteenth-century America? Douglass believed the central issue for African Americans was not when they would leave the country, but, rather, when they would achieve equal citizenship rights with all other Americans. He felt that this task was their greatest struggle and their chief concern. Douglass believed that blacks had to protect the right to vote. Thus, Douglass throughout his career was opposed to migration to Africa, yet he appreciated the historic importance of Africa to black Americans and the contributions of African peoples in world history, especially Egypt and Ghana. However, he does not appear to have been willing to extend his own African consciousness much beyond this position. Like many in his generation, Douglass absorbed the white Western world's stereotypes of Africans and does not appear to have placed much importance on Africans' lives, cultures, histories, and impact of geography on African peoples across the African continent. This perspective is indicative of typical black identity issues which faced the black community.

This was a major concern for blacks both on the continent of Africa and throughout the world. All of them had to contend with the effects of European underdevelopment of the African continent, including the forced mass migration of millions of Africans away from the continent across five centuries and the deaths by slavery of millions more in Africa, on the Middle Passage, and in the New World. Collectively, these events helped to destroy large aspects of the social, political, economical, cultural, and psychological wellbeing of the global African community.

There was a strong connection between the freedom struggles in Africa, in America, and elsewhere during Douglass's years as a black leader. As historian John Henrik Clarke (1915–1998), reminds us, "Frederick Douglass was the noblest of all Americans. This great abolitionist's civil rights views are as valid today as they were a century ago."

Further Reading

Blight, David W., ed. *Narrative of the Life of Frederick Douglass.* New York: Bedford/St. Martin's, 1993, 16.

Clarke, John Henrik. *Africans at the Crossroads: Notes For An African World Revolution.* Trenton, N.J.: Africa World Press, 1991.

———. *African people in World History.* Baltimore: Black Classic Press, 1993.

Douglass, Frederick. *Life and Times of Frederick Douglass.* New York: Collier Books, 1969.

Harris, Joseph E. *Africans and Their History.* New York: New American Library, 1987.

Martin, Waldo E., Jr. *The Mind of Frederick Douglass*. Chapel Hill: The University of North Carolina Press, 1984.

Sundquist, Eric J., ed. *Frederick Douglass: New Literary and Historical Essays*. New York: Cambridge University Press, 1990.

Thompson, Julius E. *Hopes Tied Up In Promises: Poems*. Philadelphia: Dorrance & Co., 1970. (Song of Innocence reprinted by permission of Julius E. Thompson, ca. 1970)

Ward, Jerry W., Jr., ed. *Trouble the Water: 250 Years of African-American Poetry*. New York: New American Library, 1997.

—*Julius E. Thompson*

African Aid Society (AAS)

The African Aid Society (AAS) was a British organization advocating for legal commerce with **Africa**. The AAS began in **Great Britain** on July 17, 1860, as the brainchild of Reverend Theodore Bourne, then the corresponding secretary of the African Civilization Society (ACS) which had been founded in 1858. In extending the agenda of the African Civilization Society beyond the horizons of emigration, Bourne suggested early on that the purpose of the AAS would be promoting Christian civilization in Africa and instructing the people there in both basic and technologically advanced farming theory and skills. The chairman of the AAS, Lord Randolph Churchill, proposed the nascent agenda of the society as a joint-stock company. With proposed branches of the AAS all over Great Britain to aid the ACS, the AAS represented a systematic organizational gathering of prominent British businessmen and philanthropists looking to invest in economic ventures in West Africa. To reduce economic uncertainties provoked by the instability of slavery in the Southern United States in the 1850s and to maximize long-term security of cotton exports to British markets, the AAS was a new and experimental entity uniquely designed to support persons and institutions willing to facilitate the opening up of the African continent to "legitimate commerce."

The understanding of political and historical events in the United States, especially those of the recent past in the 1850s after the passage of the **Fugitive Slave Act** (1850), convinced some African Americans to develop an emigration exposition as a rational course of action. Henry Highland Garnett and Martin R. Delany were two of the most prominent African American abolitionists interested in defining both the general principles and concrete details of emigration. For this reason, both Garnett and Delany eventually became involved in the efforts of the AAS as a means to advance their objectives. Henry Highland Garnett realized the great economic strength of the South that stemmed from slave-grown goods, and he consistently emphasized and supported creative solutions to undermine this oppressive economic enterprise. In his search for solutions, Garnet became an avid advocate of what came to be known as the Free Produce movement, which focused on the development of alternative markets in Africa and the West Indies to produce cotton and other slave-grown goods with free labor which would completely destroy the institution of slavery.

As the president of the ACS, Garnet forthrightly asked Frederick Douglass to explain his opposition to a movement that simply promoted agriculture, lawful trade, and commerce in Africa. Douglass argued that the ACS was a diversionary effort akin to the American Colonization Society that perpetuated the mistaken notion of Africa, and not America, as the true home of the Negro. Douglass was unconvinced that living and working in Africa would appreciably be more effective in abolishing the slave trade because the "savage chiefs" in West Africa were little different than slave traders in America in terms of morality and economic interests. In countering the argument that the cultivation of cotton in Africa would undermine slavery in the United States, Douglass asserted that slave labor was not limited to cotton production, but could be used to produce anything. Douglass argued that producing cotton in Africa would have no impact on the "Cotton Kingdom" in America. As a private venture, Douglass expressed no opposition to the organizational ambitions of the ACS and AAS, but as public ventures soliciting funds and seeking to recruit thousands, they could not be supported. Douglass believed that colonization and emigration schemes were pessimistic solutions to the problems of slavery that could never be applied to alleviating the conditions of four million slaves. He felt that optimal solutions must address the immediate needs and realities of the slave population within the context of American constitutional and democratic principles. As a prominent argument against emigration and organizations such as the AAS, Douglass emphasized the inherent and unique advantages that African Americans had from being exposed to and absorbing the enlightened ideas, information, and technological skills of a powerful American civilization that could elevate and potentially improve the lives of slaves in ways that separatist schemes of emigration never could.

Douglass also critiqued the efforts of his former coeditor of the *North Star*, Martin R. Delany. As head of the upstart Niger Valley Exploration Party, Delany traveled to Yorubaland in West Africa in 1859 where he personally conducted investigations, gathered facts, examined evidence, and eventually signed a treaty with an African chief of Abeokuta in hopes of establishing a colony that would settle skilled African Americans. Delany envisioned a harmonious economic coexistence between the colonists, British capitalists, and African landowners with complete equity in profit-sharing. Upon returning from Yorubaland, Delany distinguished himself on the lecture circuit in Great Britain in 1860 by sharing his findings and actively soliciting financial support for his plans. His efforts resulted in a promise of monetary support by the AAS to transport blacks from the United States and Canada to Yorubaland. In responding to Delany's plans, Douglass felt vindicated when Delany did not succeed in promoting cotton production in Yorubaland as a legitimate means to end slavery.

With the coming of the Civil War, Delany and Garnet, like Douglass, all recognized the immediate moment as an important turning point having the potential to completely free the slaves and shift focus away from agendas promoted by the AAS. Some of the naïve assumptions of Garnett and Delany regarding British economic interests in West Africa were quickly revealed as Great Britain and the AAS fomented successful efforts to occupy Lagos in 1861, convincing the African chief to repeal the treaty with Delany and thus laying the foundation for British colonialism. The AAS would continue to help promote British colonial interests throughout the nineteenth century through its organ, the *African Times*.

Further Reading

Blackett, R. J. *Building an Anti-Slavery Wall: Black Americans in the Atlantic Abolitionist Movement, 1830–1860*. Baton Rouge: Louisiana State University Press, 1983.

Foner, Philip, ed. *The Life and Writings of Frederick Douglass*. New York: International Publishers, 1950.

Griffith, Cyril E. *The African Dream: Martin R. Delany and the Emergence of Pan-African Thought*. University Park: Pennsylvania State University Press, 1975.

—*Mario H. Beatty*

African American Presses

In struggling to advance African American people, black publishers and journalists established over 40 black-owned publications in the United States between 1827 and 1860. This occurred during the height of American slavery and the struggles of free blacks to expand their rights and opportunities in this country. Frederick Douglass was certainly a major figure among the dozens of black press personalities who emerged in this 33 year period, all of whom made sacrifices to help develop the black press for their communities. The contributions of the black press for this era are historic in nature and defined the challenges which faced this generation of African Americans.

Some early black papers in this country were the *Weekly Advocate*, New York City, 1847, edited by Willis A. Hodgen; the **North Star**, Rochester, New York, 1847, edited by Frederick Douglass (later renamed *Frederick Douglass's Paper* after merging with the *Liberty Party Paper*, in 1851); the *Pittsburgh Mystery*, 1843–1847, edited by Martin R. Delany; and the *Mirror of Liberty*, a quarterly magazine, New York City, 1847–1849, edited by David Ruggles. The black church was also influential in the early development of the black press. The **African Methodist Episcopal Church** established the *Christian Herald*, a weekly magazine, in 1847; the name was changed in 1852 to the *Christian Recorder*.

The early black press in the United States emphasized three key themes: the abolition of slavery; an end to discrimination, or second-class citizenship rights, for free blacks, especially in the areas of voting, public education, and employment; and the reformation of American society. Each editor of a black press organ approached these issues from their own personal perspectives, but the common objective remained to secure freedom for all African Americans and the advancement of all black people in the United States.

Yet the black press faced many difficult problems during the antebellum period. First, most African Americans were poor, and lacking money as well as financial backing created economic hardships for many black press organs. Secondly, most black papers lacked enough staff members to produce a newspaper. In spite of these chronic burdens, there was some early support for the black press from such important groups and individuals as the abolitionist movement, free blacks, the personal resources of editors, advertisements, copies of papers sold on the streets, and subscriptions sold in Europe among antislavery supporters. Thus, although many papers were short-lived, others survived for many years, and all contributed to giving black expression global visibility.

During this period, Frederick Douglass's journalism carried on the tradition in which African Americans and other supporters of **abolition** sought media expression outside mainstream newspapers. This tradition had begun in 1827 as John B. Russwurm and Reverend Samuel Cornish established the first newspaper published by African Americans in the United States, *Freedom's Journal* (Cornish changed the name to *Rights of All* in May 1829). "We wish to plead our own cause," they wrote, "too long have others spoken for us." Frederick Douglass created three black press organs to reach the public over a 12-year period from 1847 to 1859. His work was reflected in the *North Star* (1847–1851); *Frederick Douglass's Paper* (1851 to 1859); and *Douglass's Monthly* (1859 to 1863). Douglass was perhaps the most famous and influential black journalist of his day. Like the rest of the black press, Douglass's main objective was ending American bondage in his lifetime and advancing the African American community to full and equal citizenship rights in the United States. This was the central message of the early black press in this nation, and Douglass was its chief spokesperson.

Abolitionist **William Lloyd Garrison**, a leading European-American activist, had founded his own newspaper, the *Liberator*, in 1831 with the express purpose of producing a public backlash against slavery. Douglass was employed by the *Liberator* briefly during the early 1840s before he founded the *North Star*. Garrison objected to Douglass's editorship of the *North Star*, arguing that Douglass's talent as an orator would be wasted if he used his time as a journalist. Garrison also believed that Douglass's *North Star* would compete with his *Liberator*, the *National Anti-Slavery Standard*, and Marius Robinson's antislavery *Bugle*. The split between Garrison and Douglass had ideological roots. Douglass came to believe, for example, that the U.S. Constitution could be used to support antislavery arguments, reversing his earlier stand that it was pro-slavery. Garrison, who continued to believe the Constitution was pro-slavery, demonstrated his opinion by burning copies of it in public. Douglass's change of position on the Constitution was one facet of a division that emerged in the abolitionist movement after the publication in 1846 of a book by Lysander Spooner, *The Unconstitutionality of Slavery*.

In the years after the Civil War to the end of the nineteenth century, African Americans produced several hundred black-owned publications, a great increase from the days of the early black press. Important papers during the new period included the *New Era* (1870), Washington D.C.; the *Cleveland Gazette* (1883); the *New York Age* (1887); the *Afro American* (1892), Baltimore; and others including the New Orleans *Louisianan* (1870). After Reconstruction, an era of **Jim Crow** laws and segregation settled in over the South, and Northern blacks suffered *de facto* segregation and discrimination. It was a harsh economic period too. Yet, perhaps the greatest social injustice during these decades was the **lynching** of thousands of blacks

("The Age of Lynching"), which was highlighted by the black press. The black press' coverage of social injustices was vital in the continuing struggles of African American people to overcome racism, discrimination, and inequality in society.

These were also the last years for Frederick Douglass. He continued his work with *Douglass's Monthly* (1859 to 1863) and the *New National Era* (1870 to 1873), whose central themes now shifted to securing equal citizenship rights for blacks in society; offering resistance to the domination of the white South; and seeking an end to outright mistreatment of African Americans, as demonstrated by the lynching crisis, issues of peonage, and women's suffrage. Douglass remained at the forefront of the battle on these issues until his death in 1895.

Between 1827 and 1899, African Americans created over 600 black publications in the United States. These organs were devoted to promoting a better life for black people in American society, reforming the American nation in order to live up its creeds, and the universal standards of human and civil rights which blacks believed belong to all people. Frederick Douglass, as a leader among black journalists, helped to advance these principles of the black press. Collectively, the black press carried a message of freedom, equality, and justice in its struggle to secure equal rights and quality of life for all Americans.

Further Reading

Bullock, Penelope I. *The Afro-American Press, 1838–1909*. Baton Rouge: Louisiana State University Press, 1977.

Dann, Martin E., ed. *The Black Press, 1827–1890: The Quest for National Identity*. New York: G. P. Putman's Sons, 1971.

Huton, Frankie. *The Early Black Press in America, 1827 to 1860*. Westport, Conn.: Greenwood Press, 1993.

Jacobs, Donald M., ed. *Antebellum Black Newspapers*. Westport, Conn.: Greenwood Press, 1978.

Penn, I. Garland. *The Afro-American Press and Its Editors*. Springfield, Mass.: Willey, 1891; reprint. Ed., New York: Arno Press and the New York Times, 1969.

Perry, Patsy Brewington. "Before The North Star: Frederick Douglass's Early Journalistic Career." *Phylon* 35, 1(1974): 96–107.

Pride, Armisted S. and Clint C. Wilson II. *A History of the Black Press*. Washington, D.C.: Howard University Press, 1997.

Suggs, Henry L., ed. *The Black Press in the South, 1865–1979*. Westport, Conn.: Greenwood Press, 1983.

Thompson, Julius E., "The African American Press," in Arvah E. Strickland and Robert W. Weems, Jr., eds. *The African American Experience: An Historiographical and Bibliographical Guide*. Westport, Conn.: Greenwood Press, 2001.

Woseley, Roland E. *The Black Press, U.S.A.*. Ames, Ia.: The Iowa State University Press, 1971.

—*Julius E. Thompson and Bruce E. Johansen*

African Methodist Episcopal (AME) Church

The African Methodist Episcopal church was founded by **Richard Allen** in the late eighteenth century. Richard Allen was born in Philadelphia, one of four children, in 1760. He and his family were enslaved by a Mr. Benjamin Chew who sold them when Richard was a young child to another enslaver, Stokely Sturgis, who lived near Dover, Delaware. Before he was 20, his mother and younger siblings were sold away by Sturgis. Around the same time, in 1777, he was converted to **Methodism** and began preaching to his African brethren in the clearings of the Delaware woods. Later, he would travel and preach to both black and white audiences.

Allen settled in Philadelphia in the 1780s and began organizing church meetings with other Africans in the area. At this time most churches were segregated; Africans were made to sit or stand in the back of the church or attend separate services. Because of these conditions, Allen and Absalom Jones organized a boycott in the form of a walkout. In November 1787, Richard Allen, Jones and other members were forced from their knees while praying at the front of the newly renovated St. George's Methodist Church. After this humiliating treatment, all the Africans left St. George's Methodist Church to formally organize their own body of worship, the Mother Bethel Methodist Church which voted on April 6, 1791, to become the African Methodist Episcopal (AME) Church.

Before the end of the decade (or the beginning of the nineteenth century), the African Methodist Episcopal Zionist (AMEZ) Church was founded in New York City by Reverend James Varick. This church had doctrinal and historical differences from the AME Church, but both were successful in breaking from the European-controlled Methodist churches with their racist doctrine. Douglass never became a member of the AME congregation; he was however a Methodist, and 1839 he was ordained as a preacher for the AMEZ Church.

The AME Church continued to struggle against St. George's Church and with its own low attendance and growth in Philadelphia's African American community during the early nineteenth century. Initially Richard Allen's and Absalom Jones' churches were organized as nondenominational churches, separate from the white churches of Philadelphia. They referred to themselves as the Free African Society (FAS), a *de facto* group in which Allen and Jones attempted to tend to the spiritual needs of their black congregations who were not recognized at the segregated churches. Allen was a strong Methodist and because of this, attendants of the Free African Society saw Allen and his Quaker's methods as problematic to the movement. Members desired to be spiritually fed but not religiously bound in a strict sense to either Quakerism or Methodism. Therefore, Allen was removed from the Society where Jones was left to tend to the people's needs.

Allen, however, did not give up his mission, nor did he stop his work with the Free African Society. He continued organizing with the African population of Philadelphia, and in fact was given the responsibility of finding land for the church that would be built to support the FAS community of Philadelphia. St. George's would oppose the efforts of Allen, Jones, and the FAS, but despite this opposition, St. Thomas Episcopal Church was voted into existence shortly after the turn of the century with Jones as its first priest. This was a big step toward the AME Church becoming a fully recognized institution. It would also make Jones the first black Methodist priest of the United States at that time. However, Allen's Methodist vision was not yet fully realized until 1816. Officially, St. Thomas was not Methodist; it was Episcopalian because St. Thomas's congregation voted against including Methodism as a part of their church's doctrine. This was problematic for many African Methodists of the region and was not resolved until the unification of the black Methodist churches in 1816, when the African Methodist Episcopal (AME) Church was founded and recognized as a religious institution with Richard Allen as its first bishop.

Frederick Douglass was connected to the AME Church through his writing, particularly through a family friend, Pete Humphries Clark. Clark, who was very involved in the Church, would become a great writer, publisher and speaker of the time, catching Douglass's attention. Clark founded the *Herald of Freedom*, an African news publication, which stayed in business less than four months, but the work of the *Herald* earned him a job working as secretary of the 1853 National Convention of Colored Men. He also was appointed by Douglass to work on the *Frederick Douglass's Paper*, formerly called the **North Star**. In connection to the AME Church as well, Douglass's article, "The Negro in the Present Campaign," was published in the *AME Church Review* (1892 edition).

The African Methodist Episcopal Church, like Douglass, worked against the efforts of the American Colonization Society (ACS), an organization trying to send all free Africans in America back to Africa, a practice seen by many as malevolent and futile. Douglass and members of the AME Church were more interested in staying in America and improving their lives and futures, rationalizing that as slaves, they had invested in its establishment and thus were important elements of America and its heritage. Once again, however, despite sharing the philosophy of activism with the AME Church, Douglass was not closely involved or connected with it.

Further Reading

Allen, Richard. *The Life Experience and Gospel Labors of the Rt. Rev. Richard Allen*. New York and Nashville: Abingdon Press, 1960.

Douglass, Frederick. *A Narrative in the Life of Frederick Douglass*. Oxford and New York: Oxford Press, 1999.

Meier, August, and Leon Litwack, eds. *Black Leaders in the Nineteenth Century*. University of Illinois Press: Urbana and Chicago, 1991.

—*Paul Easterling*

Allen, Richard (1760-1831)

Richard Allen, who went on to found the **African Methodist Episcopal (AME) Church,** was born in Philadelphia into bondage to a Mr. Benjamin Chew. As a child,

Allen, his parents, and four of his siblings were sold to Mr. Stokely Sturgis, who lived close to Dover, Delaware, where Allen lived until he was about 20 years old. His mother had three more children after moving to Delaware, and the four of them (mother and three children) were sold away before Allen was 20. Before Philadelphia passed the first emancipation bill in 1780, Allen was converted to **Methodism** and began his proselytizing mission. This era, the Revolutionary period of America's early history, was also characterized by evangelism and religious revival.

The American Northeast, particularly Philadelphia, Delaware, and **Maryland**, was a hotbed for American Methodist conversion. Many Methodists in the region also sought to convert Africans to Methodism. Africans in the Northeast were more attracted to Methodism not just because of the dramatic preaching style reminiscent of African communication but because the Methodists were intimately involved in the antislavery movement. Despite the fact that Allen was still in bondage at the time of his conversion, he was allowed to attend Methodist services with his family. After the American Revolution, he was able to travel as a preacher and preach to African, European, and even some **Native American** congregations in Maryland, Delaware, Pennsylvania, **South Carolina**, and New York.

After 1785, Allen settled in Philadelphia, a city with a growing African population, where he found employment and later joined St. George's Methodist Church. At this time whites did not allow Africans full access into their churches; instead Africans were forced to attend segregated services or were made to sit in the balcony. Also, Philadelphia did not have a church for the African community to meet and congregate in. Seeing this void, Allen was convinced that a separate place of worship for Africans would be the better option. Only four Africans from St. George's Methodist Church, Doras Giddings, William White, Absalom Jones, and Richard Allen, showed any desire to develop a church of their own.

Allen did not receive much initial support from the church or the community, but that would change on the famed Sunday morning of 1787 when African members of St. George's Methodist Church were instructed to sit in the newly constructed gallery which was segregated from the rest of the congregation. Jones, who initially left St. George's Church with Allen to organize an autonomous place of worship, led the black congregation of the Church to the front to pray. After being physically forced to leave by the white members of the congregation, the African members of the church and community were galvanized into organizing their own body of worship. This incident gave the African community in Philadelphia the urgency Allen and Jones needed to move Allen's plans for autonomous worship into action.

This was the beginning of the foundation of the African Methodist Episcopal (AME) Church, a very important development in African religious history in America. Further, the AME Church became institutionally recognized in 1816, a year before Frederick Douglass was born. Douglass never met Richard Allen in person, nor did he attend the AME Church. He encountered Methodism early in his life while he was enslaved by "Captain" Auld, who himself was converted. Douglass at the time hoped Auld's conversion would inspire Auld to emancipate Douglass or at least that it would make him a kinder "master." Unfortunately, this was not the case; despite the conversion Auld remained cruel toward African people.

Later in Douglass's life he would encounter Mr. Covey, a reputed "slave-breaker." The irony here is that even though Covey was a deeply religious man and a professor of religion, he felt no mercy for slaves and was especially cruel and inhumane toward them. Douglass physically fought Covey in order to maintain his humanity and self-respect. After this experience, Douglass would later remark that the religious and pious "slave masters" were the most cruel and inhumane toward African people. Despite these experiences, Douglass was ordained as a preacher in the African Methodist Episcopal Zion (AMEZ) Church, which was founded in 1796 by James Varick in New York City. Douglass did not have close ties to Allen's AME Church, though the AMEZ Church was founded under similar circumstances, and Douglass would become an important part of the church and its history.

Toward the end of Richard Allen's life, Douglass was maturing intellectually. In the 1830s when Douglass was hired out by his enslaver to work at a shipyard, he was secretly learning to read and write, away from those who considered such actions a crime. The year Allen died, 1931, Douglass graduated to reading antislavery and **abolitionist** literature. News articles that dealt with former President John Quincy Adams's petitions to Congress concerning antislavery laws particularly interested him. Despite the fact that Douglass was just a teenager when Allen passed, Douglass would honor him many years later, just before he himself died, by writing an article praising Allen and his movement in the Allen memorial edition of the *Christian Recorder*, February 22, 1894.

Further Reading

Allen, Richard. *The Life Experience and Gospel Labors of the Rt. Rev. Richard Allen*. New York and Nashville: Abingdon Press, 1960.

Douglass, Frederick. *A Narrative in the Life of Frederick Douglass*. Oxford and New York: Oxford Press, 1999.

Meier, August, and Leon Litwack, eds. *Black Leaders in the Nineteenth Century*. University of Illinois Press: Urbana and Chicago, 1991.

—*Paul Easterling*

American Colonization Society (ACS)

In 1816, around the same time of Frederick Douglass's birth in **Maryland**, Rev. Robert Finely of New Jersey established the American Colonization Society (ACS). The Society's solution for the problem of slavery in America was the emigration of America's free African population to the continent of **Africa**. Douglass had a philosophical disagreement with the American Colonization Society because he felt Africans had an investment in the United States by virtue of being an integral part of its foundation and expansion. However, there were certain groups in America who had vested interests in the emigration of the free black population. One group consisted of **abolitionists** and clergy who wanted to free African slaves and return them to Africa to civilize the Africans on the continent. Another group consisted of enslavers who feared the presence and potential power of the free African population in America. Free

Africans were thought to be "troublemakers" in the growing country, a threat to the power structure. With about 10 percent of the African population in America already free, many other groups felt that newly freed Africans would not be able to successfully integrate into American society. Others in America did not want to remove the African population because a large part of the American economy was dependent on the free African labor.

The ACS in part rode Paul Cuffe's emancipation/migration bandwagon from his 1815 voyage to Sierra Leone which transported 38 Africans back to the continent. Cuffe's efforts, however, were not based on solving the problem of slavery; rather, his efforts were based on the emancipation of Africans from the oppression of America. For him, America was the problem, not Africans. In juxtaposition, supporters of the ACS just wanted to rid themselves of the African problem in America. With that, on December 21, 1816, a group of exclusively white upper-class males including would-be Presidents James Monroe and General Andrew Jackson, Associate Justice of the United States Supreme Court Bushrod Washington, Treasury Secretary William Crawford, Senator **Daniel Webster**, and Francis Scott Key met at the Davis Hotel in Washington D.C. with Speaker of the House of Representatives Henry Clay presiding over the meeting to map out plans for the emigration of America's African population. This group constructed a constitution for the organization and began raising money. In 1817 the ACS received the support of Congress and President James Monroe (elected in 1817) in the form of $100,000.

In January 1920 on a ship named *Elizabeth*, 3 white agents of the ACS and 88 free Africans traveled to Liberia to establish a resettlement colony. The group suffered major casualties; 22 Africans and all 3 agents died from yellow fever. However, this American resettlement campaign continued to send free Africans to Liberia and eventually opened the door to enslaved Africans who had received manumission, making Liberia America's only African colony. After 1827 some enslaved Africans who were manumitted expressly for the purpose of emigration were taken to the Liberian colony. By 1830 the ACS had settled 1,420 Africans of the American Diaspora in the colony. Some slaveholding states also began to give the ACS support. For instance, Maryland, Virginia, and Kentucky had officially legislated their support for the efforts of the ACS, while other states such as North Carolina and **Mississippi** had organized their own local colonization societies.

Douglass felt that the ACS was a waste of time and energy because the majority of Africans in America did not want to leave the country for Africa; emigration, for him, was a futile endeavor that only wasted the energy, time, and money of the American people. While whites felt Africans would not be able to successfully integrate into American society and therefore should emigrate back to the continent of Africa, Douglass felt that, despite the horrors of enslavement, Africans in America could and would improve due to Western civilization, more so than if they were sent back to Africa. Contact with the white race, he believed, had done more to benefit African life in America than slavery and oppression had done to destroy African life.

Liberia was not the only place where Africans were encouraged to emigrate. Haiti, Canada, South America, Mexico, and even the American West were locations the ACS sought to transport the African American population. However, despite a population of 2 million Africans within the growing country, only 15,000 emigrated out of the United States (12,000 to Liberia). Further, many American emigration supports were discouraged by the cost of transporting millions of people to Liberia or any other place in the world. The cost of such an effort was potentially astronomical, and there were not enough supporters of the emigration idea to give it a chance of success. Due to this and the severe opposition by Europeans and Africans, the ACS and its mission were never fully realized. Through the efforts of the ACS, however, Liberia was to become one of the first republics in Africa. Ironically, Liberia would also have one of the worst civil wars on the African continent. Because Liberia was an American colony, many of the transplanted African Americans who had been sent there by the ACS on civilizing missions thought themselves to be superior to the indigenous population. These social pressures would simmer and eventually erupt into a bloody civil war in Liberia in the late twentieth century.

Further Reading

Douglass, Frederick. *A Narrative in the Life of Frederick Douglass*. Oxford and New York: Oxford Press, 1999.

Foner, Philip S., ed. *Frederick Douglass: Selected Speeches and Writings*. New York: Lawrence Hill Books, 1975.

Meier, August and Leon Litwack, eds. *Black Leaders in the Nineteenth Century*. University of Illinois Press: Urbana and Chicago, 1991.

—*Paul Easterling and Malachi Crawford*

Anthony, Susan B. (1820–1906)

Suffragist and reformer Susan B. Anthony was born the second of six children to Daniel and Lucy Read Anthony in Adams, **Massachusetts**. Daniel, a prosperous cotton mill owner and a Quaker, ensured that Susan acquired an excellent education that, with the Quaker influence, created in her a sense of social justice and equality. Daniel suffered financial reversals after the panic of 1837, so his daughters helped to save his gristmill by teaching. In 1845 Daniel used money from an inheritance of Lucy's to buy a farm in Hardscrabble, New York, near **Rochester**.

During the early to mid-1850s Rochester was a center of intense reform activity that included **abolition**, temperance, **women's suffrage** and women's rights. In Rochester, the Anthony family met and worked with Frederick Douglass, **William Lloyd Garrison**, and Amelia Bloomer. Susan met another reformer, Elizabeth Cady Stanton, who had helped organize the first Woman's Rights Convention at Seneca Falls, New York, in 1848. While both Anthony's parents and a sister attended the convention, Susan couldn't because she was teaching. Anthony and Stanton became friends and were partners in the fight for woman's suffrage for five decades.

Anthony's early reform work focused on temperance, and she was dismayed by the reluctance of men's temperance organizations to work with women. In response, Anthony helped found the Woman's State Temperance Society of New York. As her friendship with Stanton deepened, Anthony devoted more energy toward women's rights. Anthony and Stanton supported Bloomer's dress reform, even wearing the pantaloons for a time until they concluded the controversial dress distracted from their more important reform issue, the fight for women's suffrage. Anthony also worked for abolition through the American Anti-Slavery Society and formed another antislavery organization, the Women's National Loyal League. During the Civil War, Anthony and Stanton suspended women's rights reform to concentrate on the war effort and antislavery. Through the Loyal League they worked to secure 400,000 signatures to petition Congress to support the Thirteenth Amendment.

After the Civil War and with the end of slavery, the women devoted their energies toward women's suffrage. Women fully expected to be granted the franchise with freed slaves. However, the Fourteenth and **Fifteenth Amendment**s gave the vote to freed men when the word male was written for the first time into the Constitution. Some reformers, including Frederick Douglass, Henry Blackwell, and Lucy Stone believed it was imperative for African American men to gain the vote first and supported passage of the Fourteenth and Fifteenth Amendments. They supported female suffrage but thought it should come after black male suffrage. Anthony and Stanton disagreed and agitated for women to be included in the amendments and spoke against passage, and they formed a rival suffrage organization. The two groups united in 1889 to become the National American Woman Suffrage Association.

From 1868 to 1870, Anthony published the liberal weekly newspaper, the *Revolution*, which printed a variety of articles about the oppression of women. During this time Anthony helped organize the New York Working Women's Association. In 1872 Anthony led a group of women to the polls to test the right of women to vote. She was arrested two weeks later and, while awaiting trial, went on a highly publicized lecture tour. She was tried and convicted, but she refused to pay the fine and the issue was dropped. Anthony then worked tirelessly for a federal amendment granting women the franchise. With Stanton and Matilda Joslyn Gage, Anthony wrote the detailed record of the fight for the vote, *The History of Woman Suffrage* (1881–1902).

Toward the end of her life, the public, which had often been hostile toward Anthony, began to embrace her. In 1883 Anthony traveled to Europe and was amazed to find herself a celebrity. In 1888 she organized the International Council of Women. At the **World's Columbian Exposition** in 1893, Anthony spoke to huge crowds about female enfranchisement. In 1904 she traveled to Berlin and formed the International Suffrage Alliance. When she died at 86, flags flew at half-staff. 14 years later the Nineteenth Amendment gave all American women the vote and was known popularly as the Susan B. Anthony Amendment.

Further Reading

Barry, Kathleen. *Susan B. Anthony: A Biography of a Singular Feminist*. New York: New York University Press, 1988.

Kugler, Israel. *From Ladies to Women: The Organized Struggle for Woman's Rights in the Reconstruction Era*. Westport, Conn.: Greenwood Press, 1987.

Lutz, Alma. *Susan B. Anthony: Rebel, Crusader, and Humanitarian*. Boston: Beacon Press, 1959.

—*Minoa Uffelman*

Artistic Representations

Frederick Douglass has long been an inspirational artistic subject. Probably the best known images of Douglass can be found in the Library of Congress' collection, including several images of him both as a youth and an old man. These images, often used by historians, were most likely produced by **abolitionist** artists and publishers and can be found in such books as *Frederick Douglass* by Benjamin Quarles (published in 1948), and in *The Life and Writings of Frederick Douglass* by Philip S. Foner (published in 1950).

One of the earliest visual images of Douglass is an 1882 drawing (artist unknown) depicting Douglass as a child seeing his mother for the last time, a situation Douglass refers to in his ***Narrative of the Life of Frederick Douglass***. In 1883, Sarah J. Eddy produced the only formal portrait for which Douglass actually sat. Several twentieth-century artists portray Douglass as a subject of historical importance. Renowned artist Jacob Lawrence's *Frederick Douglass* series (1938–1939) presents a visual biography of Douglass in 32 panel paintings which harmonizes with Douglass's *Narrative* by creatively depicting his life as a child, a runaway slave, an abolitionist, a spokesman, a writer, a publisher, an editor, and as a diplomat.

Visual artist Charles White uses Douglass as a vivid pictorial symbol. White's creative research on Douglass results in *Frederick Douglass Lives Again* (date unknown), *Frederick Douglass* (1950), and *Contribution of the Negro to Democracy in America* (1943). White reflects Douglass as a heroic African figure. He not only celebrates Douglass as a great historical figure, but through his strong bold portrait of Douglass, he maintains Douglass's immortality as a powerful leader. For the artist, Douglass is more than a didactic visual image; he is an inspiration, hero and timeless subject.

Further Reading

Foner, Philip S. *The Life and Writings of Frederick Douglass*. Volumes I and II, New York: International Publishers, 1950.

Lawrence, Jacob. The *Frederick Douglass* and *Harriet Tubman* series of casein tempera paintings, 1938–40.

Lewis, Samella. *African American Art and Artists*. Berkeley: University of California Press, 1990.

—*Najjar Abdul-Musawwir*

A portrait of Frederick Douglass. Library of Congress, Prints and Photographs Division, LC-USZC4-3623.

B

Bailey, Harriet (1792-1825)

Frederick Douglass's mother, Harriet, was the second child of freedman Isaac and slave Betsey Bailey, owned by Aaron Anthony of **Talbot County** in **Maryland**. For most of her life she worked as a field hand and was often hired out to neighboring farms. Bailey gave birth to Douglass in 1818, her fourth of six or seven children. As was often customary in enslavement, Douglass and Bailey were separated shortly after his birth.

Much of what is known about Harriet Bailey emerges through Douglass's two autobiographies, representing for him the central injustices of enslavement: separation of families and the cruel effects of slavery on motherhood. Though raised by his maternal grandmother and amongst extended family, Douglass lamented the separation from his mother. Moreover, Douglass's inability to prove his father's identity, rumored to be that of his owner, Aaron Anthony, troubled him throughout adulthood. Though only 12 miles away from Douglass's childhood home, Bailey managed only four or five visits to see him, all of which occurred at night. The last visit remained vivid in Douglass's mind when she intervened on Douglass's behalf during a punishment inflicted by the house cook. However strained their familial relationship was due to the circumstances of slavery, Harriet Bailey in Douglass's memories proved an affectionate, caring, and dedicated mother whose literacy inspired Douglass's own quest for knowledge and racial justice. After a lengthy illness, Bailey died serving on the Holme Hill Farm (Tuckahow Creek) in late 1825 or early 1826.

Further Reading

Douglass, Frederick. *My Bondage and My Freedom*, 1855 ed. Black Rediscovery series. Philip S. Foner, ed. New York: Dover Publications, Inc., 1969.

———. *The Frederick Douglass Papers*. John R. McKivigan, John W. Blasingame, Peter P. Hinks, eds. Volume 1 "Narrative," *Series Two: Autobiographical Writings*. New Haven: Yale University Press, 1999.

McFeely, William S. *Frederick Douglass*. New York: W. W. Norton & Co., 1991.

—*Marisa J. Fuentes*

Black Codes

Statutes specifically aimed toward limiting civil rights and civil freedoms for newly freed black Americans. Black Codes were first introduced in 1865 with the ratification of new state constitutions in the former confederacy following the U.S. Civil War. These statutes defined the legal position of black Southerners, signifying efforts on the part of state legislatures to ensure that blacks would remain socially, economically, and politically inferior despite their newly-freed status. Although the statutes were inconsistent from state to state, all represented the refusal of whites to accept blacks as their equals in society, stifling the efforts of blacks to enjoy the benefits of full citizenship.

Examples of Black Codes included those established in **South Carolina** which, in ratification of its new constitution, failed to give blacks the right to vote. All other states established poll taxes that further restricted blacks from exercising the franchise. Florida explicitly declared that only white men were eligible to be elected to the State House. Statutes also restricted the liberties of blacks in issues pertaining to everyday life such as those imposed in the small town of Opelousas, Louisiana, prohibiting blacks from renting or owning homes within the town limits. Black Codes in Mississippi prohibited unemployed blacks from assembling for any purpose and levied fines for blacks who violated this statute. Individuals, both black and white, who violated these provisions were deemed vagrants. Moreover, in **Mississippi**, Black Codes restricted the rights of blacks in employment, establishing contracts for length of employment, which if terminated by blacks, would result in the forfeiture of all wages earned prior to termination of employment. Black Codes in many states did not explicitly mention race but instead addressed blacks in general terms such as those that spoke to occupations and situations that only pertain to freed blacks.

Heavily involved in the movements for **abolition, women's suffrage**, and expansion of rights and freedoms for blacks, Douglass fervidly opposed Black Codes and objected to their existence as part of the core racism in the American South, thus further challenging the structure of a country that allowed these overtly racist statutes to exist.

Further Reading

Wilson, Theodore Brantner. *The Black Codes of the South*. Tuscaloosa: University of Alabama Press, 1965.

—*Ronald Williams II*

Black Existentialism

Black Existentialism is an area of Africana thought in which Frederick Douglass is one of the canonical figures. Africana thought is also known as African diasporic thought. Africana thought includes critical studies of the ideas and problems faced by black people in the modern world. Such study also includes the concepts of race and racism. Douglass's thought is part of the African American contingent of such inquiry. Existentialism is a form of thought that explores the implications of "existence," which refers to life and emergence. The term is from the Latin expression *ex sistere*, which means to stand out, which also means to emerge. In this sense, to exist means to appear, which brings problems of visibility and invisibility, crucial to any study of the modern black experience, to the fore.

Frederick Douglass (1818–1895) was born in slavery. He lived through the horrors of the system in Maryland before standing up against a slave-breaker and eventually escaping to New York where he became one of the main spokespersons of the abolitionist movement led by **William Lloyd Garrison** (1805–1879). Douglass wrote about his experiences as a slave through three autobiographies. He went to Ireland and then on to Scotland and England at the publication of the first, ***Narrative of the Life of Frederick Douglass, an American Slave, Written By Himself*** (1845), to avoid extradition to the South under the fugitive slave laws. Given the protections afforded his book under the copyright laws of the land, he was living the ironic situation of his text having more rights than he. Douglass's speeches in Europe drew large crowds and rallied much support for the abolitionists and brought his cause to the attention of some English benefactors who paid Hugh Auld, his former owner, and thereby manumitted him and enabled him to return to the United States as a freed man. He subsequently dedicated his life to a variety of journalistic, social activist, and government service, which included his tenure as the minister-resident and consul-general to Haiti (1889–1891).

Douglass's primary contribution to Black Existentialism is the theory of freedom implicit in his narratives and his radical egalitarianism. He defended the rights of women and was a known activist in the suffragette movement. His view of freedom was articulated through several developmental stages in his narratives, many of which foreshadow what was to come in the twentieth-century reflections of W. E. B. Du Bois (1868–1963), Richard Wright (1908–1960), and Frantz Fanon (1925–1961). Douglass argued in his three biographies that the love offered by his slave mother, who risked her life to spend time with him during his infancy, kindled his sense of self-worth. His acquiring literacy later on in his youth transformed him. It made him realize that literacy was not a uniquely divine ability of whites. This reminded him of his humanity and made more intense his realization of the scale of harm done to him and many others by slavery. His masters responded by unleashing a more dehumanizing effort to affirm his bondage and thereby continue to "make" him into a slave. Although literacy offered a new understanding of slavery and freedom, Douglass also solicited the aid of supernatural forces, through the aid of a roots amulet from a fellow slave, to protect him. He eventually realized, however, that he could only claim his freedom through fighting for it, through risking his life. He resisted the slave-breaker Covey, which led to a physical altercation in which Douglass defended himself without killing the man. The situation was such that to fight Covey at all was to risk death, and it was also so in allowing Covey to live. As Paul Gilroy observed in *The Black Atlantic: Modernity and Double Consciousness*: "For [Douglass], the slave actively prefers the possibility of death to the continuing condition of inhumanity on which plantation slavery depends" (p. 63).

The battle with Covey can also be understood in existential philosophical terms. Douglass's preference for the *possibility* of death is governed by his realization of the affirmation of life. The existential paradox here is that he must be willing to die in order to live. This was not a trivial matter under legalized slavery. The fight held within it a form of infinite resignation, where he had every reason to believe that his life was over while he was fighting for its continuation. The conflict was liberating. From that moment onward he was able to plot his path to liberty, although he searched for his freedom for the rest of his life. In Douglass's experiences, the distinction between liberty and freedom was crucial: The former was the absence of an impediment; the latter required the conviction of his self-worth, responsibility, and dignity in the face of death. Others could enable his liberty, as the patrons who manumitted Douglass attested, but only he could secure his freedom. In Douglass's view, seizing one's freedom is something one is responsible for alone. Liberty is external; freedom is internal and constitutive of what one is or wishes to become.

Douglass's portrait of his understanding of freedom as a movement from childhood love to the impact of literacy to the struggle for recognition in the face of death has had an impact on many Africana existential thinkers. Du Bois, another canonical figure, explored the movements in the struggle for recognition as a lived experience of conflicting duality. The black American, in Du Bois's view, sees him- or herself through the eyes of white America as in contradiction with America. This conflict takes the form of a double consciousness and political twoness. The former is awareness of dual perspectives; the latter is the notion that a real American must be white, or at least not black. The consequence, Du Bois further argued, is that the existential condition of the black American becomes one of being a problem instead of living with problems. As a problem, the conflict becomes one in which the society functions as Covey.

Douglass's insight on the importance of resistance is also taken up in the thought of one of the most influential existential novelists of the twentieth century: Richard Wright. Wright presents the black experience as what existentialists such as Jean-Paul Sartre and Simone de Beauvoir call a *situation*, which refers to what emerges from human encounters, which they describe as a conflict of freedoms. Such encounters often generate unintended meanings. In Wright's novel *Native Son*, the protagonist Bigger Thomas finds himself "in a situation," when he helps his employer's drunken daughter to her bedroom after chauffeuring her and her boyfriend round town and realizes that he, with her in his arms, was at risk of being "discovered." Wright explores the relationship between choice and options for those who are denied normality in the modern world, who continuously find themselves in "situations" they would rather avoid, a situation that Abdul Jan Mohamed, in his study of Douglass and Richard Wright, calls "death-bound subjectivity." He outlines many of the classic existential problems of freedom and responsibility that follow. In "How Bigger Was Born," his famous introduction to the 1940 edition of *Native Son*, he argued that American society "makes" Bigger Thomases, people who, in attempting to be humane, become viewed as troublemakers who need to be put "into their place" while being held responsible for their actions. Wright takes issue with the system that imposes this on people, while at the same time upholding accountability, even under unjust systems, as a necessary condition for human dignity and maturity. In his last novel, *The Outsider*, this theme is explicitly made through the antihero, Cross Damon, who is unable to take on responsibility because society inhibits his moral development and maturation. His greatest fear is realized when he dies confessing a feeling of "innocence" after having killed several people.

The theme of eventual conflict is also linked to the existential interpretation of black invisibility, a subject that has become almost synonymous with the name Ralph Ellison. Here, black invisibility is a function of hypervisibility. It is a form of being what Frantz Fanon called a phobogenic object, an object that stimulates anxiety. Ellison mourns the plight of educated blacks, who believed their achievements would bring about inclusion (visibility) in U.S. society rather than the heightened exclusion (invisibility) from a social world in which they exemplify the "impossible."

Douglass's influence is particularly pronounced in the black liberation thought of the 1950s and 1960s. Frantz Fanon, the Martinican psychiatrist and philosopher, used a mixture of autobiographical and theoretical reflection to present a portrait of the struggle for freedom as one against a social world riddled with contradictions. This effort first takes the form of mastering language, seeking refuge in love, and then realizing that freedom must be seized instead of given. In *Black Skin, White Masks*, Fanon articulates the movements from language to love as failed efforts at recognition. Like Douglass and Du Bois, he shows that the objective is to transcend a world in which one is judged by a standard that can never be one's own. As well, Angela Y. Davis, in her "Unfinished Lecture on Liberation—I," challenges conceptions of freedom that do not take seriously the perspectives of enslaved people. She argues against metaphysical conceptions of freedom that fail to account for the concrete conditions of their possibility. Davis drew directly upon Douglass's thought as inspiration for her lecture.

Douglass's influence on black existential thought is explicit in work at the end of the twentieth century. Molefi K. Asante, a scholar of Afrocentricity, draws explicitly on Douglass's thought in such works as *The Afrocentric Idea* and more recently *An Afrocentric Manifesto*. In each instance, Asante argues for the agency of African people in history. The reason his thought is included here is because of his proviso that agency is paramount. In effect, Asante's argument requires rejecting a concept that yokes agency. As a transcending category, agency, in effect, precedes any essence or concept. Douglass's thought is also brought to the fore in existential analyses by authors in the anthology *Existence in Black* and by Lewis R. Gordon in *Existentia Africana*, where the chapter, "Douglass as an Existentialist," develops the themes of this entry.

Further Reading

Davis, Angela Y. *The Angela Y. Davis Reader*. Joy Ann James, ed. Oxford: Blackwell Publishers, 1998.

Douglass, Frederick. *The Life and Writings of Frederick Douglass*. Philip S. Foner, ed. New York: International Publishers, 1950.

Du Bois, W. E. B. *Darkwater: Voices from within the Veil*. New York: Harcourt, Brace, and Howe, 1920.

———. *The Souls of Black Folk*. New York: New Library, 1982.

Ellison, Ralph. *Invisible Man*. New York: Vintage, 1990.

Fanon, Frantz. *The Wretched of the Earth*. Trans. Constance Farrington. New York: Grove Press, 1963.

———. *Black Skin, White Masks*. Trans. Charles Lam Markmann. New York: Grove Press, 1967.

Gilroy, Paul. *The Black Atlantic: Modernity and Double Consciousness*. Cambridge, Mass.: Harvard University Press, 1993.

Gordon, Lewis, ed. *Existence in Black: An Anthology of Black Existential Philosophy*. New York: Routledge, 1997.

———. *Existentia Africana: Understanding Africana Existential Thought*. New York: Routledge, 2000.

JanMohamed, Abdul R. *The Death-Bound-Subject: Richard Wright's Archaeology of Death*. Durham, N.C.: Duke University Press, 2005.

Wright, Richard. *The Outsider*. New York: Harper & Row, 1953.

———. *Native Son*. New York: Harper & Row, 1960.

—*Lewis Gordon*

British Antislavery Movement

The British antislavery movement of 1834–1895 birthed the Western antislavery movement. The first British antislavery organization was founded in 1783. Until 1833, when slavery was abolished throughout the British Empire, the movement's main focus was on the campaigns against the slave trade and slavery in the British colonies. Once this task had been accomplished, it was possible to assume a more comprehensive point of view. To mark this new departure, in 1834 a new antislavery alliance was forged, the British and Foreign Society for the Universal Abolition of Negro Slavery and the Slave Trade, whose main focus was the struggle against slavery which existed in foreign countries and over which the British government exercised no direct control. This, in turn, necessitated a shift in orientation and tactics away from the familiar work of lobbying politicians at Westminster to the more challenging and indeterminate task of mass mobilization and agitation among the population at large. To be sure, mass mobilization had always been an important part of the antislavery strategy but, from the late 1820s onward, it assumed an increasingly central place in the movement armory.

The period from 1828–1833 had been a stirring moment in the history of British liberalism, when Catholic Emancipation, constitutional reform, and franchise extension had all been wrested by an aroused people from an increasingly beleaguered, aristocratic oligarchy. Antislavery had figured significantly in this panoply of liberal causes. Indeed, as David Brion Davis has persuasively argued, it was often embraced by the moderate middle-class progressives as an antidote to more radical and domestically divisive causes such as factory reform or universal adult male suffrage. Emboldened by what they perceived as liberal hypocrisy, a few reactionary populists such as William Cobbett and Richard Oastler tried to drive a wedge, during the 1830s and 1840s, between the middle class abolitionists and the organized working class. Generally speaking, these divisive efforts ended in failure. Nevertheless, from the 1830s onward, the British antislavery movement became increasingly diverse and heterogeneous, as a plethora of local, sectional, and religious denominational organizations proliferated, intermittently combining and recombining in a profusion of transitory ways.

Not surprisingly, from the mid-1830s onward, attention was gradually refocused on the gathering struggle against slavery as it continued to exist in the United States. By the end of that decade, the leading British movement activists had been absorbed in an "Anti-Slavery International" with their American cousins, which revolved around the twin poles of Boston and London. The high point of this cosmopolitan alliance came in 1840 when a world Anti-Slavery Congress was held in the British capital, with delegates from many nations around the globe. A year later, however, when the American **abolitionists** split between Garrisonian radicals and conciliatory moderates, the British abolitionists followed suit. The London-based British and Foreign Society took care to preserve its respectable image, while the more grass-roots-based movements in Ireland, Scotland, and the industrial north were more inclined to line up with the American radicals.

Throughout this period, there was much traffic across the Atlantic, as British antislavery activists traveled to America, and the American leaders made pilgrimages to Britain. A high point in this interchange came in 1845–1847 when Frederick Douglass toured the British Isles. Traveling and lecturing in most major cities, Douglass quickly achieved celebrity status, and his appearances were extensively reported in the British press. "I have spent some of the happiest moments of my life since landing in this country," Douglass wrote to **William Lloyd Garrison**, back home:

> I live a new life. The warm and generous cooperation extended to me by the friends of my despised race, the prompt and liberal manner with which the press has rendered me its aid, the glorious enthusiasm with which thousands have flocked to hear the cruel wrongs of my down-trodden and long-enslaved fellow-countrymen portrayed contrasted so strongly with my bitter experience in the United States, that I look with wonder and amazement on the transition. (Douglass, 1855)

The British abolitionists who hosted Douglass's visit reciprocated with equal enthusiasm, although one white male activist from Bristol, John Estlin, betrayed a hint of jealous unease at the black orator's stunning effect on the white women who came to hear him:

> While observing him at Liverpool, I could not but tremble for his future domestic comfort when he returns to the U.S. You can hardly imagine how he is noticed,— *petted* I may say by *ladies*. Some of them really a little exceed the bounds of propriety, or delicacy, as far as appearances are concerned; yet F. D.'s conduct is most guardedly correct, judicious and decorous. I doubt if he forms intimacies much with gentlemen.... My fear is that often associating so much with white women of education and refined taste and manners, he will feel a 'craving void' when he returns to his own family. (Midgley, 1992)

One can only wonder what Estlin thought about the British antislavery activist Julia Griffiths who was so impressed by Douglass that she went to America to work as his assistant. In all likelihood, however, the chance to feel virtuous and superior to the brutal Americans without entirely abandoning a residue of racial prejudice was probably attractive to many British liberals of both sexes. Through this, and perhaps other, less self-serving, motives, the British abolitionist movement remained strong through the 1850s as the debate on American slavery reached its climax.

The outbreak of the American Civil War in 1861 created a crisis for the British abolitionist movement. The failure of the federal government to mount a crusade against slavery made it difficult initially to rally support for the Union cause. That the British government desisted from openly recognizing the Confederacy was probably due more to the forbearance of Lancashire's cotton workers than to any decisive action by the antislavery organizations. In 1862, however, a new round of Emancipation Committees was established in London and many provincial cities. Then, after 1863 when President **Abraham Lincoln** issued the **Emancipation Proclamation**, there was a fresh groundswell of enthusiasm for the Northern cause throughout the British Isles. After the war, thousands of pounds were subscribed to Freedman's Aid Societies, which were dedicated to helping the ex-slaves to adjust to the vicissitudes of freedom.

And yet, paradoxically, the final abolition of slavery in the United States corresponded with a notable diminution in British sympathies for the extension of Negro rights in Britain's own colonies. As black people gained more *de facto* economic independence and began to grow restive with white social and political control, the older, sentimentalized image of the Negro as pure victim began to give way to a more complex picture. The Indian Mutiny of 1857, the Jamaica Rebellion of 1865, and the Maori, Afghan, and Zulu wars of the 1860s and 1870s all contributed to a growing fear of colored peoples. During the late 1860s and 1870s, racial attitudes began to harden, and the philanthropic liberalism of the early nineteenth century became less fashionable. This was an inauspicious augury for the future. Over the next 30 years race relations would continue to deteriorate as Britons sought to justify a wave of fresh imperial conquests and to impose new disciplinary controls over restive natives in the colonies.

Nevertheless, it would be a mistake to exaggerate the significance of late Victorian racism in Britain. The brutal suppression of the Jamaican insurgents by the vindictive Governor Eyre unleashed a vituperative campaign of racist propaganda. But it also sparked British liberals, like John Stuart Mill, to go beyond the old antislavery sentimentalism to a vigorous endorsement of the principle of black civil rights. By the time Frederick Douglass died, in 1895, there was not much left of the old condescending sympathy for the distant, suffering slave. The abstract humanitarianism which Douglass had so perfectly embodied, and which his testimony had so powerfully evoked, was no longer sufficient in an increasingly complex and interconnected capitalist world. In the short-run, the "new racism" appeared to be the beneficiary of these circumstances. In the long run, however, a new and more difficult challenge had begun: No longer the mere conceit of white benevolence and protection, twentieth-century blacks in their struggles would look beyond the confines of antislavery, insisting on unconditional racial justice, integration, and equality.

Further Reading

Bolt, Christine. *The Anti-Slavery Movement and Reconstruction: A Study in Anglo-American Co-operation, 1833–77*. London: Oxford University Press, 1969.

Davis, David Brion. *The Problem of Slavery in the Age of Revolution, 1770–1823*. Ithaca, N.Y.: Cornell University Press, 1975.

Douglass, Frederick. *My Bondage and My Freedom*. New York: Miller, Orton, and Mulligan, 1855.

Drescher, Seymour. *From Slavery to Freedom: Comparative Studies in the Rise and Fall of Atlantic Slavery*. New York: New York University Press, 1999.

Foner, Philip S. *British Labor and the American Civil War*. New York: Holmes and Meier Publishers, 1981.

Midgely, Clare. *Women Against Slavery: The British Campaigns, 1780–1870*. London and New York: Routledge, 1992.

Lorimer, Douglas A. *Colour, Class and the Victorians: English Attitudes to the Negro in the Mid-Nineteenth Century*. New York: Leicester University Press, and Holmes and Meier Publishers, 1978.

Semmel, Bernard. *The Governor Eyre Controversy*. London: MacGibbon and Kee, 1962.

—Theodore Koditschek

C

Catholicism

In the histories of race, the slave trade, and slavery as an institution, Catholics figure as exceptionally problematic agents. Such nominally Catholic nations as Spain, France, and Portugal rationalized the contradictions between the tenets of their Roman Catholicism and the economic ends of appropriating lands and exploiting human populations. In the struggles for political dominance in the New World, the necessary conflict between Catholics and Protestants engendered attitudes of mutual suspicion, a cultural thread that runs through both the colonial and postcolonial fabric of the United States. It is noteworthy that in locations where Catholics were a minority presence, they were sometimes subject to legal discrimination. Anti-Catholic hostility was particularly noticeable in the pre–Civil War decades. The fact that Catholics were a minority within a Protestant America and that black Catholics, slave or free, were a minority within a minority helps to explain why Catholic voices were relatively muted in **abolitionist** discourses. The habitual character of American Roman Catholicism in accommodating itself to prevailing social and political mores regarding race may also explain, in part, why Catholics were not exceptions in the trenchant critiques of Christianity in antislavery literature.

Further Reading

Billington, Ray A. *The Protestant Crusade 1800–1860*. Gloucester, Mass.: P. Smith, 1963.

Dinnerstein, Leonard, Roger Nichols, and David Reimers. *Natives and Strangers: Blacks, Indians, and Immigrants in America*. New York: Oxford University Press, 1990.

Hall, Gwendolyn Midlo. *Africans in Colonial Louisiana*. Baton Rouge: Louisiana State University Press, 1992.

—*Jerry W. Ward, Jr.*

Childhood

Frederick Douglass's childhood consisted of life as a slave. Even at a young age he questioned the "why" of his situation—why was he born a slave? Why were some people slaves and others masters? As a child, he was told that the "God up in the sky" who knew what was best for all of humanity had deemed that blacks would be enslaved and whites would have hegemony over them (Douglass 1982). As a youngster, Douglass knew that not all persons of African descent were enslaved and not all whites were slave owners. Such astute observations are the reflections of an unusual child who came of age in bondage but never accepted the notion that enslavement was normal for African Americans. Slavery was an anomaly and nothing, wrote Douglass, could "atone for taking my liberty from me." He concluded that liberty was the natural and inborn right of every member of the human family. Therefore, he began, even as a child, to earnestly consider and devise plans for his freedom.

Frederick Douglass, seated right, beside a grandson. Library of Congress, Prints and Photographs Division, LC-USZ62-51528.

Born on Virginia's Eastern Shore in 1817 (or 1818, depending on the source), Frederick Douglass experienced the most unsettling aspects of bondage, separations, and whippings, before reaching 18 years of age. Under the circumstances, his comment, "Children have their sorrows as well as men and women; and it would be well to remember this in our dealings with them. SLAVE-children **are** children, and prove no exceptions to the general rule" (Douglass, 1969:39) is understandable.

Frederick Douglass's earliest memories were those in the humble cabin of his loving grandparents, Betsey and Issac Bailey, rather than with his own parents and siblings. Douglass had no association with his father, a white man, or his brother and sisters, Perry, Sarah, and Elizabeth, who lived on another plantation. But, the child had an indelible impression of his mother, **Harriet Bailey**, whose owner hired her out on a distant plantation. Douglass did not remember ever seeing her "by the light of day" because it was 12 miles between her workplace and his abode. Despite the grueling walk, she made brief sporadic visits to see him after her workday ended and left early enough the following morning to resume her tasks anew. The timing of her appearances suggests that she traveled to see her son without permission.

Living with his grandparents and seeing his mother only occasionally was not extraordinarily troublesome for the youngster, who did not know he was enslaved. Aside from his age as a contributing factor, his grandparents probably insulated him from the fact. The moment of truth came when Betsey Bailey, acting under the direction of their owner, carried her little grandson to another plantation where he was to perform tasks considered appropriate for his age.

The child's journey into the unknown effectively ended the idyllic facet of his life. He described the agony of parting from his grandmother and was inconsolable. It is difficult to tell which was more painful for the seven-year-old boy, the actual separation or the belief that his grandmother had deceived him. Douglass was angry, felt abandoned, and saw himself as a stranger in a strange land. His siblings, themselves enslaved, understood his plight because they too had been separated from the old woman as soon as they were old enough to perform simple tasks. Douglass's brother, Perry, begged him to stop crying and offered peaches and pears to soothe him, but the younger child flung the fruit away. He was indignant and hurt. If he were so acutely distressed, his grandmother's pain must have been more intense since she had committed her other grandchildren to similar fates.

Douglass did not adjust well and grieved over the disengagement from his family and friends. As a lonely child, he aggravated the plantation cook, "Aunt Katy," but could not recall the exact nature and "heinousness" of his offenses. Her "favorite" mode of punishment was to make him "go without food all day . . . after breakfast." Apart from withholding his allotted nourishment, Douglass remembered that Katy threatened him "with a scowl well suited to its terrible import," and conveyed, he wrote, "that she 'meant to *starve the life out of me!*' " Katy frightened the small boy further by "brandishing her knife" while slicing bread for the other youngsters in his presence.

The young boy's sorrow turned to joy with an especially memorable visit from his mother. She arrived for a brief stay while the hungry child, who considered himself "friendless" and "in his extremist need," ate a few grains of corn pilfered from the kitchen. After recounting the details of his plight, he saw an indescribable expression on his mother's countenance. Her eyes reflected pity for him and "fiery indignation" for Aunt Katy. In a confrontation between the two women, the younger woman "read Aunt Katy a lecture which she never forgot," according to Douglass. Of greater significance, his mother threatened to tell their owner about Katy's behavior toward the child. Douglass believed his owner, Captain Aaron Anthony, would not have tolerated Katy's "meanness, injustice, partiality, and oppressions."

His mother's intercession on his behalf taught him that he "was not only a child, but *somebody's* child." He remembered being upon his mother's knee at that moment made him prouder than being a king upon a throne. Sadly, his mother had to return to her work and left her young son virtually alone again. Shortly thereafter, she sickened and died. He was then more alone than ever.

By the time he was seven years old Douglass had entered a new stage of his life that would truncate childhood as he knew it. It was a bittersweet period. On the one hand, he witnessed a merciless beating of a young enslaved woman which "opened [his] eyes to the cruelties and wickedness of slavery." Seeing the flogging terrified, stunned, and bewildered him. Similarly, the whipping of a woman called Aunt Ester, for "impudence," was equally disturbing. But, on the other hand there were mitigating factors. He was not yet old enough to perform the most arduous tasks associated with enslavement. Instead, he herded cows, swept the yard, and ran errands. Furthermore, Lucretia Auld, daughter of Captain Auld and wife of Thomas Lloyd, whom Douglass called his "young mistress," was "kindly disposed" toward him, and he enjoyed an esprit de corps with Daniel Lloyd, the youngest son of Colonel Edward Lloyd. On occasions Daniel gave Frederick cake and protected the young slave from the "bigger boys." When taken together, these acts were extraordinarily meaningful for Douglass who wrote:

> For such friendship I am deeply grateful, and bitter as are my recollections of slavery, it is a true pleasure to recall any instances of kindness, any sunbeams of humane treatment, found way to my soul, through the iron grating of my house of bondage. (Douglass, 1962:71)

To be sure, the "sunbeams of humane treatment" were rare for a child who ordinarily experienced hunger, cold, nakedness, and physical abuse. The greatest ray of hope came when Captain Auld decided to send Douglass to Baltimore to stay with Hugh Auld as a companion for his young son.

Living in Baltimore was a wonderful and liberating experience for Douglass since it opened the doors of literacy and fortified his belief in the wrongs of slavery. Hugh Auld's wife provided the initial reading lessons but stopped when her husband objected, thinking education would ruin a slave, making him discontented and unhappy. Auld's decision only slowed the learning process for the child who quickly devised a clever scheme to further his own education. Whenever he met any boy whom he knew could read and write, he claimed that he could read and write as well. This set a harmless one-upmanship in motion. Knowing only four letters of the alphabet, Douglass wrote them, and then challenged the boys to "beat that." "In this way," he recalled, "I got a good many lessons in writing." The ploy shaped Douglass's early concept of barter. He used bread taken from his owner's kitchen to pay for the lessons, thereby establishing a trade relationship which benefited all parties.

Perhaps the most significant event associated with Douglass's literacy and interactions with his young teachers was his purchase of the *Columbian Orator*, a book he heard the boys discuss. The 13-year-old slave read and reread its contents, especially a brief dialogue between a slave and slaveholder which actually served as a forum for pro- and antislavery arguments. Although he had once said he was born insolent, the *Columbian Orator* and his conversations with white boys on the street, who agreed that he had as much right to freedom as they, made Douglass more restive with his legal status as a slave. The extent of that restlessness intensified when Captain Anthony died intestate, and Douglass eventually left Baltimore and returned to bondage on a plantation in St. Michaels, **Maryland**.

"The rigors of a field," remembered Douglass, "less tolerable than the field of battle, awaited me." His new situation contrasted sharply with his days in Baltimore. "We were worked in all weather," he remembered. "It was never too hot or too cold; it could never rain, blow hail, or snow, too hard for us to work in the field," according to Douglass. Finally, he said, "Work, work, work, was scarcely more the order of the day than of the night." Work can be rightly called the thief who stole the childhood of youthful bondservants. Slave owners initially used children to complement workers, but as they both grew older, children became experienced substitutes for aging adult laborers and finally replaced them.

Such an arduous life reminded him of the successful escape of an enslaved man and woman, whom he called Uncle Noah and Aunt Jennie, nearly a decade earlier. Douglass admitted that their flight had made him think seriously of running away. "I was already, in spirit and purpose, a fugitive from slavery," he wrote. The concept of natural freedom had piqued Frederick Douglass's imagination early on when he contrasted his status with that of birds. He believed they were "so happy" as he listened to their "sweet songs." "Their apparent joy," wrote Douglass, "only deepened the shades of my sorrow."

His hatred of enslavement never subsided, nor did any amount of punishment curb his desire for liberty from the hated labor, physical abuse, and bondage. Douglass made an initial assault upon the institution of slavery by objecting to regular whippings intended to make him submissive. When his owner found the 16-year-old "unsuitable," he hired him out to Edward Covey, a tenant farmer known as a slave-breaker. Covey's determination to make Douglass a slave matched the adolescent's tenacity for resisting. Douglass described the battle which ended the harassment:

> The brute was endeavoring skillfully to get a slip-knot on my legs . . . As soon as I found what he was up to, I gave a sudden spring, and as I did so, he holding to my legs, I was brought sprawling to the stable floor. Mr. Covey seemed now to think he had me, and could do what he pleased; but at this moment—from whence came the spirit I don't know—I resolved to fight. (Douglass, 2004:51)

Reacting with heretofore unknown strength, Douglass flung Covey to the ground and drew blood. After a tug-of-war which lasted nearly two hours, each combatant recognized a winner and loser in his own way. Covey claimed that if Douglass had not resisted, he would not have beaten him. Douglass knew otherwise, but neither wished to push the matter further. The fight, a turning point in the youngster's life, "rekindled the few expiring embers of freedom." Exhilarated and full of renewed self-esteem over his physical and mental victory Douglass said, "I was nothing before; *I was a man now.*"

At sixteen, Douglass considered himself a man rather than chattel; making that distinction more meaningful required that he also liberate himself from bondage. His first attempt at freeing himself came when he was 19. He and several friends planned to steal a canoe and row away. Before taking any action, they were arrested upon suspicion of plotting to abscond. The would-be fugitives conducted themselves as mature adults and were released without punitive actions. Perhaps the embarrassment of a 19-year-old plotting an escape for him and several other young males valued at thousands of dollars saved them from punishment. It is also possible that the suspicion was not taken seriously since Douglass and his friends were not viewed as adults. Nevertheless, the failure to escape did not dissuade the insolent Frederick Douglass nor snuff out his imagination for another attempt to secure his liberty.

Further Reading

Douglass, Frederick. *Life and Times of Frederick Douglass, Written by Himself, His Early Life as a Slave, His Escape from Bondage, and his Complete History*. New York: MacMillan Publishing Company, 1982.

———. *Life and Times of Frederick Douglass, Written by Himself His Early Life as a Slave, His Escape from Bondage, and his Complete History*. New York: Collier MacMillan Publishing, 1962.

———. *Narrative of the Life of Frederick Douglass: An American Slave*. New York: Kessinger Publishing, 2004.

———. *My Bondage and My Freedom*. New York: Dover, 1969.

Preston, Dickson J. *Young Frederick Douglass: The Maryland Years*. Baltimore: Johns Hopkins University Press, 1980.

—*Wilma King*

Christianity

Douglass's religious life started in his youth and was ignited by his spiritual mentor and father figure, Rev. Charles Lawson, providing him with the bedrock of his ethical and moral nature. His Christian beliefs fortified him during periods of duress. He felt it was his Christian faith that inspired him to defeat the slave-breaker, Edward Covey.

It had been said about Douglass "that the Lord had chosen him for a 'great work.'" But as a Christian, Douglass found ambiguity in the Christian teachings. Many in the abolitionist movement would rather have waited for divine intervention to free Africans, but as a leader in the abolitionist movement, Douglass advocated from moral as well as Christian perspectives for freeing enslaved Africans. But, when necessary, **abolitionists** including Douglass himself separated themselves from proslavery churches because of those churches' immorality.

Douglass applied this same evangelical fervor to his fight against slavery. Like most abolitionists, Douglass believed that slave owners could be influenced by appealing to their Christian morals. Religiosity had been a major part of the struggle for liberation for Africans in America. Douglass exemplified Christian ethics in the abolitionist struggle and modeled those ethics to influence the morality of the enslavers.

Further Reading

Meier, August and Leon Litwack, eds. *Black Leaders in the Nineteenth Century*. Urbana and Chicago: University of Illinois Press, 1991.

—*Ivory Phillips*

Civil Rights Acts

Though he had always questioned the institution of slavery, Frederick Douglass's views on civil rights began to form when he settled in New Bedford, **Massachusetts**, and became affiliated with the abolitionist movement. With the help of his future wife, **Anna Murray**, Douglass had escaped to the North, traveling through Delaware, Pennsylvania, and New York before settling in New Bedford, where he changed his surname to Douglass. Initially adopting the antislavery philosophy of **William Lloyd Garrison**, whom he had met in New Bedford, Douglass soon realized that many **abolitionists** who advocated against slavery were also against granting African Americans full and equal rights.

Douglass was a dynamic civil rights scholar who understood the sociopolitical complexities of American constitutionalism. When rumors of a civil war began, Douglass realized that the Northern states would never abolish slavery if that goal could only be achieved by refuting the Constitution and dismantling the United States. Using a moralistic paradigm, Douglass keenly exposed how American ideology was corrupted when equality was not enforced or discriminatory laws were applied. For example, in a speech given in **Rochester, New York** on July 4, 1852, Douglass pointed out how differently blacks and whites viewed Independence Day: **"What to the Slave is Your Fourth of July? (The Meaning of July Fourth for the Negro)"**. With his deep baritone voice, Douglass proclaimed the hypocrisy of American white supremacy.

The Thirteenth Amendment, which outlawed slavery, was certified on December 18, 1865. At the end of the Civil War, Congress passed the Civil Rights Act of 1866 to ensure that newly freed African Americans would not be re-enslaved. There was significant progress during this time. Congress passed the Reconstruction Acts, allowing Congress to divide the South into five military districts and laying out strict guidelines for the readmission of the Confederate states into the Union. Reconstruction laws required former Confederate states to ratify the Fourteenth

Amendment and to guarantee blacks the right to vote. Between 1868 and 1870, the Southern states were readmitted to the Union, and large numbers of blacks were elected to the state legislatures. Despite these advancements, Douglass became increasingly concerned about the status of newly emancipated African Americans and appealed to members of the Thirty-ninth Congress to grant further measures to erase the sediments of slavery. He was especially alarmed by the emergence in many Southern states of laws called **Black Codes**. These laws allowed for legal discrimination based on race and were passed in order to keep blacks as second-class citizens.

Douglass held firm to his belief that the Constitution is the bedrock of Americanism, guaranteeing freedom, equality, and justice for all. He understood that the Civil Rights Act of 1866 encompassed the sprit of equality and helped ease the difficult transition of African Americans from slavery to freedom. Douglass considered the Act an important factor in the protection of the rights of African Americans. Using the Act as a framework, Douglass effectively defined the status of African Americans in the post-Civil War years. Though many blacks rejoiced during Reconstruction, Douglass remained cautious. He was pleased that Congress passed the Civil Rights Bill of 1875, which gave blacks the right to equal treatment in theaters, inns, and other public places; nevertheless he was not surprised when the **U.S. Supreme Court** ruled the Act unconstitutional in 1883 because it exceeded the limits of Congress's authority.

The success of Reconstruction began to be curtailed in the mid-1870s. Douglass outlined several reasons for the erosion of the new rights bestowed on African Americans. He argued that abolitionists failed to challenge the Black Codes and other Southern laws that were discriminatorily applied against blacks. He cited the failure of religious leaders to maintain public protest regarding the second-class citizenship of blacks. He pointed out that many government leaders were tired of the "Negro Question," and the federal government became complacent and failed to curtail discrimination against African Americans. Douglass's goal of equality was doomed when the Supreme Court ruled in *Plessy vs. Ferguson* that "separate but equal" was the law of the land. He died at the age of 77 of a heart attack in Washington, D.C.

Overall, Douglass was correct in his sociolegal assessments. Though the Civil Rights Act of 1875 was declared unconstitutional, the Civil Rights Act of 1866 was upheld. Over the years, the Civil Rights Act was never successfully challenged in the courts. As the years passed, the Civil Rights Act of 1866 came to be regarded as a fundamental part of contemporary civil rights in America, and exists today as section 1981 of the United States Code.

Further Reading

Douglass, Frederick. *My Bondage and My Freedom*, 2003, reprint of the original 1855 edition. John W. Blassingame and John R. McKivigan, *The Frederick Douglass Papers, Series One: Speeches Debates, and Interviews, Vol. 4: 1864–1880 & Vol. 5: 1881–1895*. New Haven, Conn.: Yale University Press, 1999.

Hall, James C., ed. *Narrative of the Life of Frederick Douglass*. Approaches to Teaching Series. New York: Modern Language Association of America, 1999.

—*Otis Grant*

Cleveland, Stephen Grover (1837-1908)

Grover Cleveland, who served as President of the United States from 1885 to 1889, and from 1893 to 1897, was born in Caldwell, New Jersey, to Ann Neal and Richard Cleveland. He rose to national power in the 1880s, a time when the rights of African Americans were being increasingly limited. In 1885 he was inaugurated to his first Presidential term, 20 years after the Civil War and during the Southern Reconstruction period. Unlike many other Democrats, however, he did not advocate **lynching** or most other harsh aspects of the **Jim Crow** system. And, Cleveland never publicly attacked the Fourteenth or **Fifteenth Amendments**. But he did believe the revisionist history of Reconstruction, which held that blacks had helped radical **Republicans** subjugate the South. Cleveland also believed that African Americans were ignorant, wasteful, and had no respect for property rights.

Given these public statements by Cleveland, and the fact that he was a Democrat, it is not surprising that the Republican Frederick Douglass campaigned against Cleveland when he ran for president in 1884. But the relationship between the men proved to be complex. Upon becoming president, Cleveland initially allowed Douglass to remain as **Recorder of Deeds** for Washington, D.C. However, in 1886, Cleveland asked Douglass to resign his office. Douglass complied, after which Douglass toured Europe and Egypt. In Egypt in 1886–1887, Douglass compared Egyptians and blacks in America, angering critics who attempted to discredit him.

Also in 1887, Cleveland signed the Interstate Commerce Act which allowed railroads that crossed state lines from the North to the South to discriminate against blacks. Republican senators charged Cleveland with racial discrimination, but Douglass refused to join in the attacks on Cleveland. The civil rights leader in fact praised the President for having invited him to White House functions. By contrast, recent Republican Presidents James Garfield and Chester Arthur had not issued such invitations to Douglass. However, Cleveland, who believed that it was the responsibility of moderate white Southern leaders to protect blacks in the South from the "Jim Crow" system, allowed racial discrimination to exist during his presidencies. Douglass steadfastly called for federal intervention to stop discrimination. Douglass campaigned against Cleveland during his unsuccessful reelection bid in 1888.

During President Cleveland's intermission as president, in 1889, Douglass was appointed by President Benjamin Harrison to the position of Haiti's Minister and Consul General. Douglass resigned from this position in 1891. Grover Cleveland was reelected to the presidency in 1893. During both presidencies Cleveland did not seriously address the "Negro" question, and he had limited contact with Douglass. He mainly addressed Native American issues. Frederick Douglass died during Cleveland's second term on February 20, 1895 in New York.

Further Reading

Chesebrough, David D. *Frederick Douglass: Oratory from Slavery*. Westport, Conn.: Greenwood Press, 1998.

Foner, Philip S. *Frederick Douglass, a Biography*. New York: Citadel Press, 1964.

Welch, Richard E. Jr. *The Presidencies of Grover Cleveland*. Lawrence, Ks.: University of Kansas Press, 1988.

—*Russell Benjamin and Paul Easterling*

Compromise of 1850

Enacted as legislation to balance interests between states after the Mexican-American War, the Compromise served only as a small bandage to the enormous wound of the sectional crises. The series of bills is best known for the Fugitive Slave Law, which required all citizens to assist in the capture of runaway slaves, even in states where slavery was not legal.

By 1848, the United States contained an equal number of free and slave states: 15 each. The American victory in the Mexican War resulted in the signing of the Treaty of Guadalupe Hidalgo in 1848. The Treaty resulted in the United States acquiring a vast amount of territory, which threatened to upset the balance of the Union. The implications of "free soilism," the Wilmont Proviso (which insisted that Congress bar slavery in the territories ceded by Mexico), and the idea of extending the Missouri Compromise line, 36° 30´, were contested either by Northerners or Southerners.

Offering a set of compromise proposals to resolve the contention of the impending sectional crises, Henry Clay played the role of intermediary, as he had during both the controversy over Missouri in 1820 and again during the nullification crisis in the early 1830s. The Compromise of 1850 also called for federal assumption of the Texas debt, abolition of the slave trade in Washington D.C., and a new fugitive slave law.

The North saw victories in winning California as a free state, in New Mexico and Utah as likely future free states, a favorable settlement of the Texas-New Mexico boundary, and the abolition of the slave trade in the District of Columbia. As an abolitionist and former slave, Douglass would have definitely favored the clauses in the Compromise that added these additional territories as free states and that called for the abolition of the slave trade in Washington D.C. The uncertainty of popular sovereignty made the South's benefits hazier. One definite Southern victory was a more stringent **Fugitive Slave Act** which authorized Southerners to pursue fugitive slaves on Northern soil. Like many Northerners, Douglass, a former fugitive, despised that aspect of the Compromise.

Further Reading

Gates, Henry Louis, ed. *The Classic Slave Narratives*. New York: Signet Classic, 2002.

Stewart, Jeffrey C. *1001 Things Everyone Should Know about African American History*. New York: Doubleday, 1996.

—*Kelton R. Edmonds*

Crummell, Alexander (1819–1898)

Alexander Crummell was a leading nineteenth-century black intellectual and advocate of emigration to **Africa**. Crummell was born free in New York City to a free mother and a father who identified himself as a descendant of West African royalty. Alexander Crummell attended interracial schools in New Hampshire and New York State run by **abolitionists** that emphasized both manual and liberal-arts-oriented education. His theological studies were done privately, and he would become an ordained Episcopal minister in 1844. In 1848 Crummell traveled to **England** to raise money for his church, but would soon matriculate at Queens College of Cambridge University in Cambridge, England, where he would receive his degree (A.B.) in 1853. Crummell went to Liberia, living there for 20 years before returning to the United States around 1873. He became pastor of Saint Luke's Episcopal Church in Washington D.C., serving in that capacity from 1879 to 1894. Throughout his professional career, Crummell lectured, attended conferences, and participated in debates on Reconstruction with many notable figures such as **Booker T. Washington** and W. E. B. Du Bois. He wrote extensively on issues of race, religion, spirituality, and the social and moral conditions in the United States and beyond. He cofounded the American Negro Academy in Washington, D.C. which functioned as an outlet for scholars, researchers, and artists to research and engage in intellectual inquiry and discussion of ideas in order to propose solutions to existing African American problems in the United States.

As a result of conflict within the black Episcopal Church, Crummell promoted greater independence of the church within the white Episcopal structure instead of separating from it. When in trouble at his home church of St. Mary's, he cited Frederick Douglass as a character witness to buttress those who opposed him, which derailed attempts to remove him from his church.

With Frederick Douglass as both a contemporary and an influence, Crummell advocated for full civil and political rights for African Americans. He championed the cause of black masses gaining self-determination instead of just focusing on the civil rights of the privileged few African Americans, or one-eight, that he believed would be the only beneficiaries of the integration in public hotels and theaters.

At the National Convention of Colored People in Washington, D.C. (1873) Crummell stated his beliefs: he believed in focusing on the masses along with the middle class, but that the middle class would have to be convinced they had a special responsibility of service; second, that the end of slavery did not end the effects of bondage; third, that black people had a crucial role in improving their condition and that black education would mean the spreading of knowledge to the masses; and finally, that the role of refined women in this movement would be crucial.

Crummell initially disagreed with the "mulattos" who favored assimilation of the black race into white society and was against the use of the term "Afro-Americans" instead of "Africans." Crummell placed civil rights and the eradication of segregation laws very low on his agenda. He was distrustful of the political process and did not favor the social accommodations of Booker T. Washington. He did favor the economic and labor integration of black people, but did not go as far as

Edward W. Blyden at condemning African American participation in the political process.

In a speech at Storer College in **Harpers Ferry**, West Virginia (1885), and with Frederick Douglass present, Crummell gave an address titled "The Need for New Ideas and New Aims for a New Era." Crummell believed black people should not dwell on slavery in the past but instead on their duty and service. Frederick Douglass rose to disagree and stated that this history should always be present in black people's memories. Crummell advocated for common leadership for black people, whether it be behind Frederick Douglass or Henry Highland Garnet. With Garnet's death in 1881, Crummell supported Frederick Douglass, who was under attack for his active support for the **Republican Party**. Crummell believed that Frederick Douglass was the best person to represent the leadership of black people in the late nineteenth century and feltDouglass's name and work had a profound impact on African Americans. He also rebuked young black leaders who did not appreciate the significance of Frederick Douglass's leadership. Douglass in turn remarked shortly before his death in a pamphlet, *The Lesson of the Hour*, that Crummell and other blacks of great intellect were overlooked by society who favored instead the public oration of former slaves recounting their experiences.

Though they differed ideologically on various issues over the course of their careers, Douglass and Crummell had mutual respect for each other that continued until Douglass's death in 1895. Crummell provided a prayer offering at Douglass's funeral, using that moment to reflect on Douglass's accomplishments and the significance of his leadership.

At the very end of his life Crummell expressed optimism for black people and pessimism about black leadership: "I have no fear of the future of the American Negro, for he belongs to a prolific, hardy and initiative race, and areas of glorious future before him; but I do dread his leaders, because most of them are unscrupulous, ambitious, and ungodly men, who care nothing for the race." Crummell expressed concern for "Super Scholars" who were more concerned about being in the spotlight than their willingness to work unnoticed in trying to help the larger population of African Americans in need. He also believed that black leadership should be prepared for service, and he defended the practical industrial-based education as a greater need than the liberal arts education for the masses of black people. However, he disagreed with Booker T. Washington's extreme advocacy of **industrial education**, aware that whites would use this to advocate racial discrimination, an issue he spoke about in 1881. Crummell also articulated the concept of the "Talented Tenth" theory of black leadership espoused by advanced black institutions like Fisk University and Spelman College, but stated that black education should strive for excellence not for its own sake but for its function in helping the masses of African Americans. This explication of his position was recognized in the later writings of W. E. B. Du Bois over 20 years later.

Alexander Crummell's pan-African vision at the end of his life entailed the consolidation of African Americans across class lines. He was not for separation of races as much as the promotion of black unity that would lead to unity in the African Diaspora, according to his biographer, Gregory Rigsby. Viewed as a complex man of great intellect, he wrote extensively about the optimistic future of black people tempered with the pessimistic view about human nature. Overall, his biographer, Wilson J. Moses, observes that Crummell's influence would later surface in the use of black protest ethic to explore solutions related to the plight of African Americans in the twentieth century. This would later serve as an ideological influence for organizations like Marcus Garvey's Universal Negro Improvement Association and the Nation of Islam under the leadership of the Honorable Elijah Muhammad in the twentieth century.

Further Reading

African American World. Reference by Encyclopaedia Britannica: http://www.pbs.org/wnet/aaworld/reference/articles/alexander_crummell.html, September 8, 2003.

Cowan, Tom and Jack Maguire. *Timelines in African-American History.* New York: Roundtable Press, 1994.

Crummell, A. "An Address to the British Anti-slavery Society" (1851) in *Against Slavery: An Abolitionist Reader.* Mason Lowance, ed. New York: Penguin Books, 2000.

Moses, Wilson J. *Alexander Crummell: a Study of Civilization and Discontent.* New York: Oxford University Press, 1989.

Rigsby, Gregory U. *Alexander Crummell: Pioneer in Nineteenth Century Pan-African Thought.* Westport, Conn.: Greenwood Press, 1987.

—*Andrew Smallwood*

D

Davis, Jefferson (1808-1889)

Jefferson Davis was a colonel in the U. S. Army, a representative and senator from Mississippi, and President of the Confederate States of America. Davis was born in Christian County, Kentucky, as the tenth child of Revolutionary War cavalryman Samuel Davis and Jane Cook Davis. The Davis family then moved to a plantation in Wilkinson County, **Mississippi**, while Jefferson was in his infancy. Davis entered Transylvania College in Kentucky in 1821, transferred to **West Point** in 1824 following a nomination from President Monroe, and graduated in 1828. He entered the military following graduation and fought in the Black Hawk War of 1831–1832. Davis married Sarah Knox, the daughter of Colonel Zachary Taylor, three years later on June 30, 1835 and moved near Vicksburg, Mississippi, to become a cotton farmer. Sarah died three months later of malarial fever.

By 1843 Davis had become involved in politics and was elected to the House of Representatives from Mississippi in 1845. That same year Davis married his second wife, Varina Howell. The next year Davis broke a promise to his wife not to join the military; he resigned from Congress to join the Mexican-American War in the rank of Colonel of the First Mississippi Volunteer Rifles. During his military service, Davis left enslaved laborer James Pemberton in charge of his farm. Following the war Davis was offered a presidential promotion to brigadier general that he declined to pursue a career in the **U.S. Senate**. Davis received a gubernatorial appointment to the Senate and was confirmed in August of 1847. Davis was reelected to the Senate in 1850 and in 1856. He formally withdrew on January 24, 1861, upon receiving notice of Mississippi's succession from the Union. Offered the rank of commander in -chief of the army of Mississippi, Davis instead accepted the Presidency of the Confederate States of America. He took office on February 18, 1861. During his tenure in office, Davis used only free black labor in his White House and entertained the notion of abolishing slavery in the Confederate States in return for military aid from **England** and France. At the end of the Civil War, Davis tried to flee the country but was captured by the Federal cavalry at Irwinville, Georgia, on May 10, 1865. Although never brought to trial, Davis was held in prison for two years and became a symbol of the "lost cause" of the Confederacy. Davis was released with a *nolle prosequi* in December 1868.

He became the president of an insurance company in Memphis, Tennessee. Upon receiving the estate of his friend Mrs. Sarah A. Dorsey in her will in 1879, Davis left the insurance business and moved to Beauvoir, Mississippi, to manage that estate. Davis spent much of his time in literary pursuits writing a two-volume defense of the Confederacy titled *The Rise and Fall of the Confederate Government*. Davis died December 6, 1889, surrounded by friends and family.

Further Reading

Allen, Felicity. *Jefferson Davis, Unconquerable Heart*. Columbia: University of Missouri Press, 1999.

Cooper, William J., Jr. *Jefferson Davis, American*. New York: Knopf, 2000.

Davis, William C. *Jefferson Davis: The Man and His Hour*. New York: HarperCollins, 1991.

Hattaway, Herman, and Richard E. Beringer. *Jefferson Davis, Confederate President*. Lawrence, Ks.: Univeristy of Kansas Press, 2002.

—*Orville Vernon Burton, Beatrice Burton, and Matthew Cheney*

Douglass, Annie (1849–1860)

Annie Douglass was the youngest daughter and last child of Frederick and Anna Murray Douglass. Born in **Rochester, New York**, Annie attended public school in Rochester. As the youngest member of the Douglass household, Annie was doted on by her parents and siblings. Intellectually curious, she was an avid reader and writer. In December 1859, Douglass's oldest daughter, **Rosetta,** in a letter to her father reported that Annie was attending school regularly and that she was the best student in her class. Annie had also written to her father in December 1859 telling him proudly about her good work in school.

In March 1860, after three months of illness, Annie, aged 10, died nine days before her eleventh birthday. Word of her death reached her father in Glasgow, Scotland. He decided to return to Rochester immediately to join his grief-stricken family. Frederick, who had fled the United States after being named as an accomplice in John Brown's raid at **Harpers Ferry,** had been touring **England** since November 1859. In January 1860, a **U.S. Senate** inquiry had implicated him directly in John Brown's raid. Deeply affected by Annie's death, Frederick ignored the risk of being imprisoned and returned home. Annie Douglass is buried in Mount Hope Cemetery, Rochester, New York.

Further Reading

Douglass, Frederick. *Life and Times of Frederick Douglass, Written by Himself*. Hartford, Conn.: Park Publishing, 1881.

———. *Douglass's Monthly*. June 1860.

McFeely, William S. *Frederick Douglass*. New York: Norton, 1991.

—*Gregory P. Lampe*

Douglass, Frederick, Jr. (1842–1892)

Few individuals born into the world have had their lives more front-loaded than did Frederick Douglass, Jr., a social activist and the second son of Frederick Douglass. By bearing the name of the world's most noted abolitionist, many could argue that Frederick Douglass, Jr., was destined to be a "race man." However, such explanations of his future development are relatively incomplete, particularly as they fail to incorporate the most important influence in his development, his mother **Anna Murray-Douglass**. Although many people would erroneously trace the social activism of the Douglass children to their father, such reconstructions fail to consider that not only was the family patriarch away for extended periods of time working against the pernicious system of slavery and therefore limited in his interaction with his offspring, but also Anna Murray-Douglass was as much an activist as her much more renowned husband.

Born on March 3, 1842, in New Bedford, **Massachusetts**, during the tumultuous pre-Civil War period, Frederick Douglass, Jr., was impacted by the social activism that he saw occurring all around him. As a child Douglass witnessed his mother's prominent role in the Massachusetts abolitionist movement with figures such as Wendell Phillips and **William Lloyd Garrison**. It would be this tradition that most propelled the Douglass male children to serve on the Union Army side during the Civil War. Frederick Douglass, Sr. had served as one of the initial recruiters for the **Fifty-fourth Regiment of Massachusetts Volunteer Infantry**, and Douglass, Jr., mirrored his father most when he followed his example and served as a recruiter for the Union Army.

In addition to serving as a soldier and recruiter for the Union Army, Frederick Douglass, Jr., married Virginia M. Hewlett and fathered seven children: Frederick Aaron, Jean Hewlett, Lewis Henry, Maud Ardelle, Charles Paul, Gertrude Pearl, and Robert Small.

Frederick Douglass, Jr., the second son and third child of Frederick and Anna Douglass. c. 1867–1870. Carte-de-Visite. S. M. Fassett, Chicago, IL. Courtesy National Park Service, Museum Management Program and Frederick Douglass National Historic Site, FRDO 4954. http://www.cr.nps.gov/museum.

Further Reading

Foner, Philip S. *The Life and Writings of Frederick Douglass: Early Years 1817–1849.* New York: International Publishers, 1950.

The Frederick Douglass Papers Project: Frederick Douglass Family Tree. Manuscript Division, Library of Congress, Washington, D.C.

Thomas, Sandra. A biography of the life of Frederick Douglass. University of Rochester. http://www.history.rochester.edu/class/douglass/home.html.

—*James Jones*

Douglass, Helen Pitts (1838–1903)

Helen Pitts was the second wife of Frederick Douglass. She was born into a white family in Honeoye, New York, and may have met Douglass during her childhood, as her father had known him during the 1840s. Pitts graduated from Mt. Holyoke Seminary (now Mt. Holyoke College) in 1859. After working for the American Missionary Association teaching former enslaved people in Norfolk, Virginia, during the Civil War (1862–1864), Pitts eventually moved to Uniontown in the 1880s to live with her uncle and worked with Dr. Caroline Winslow of the Moral Education Society on the *Alpha*. Her uncle lived next door to Douglass, who hired her as his clerk; Douglass was the recorder for the district. Douglass and Pitts had a romantic relationship about which he did not tell his offspring until the day of his marriage.

When Pitts married Frederick Douglass on January 24, 1884 at the age of 45, it was her first and only marriage. Pitts was disowned by her family; her ancestors had been on the Mayflower, giving her family high social status, and her father was outraged by her marriage to a former slave. In spite of a generation (20 years) separating them, they appeared to have common interests regarding women's suffrage. Douglass's children did not attend the wedding, but had an awkward reception for them afterwards. There were outspoken critics of the union in both black and white societies. Douglass justified his actions by saying he had first married someone the color of his mother and was now married to someone the color of his father. Black society saw his standing in the black community as compromised and many wondered aloud why no "colored" woman was good enough.

Helen Pitts Douglass, Frederick Douglass's second wife, 1880. By J. H. Kent, Rochester, New York. Courtesy National Park Service, Museum Management Program, and Frederick Douglass National Historic Site, FRDO 22814. http://www.cr.nps.gov/museum.

Douglass kept letters he received in reaction to his marriage, but remained steadfast about his decision. After honeymooning, Pitts and Douglass traveled to Europe and **Africa**, after he officially retired from his appointment as U.S. Recorder of Deeds. They spent almost two weeks in Cairo, Egypt. When they returned to the United States, Douglass was designated Minister to Haiti. In 1889 when the couple went there, Pitts, being able to speak French, assisted Douglass during their time in Haiti.

In their marriage, Pitts' family called him Uncle Fred, but she remained Mrs. Douglass to his children and grandchildren, who were encouraged to give her the silent treatment. Some believed that the marriage was happy because they were compatible; it helped that Pitts thought very highly of her husband and was amazed at his principled ways. After resigning as Minister to Haiti, Douglass continued to lecture nationwide. They attended the **World's Columbian Exposition in Chicago in 1893**, with Douglass representing Haiti. He succumbed to a heart attack on February 20, 1895.

Frederick Douglass, Helen Pitts Douglass, and Eva. Courtesy National Park Service, Museum Management Program and Frederick Douglass National Historic Site, FRDO 3912. http://www.cr.nps.gov/museum.

Pitts was instrumental in making sure Douglass's memory was preserved. She asked Congress to establish the Frederick Douglass Memorial and Historical Association (FDMHA) and deeded Cedar Hill to it. She continued to advocate for people of African descent and women after he died. For instance, Pitts spoke at the National League of Colored Women's first meeting. In 1896 she criticized the women's movement convention because they allowed racist women to suggest that the right to vote would help the cause of white supremacy. Helen applied to the Mayflower Society of the District of Columbia, an organization of Mayflower descendents, but her application was delayed as she was Douglass's widow. She wrote a letter of protest in September 1900.

The National Association of Colored Women's Clubs partnered with the FDMHA to make the Cedar Hill location available to the public in 1916 and helped pay the mortgage. By then, Pitts had died of heart disease on December 1, 1903. She is buried at Mt. Hope Cemetery. Before she died, she wanted to have Douglass's body moved to Cedar Hill where she wished to be buried beside him. Douglass's son, Charles, objected, but did not object to her being buried in the family plot in Rochester.

Further Reading

McFeely, William. *Frederick Douglass*. New York: W. W. Norton & Co., 1991.

Selected papers from Mt. Holyoke College.

—*Marilyn D. Lovett*

Douglass, Lewis Henry (1840–1908)

Frederick Douglass's oldest son, Lewis Henry, was born in New Bedford, **Massachusetts**. He proved to be a credit to his father, although Frederick Douglass often lamented the racial and social barriers that stunted the success of his children. Like his brother Charles, Lewis responded to his father's call in the *North Star*, "Men of Color, to Arms!" (1863) and became a sergeant major in the **Fifty-fourth Regiment of Massachusetts Volunteer Infantry**. Lewis also accompanied his father in 1866 as part of a delegation of black leaders who met with President Andrew Johnson to protest the Southern states' institution of **Black Codes**.

Much is recorded about Lewis's diverse employment record, and he is considered to be the most ambitious and resourceful of Douglass's children. Lewis taught school for a brief period after the Civil War, and in 1866 he moved to Denver, where he worked for a mining company, serving as secretary for the company at one point. In 1869 he moved to Washington, D.C. and worked in the Government Printing Office. Lewis was a typographer by trade but experienced discrimination in the

Washington typographers' union. In 1873 his father corrected this injustice by employing him for his paper, *New National Era*. Lewis did work with black labor conventions and served as his father's representative at various social and political engagements. Lewis also worked in the Recorder's office and in real estate, and in the late 1870s he was employed as a deputy-marshal under his father (while Frederick Douglass served as Marshal of the District of Columbia) during the Rutherford B. Hayes administration. Frederick Douglass depended on Lewis to handle his affairs in the later years of his global travel and activism.

Further Reading

Huggins, Nathan Irvin. *Slave and Citizen: The Life of Frederick Douglass*. Boston: Little, Brown, 1980.

McFeely, William S. *Frederick Douglass*. New York: W. W. Norton & Co., 1991.

Quarles, Benjamin. *Frederick Douglass*. Englewood Cliffs, N.J.: Prentice-Hall, 1968.

—*Christel Temple*

Lewis Douglass, the eldest son and the 2nd child of Frederick and Anna Douglass. Lithograph. Courtesy National Park Service, Museum Management Program, and Frederick Douglass National Historic Site, FRDO 116. http://www.cr.nps.gov/museum.

Douglass Sprague, Rosetta (1839–1906)

Frederick Douglass's oldest child, Rosetta, was born in New Bedford, **Massachusetts**, shortly after her parents settled into freedom. Having a daughter made her father more aware of the complexities of racial and gender oppression, the hypocrisy of the North, and the struggles of black parents trying to ensure the success of their children. He sent her away for private tutoring from age seven through her teenage years, which built noticeable gaps in her relationship with her mother. Frederick Douglass sought to ensure Rosetta's early intellectual development, but her schooling necessarily coincided with his activist journalism. In 1848 Rosetta passed entrance exams and was admitted to the prestigious Seward Seminary in **Rochester, New York**. Frederick Douglass was infuriated that Rosetta was segregated away from the white students. He championed her cause in his newspaper, *North Star*.

Rosetta Douglass, daughter of Frederick Douglass and Anna Douglass. Courtesy National Park Service, Museum Management Program and Frederick Douglass National Historic Site, FRDO 4812. http://www.cr.nps.gov/museum.

Rosetta and her father shared a close relationship. He liked hearing her play the piano for visitors at his home. Even though she was a liberal freethinker like he was, she discovered firsthand how gender limited her options. Ironically, as the eldest child of a famous leader, society placed impractically high standards and expectations upon her. She attended Oberlin College's Young Ladies Preparatory and New Jersey's Salem Normal School, but did not attend college. She worked primarily as a teacher before becoming a wife and homemaker. Rosetta is credited with having a keen sense of racial justice, inherited from her father's example of activism and from her experience as a woman in antebellum and Reconstruction America. She advised Frederick Douglass against accepting the presidency of the Freedman's bank and did not support his interracial marriage, after her mother's death. Rosetta was a founding member of the National Association of Colored Women.

Further Reading

McFeely, William S. *Frederick Douglass*. New York: W. W. Norton & Co., 1991.

Quarles, Benjamin. *Frederick Douglass*. Englewood Cliffs, N.J.: Prentice-Hall, 1969.

Sprague, Rosetta Douglass. "Anna Murray Douglass—My Mother As I Recall Her," *Journal of Negro History*. 8 (1923): 93–101.

—*Christel Temple*

E

Emancipation of the West Indies

Frederick Douglass was an emancipationist who rejected any color-based rights. This is why his paper, the ***North Star***, had the following masthead: "Truth is of no color." Douglass used the emancipation of blacks in French and British territories and the theory of African origin of the ancient Egyptians to strengthen his moral, political, philosophical, and intellectual stance against enslavement in the United States. He became a powerful black leader at the end of the Civil War, which earned him some political appointments.

Douglass, fighting for emancipation and equality of blacks in the United States, was inspired by the emancipation of blacks in West India and Haiti. He saw the possibilities of using these countries as political tools against the slaveholding government of the United States.

Douglass was proud of Haiti because it was the first free black republic in the world. Using the idea of "Liberty" proclaimed in the French Revolution of 1789–1799, enslaved blacks from Haiti revolted in 1791 under the leadership of **Toussaint L'Ouverture**. The revolt led to the fall of the colonial government, the end of enslavement, and the proclamation of the independence of Haiti in 1804 by Jean Jacques Dessalines. Douglass considered Haiti a role model and a source of pride for blacks in the United States. The creation of Haiti, a black republic, vindicated blacks who fought for freedom and equality. It also vindicated **abolitionists** against all enslavers who made untrue assertions about black racial, mental, and organizational inferiorities. In May 1861 Douglass announced in the *Douglass Monthly* his plan for a weeks-long trip to Haiti to report on the status of that country. For Douglass the trip would serve partly as an inspiration:

> We are drawn towards the sunny region at this time by other considerations than those of pleasure ... Born a slave as we were, in this boasted land of liberty, tinged with a hated color, despised by the rulers of the State, accustomed from childhood to hear the colored race disparaged and denounced, their mental and moral qualities held in contempt, treated as an inferior race, incapable of self government, and of maintaining, when left to themselves, a state of civilization, set apart by the laws of our being to a condition of slavery—we, naturally enough, desire to see, as we doubtless shall see, in the free, orderly and Independent republic of

Haiti, a refutation of the slanders and disparagements of our race. (Foner, 1999:440)

Unfortunately, the trip was cancelled due to the Civil War in the United States.

Beside Haiti, Douglass was also proud of the developments in West India which he saw as an example of true republic and the positive effect of the antislavery movement. West India is an archipelago sometimes called the Antilles. In the nineteenth century, West India, in addition to Puerto Rico and the Virgin Islands, was divided into British, French, and Dutch territories. In the British West Indies, pressure from the abolitionists combined with enslaved blacks' unrest led the British Parliament to pass in 1833 the Abolition of Slavery Act, which provided for the gradual emancipation of the enslaved. This led to the emancipation of all enslaved by 1838. Douglass marveled at the combined action of the British abolitionists and Parliament to end enslavement in the British West Indies. In a speech delivered in 1857 in New York to commemorate the twenty-third anniversary of emancipation in West India , Douglass stated:

> The day and the deed are both greatly distinguished... But to no people on the globe, leaving out the emancipated men and woman of the West Indies themselves, does this address itself with so much force and significance, as to the people of the United States... Slavery in America, and slavery everywhere, never received a more stunning and killing condemnation. (Foner, 1999: 358–359)

Douglass also used the emancipation of blacks living in French West India (Martinique) in his campaign against the slaveholding system in the United States. The French Revolution of 1848, which overthrew the monarchy and established a republic, combined with enslaved revolts led to the emancipation of enslaved blacks in French West India by the Provisional Government of the French Republic. Douglass compared the Provisional Government that emancipated the enslaved blacks in accordance to its motto "Liberty, Equality, and Fraternity" to the American Republic, which was full of contradiction and lacked the courage to meet its responsibility to free its enslaved. Even though the Provisional Government of the French Republic. and the United States Republic came to power after revolution against royal oppression and domination, the former was more progressive than the latter because it offered freedom to everybody (specifically the enslaved blacks of West India) in the name of Justice and Liberty.

Douglass was optimistic that the French Revolution that sparked other popular revolts by the underclass and the oppressed against tyrants and monarchies in Europe, would reach the United States. He felt slaveholders and their government could not stop that powerful wind of freedom and equality.

In **Africa**, anthropology was the child of the colonial enterprise. Wrong anthropological theories were promoted that argued for the racial and cultural inferiority of primitive blacks. This false interpretation of African culture and history was frequently used by enslavers and European colonial powers to justify their oppression in the name of the "White Man's Burden." Neo-evolutionary theories using a social Darwinist approach classified mankind into racial hierarchies, most of which put blacks at the bottom of the hierarchy, considering them primitive and having no civilization and no historical achievement. Douglass rejected that misinterpretation of

African history that denied Africans all their historical achievements. In a speech delivered at Western College in 1854, Douglass blamed ethnologists such as Morton (1839), who had stipulated an inferiority of the black race. Douglass was among the earliest blacks to demonstrate that ancient Egypt was African and black. He referred to eyewitness accounts from classical authors as well as linguistic (philological), ethnographical, and physical anthropological data from scholars such as Prichard (1843) and Latham (1850) to state that Africans were the founders of great civilizations such as ancient Egypt and Nubia. Douglass stressed that blacks are human beings and as such, they should have the same rights, such as freedom, justice, and equality, given to other humans. He argued that Africa, through Egypt, is the mother of the Western classical civilizations such as Greece. This same conclusion was made decades later by other scholars such as Ben-Jochannon (1971), Diop (1974, 1991), and Bernal (1991). In both content and style, Douglass can be considered the precursor of Cheikh Anta Diop. They have similar views on ancient Egypt and its achievements, and both have a similar powerful debative oratory style, quoting opponents to demonstrate the inherent weakness in their opponents' assertions.

Douglass also used his own genealogy to further argue for the black origin of African civilization. He stated that his own mother looked like the head of the figure of the Egyptian found by Prichard. By showing that ancient Egypt was black and that Africa played a major role in the birth of European classical civilizations, Douglass asserted that anthropological theories of primitive black societies were not only inaccurate but were ideological tools used to justify the oppression of blacks.

Despite being proud of African historical achievements, Douglass was against the return of blacks to Africa. He felt it was the right of blacks to live in America because they helped build it. In fact, he denounced the **American Colonization Society**, a group that advocated the return to Africa. For Douglass, returning to Africa meant exile and a denial of blacks' rights.

Douglass considered the Civil War as an opportunity and a means to abolish enslavement. He gained support from **Republicans** in Congress and, later, from President **Abraham Lincoln** (for whom he had campaigned) in his fight to abolish enslavement. By the end of the Civil War, Douglass had become a powerful black leader, earning him important positions.

In 1871, President Ulysses S. Grant appointed Douglass Secretary of the Commission on the Annexation of San Domingo (Dominican Republic). Douglass accompanied the Commission to Santo Domingo and supported the Commission's recommendation to annex Santo Domingo. Douglass believed Santo Domingo would gain more by becoming part of the United States. However, the recommendation to annex was rejected by the **U.S. Senate**.

In 1889, Douglass was appointed Minister Resident and Consul General to the Republic of Haiti by President Benjamin Harrison. At that time the diplomatic service was socially advanced on the issue of hiring blacks. More than a dozen blacks were nominated ambassadors to Haiti and Liberia by the end of the nineteenth century. Douglass succeeded John E. W. Thompson (1885–1889) and Ebenezer Don Carlos Bennett (1869–1877) as the third black to serve as United States Minister to Haiti. Even though this nomination drew criticism from the American press, Douglass welcomed his new position. He admired Haiti as a free and independent black nation, and this new position would allow him to work for racial equality. He attributed criticism to racial prejudice and economic pressure to obtain for the

Frederick Douglass at his desk in Haiti. Courtesy National Park Service, Museum Management Program and Frederick Douglass National Historic Site, FRDO 3899. http://www.cr.nps.gov/museum.

United States an advantage he was not ready to give. Some people were also concerned about Douglass's age and the health challenges of living in tropical conditions. One of the main reasons Douglass was nominated was that the United States wanted a coastal station for American vessels at Môle St. Nicolas.

However, Haitians were unwilling to accede part of their territories, rationalizing this with a loss of sovereignty that they had fought so hard for. Haitians did not want to keep talking with U.S. Admiral Gherardi (chief U.S. negotiator for Môle St. Nicolas) because his words were not binding. Haiti wanted a direct talk between President Harrison of the United States and President Hyppolite of Haiti. In 1891 Douglass resigned, disgusted by maneuverings from the State Department and American business groups to acquire Môle St. Nicolas. His resignation saddened Haitians, who viewed him as a great black leader and a compassionate defender of his race and people. Haiti designated Douglass as Haitian Commissioner at the **World's Columbian Exposition in Chicago in 1893.** He was the only black official present.

Further Reading

Andrews, W. L., ed. *The Oxford Frederick Douglass Reader*. Oxford: Oxford University Press, 1996.

Ben-Jochannon, Yosef A. A. *Africa: Mother of Western Civilization*. New York: Alkebu-Lan Book Associates, 1996.

Bernal, M. *Black Athena: The AfroAsiatic Roots of Classical Civilization*. New Brunswick, N.J.: Rutgers University Press, 1991.

Brown, N. *A Black Diplomat in Haiti: The Diplomatic correspondence of U.S. Minister Frederick Douglass from Haiti 1889–1891*.vols. 1 & 2. Salisbury, N.C.: Documentary Publications, 1977.

Deme, A. *Africa and the Theoretical Debate in Anthropology*. Unpublished M. A. paper. Rice University: Department of Anthropology, 1997.

Douglass: F. *My Bondage and My Freedom*. New York: Miller, Orton, and Mulligan, 1855.

Diop, C. A. *Civilisation ou Barbarie*. Paris: Présence Africaine, 1981.

———. *The African Origin of Civilization: Myth or Reality*. Westport, Conn.: Lawrence Hill and Co., 1974.

Foner, P. S. *Frederick Douglass: Speeches and Writings*. Chicago: Lawrence Hill, 1999.

Gobineau, J. A. Comte de, *Essai sur l'inégalité des races*. Paris: Didot, 1853.

Latham, R. G. *The Natural History of the Varieties of Man*. Paternoster Row, London: John Van Voorst, , 1850.

Lubbock, J. *The Origin of Civilization and the Primitive Condition of Man*. London: Longmans, Green and Co., 1889.

———. *Prehistoric Times, As Illustrated by Ancient Remains and the Manners and Customs of Modern Savages*. London: Williams and Norgate, 1872.

Morton, S. G. *Crania Americana*. Philadelphia: Dodson, 1839.

Prichard, J. C. *The Natural History of Man*. London: H. Bailliere, 1843.

Quarles, B. *Frederick Douglass*. Washington, D.C.: The Associated Publishers, Inc., 1948.

Tylor, E. B. *Researches into the Early History of Mankind and the Development of Civilization*. London: John Murray,1878.

Wolf, E. R. *Europe and the People Without History*. Berkeley: University of California Press, 1982.

—*Alioune Deme*

Emancipation Proclamation

Issued in 1863, the Emancipation Proclamation was an executive order that declared the abolition of slavery in all Confederate states, i.e. those not under Union control. During the early years of the Civil War, Douglass argued vehemently that the overarching mission of the war was to liberate the slave and save the Union. On the other hand, President **Abraham Lincoln** feared that if he advocated for the emancipation of slaves, it would have a devastating effect; he would risk alienating Northern Democrats and conservative Republicans. Furthermore, the four border states, Delaware, **Maryland**, Kentucky, and Missouri would abandon him by joining forces with the rebels. To avoid an anti-emancipation backlash, Lincoln proclaimed that the chief purpose of the war was to preserve the Union, not to liberate the slaves.

Despite Lincoln's staunch position on the war, Douglass also postulated that the Union cause would be strengthened if blacks were able to enlist in the Union army. Perturbed that runaway slaves were being returned to their slaveholders, Douglass insisted that Union officers needed to put the runaways to work.

To Douglass's dismay, Lincoln, who was personally against slavery and who believed in colonizing blacks in other countries, was in favor of compensating the slaveholders for their slaves. In fact, Lincoln proposed that Delaware legislators adopt a plan to recompense slaveholders. Clearly the abolitionists were enraged. The bill was not introduced to Congress.

In 1861, Douglass was pleased to learn that General John C. Frémont had imposed martial law; he freed the slaves of rebels in Missouri. Lincoln overturned Frémont's order under the Confiscation Act and removed him from his post. Touched by Frémont's act of bravery, Douglass prophesied that he would rise again and that his war horse would descend upon the rebels.

After a number of military defeats and casualties, Douglass and other abolitionists convinced **Republicans** in Congress that slavery was immoral and that slave labor made the Confederacy stronger. In April 1862, Congress passed an act abolishing slavery in the District of Columbia. Months later, slavery was banned in territories. In July, all slaves of rebel masters were declared forever free of their servitude under the Second Confiscation Act. Because Lincoln did not have authority in the slave states, the act obviously did not free the slaves.

Douglass soon learned that Lincoln would issue the Preliminary Emancipation Proclamation on September 22, 1862. It declared that unless the Confederates discontinued their rebellion as of January 1, 1863, all slaves in the areas that were still rebelling against the Union would be free. Slavery would remain intact in the other slave states. Lincoln waited until after the Union won the battle at Antietam to make the announcement about the Emancipation Proclamation that would be executed on January 1, 1863. He also declared that the federal government was in favor of using the black soldier in the Union army.

Joyful over the news, Douglass praised Lincoln. On January 1, 1863, Douglass and other black and white abolitionists met at Boston's Tremont Temple. They waited for Lincoln to issue the Emancipation Proclamation. Although Douglass was optimistic, he was not sure if Lincoln would keep his word. With excitement, messengers waited near the telegraph office and on the stage of the Tremont Temple. While they waited for the announcement, several speeches were given. Douglass waited, as he stated in his autobiography, for a bolt from the sky which would break the chains of 4 million slaves. Several hours later, the crowd grew tired until they heard that the Proclamation had arrived. Charles W. Slack, a white abolitionist, read the Proclamation as the audience celebrated by shouting and crying.

Several hours later Douglass had a chance to critique the Proclamation. It had blatant limitations; it did not promise liberty throughout all the land. Instead, the executive order abolished slavery in areas where slavery no longer existed. Slavery would continue where it did exist. It was clear to Douglass that Lincoln wanted to satisfy loyalists, who were adamant about preserving the Union. Nevertheless, as an optimist, Douglass believed the Proclamation had promise and engendered a sense of hope.

Uplifted, Douglass praised the Proclamation. In a speech titled "The Proclamation and the Negro Army," delivered February 6, 1863 in New York City at the Cooper Institute, he stated that the Emancipation Proclamation liberated blacks and whites and the brave men fighting the battles of their country against rebels and traitors. He said the Proclamation emanated a mesmerizing power and spirit that lifted the oppressed from serfdom to absolute citizenship. He compared the Emancipation Proclamation's inspirational power to Independence Day, to Catholic Emancipation, and to the British Reform Bill. To Douglass, the issuance of the Emancipation Proclamation was the glorious first step to America's liberty.

Further Reading

Chesebrough, David B. *Frederick Douglass: Oratory from Slavery*. Westport, Conn.: Greenwood Press, 1998.

Franklin, John Hope. *The Emancipation Proclamation: An Act of Justice*. Garden City, NY: Doubleday & Company, 1963.

The U.S. National Archives & Records Administration. Summer 1993, vol. 25, no. 2

McFeely, William S. *Frederick Douglass*. New York: W. W. Norton & Co., 1991.

Miller, Douglas T. *Frederick Douglass and the Fight for Freedom*. New York: Facts On File, 1988.

Oakes, James. *The Radical and the Republican: Frederick Douglass, Abraham Lincoln, and the Triumph of Antislavery Politics*. W. W. Norton & Company: New York, 2007.

—Della Scott

Emerson, Ralph Waldo (1803–1882)

The poet, philosopher, essayist, literary critic, and minister Ralph Waldo Emerson was born May 25, 1803 in Boston, **Massachusetts**, the fourth of eight children born to William Emerson and Ruth Haskins. Emerson's formal education began at Boston Latin School at the age of nine. In 1817, he earned unconditional admittance into Harvard College after passing the school entrance exams. Although Emerson held a scholarship, a rise in tuition costs at Harvard that year forced Emerson to defray the expense of his education through various jobs as waiter, teacher, and messenger.

Emerson graduated from Harvard in 1821 and earned the objectionable title of class poet at the school's commencement in August. He spent the next four years teaching theology in different locations around Canterbury, Massachusetts. Emerson worked for his older brother, William, at a school for young ladies in Gehenna for three of these years. In 1825, he entered Divinity School at Harvard and was approved to teach as a Unitarian minister the following year. Emerson married his first wife, Ellen Tucker, in 1829. His life in the clergy progressed and he was ordained as a junior pastor of Second Church in Boston.

Influenced by the ideas of German philosophers, Emerson started formulating his own thoughts and began a new career as a lecturer in 1834. The next year, Emerson moved to Concord, Massachusetts, where he married for a second time, in mid-September to Lydia Jackson. His career as a writer and speaker soared after the critical reception of a series of lectures he gave at Harvard, "The American Scholar" (1837) and "Divinity School Address" (1838), and his first major publication, *Nature*, in 1836.

Emerson was intermittently active in the social issues of his day. During his brief career as a minister, he preached social reform through moral suasion. His knowledge of the world, philosophy, and nature grew significantly between 1825 and 1834, and he began to articulate his insights on humanity and culture. In the 1840s, he established and led the philosophical movement called transcendentalism which focused on self-reliance, individuality, and the use of the soul as a moral and ethical compass. From 1841 to 1844, Emerson edited the *Dial*, a literary journal that underscored his transcendental philosophy. By 1860, Emerson published several works that cemented his renown as one of America's foremost intellectuals: *Essays: First Series* (1841), *Essays: Second Series* (1844), *Poems* (1846), *Representative Men* (1850), *English Traits* (1856), and *The Conduct of Life* (1860). Still, Emerson was altogether reluctant to address the major social issue of his day—the abolition of slavery.

At the coercion of his peers, Emerson found occasion to speak out against the physical cruelties associated with slavery, but saw nothing morally inconsistent with American race prejudice and counted Southern slaveholders among his human "brothers." Likewise, Emerson never considered himself an **abolitionist** and eschewed this class of reformers on the whole. His opinion of African Americans was considerably less still. When James Russell Lowell proposed Frederick Douglass's name for membership in the Town and Country Club, an intellectual society that Emerson cofounded in 1849, Emerson was chief among those objecting to Douglass's admission.

Emerson remained widely traveled throughout his lifetime. In 1826, he took his first trip abroad to St. Augustine. Six years later, in 1832, Emerson traveled to Europe and **England**. A second trip to Europe came in 1847, when Emerson visited England and France. In 1873, Emerson made a third voyage to Europe and visited Egypt in **Africa** as well. He continued to write, publish, and lecture until his death from pneumonia on April 27, 1882. His later works include *May-Day and other Pieces* (1867), *Society and Solitude* (1870), *Parnassus* (1874) and *Letters and Social Arms* (1875).

For the duration of his career, Emerson was known as America's most original writer. His work as a poet, philosopher, and essayist led scores of writers in his era to call him the "sage of Concord." His writings explored a range of themes such as religion, spirituality, nature, politics, and culture.

Further Reading

Emerson, Ralph Waldo, ed. *Emerson's Anti-slavery Writings*. New Haven, Conn.: Yale University Press, 1995.

McAleer, John. *Ralph Waldo Emerson: Days of Encounter*. Boston: Little, Brown and Company, 1984.

Richardson, Robert D. *Emerson: The Mind on Fire*. Berkeley: University of California Press, 1995.

—*Malachi Crawford*

England

For his **European lecture circuit**, Douglass traveled to England on three separate occasions. Fearing rendition after the publication of his *Narrative* in 1845, Douglass embarked for England with James Buffum on board the *Cambria* for a lecture tour on behalf of the American Anti-Slavery Society in the fall of 1845. After stops in Belfast, Glasgow, and Edinburgh (see **Great Britain**), in May of 1846, Douglass lectured to great acclaim in London to various organizations, including the British and Foreign Anti-Slavery Society. Aside from slavery, other pressing issues of which Douglass took note were the debates over repeal of the Corn Laws, the repeal of the union between England and Ireland, and Chartist concerns about wage slavery. Among reformers, Douglass spoke most glowingly about Richard Cobden and John Bright, energetic members of Parliament who were both advocates for repeal of the Corn Laws. On August 17, 1846, Douglass, along with William Lloyd Garrison and Chartists William Lovett and Henry Vincent, announced in London the formation of a new Anti-Slavery League. The next day, in the company of Garrison and George Thompson, Douglass visited Thomas Clarkson, the great abolitionist who was then in his eighty-seventh year. Douglass was much impressed by the great man who received him very warmly and who warned him against contaminating and diffusing the cause of **abolition** with other reforms.

In July of 1846 Douglass stayed with the Richardson family in Newcastle-upon-Tyne. Sensitive to Douglass's concerns about whether it was safer for him to go home or better to have his family move to Britain, Ellen Richardson began making arrangements to raise money for the purpose of buying Douglass's freedom. Spurred on by a check for 50 sterling from John Bright, Miss Richardson initiated inquiries that eventually led to the purchase of Douglass from his master, Hugh Auld, on December 12, 1846, for the price of 150 sterling (approximately $1,250). Abolitionists on both sides of the Atlantic criticized the sale, with purists claiming that it violated the very essence of abolition by implicitly recognizing the right of one man to own another. While conceding that he could have avoided rendition by residing in England indefinitely, Douglass insisted that the United States was the proper place for him to work on behalf of abolition, and he could not do that work unless he were free. During Christmas of 1846, the Richardsons introduced Douglass to Julia Griffiths, who would later become a partner in the publishing of the *North Star*, as well as a lifetime companion and confidant of Douglass. With 500 donated by British friends to start his own abolitionist paper, Douglass returned to Boston in the spring of 1847 on board the *Cambria*, which, by refusing him full access to its amenities, reminded him once again of the great and ironic disparity between republican America and monarchical England in the treatment of black folk.

A second lecture tour to England had already been scheduled when John Brown attacked the armory at **Harpers Ferry** on October 16, 1859. Authorities found correspondence and witnesses that linked Douglass to Brown, and his arrest was imminent. Douglass fled to Canada, and on November 12, 1859, embarked for England aboard the *Nova Scotian*, arriving in Liverpool on November 24. Douglass spent Christmas and January with Julia Griffiths and her husband, the Rev. Dr. H. O. Crofts in Halifax, Yorkshire. After spending six months in England and Scotland lecturing and renewing old acquaintances, Douglass learned of the death of his youngest daughter, **Annie Douglass**, who had died on March 13, 1860, nine days shy of her eleventh birthday. Departing immediately for the United States, Douglass was back in **Rochester** with his family by April.

In the fall of 1886, accompanied by **Helen Pitts Douglass**, whom he had married in January 1884, Douglass once again visited England. The couple departed New York in September 1886 and arrived in Liverpool later that month. After visiting Julia Crofts, widowed since 1880, as well as Mrs. Anna Richardson and Ellen Richardson, both now in their eighties, the Douglasses proceeded to Paris to commence the tour that would take them as far as Egypt and Greece. Douglass returned to England to give a series of lectures in the summer of 1887, and was back at Cedar Hill by August.

Further Reading

Douglass, Frederick. *My Bondage and My Freedom*. New York: Arno Press, 1968.

———. *The Life and Times of Frederick Douglass*. Hartford, Conn.: Park Publishing Co., 1888.

McFeely, William. *Frederick Douglass*. New York: W. W. Norton & Co., 1991.

—Stephen Andrews

European Lecture Circuit (1845–1847)

After publishing the *Narrative of the Life of Frederick Douglass* in the spring of 1845, Douglass sensed that his chances of being returned to a state of slavery had increased, and he arranged passage on a British vessel, the *Cambria*, going to **England**. However, his friend James N. Buffum told him that he could not board the ship and have a cabin like the white passengers. Instead, Douglass was relegated to the ship's steerage section.

He was an instant celebrity among the other passengers, except for two drunken passengers from New Orleans and Georgia who objected to the speech on slavery that other passengers had urged him to give. The ship's captain, Captain Judkins, instructed his crewmen to put the two Southerners in irons, and they fled back to their cabins without offering any further protest until the ship reached Liverpool, England. This incident was recanted to the British press by the Southerners, and Douglass contended that the publicity worked in his favor, as the antislavery British public condemned the Southerners; the incident also attracted a national audience for his antislavery message.

In January 1846, Douglass wrote a letter to **William Lloyd Garrison** describing some of his experiences in England and Ireland, noting that he was not publicly discriminated against, and that in some cases, he was actually favored. Douglass was surprised and refreshed by the change, as he was used to being despised and hunted because of his skin color in the United States. Douglass told Garrison that after his landing in England, he felt true happiness and became transformed by it, contrasting the latter with his long, bitter American experience. Douglass dined with the Lord Mayor of Dublin, Ireland, and he visited the home of the Marquis of Westminster at Eaton Hall in England as well.

Douglass lectured in almost every major city of the United Kingdom during his stay, and during that time Mrs. Henry Richardson successfully raised enough funds, 150 pounds sterling, to purchase Douglass's freedom from Hugh Auld of **Maryland**. Douglass revealed in *My Bondage and My Freedom*, published in 1855, that he went to England to raise the British public's religious and moral oppositions to American slavery. Douglass told Europeans candidly about American slavery during one of his characteristic speeches at Finsbury Chapel in Moorsfields, England, on May 12, 1846; he stated that in Virginia, a "colored" man could be executed for 71 crimes, while a "white" man could be executed for only three of them. He also noted that a "colored" woman could be executed on the spot for resisting the sexual advances of her master, and such an execution would not be considered a crime.

Douglass and his supporters, Joseph Sturge and George William Alexander, rallied against churches in the United Kingdom—especially the Free Church of Scotland in Edinburgh, which were accepting funds from American slaveholders and slave traders—arguing that slavery was a crime against God and humanity. Douglass was encouraged to move his family to England and take up residence there on numerous occasions. He could have led a life of luxury there, but Douglass resolved to return to America to work toward the emancipation of his people. Thus, in the spring of 1847, after spending about 21 months in the United Kingdom, Douglass returned to America as a free man with $2,500 that had been raised to start an antislavery newspaper, the **North Star**. On his return voyage aboard the *Cambria*, Douglass caused the *Cunard* steamship line to end its discriminatory policy toward "colored" people forever, and he had first-class cabin accommodations. As a result of his sojourn, Frederick Douglass became a model for abolitionist philosophers around the world.

Further Reading

Douglass, Frederick. *My Bondage and My Freedom*. New York: Arno Press, 1968.
Bennett, Lerone. *Before the Mayflower*. New York: Penguin Books, 1993.

—Larry Ross

F

Fifteenth Amendment

The Fifteenth Amendment to the U.S. Constitution, ratified on February 3, 1870, guaranteed voting rights to African American men, including those who had previously been enslaved. This amendment, like the Thirteenth and Fourteenth Amendments, would empower Congress to pass laws to enforce it. This empowerment of Congress to pass additional laws in support of amendments had not existed before the passage of the Thirteenth, Fourteenth, and Fifteenth Amendments, commonly called the Reconstruction Amendments. Additionally, the Union Army remained in the South for several years to help enforce these three amendments.

Frederick Douglass was a major supporter of the enactment and enforcement of the Fifteenth Amendment, as well as its two predecessors. Soon after slavery was ended, Douglass began to argue that the freedmen needed the right to vote. He felt that unless black men had the right to vote, they would not truly have freedom. Douglass and other black leaders met with President Andrew Johnson in early 1866. Johnson, however, wanted blacks to be sent out of the country. At the urging of those who had accompanied Douglass to the meeting with the president, Douglass wrote a rebuttal to Johnson's proposal.

Once the opposing views of Johnson and Douglass and his associates became public, the **U.S. Senate** began to debate the enfranchisement of the freedmen. The issue of blacks gaining voting rights was eventually resolved by newly elected President Ulysses S. Grant and the **Republican Party**, who supported what became the Fifteenth Amendment.

Even before the Fifteenth Amendment was ratified, the fact that it would specifically provide for black men to have the right to vote caused a rift between Douglass and white **women's suffragists**. Douglass and a significant number of black activists had supported rights for women, while white feminists had supported the abolition of slavery. The alliance between the groups had had the common goal of race and gender equality. However, some prominent white suffragettes were offended that black men, whom they considered inferior to white women, would be the first of the disenfranchised groups to gain the right to vote.

Douglass had the unique position of being the leading advocate of the Fifteenth Amendment, while also serving as vice president of the Women's Equal Rights

League, an organization opposed to the measure. Douglass argued that African Americans had a greater immediate need for the amendment because blacks were experiencing far more extensive oppression than were white women. Despite the arguments made by Douglass, the alliance between the women's suffrage movement and the black rights movement never recovered. However, while Douglass felt there was a more pressing need for black enfranchisement, he would press for suffrage to be extended to women throughout his life.

The Fifteenth Amendment resulted in black men being elected to public office at the federal, state, and local levels. Although Douglass never held elective office, he was seen as a major black political leader. He also held several highly visible appointed positions after the ratification of the amendment. These included **Recorder of Deeds** for the District of Columbia, member of the Council for the District of the District of Columbia, and Marshal of the District of Columbia.

In terms of long-term federal government support of the Fifteenth Amendment, Douglass became disappointed with the Republican Party, which controlled Congress and the presidency during Reconstruction and for decades afterward. Even before the Hayes Compromise of 1877, the national government had become less supportive of the Fifteenth Amendment, and of Reconstruction.

After the Hayes Compromise of 1877, Southern states adopted several policies, including the grandfather clause, poll tax, literacy test, and the white primary, to thwart the enforcement of the Fifteenth Amendment. All of these measures were enforced by violence, primarily **lynchings**. During Douglass's lifetime, the federal government refused to attempt to stop these practices. For the remainder of his life, Douglass continued to campaign for the enforcement of the Fifteenth Amendment.

Further Reading

Douglass, Frederick. *Life and Times of Frederick Douglass: Written by Himself* (with a new introduction by Rayford Logan). New York: Collier Books, 1962.

Walton, Hanes Jr., and Robert C. Smith. *American Politics and the African American Quest for Universal Freedom*. New York: Longman, 2000.

Welch, Susan, John Gruhl, John Comer, and Susan Rigdon. *Understanding American Government*. St. Paul: West Publishing Co., 1991.

—Russell Benjamin

Fifty-fourth Regiment of Massachusetts Volunteer Infantry

Sparked by Frederick Douglass's powerful oratory and recruiting efforts, the Fifty-fourth Massachusetts Regiment was formed successfully in 1863. As the first all-black volunteer regiment of the North's Union Army during the Civil War, it exceeded all expectations. The enactment of the **Emancipation Proclamation** on

December 31, 1862 by President **Abraham Lincoln** was a war-bargaining policy, threatening to emancipate all slaves in the Confederate states if the states did not surrender. Frederick Douglass's previous oratorical denunciation of President Lincoln's policies on not enlisting blacks into the military finally turned to recruitment efforts after Lincoln and his administration were unsuccessful in getting the South to surrender. Efforts by **Massachusetts** Governor John Andrew and abolitionist George L. Stearns to organize prominent black leaders as recruiters of Northern blacks meant Frederick Douglass was almost immediately picked for a leadership role in the recruitment process. His recruiting efforts took him to street and church platform meetings throughout major Northern cities. Significant concentrated efforts were focused on encouraging free blacks' enlistment into the Union Army in order to ensure a Confederate loss in the Civil War. Thus, the Fifty-fourth Massachusetts Regiment recruitment began February 9, 1863. Among the first recruits to enlist out of New York were two of Frederick Douglass's own sons, **Lewis** and **Charles Douglass**. In one of his recruiting meetings, Douglass spoke of not denying the right of citizenship for blacks who wore the brass U.S. letters on their uniforms, eagles on their buttons, and muskets on their shoulders with bullets in their pockets. In addition to his oratories from street platforms and church meetings, Frederick Douglass wrote a widely published newspaper editorial, "Men of Color, To Arms."

Charles Douglass, the fourth child and youngest son of Frederick and Anna Douglass. Carte-de-Visite, By Rice, Washington, D.C. Courtesy National Park Service, Museum Management Program and Frederick Douglass National Historic Site, FRDO 3908. http://www.cr.nps.gov/museum.

Recruiting efforts to sign up free blacks from some major Northern cities for the Union Army were not an immediate success. The little wealth and freedom they already had were not considered worth jeopardizing. With the Civil War came greater employment opportunities in some of these same cities, contributing to blacks' hesitation to enlist. Also, full citizenship for blacks who enlisted in the Army, while endorsed by Douglass, was strongly opposed by Northern whites.

Equal pay for the black recruits became the next focus of Frederick Douglass's oratorical denunciation of President Lincoln's administration. Supported by Massachusetts Governor Andrew, Douglass traveled throughout the North denouncing the plight of black soldiers fighting in defense of the Union for less pay than their white counterparts. For over a year this fight for equal pay waged on. Not even legislation by Massachusetts Governor Andrew increasing the pay of the black Union soldiers would prevent the Union government from enforcing half pay for the black recruits. Within the ranks of the black recruits themselves, they protested by not accepting any pay at all until authorized to receive pay equal to white recruits. This protest lasted until 1864 when the policy eventually changed.

Another debate that engaged Frederick Douglass was blacks not commissioned as officers in the Union Army. President Lincoln's policy called for white officers to lead black recruits of the Fifty-fourth and later the Fifty-fifth Massachusetts Regiments. White Northerners simply did not believe in black leadership at any level. Frederick Douglass was unable to convince President Lincoln and his administration otherwise. Even a proposed commissioning for Frederick Douglass by the Secretary of War was successfully opposed; the Union had a clear preference to only use blacks in non-authoritative positions of rank.

The performance of the Fifty-fourth Massachusetts Regiment on the battlefield would set a precedent affecting hundreds of thousands of blacks in future regiments. Though there were other black regiments formed prior to 1863, mostly in the South, the Fifty-fourth Massachusetts was the first to receive a presidential endorsement. One well-documented, epic battle occurred in July 1863. The Union Army assault on a Confederate stronghold, Fort Wagner on Morris Island in **South Carolina**, would not only be remembered as a historical landmark for the Fifty-fourth Massachusetts Regiment, but both a collective victory and defeat for all future black regiments thereafter. Any doubt about blacks' loyalty and courage in battle would be dispelled by this epic battle on July 18, 1863. In a letter written by one of Frederick Douglass's sons, Lewis, to his future wife Amelia, he describes the pride of the Fifty-fourth Massachusetts Regiment, "to a man this regiment did proud, all in the fight waged on at Fort Wagner." Not once, but several times the Fifty-fourth Massachusetts led the charge against the Confederate fortress, which up until then had never been penetrated. What Northern white news reporters wrote about the heroism of the Fifty-fourth Massachusetts Regiment in the assault on Fort Wagner would later be chronicled as the Regiment battled to the end. Even though they failed to capture and hold the Confederate fortress, the success of the Fifty-fourth Massachusetts Regiment paved the way for blacks in the Union Army.

Frederick Douglass's oratorical leadership, sacrifices, and commitment to recruit and speak for thousands of black recruits highlights the origin of the Fifty-fourth Massachusetts Regiment. Not only his efforts, but also his sons', proved to both the Union Army and the Confederacy that the will for freedom, placed squarely on the shoulders of blacks, would withstand the depths of any battle.

Further Reading

Astor, Gerald. *The Right to Fight*. Novato, Calif.: Presidio, 1998.

Blatcher, Charles, III. *Of Thee I Sing*. Oakland, Calif.: National Minority Museum Foundation, 1997.

McPherson, James M. *The Negro's Civil War*. Urbana: University of Illinois Press, 1982.

Russell, Sharman Apt. *Frederick Douglass*. New York: Chelsea House Publishers, 1988.

Russell, Sharman Apt, and Nathan Irvin Huggins. *Black Americans of Achievement: Frederick Douglass*. New York: Chelsea House Publishers, 1988.

—*Emerson Mungin, Jr.*

Freedman's Savings and Trust Company (Freedman's Bank)

Although most African Americans entered "freedom" with little more than the clothes on their backs, not all ex-slaves were penniless. Thousands had served in the Union Army and many managed to accumulate several hundred dollars.

Consequently, white businessmen, together with the U. S. government, chartered the Freedman's Savings and Trust Company (Freedman's Bank) for use by black Union soldiers. The whites associated with the Freedman's Bank, similar to those associated with schools for African Americans established after the Civil War, viewed themselves as missionaries. They believed the Freedman's Bank would instill in newly-freed blacks the virtues of savings and thrift. Between 1865 and 1870, the Freedman's Savings and Trust Company established branches throughout the country. Furthermore, not only ex-soldiers deposited their pay in this institution, but other blacks as well. In fact, the majority of accounts had balances under $50 and some amounted to only a few pennies. Nevertheless, regardless of the balance of one's account, African Americans viewed the Freedman's Bank as an institution whose purpose was to stimulate black wealth accumulation.

Unfortunately, by the early 1870s, the white directors of the Freedman's Bank lost sight of their earlier missionary intent and became caught up in the speculative fever of the period. Using the savings of African Americans, the bank's officers engaged in a number of questionable financial maneuvers, including granting large, unsecured loans to railroads and other white corporations. With the onset of the Panic of 1873, the Freedman's Savings and Trust Company lost huge sums of money (in the form of bad loans). Yet, the bank's directors intentionally kept this information from the general public and the institution's black depositors.

In the short term, the white directors of the Freedman's Bank were able to cover up their misdeeds. Yet, by early 1874, an increasing number of African American depositors became increasingly suspicious of the bank's operations. Consequently, to allay the fears of grassroots African American patrons, the bank's directors appointed the venerable Frederick Douglass as president of the institution. Moreover, the directors encouraged Douglass, who was not informed of the bank's crisis situation, to make a well-publicized personal deposit (to help maintain depositor confidence).

This tragic charade ended in June 1874 when an audit forced the Freedman's Savings and Trust Company to close its doors. The $31,000 in available cash deposits must have shocked Douglass and the institution's 61,000 other depositors because their passbooks verified that African Americans had deposited nearly $3.3 million in the Freedman's Bank.

In 1874, deposits in U.S. banks, unlike today, were not insured. Consequently, the Freedman's Saving and Trust Company's demise carried especially troubling implications for its depositors. Still, because African American depositors had been given the impression that the federal government cosponsored the Freedman's Bank, many believed the United States Congress would reimburse them for their losses.

Unfortunately, this expectation, similar to the expectation generated by the land distribution clause of the Freedman's Bureau Bill, would not materialize.

Ultimately, about half the creditors (depositors) of the Freedman's Savings and Trust Company received partial compensation of approximately $18.51 each (under normal bankruptcy procedures). The remainder, who failed to follow the procedures necessary to get their partial reimbursement, received nothing. Moreover, Freedman's Bank depositors, well into the twentieth century, sent appeals to Washington, D.C. seeking the balance of their funds. Yet, as historian Eric Foner has poignantly noted, "their letters now gather dust in the National Archives."

It would be difficult to overestimate the negative effect the demise of the Freedman's Bank had on the psyche of not just its unfortunate depositors but the entire African American community. As Carl R. Osthaus asserted in his book, *Freedmen, Philanthropy, and Fraud: A History of the Freedmen's Savings Bank*:

> Founded to encourage saving and economic enterprise, the Freedmen's Bank left an entirely different legacy. Observers of every type recorded their impression that many black depositors and their friends, who had accepted the maxims of work and thrift, lost faith in frugality and accumulation as a means toward improvement.

Further Reading

Foner, Eric. *Reconstruction: America's Unfinished Revolution, 1863–1877.* New York: Harper and Row, 1988, 531.

Franklin, John Hope, and Alfred A. Moss. *From Slavery To Freedom: A History of African Americans.* 7th ed. New York: McGraw-Hill, 1994, 236–237.

Osthaus, Carl R. *Freedmen, Philanthropy, and Fraud: A History of the Freedmen's Savings Bank.* Urbana: University of Illinois Press, 1976, 26.

—*Robert E. Weems, Jr.*

Fugitive Slave Act

The Fugitive Slave Act proved to be a contentious component of the **Compromise of 1850**. Northern moderates conceded to the Fugitive Slave Act as the cost the North had to pay to save the Union. The law, however, included several features that were repulsive to many antislavery Northerners. It denied trial by jury to alleged fugitives; it did not allow accused fugitives to testify in their own behalf; it permitted their return to slavery based simply on the testimony of the claimant; and it enabled court-appointed commissioners to unfairly collect $10 if they ruled in favor of the fugitive. Many felt that the law threatened to turn the North into a big pursue-and-capture area by authorizing federal marshals to gather posses to hunt fugitives on Northern soil. Furthermore, the law targeted not only recent fugitives, but also runaways who had fled the South decades earlier. For example, it allowed slave-catchers to take a former slave from his family in Ohio in 1852 and return him to his master from whom he had fled in 1831. Above all, the law oddly highlighted the irony that slavery was based on Northerners' complicity. By legalizing slave-catchers' activities on Northern soil, the law reminded Northerners that slavery was a national problem, not merely a peculiar Southern institution.

Northerners used legal tactics and occasionally resorted to violence in responding to the Fugitive Slave Act. Vigilance committees sprang up in many Northern communities to protect endangered blacks by organizing safe havens into Canada. Sympathetic Northern lawyers used obstructive legal tactics, extending court proceedings as long as possible, thus raising the slave-catchers' expenses. In another attempt to dilute the Act, nine Northern states passed "personal-liberty" laws banning state officials from enforcing the law. In the eyes of most Southerners, the South had gained little from the Compromise of 1850 other than the Fugitive Slave Act, and doubts soon surrounded even that Northern concession. Frederick Douglass, a former fugitive himself, understood the dangers the Act posed. He knew the blacks in the North could be snatched from their new lives and families, as he explained in his slave narrative. In fact, after escaping from Baltimore, Douglass became a key speaker on the abolitionist lecture circuit in addition to authoring his autobiography. This publicity caused his former owners to seek him out. The Fugitive Slave Act ordained their efforts, and Douglass ultimately fled the country until friends purchased his freedom.

Further Reading

Gates, Henry Louis, ed. *The Classic Slave Narratives*. New York: Penguin, 1987.

—Kelton R. Edmonds

G

Garnet, Henry Highland (1815-1882)

A clergyman and antislavery spokesman, Henry Garnet "organized [at 20] a 150 youth into the Garrison Literary and Benevolent Association, a group more bent on revolution than benevolence." Born into slavery in New Market, **Maryland**, Garnet escaped with his parents at the age of nine from a Maryland plantation. They relocated to New York in 1824. There he attended a private school, which had been controlled and operated by the black community, and became known for his "speechmaking abilities." As an adult he traveled throughout the United States and **Great Britain** speaking against the slave trade. Garnet advocated closer ties among Africans in the United States and Africa, and called upon African Americans to immigrate to African nations.

Garnet's formal education began and continued for 14 years. In 1835 he was set to begin schooling at an academy in Canaan, New Hampshire, but the townspeople "burned the school down when he showed up." Instead, he attended and eventually graduated from Oneida Institute in Whitesboro, New York, in 1840. Three years later, he was ordained a minister and appointed pastor of the Liberty Street Presbyterian Church in Troy, New York. Later, he led congregations in Kingston, Jamaica. He later returned to the United States, settling first in New York City, where he preached for Shiloh Presbyterian Church, and later in Washington, D.C. Though he lived in New York, he remained concerned about the problem of slavery in the South. Preaching against slavery, agitating for slave insurrections, and condemning complacent Northerners were the activities closest to Garnet's heart. This also marked Garnet's fierce, penetrating, and fiery rhetorical stance. His use of bold and forceful language, which was Garnet's aim, "appealed to the example of the American Revolution as he decried the slaves' voluntary submission to cruelty."

Before entering the ministry Garnet had identified himself with the movement against slavery, lecturing at the annual meeting of the American Anti-Slavery Society in 1840. The same year, he attended the first annual meeting of the American and Foreign Anti-Slavery Society. At the National Convention of Colored Citizens, a convention for free African Americans held in Buffalo, New York, in 1843, Garnet delivered "An Address to the Slaves of the United States." Among the more than 70 delegates were such notable antislavery advocates as Frederick Douglass, Charles Lenox Remond, and William Wells Brown. Undisturbed by the presence of these antislavery giants, Garnet urged the slaves to protest for their lives and liberties. Garnet noted "it would be better for slaves to die seeking freedom than to live in captivity." Tackling the issue of a "diabolical injustice," Garnet stated: "Neither God nor angels, or just men, command you to suffer for a single moment. Therefore, it is your solemn and imperative duty to use every means, moral, intellectual, and physical, that promises success." Although the speech he delivered became well known and thrust him into the limelight as a ranking antislavery orator, there was debate among some of the delegates as to whether to accept it "as a resolution to be transmitted to the South." The proposed resolution was rejected by one vote. Many of the delegates considered his language too militant. Garnet had spoken in the tradition of his mentor, David Walker, as he delivered one of the most militant speeches of the day.

By 1848 Garnet had developed into a leading revolutionary. He published a volume, which contained David Walker's Appeal to the Colored Citizens of the World and his Address to the Slaves of the United States. He also delivered another speech, "The Past and the Present Condition and the Destiny of the Colored Race," continuing the circulation of his radical ideas as he critiqued the contemporary use of the concept of colonization as a solution to the problems of the day. In the delivery of this speech, Garnet noted:

> There are those who, either from good or evil motives pleads for the utopian plan of the Colonization of a whole race to the shores of Africa. We are now colonized. We are planted here, and we cannot as a whole people, be re-colonized back to our fatherland. It is too late to make a successful attempt to separate the black and white people in the New World. They love one another too much to endure a separation. (Royster, 2007: 23)

Garnet later wrote and spoke of "the ancient fame of our ancestors," praising Africa as an age-old leader in peace and war. Garnet often cited the role African Americans played in the American Revolution, and the accomplishments of Haitian leaders such as **François Dominique Toussaint-Louverture**. In 1858, he founded the African Civilization Society (ACS) with the mission of encouraging African Americans to immigrate to Africa. Although the organization dissolved before the end of the Civil War, Garnet continued to maintain a strong interest in Africa.

Near the end of the American Civil War (1861–1865), Garnet addressed the House of Representatives, encouraging a final end to slavery. In 1881, he was appointed U.S. minister and consul general to Liberia.

Further Reading

Garnet, Henry Highland. "Address to the Slaves of the United States of America," 1848.

Garnet, Henry Highland. *The Past and the Present Condition, and the Destiny, of the Colored Race (1848)*. Paul Royster, ed. Available at http://digitalcommons.unl.edu/etas/13.

Smith, Arthur L. (a.k.a. Molefi Kete Asante) and Stephen Robb, eds. "Henry Highland Garnet," in *The Voice of Black Rhetoric: Selections*. Boston: Allyn and Bacon, 1971.

Smith, Arthur L. "Henry Highland Garnet: Black Revolutionary in Sheep's Vestments." *Central States Speech Journal*. Vol. XXI, No. 2 (Summer 1970): 5–14.

—*Ronald J. Stephens*

Garrison, William Lloyd (1805–1879)

William Lloyd Garrison was born on December 10, 1805 (although some sources cite his birth date as December 12) in Newburyport, **Massachusetts**, and passed away on May 24, 1879 in New York City. He was buried in Forest Hills Cemetery in Boston, Massachusetts. His father, Abijah, a merchant sailor, and his mother (only identified as having the maiden name of Lloyd) were residents from the British province of New Brunswick. The Garrison family was challenged with the *Embargo Act* of 1805, in which Garrison's father left his family, went to sea, and was never heard from again. This hardship and instability placed the Garrison family in an awkward position to acquire resources. His mother died in 1823.

Some documents note he was indentured at the age of 14 to Ephraim W. Allen, the owner of the *Newburyport Herald* (also documented as the *Newburyport Free Press*). Ironically, Garrison was later himself the editor of this newspaper in 1824. Selected sources indicate that Garrison owned this paper and that the paper discontinued publication in 1826. By 1828, Garrison was then named the editor of the *National Philanthropist*, located in Boston. Equally important, in 1829 Garrison, in partnership with Benjamin Lundy, a Quaker and an activist in the **Anti-Slavery Society**, became the coeditor of the newspaper, *Genius of Universal Emancipation*. Ironically, Garrison served a short prison sentence, an estimated seven weeks, after being convicted of libel for an article he wrote criticizing a merchant involved in enslaving Africans.

By the time Garrison reached the age of 25, he had joined the abolitionist movement in the United States. By 1828, Garrison had established the journal newspaper, *Journal of the Times*, in Bennington, Vermont, whose purpose was to support the reelection of John Quincy Adams as president of the United States. Later, in 1830, he was a participant and activist addressing issues related to the **American Colonization Society**; in 1831, he addressed the New England Slavery Society; and in 1833, he addressed the American Anti-Slavery Society.

During 1832–1833, he was active in organizing alliances concerned with the abolition of slavery and helped establish the Anti-Slavery Society with fellow abolitionists Arthur Tappan, Lewis Tappan, and Theodore Dwight Weld.

William Lloyd Garrison, editor of the antislavery newspaper, *Liberator*. John Sartain. Courtesy National Park Service, Museum Management Program, and Frederick Douglass National Historic Site, FRDO 3124. http://www.cr.nps.gov/museum.

He served as president of the American Anti-Slavery Society from 1843–1865. During 1840 there was an ideological spilt in the Anti-Slavery Society, and Garrison with his supporters advocated developing a government branch in the United States which forbade enslaving Africana people. The Liberty Party was formed. Additionally, Garrison worked with **Susan B. Anthony** and others in advancing the cause for the **women's suffrage** movement.

In 1838, Garrison's first son, William Lloyd Garrison, was born (1838–1909) and in 1840, his second son, Wendell Philips Garrison, was born (1840–1907). Unfortunately, by 1876, Garrison's wife, Helen Eliza Benson, died. During the latter years of Garrison's life, he focused his activism more toward the women's suffrage movement and pacifism. Garrison died two years after his wife in 1879, in New York City.

Further Reading

Africans in America, http://www.pbs.org/wgbh/aia/part4/4p1561.html.

William Lloyd Garrison: NNDB http://www.nndb.com/people/966/000049819/.

———. Ohio History Central http://www.ohiohistorycentral.org/entry.php?rec=167.

———. Spartacus Educational http://www.spartacus.schoolnet.co.uk/USASgarrison.htm.

—*James L. Conyers*

German Enlightenment

The most direct, personal influence of Germany on Frederick Douglass was by way of Ottilie Assing, who was born in Hamburg in 1819 and emigrated to the United States in 1852. One of many disillusioned intellectuals who left Germany after the failure of the Revolution of 1848, Assing visited Douglass in **Rochester, New York** in 1856 in her role as a reporter for the German periodical, *Morgenblatt*, with the express intention of translating Douglass's autobiography into German. Thus began a 28-year personal relationship that was mutually beneficial in both professional and intellectual ways. Published in 1860 by the Hamburg firm of Hoffman und Campe, Assing's translation of **My Bondage and My Freedom**, as well as numerous articles about Douglass and the American scene, spread the gospel of **abolitionists** to the German-speaking world, while her professional connection to Douglass enhanced her portfolio in her adopted country.

Aside from Ottilie Assing's direct influence, the indirect impact of German Enlightenment and Romantic thinkers on cultural issues pertaining to Douglass was enormous. Contemporary philosophers such as Emmanuel Eze and Robert Bernasconi find convincing evidence that our modern-day concept of "race" as a transcendental signifier of human worth and value can be traced to Immanuel Kant (Konigsberg, 1724–1804). Kant's popular lectures on anthropology, the study of the inner man, and geography, the study of physical characteristics, were collected in his *Anthropology from a Pragmatic Point of View*, as well as his *Observations on the*

Feeling of the Beautiful and Sublime. Skin color, for Kant, was evidence of race, and race, in turn, was evidence of natural character. Hence, the blackness of the skin of a speaker is always proof, for Kant, of moral and intellectual inferiority. Or, to put it another way, the paradigm for rational and moral perfection is the white, European male. Many of Kant's racial concepts were later elaborated and systematized by Johann Friedrich Blumenbach (1752–1840) in his treatise, *On the Natural Variety of Mankind* (1775). There, Blumenbach divides mankind into five races—Caucasian, Mongolian, Ethiopian, American, and Malay. As with Kant, the Caucasian is imagined to be the ideal of which all others are more or less degenerated forms.

If Kant and Blumenbach develop race as a stable category of inquiry, the intellectual trajectory from Georg Hegel (1770–1831) to Karl Marx (1818–1883) and Friedrich Engels (1820–1895) becomes the impetus for its destabilization. In the *Phenomenology of Spirit* (1807) Hegel articulates his now-famous dialectic of interdependence between master and bondsman. Susan Buck-Morss, following David Brion Davis, has recently shown that Hegel's allegory of self-consciousness must now be read against the historical backdrop of the Haitian Revolution, that epic struggle for sovereignty and recognition between Napolean and **Toussaint L'Ouverture** about which Hegel was reading in periodicals available in Jena, a university city in central Germany. Hegel's dialectic famously exposes the master's dependence on the slave's recognition of his mastery, but Hegel nevertheless naturalizes the hierarchical racial categories set up by his predecessors. In the *Philosophy of History*, for example, Hegel constructs an **Africa** that is outside the teleology of Universal History, always primal, never progressive. Starting out as Left Hegelians, Marx and Engels turn from Hegel's historical idealism to Ludwig Feuerbach's historical materialism. Understanding history as a function of class struggle, Marx and Engels provide an analytical framework that, according to Orlando Patterson, will become one of two dominant methodologies in late-nineteenth and twentieth century analyses of the history of slavery.

Since the advent of the slave trade, transatlantic subjectivity has been shaped in significant ways by either slavery or race. Viewed through the prism of class-struggle, one can read eighteenth- and nineteenth-century accounts of race, as many theorists now do, as ideological effects of the material conditions of slavery, effects so pernicious that long after slavery was abolished, as Douglass would find in his latter years, race would continue to patrol the cultural spaces that slavery helped create. For that reason, the German Enlightenment, with Kant as its central figure, has had an inordinate impact on the transatlantic culture that slavery helped build.

Further Reading

Bernasconi, Robert. "Who Invented the Concept of Race? Kant's Role in the Enlightenment Construction of Race," in Robert Bernasconi, ed. *Race*. Malden, Mass.: Blackwell, 2001.

Diedrich, Maria. *Love Across Color Lines: Ottilie Assing and Frederick Douglass*. New York: Hill and Wang, 1999.

Eze, Emmanuel. "The Color of Reason: The Idea of 'Race' in Kant's Anthropology," in Katherine M. Faull, ed. *Anthropology and the German Enlightenment: Perspectives on Humanity*. Arlington, Va.: Institute for Humane Studies, Incorporated, 1995.

—Stephen Andrews

Grandfather Clause

The Grandfather Clause was a voting rights statute passed primarily by Southern legislatures in the 1890s extending voting rights to males whose ancestors had voted in the 1860s. It was included with others referenced by the term "**Black Codes**." This measure was specifically designed to exempt a segment of white male voters from literacy, residency, property, or tax requirements that otherwise disqualified them from voting. On the surface, the Grandfather Clause appeared to be a race-neutral measure, but in reality it was discriminatory in intent and impact because it was expressly and clearly designed only to protect the voting rights of white males. Grandfather Clauses selected dates, such as 1867, to be temporal markers because those dates simultaneously included previously disfranchised white males and excluded African Americans because they had been ineligible to vote prior to this date due to their legal status as slaves.

For the South, the validity of the Grandfather Clause, as with other discriminatory requirements and measures restricting voting rights, rested on a strict interpretation of the **Fifteenth Amendment**. The Fifteenth Amendment stated that the extension of the right to vote to citizens could not be denied based upon the criteria of race, color, or previous condition of servitude, but it did not affirmatively extend the right to vote to anyone, a fact not lost on Southern legislatures. In *United States vs. Reese* (1876), the Supreme Court reaffirmed the fact that the Fifteenth Amendment did not confer on anyone the right to vote and emphasized the role of the states as the primary arbiters of suffrage. Because states' rights determine voting rights, and not the federal government, Southern states were empowered to incrementally deny voting rights to African Americans.

The Grandfather Clause must be interpreted not just legally, but also within its proper historical and political context. In the aftermath of the Civil War, the nation witnessed significant and expansive constitutional changes embodied in the passage of the Thirteenth, Fourteenth, and Fifteenth Amendments. These Reconstruction Amendments were buttressed by the **Civil Rights Acts** of 1866 and 1875 and the Enforcement Acts of the 1870s. Taken together, these legal measures theoretically prevented autonomous state sovereignty and strengthened the ability of the federal government to articulate a national vision of personal liberty and civil rights. This nationalization of civil rights signaled to African Americans the promise of actualizing freedom in the concrete form of greater political participation. All across the South African Americans mobilized themselves to actively participate in shaping a new vision of civil and political society in the South that partially emerged in the context of state constitutional conventions heavily influenced by the platform of the **Republican Party**. As a consequence, thousands of African Americans went to the ballot box to exercise their voting rights, often backed by military protection. As a Republican, Frederick Douglass championed and chronicled through his speeches and writings the dynamic efforts by African Americans to attain and exercise their civil rights, especially the right to vote. Douglass did not only desire to develop and spread the ideas of the Republican Party throughout the South; he advocated imposing on the South the lofty political ideals of national citizenship and voting rights contained in the Fourteenth and Fifteenth Amendments. Without imposition from the federal government backed by an armed military presence, Douglass felt that the South would inevitably continue to resist and retreat back to the past of slavery. By 1880, under the banner of "Redemption," Douglass lamented the fact that Southern white Democrats had begun to suppress African American political participation initially through terrorist acts of violence and intimidation, but eventually by law with the implementation of poll taxes, gerrymandering, complicated voting procedures, and restrictive registration requirements which enabled white Democrats to regain control over polling places and counting ballots.

Frederick Douglass, a staunch supporter of the Fifteenth Amendment, saw voting rights for African Americans as necessary to improve their lives in all areas of their lives. Over time, Douglass's views began to reflect a growing disillusionment with the passive acceptance and lack of will on the part of the federal government and the Republican Party to effectively respond to the violence and fraud that African Americans were facing all over the South preventing them from voting. Douglass saw that the inactivity of the federal government to protect the civil rights of African Americans ultimately stemmed from the constitutional interpretation that subsumed the primary responsibility to regulate civil rights under the auspices of the states. One of Douglass's consistent critiques emphasized what he considered a narrow interpretation of the Constitution. For Douglass, the Constitution was the legal embodiment of national interests which should take precedence over states' interests, especially involving basic civil rights which he felt should be extended to citizens equally regardless of race, class, or gender. In his speeches and writings, he constantly chided the nation and the Republican Party for being morally weak in retreating from universal manhood suffrage by allowing suffrage schemes like the Grandfather Clause to taint the lofty democratic principles of the nation.

The first Southern Grandfather Clause was adopted by **South Carolina** in 1890. The most often cited Grandfather Clause originated in the Louisiana State Convention of 1898 and indicated that no male person who was entitled to vote on or before January 1, 1867 could be denied the right to vote. This right to vote was also extended to the descendants of the male person. The year 1867 was carefully considered and selected because no African American in **Louisiana** could vote prior to 1868. In 1915 the Supreme Court, in *Guinn vs. United States*, ruled that the Grandfather Clause was unconstitutional, but it continued to acquiesce to most Southern disfranchisement schemes. Douglass saw that the restoration of white Democratic rule in the South and the resulting end of federal intervention was accomplished at the expense of African American freedom and equal rights.

Further Reading

Blassingame, John W. and John R. McKivigan, eds. *The Frederick Douglass Papers*, vol. 5. New Haven, Conn.: Yale University Press, 1999.

Hahn, Steven. *A Nation Under Our Feet: Black Political Struggles in the Rural South from Slavery to the Great Migration.* Cambridge, Mass.: Belknap Press of Harvard University Press, 2003.

Keyssar, Alexander. *The Right to Vote: The Contested History in the United States.* New York: Basic Books, 2000.

—*Mario H. Beatty*

Great Britain

British participation in the slave trade rose dramatically after the Treaty of Utrecht (1713), which formally ended the War of Spanish Succession in which Great Britain was granted the *asiento*, or exclusive right to supply slaves to Spain's New World colonies. As a result, London, Bristol, and Liverpool became dominant British slave ports in the eighteenth century, and profits from the slave trade helped found banks, created new factories, gave impetus to shipbuilding, and increased demand for textiles manufactured in places such as Manchester. In addition, the eighteenth century European mania for sugar and tobacco, both produced by slave labor in the Americas, helped ensure that trade in slaves would be an integral part of the British economy until slavery was abolished.

Even as fortunes were being made, abolition was being encouraged in some religious and philosophical circles. Quite simply, slavery was at odds with the burgeoning eighteenth-century discourse of individual liberty that placed increased value on intellectual, religious, and political freedom. In religion, the Society of Friends, or Quakers, led the **abolitionist** charge, becoming the first sect in Britain to prohibit members from trading in slaves (1781), thus putting pressure on other denominations to follow suit. Arguably the greatest advocate for abolition was the Englishman Thomas Clarkson, who made abolition his life's work. In 1787, Clarkson, along with Granville Sharp, helped found the Committee for Effecting the Abolition of the Slave Trade, of which Quakers made up the majority. Clarkson was able to convince Member of Parliament William Wilberforce to enjoin abolitionist causes in the House of Commons on behalf of the Committee. The triangulation of cultural forces embodied by the Quakers, Clarkson, and Wilberforce would eventually lead to outlawing the slave trade in 1807. By that time, English and British vessels had made approximately 12,000 voyages and delivered between 3 and 4 million slaves to the New World. The abolition of slavery in the British West Indies on August 1, 1833, provided a beacon of hope for abolitionists in the United States, as British abolitionists remained resolute in their quest to rid the world of slavery.

Douglass's **European lecture circuit** included three separate lecture tours in Great Britain: 1845 to 1847; 1859 to 1860; and 1886 to 1887. The first and second tours are the more significant as they occurred when slavery had not yet been abolished in the United States and during times when Douglass was in fear for his safety. In January 1846, the American Anti-Slavery Society sent Douglass from Belfast, Ireland, to Glasgow and Edinburgh, Scotland. The purpose of the trip was to fire up the abolitionist base in the ongoing debate between members of the Church of Scotland and the Free Church, a splinter group of Presbyterians led by Thomas Chalmers, which was accepting funds from Presbyterians in the American South who were advocating on behalf of slavery. The abolitionists' motto "Send back the money" became a catchphrase that galvanized the faithful and helped bring new converts into the abolitionist cause, and Douglass became something of a folk hero in Scotland. On his second trip, Douglass gave an important speech in Glasgow in March 1860, defending the U.S. Constitution as an antislavery document, thus putting him radically at odds with **William Lloyd Garrison**. These first two visits to Great Britain not only made Douglass an international star, they also provided a model for him of the kind of social and political freedom that might be available to persons of African descent once the stumbling block of slavery was lifted.

Further Reading

Douglass, Frederick. *The Life and Times of Frederick Douglass*. New York: Collier Books, 1962.

McFeely, William. *Frederick Douglass*. New York: W. W. Norton & Co., 1991.

Thomas, Hugh. *The Slave Trade: The Story of the Atlantic Slave Trade: 1440–1870*. New York: Simon and Schuster, 1997.

—*Stephen Andrews*

Greeley, Horace (1811-1872)

Editor, journalist, and Republican Horace Greeley was born in Amherst, New Hampshire. His family later settled in Westhaven, Vermont, where he attended the district's schools. Arriving at New York City in 1831, he founded and was the editor of the *New Yorker* and the *New York Tribune*. He contributed greatly to such political legislation as the 1842 Tariff Act, the 1850 **Kansas-Nebraska Act**, and the 1862 Confiscation Act and contributed to other social and political causes. In 1860 he ran for Congress in New York; in 1861 he ran for state senator of New York, and he campaigned for President in 1872; all attempts were unsuccessful.

His opinions on such political issues as tariffs and legislation were well respected and recognized nationally. However, Greeley disagreed with many, especially Frederick Douglass, on such black issues as slavery and emigration. There are some accounts of Greeley being an abolitionist; but while Douglass was advocating for complete freedom and emancipation for blacks, Greeley was lobbying for selected and partial freedom for blacks only in New York. His opinions on race relations were at times contradictory. He felt that blacks would always be subservient to whites. Douglass strongly disagreed with Greeley on the question of black emigration to other countries, citing it as evidence of their unwillingness to uplift themselves as a collective group of people.

Further Reading

Blassingame, John W. *The Frederick Douglass Papers*. New Haven, Conn.: Yale University Press, 1979.

Isley, Jeter A. *Horace Greeley and the Republican Party 1853–1861*. Princeton, N.J.: Princeton University Press, 1947.

Stoddard, Henry L. *Horace Greeley, Printer, Editor, Crusader*. New York: G. P. Putnam's Sons, 1946.

—*Tyre Fante*

Greener, Richard T. (1844–1922)

Educator, politician, lawyer, and philosopher Richard Greener was born free on January 30, 1844 in Philadelphia, Pennsylvania. At the age of five, Greener's family moved to Cambridge, **Massachusetts**, where he received a formal education at the Broadway Grammar School until the age of 14. After a short absence from schooling, Greener spent the next two years studying at Oberlin College in Ohio and the Philips Academy in Andover, Massachusetts, preparing for admittance into Harvard University. Greener entered Harvard in 1865 at the age of 21, excelling in all areas of study and receiving academic notice in oratory and dissertation writing. He finished the coursework for the Bachelor of Arts in five years, choosing land tenures in Ireland as the subject of his dissertation. In 1870, he earned the distinction of being Harvard's first African American graduate. Reflecting on this success, he wrote a brief autobiographical sketch outlining his educational development and social origins.

Greener immediately began a career in teaching and accepted the position of principal at the male department of the Institute for Colored Youth in Philadelphia and, later, the Summer High School in Washington, D.C. In 1873, Greener was made professor of metaphysics and logic at the University of South Carolina. He taught Latin, Greek, U.S. constitutional history, and international law. Before the University closed in 1877, Greener began work toward a law degree. At the same time he participated in revising the course curricula for the entire state school system. After having completed his coursework, Greener gained admittance to practice law within the state of **South Carolina**.

Throughout his career, Greener received notoriety as one of the most powerful orators and gifted African American philosophers in America. He espoused a belief that African Americans would succeed as a race only through the individual efforts of its members. Likewise, his prominence as a leading African American orator of his time brought him into conference with Frederick Douglass on the subject of the mass exodus of African Americans then affecting the American South. At a public debate on September 12, 1877 in Saratoga Springs, New York, Greener criticized Douglass's interpretation of the exodus as being the result of political forces and insisted that the movement was a legitimate response for African Americans given their oppressed condition. Although Douglass could not attend the event, Greener correctly predicted that the exodus would continue beyond the national elections of the following year.

Greener had worked as an associate editor for Douglass's *New National Era*, a weekly paper in Washington, D.C. He had previously edited another paper in Washington, the *National Era*. He gained national attention for his involvement in the defense of Johnson C. Whittaker, a black **West Point** cadet charged with falsely accusing his fellow cadets of attempted mutilation of his ears. Although Greener enjoyed the prestige that came with his various successes, his beliefs on racial uplift by individual efforts caused him to avoid the leadership roles that such successes usually demand. In 1879, after passing the bar in Washington, D.C., Greener accepted a position as professor in Howard University's Law Department. Over the next few years, Greener became Dean of Howard's Law School while working in the office of the First Controller of the United States Treasury. In 1882 he decided to go into private practice.

At what eventually became the apex of his career, Greener accepted several Foreign Service posts in the McKinley and Roosevelt administrations. In January 1898, Greener received an appointment as consul to Bombay, India. Upon learning that the city was being ravaged by an epidemic of bubonic plague, Greener turned down the post for a more tenable offer in Russia. In July 1898, he accepted an appointment as the first U.S. Consul to Vladivostok.

During his appointment in Vladivostok, Greener would oversee British and Japanese interests in the region. In 1904, the Chinese government decorated Greener with the Order of the Double Dragon for his assistance to war victims during the Russo-Japanese War. In 1905, Assistant Secretary of State Herbert H. D. Pierce removed Greener from his post on charges of bad habits and neglect of duty. Despite the fact that Greener received international recognition for his services, Pierce's action would prove bindingly final. Although a special investigatory committee proved the allegations false, Greener was never reappointed to his former post. In the last years of his life, Greener became increasingly disillusioned with the **Republican Party's** approach toward the problems of African Americans. He retired to Chicago where he practiced law until his death on May 2, 1922.

Further Reading

Blakely, Allison. "Richard T. Greener and the "Talented Tenth's" Dilemma." *Journal of Negro History*. 59, No. 4 (1974): 305–321.

—Malachi Crawford

Grimke, Angelina Emily (1805-1879)

Noted **abolitionist** Angelina Grimke was the youngest of 14 children born to a strict Episcopalian family in the upper echelons of **South Carolina** society. Angelina followed her sister's example and converted to Quakerism against family tradition and social status. In 1834 she began to read abolitionist papers, later joining the Philadelphia Female Anti-Slavery Society. On August 30, 1835 she wrote a declaration of abolition to **William Lloyd Garrison**. Angelina's letter was published in Garrison's paper, the *Liberator*, and became a powerful piece of propaganda linking the slaveholding name of Grimke with the most famous abolitionist of the time. Angelina went on to write a pamphlet, an appeal to Southern Christian women, which also caused some controversy. She became an ardent speaker for the abolitionist cause and one of the first females to speak publicly before mixed crowds. In defending her right as a woman to speak publicly, Angelina also became known in women's rights circles. After the Civil War she continued to promote civil rights and campaigned for **women's suffrage**.

Further Reading

Lerner, Gerda. *The Grimke Sisters From South Carolina.* New York: Schocken Books, 1971.

———. "The Grimke Sisters and the Struggle Against Race Prejudice." *The Journal of Negro History.* Vol 48, No. 4 (1963): pp. 277–291.

Lumpkin, Katherine Du Pre. *The Emancipation of Angelina Grimke.* Chapel Hill: University of North Carolina Press, 1974.

—*Lia Bascomb*

Grimke, Francis J. (1850–1937)

Civil rights activist and religious leader Francis Grimke was born in Charleston, South Carolina, to Henry Grimke and his slave, Nancy Weston. Francis, upon the death of his father, was left in the care of his half-brother, Montague. Escaping his half-brother's ownership, he acted as a valet in the Confederate Army until he was recognized in Charleston and sent back to Montague. Francis was then sent to a workhouse where he became extremely ill, and upon leaving, was sold to a Confederate officer.

After the Civil War he and his older brother, Archibald, were sent north to take advantage of newly opened educational opportunities. Francis excelled in his studies, bringing him and his brother to the attention of their then-famous aunt **Angelina Grimke** Weld. Francis befriended Frederick Douglass, whom he had long admired. Douglass mentored Francis, who went on to study theology at the Princeton Theological Seminary and later became pastor of the Fifteenth Street Presbyterian Church in Washington, D.C. He remained a pastor for 50 years, becoming a prominent persona in the city and nationwide. Francis Grimke served as a trustee of Howard University as well as a founding member of the American Negro Academy.

Further Reading

Lerner, Gerda. *The Grimke Sisters From South Carolina.* New York: Schocken Books, 1971.

Woodson, Carter G. *Works of Francis James Grimke.* Washington, D.C.: The Associated Publishers, Inc., 1942.

—*Lia Bascomb*

H

Harpers Ferry

Though Harpers Ferry, West Virginia, hosted the likes of U.S. Presidents George Washington and Thomas Jefferson, played a crucial role in the outcome of the Civil War, and served as the site of the Niagara Movement's (forerunner to the NAACP) first meeting on American soil (1906), it is probably best known for the historic raid led by **abolitionist** John Brown on the city's arsenal.

In 1799 the United States Armory and Arsenal was established at Harpers Ferry, transforming the remote village into an industrial center. Inventor John H. Hall pioneered interchangeable firearms manufacture at his Rifle Works between 1820 and 1840 and helped lead the change from craft-based production to manufacture by machine. In fact, the federal government contracted Hall to manufacture his patented rifles at Harpers Ferry.

These developments created a city with industry and weapons prized by both the Union and Confederate armies; in fact, the town changed hands eight times between 1861 and 1865 because of its arms-producing capabilities, great waterpower provided by the Potomac and Shenandoah Rivers and close proximity to Washington, D.C. However, before Harpers Ferry served as a prized possession bandied about between opposing forces of the Civil War, it served as home to an event that Frederick Douglass credits with setting in motion both the war and the ultimate emancipation of enslaved Africans.

The raid on Harpers Ferry (October 16–18, 1859) was to be the initial stage of a war leading to the freedom of America's enslaved Africans. Brown's original plan was to deploy his 21-man "army of liberation" into the Blue Ridge Mountains, using the terrain as a base for guerilla warfare tactics aimed at freeing the enslaved. Brown's hopes of victory rested upon his assumption that those freed would join his army, growing it into a formidable force for his cause.

Initially, Brown had the money and manpower to launch his offensive in 1858, but postponed his war because one of his followers threatened to reveal Brown's plan. Brown went into hiding, renting a farm in Maryland—across the Potomac River from Harpers Ferry—in the summer of 1859 using the pseudonym Isaac Smith. There, Brown trained 22 men, including his sons Oliver, Owen, and Watson, in preparatory military maneuvers.

It was during this period that Brown's plan changed; instead of using the Blue Ridge Mountains as cover for his ongoing war against slavery, he would deploy his troops to seize the armory in Harpers Ferry. With the armory's 100,000 weapons in his possession, Brown thought his plan to free the enslaved was strategically sound. However, during this delay, many of his recruits changed their minds, moved away, or simply lost faith in Brown's plan. In fact, **abolitionists Henry Highland Garnet** and Frederick Douglass shared with Brown their misgivings. Garnet, who advocated insurrection as a viable option for freeing the enslaved, believed the enslaved unprepared to respond as Brown envisioned. Douglass warned Brown that attacking the armory was in effect attacking the federal government and likened the plan to walking into a trap.

Undeterred, Brown led a force of 21 men—5 free African Americans and 16 whites, including two of Brown's three sons—across the Potomac River at sundown on October 16. Reaching the city around 4:00 a.m., Brown's forces cut telegraph wires and captured the city's armory along with Hall's Rifle Works.

Brown's army then rounded up 60 of Harpers Ferry's most prominent citizens and held them as hostages; one of the captured was George Washington's great-grandnephew, Lewis Washington. At least two Africans who escaped enslavement joined Brown, although federal authorities, in an attempt to discredit Brown and quell any notions of future uprisings, reported in the raid's aftermath that none of the enslaved came forth to join Brown's crusade. To further emphasize the futility of African American and white antislavery alliances, authorities were quick to publicize the raid's first casualty, Hayward Shepherd, an African American railroad baggage handler who was killed after confronting Brown's troops.

Along with disabling telegraphic communications, Brown and his followers detained a Baltimore and Ohio train for five hours to keep word of their actions from reaching federal officials. However, after they let the train continue its journey, it arrived in Baltimore at noon the next day, and the conductor immediately alerted authorities in the nation's capital of the raid on Harpers Ferry.

President James Buchanan immediately ordered a force of Marines, led by Colonel Robert E. Lee, to Harpers Ferry to capture Brown and reclaim the federal armory. Before their arrival, local militia companies had already surrounded the armory to cut off all escape routes. When Lee's troops arrived, 8 of Brown's 22 men had already been killed, as had Fontaine Beckham, the mayor of Harpers Ferry, who was among the 60 captured by Brown.

At 6:30 a.m. on October 18, Lee ordered Lieutenant Israel Green and a group of men to storm the armory's small fire engine house, to which Brown had retreated with nine prisoners. The fire engine house would later become known as John Brown's Fort. The Marines immediately began taking prisoners. Green seriously wounded Brown, who was then taken to Charlestown, Virginia (now Charles Town, West Virginia) for trial. In the end, 10 of Brown's men, including two of his sons, were killed, seven were captured, and five escaped.

John Brown was eventually tried, convicted, sentenced, and finally hanged on December 2, 1859. Brown's brief raid failed to liberate the enslaved, but his trial and execution forced the nation to confront the issue of slavery. In fact, on May 30, 1881 during the fourteenth anniversary of Storer College, located in Harpers Ferry, Frederick Douglass delivered the keynote address that lauded Brown as a martyr and hero who, said Douglass, failed to lead an army of liberators into the mountains of Virginia and save his own life. Douglass added, however, that Brown's aim was not saving his own life, but rather bringing an end to slavery. Thus, Brown did not fail because he began the war that eventually ended slavery.

Further Reading

Anderson, Osborne. *A Voice From Harper's Ferry, 1859*. Ithaca, N.Y.: Cornell University Press, 2001.

Du Bois, W. E. B. *John Brown*. New York: Oxford University Press, 2007.

Reynolds, David S. *John Brown, Abolitionist: The Man Who Killed Slavery, Sparked the Civil War, and Seeded Civil Rights*. New York: Alfred A. Knopf, 2005.

—*Aswad Walker*

Hughes, Langston (1902–1967)

Poet, novelist, and essayist Langston Hughes is one of the most noted African American poets and Harlem Renaissance writers. His celebrated poem "Frederick Douglass: 1817–1895" was first published in *Liberator* in 1966 at the height of the civil rights movement, when African Americans continued to face strong resistance to their fight for equal treatment. The poem was also included in the posthumously published *The Panther and the Lash* (1967), a collection of 70 poems, some written as early as the 1930s and others as late as 1966. Unlike some of Hughes's earlier love poems, the poetry in *The Panther and the Lash* was "militant, angry, and defiant." Although critics ignored the book, it was very popular, selling more than 7,000 copies in its first few months in print. Not particularly militant, Hughes's "Frederick Douglass: 1817–1895" gives hope to an entire race of people, for whom at times little hope existed. The succinct, 22-line poem might have been a rallying cry for all those who worried that full freedom and equality might never be a reality. This subject of freedom was a constant theme in Hughes's poetry.

While the poem calls attention to the strength and determination of Frederick Douglass, it also calls on African Americans not to be afraid to "strike the first blow" against white oppression. At the time this poem was published, a chasm was developing between supporters of Dr. Martin Luther King Jr.'s nonviolent approach and Stokely Carmichael's and other black power groups' calls for civil rights "by any means necessary." Although Hughes had defended King from attacks by militant blacks one year earlier, in this poem he seems to be advocating a more proactive stance. The poem encourages African Americans not to walk with "wary foot" or "frightened tread" but instead to be "bold" on the route "toward freedom's goal," just as Douglass had been when he decided he would be "anything but a slave!" For Hughes, African Americans needed to not waver in their quest for freedom lest they face death, or worse yet, the loss of their souls. The last lines of the poem, "He died in 1895. / He is not dead." helps the reader understand that Douglass's courage in the face of his white masters still lives, and is alive within all of us. Like his other poetry, essays, and novels, Hughes's poem "Frederick Douglass: 1817–1895" captures African American culture by exploring the contributions of those strong black men and women who had come before him.

Further Reading

Rampersad, Arnold. *The Life of Langston Hughes*, vols. I and II. New York: Oxford University Press, 2002.

Watson, Steven. *The Harlem Renaissance: Hub of African-American Culture, 1920–1930*. New York: Pantheon Books, 1995.

—Dwonna Goldstone

I

Imperialism in the Caribbean

The public life of Frederick Douglass was so vast and its scope so immense that writers have frequently tended to emphasize certain aspects of it to the virtual exclusion of others. Such has been the case with the views and roles of Douglass in American foreign policy. While Douglass has been portrayed as abolitionist, writer, journalist, and advocate of the civil rights of blacks as well as women, he could be regarded as having an expansionist view vis-à-vis American diplomacy in the Caribbean.

In 1871, Frederick Douglass was appointed to the Commission of Inquiry for the annexation of Santo Domingo to the United States of America. With this appointment, he was cast in a new light. He was concerned not only with domestic reforms, but also with protecting American interests abroad. Douglass's appointment came somewhat as a surprise to him, at a time when he had just about given up hope of receiving a government post. Even so, he hailed the assignment as a new day for blacks: "My selection to visit Santo Domingo with the commission sent thither was another point indicating the difference between the old time and the new."

This post, needless to say, placed Douglass in a precarious position. It put him at odds with his previous political stance on the independence of countries in the Caribbean as well as with his most trusted friend, **Charles Sumner**. Douglass, who in 1868 had supported the Cuban Revolution, was in 1871 advocating the termination of another Latin American country. The "Sage of Anacostia," who had not differed with Sumner for 15 years, would now find himself in opposition to the senator over the issue of annexation.

After 1844, the island of Santo Domingo, which now bears the name Haiti, was divided into two independent states, the Dominican Republic and the Republic of Haiti. The next 50 years witnessed periods during which efforts were made to annex the island or parts of it to the United States. While these attempts to annex Santo Domingo and to acquire a naval base in Haiti were of vital interest to blacks of both the West Indies and the United States, they were of special interest to the freedom fighter, politician, and diplomat, Frederick Douglass.

The American government made three attempts to acquire Santo Domingo. The first came in 1854, the second in 1866, and the third in 1868. In all three of these ventures, the incentives for annexation were more or less the same. They included the United States' desire to acquire a naval base in the West Indies and to strengthen the Monroe Doctrine, which supposedly had been weakened in that area by European activities. There was a desire on the part of some Americans to stimulate business interest in the Caribbean. The third effort to acquire Santo Domingo is the one that involved Douglass. Douglass came to the conclusion that the miserable conditions of the people of that island were caused not by laziness, but by slavery, absentee landlords, civil wars, and the general economic condition. Because he believed that the United States could improve this situation, when Douglass was made special envoy to Santo Domingo and went to the island in 1872, he became fully convinced that its people should be made American citizens.

Given the above argument, it is not surprising that Douglass sympathized with the imperialist aspiration of Benjamin Harrison's administration for acquiring a naval base in Haiti in 1889 when he was appointed ambassador. At no time from Ambassador Douglass's arrival in Haiti on October 15, 1889, to November 30, 1889, was he instructed to negotiate for a coaling station at Môle St. Nicolas. Apparently his first knowledge of the United States' efforts to acquire Môle St. Nicolas came from reports that he had read in the newspaper in December 1889. At that time, he reported to Secretary of State J. Gordon Blaine that rumors in the American press concerning the alleged desire of the United States to acquire Môle, coupled with the reconnoitering of unauthorized warships in Haitian waters, were creating suspicion among the Haitians. "There is a feeling," he argued in a letter to Blaine, "that preliminary steps had been taken to sell the country to the Americans." In this same letter Douglass expressed doubts over the United States' intention as perceived by the Haitians. However, he would later discover that he was deceived by protocol. Not only did Blaine know the reasons why the United States' ships were at Môle, but he was also aware that William P. Clyde, a shipping magnate from New York, would seek the support of Douglass in order to promote his business interests in Haiti.

Although he was unaware at the time he arrived in Haiti that he was expected to facilitate the transaction of Môle, when he was given the assignment at a later date, he did not object to the mission. The argument that he used in the incident would be similar to the one used in the Santo Domingo controversy. That is, as long as slavery persisted in the United States, Douglass opposed or would have opposed expansion at black Haitians' expense. With slavery overthrown, the cardinal objection to American expansion disappeared. As such, Douglass saw no reason to oppose the *raison d'être* of his mission.

In a sense, one could consider Douglass a missionary, confident that he comprehended the peace and well-being of other countries better than the leaders of those countries themselves. This urge to do good, to render disinterested service, was so compelling that it motivated interference in the internal affairs of other nations. Moreover, an evangel of Democracy, Douglass thought that Americans could teach the people of the Caribbean how to elect a good and established stable government. Intervention was therefore rationalized in terms of rescuing his helpless friends from foreign dangers and internal disorder. Because Douglass thought in those terms, it did not always occur to him that he was pursuing a conventionally imperialistic course.

Further Reading

Douglass, Frederick. *Life and Times of Frederick Douglass*. New York: Collier, 1963.

Foner, Philip S., ed. *The Life and Writings of Frederick Douglass*. vol. 4. New York: International Press, 1975.

Himelock, Myra.. "Frederick Douglass and Haiti's Mole St. Nicholas." *Journal of Negro History*. 56 (July 1971): 161–180.

Logan, Rayford. *Diplomatic Relations of the United States with Haiti, 1776–1891*. Chapel Hill: Univ. of North Carolina Press, 1941.

Pitre, Merline. "Frederick Douglass and American Diplomacy in the Caribbean." *Journal of Black Studies*. 13 (June 26, 1983): 452–475.

Quarles, Benjamin. *Frederick Douglass*. Washington, D.C.: Associated Publishers, 1940; see also *Report of the Santo Domingo Commission*, Washington, D.C.: Government Printing Office, 1871.

—Merline Pitre

Industrial Education

Douglass was an early and long-term champion of industrial education for African Americans. He advocated it with all of the zeal of an educational reformer throughout most of his life. In public addresses as well as the pages of his newspaper, Douglass called upon African Americans and the nation to develop and implement an education policy that embraced their current economic needs and future aspirations in the United States.

Douglass was not the first **abolitionist** to embrace industrial education as a solution to the numerous racial barriers and economic problems confronting African Americans. Samuel Cornish outlined a plan for a manual labor school in *Freedom's Journal* as early as 1827. Delegates at the 1831 Black National Convention also endorsed such a proposal. White abolitionists of the 1830s such as Arthur Tappan and Gerrit Smith proposed such a school for free African Americans, too. Despite several attempts to found such an institution, this policy initiative encountered serious opposition from antagonistic whites as well as members of the free African American community.

The task of building support for such a school fell to Douglass, who first embraced the idea of vocational training for the uplift of African Americans in 1853. Realizing that traditional avenues such as apprenticeships for entering skilled trades were closed to African American workers because of the systemic racism of the American labor market, Douglass believed that a vocational school—as opposed to a traditional college or industrial school—offered the best means of overcoming this barrier to African American upward mobility. In his estimation, such a school would not only offer students the opportunity to learn handicrafts, but they would also acquire a traditional English education. As envisioned by Douglass, the learning of trades and traditional education in such a school would have a symbiotic relationship to one another and enhance the learning outcomes of both for students. Such an initiative would be a public effort of grand scope articulating the education of

African Americans with their economic needs and aspirations. Douglass believed that such an educational institution would, over time, prepare African Americans to help themselves and eliminate poverty, which he saw as the root cause of African Americans' problems.

Douglass also thought that industrial education would disprove notions of the mental inferiority of African Americans and help refute the pro-slavery argument against emancipation. Believing in the mental genius of African Americans, he argued that African Americans should demonstrate by their actions that they were equal to whites and hoped that such an institution would equip them with the necessary knowledge and vocational skills to do so. In his second autobiography, *The Life and Times of Frederick Douglass* (1881), he reiterated his conviction that free African Americans must possess the job skills to compete against the hordes of foreign workers then immigrating to the United States or be eliminated from all lucrative employment.

Despite delegates endorsing his proposal at the 1853 Black National Convention and subsequent black state conventions in 1854, Douglass's pre-Civil War efforts on behalf of industrial education were unsuccessful. A lack of funding, persistent opposition from anti-black elements and a lack of broad-based support among African Americans prevented its implementation. After the Civil War, however, industrial education was championed successfully by educational reformers such as Samuel Chapman Armstrong and **Booker T. Washington** and received the financial backing to found and support the Hampton and Tuskegee Institutes.

Further Reading

Blassingame, John W., ed. *The Frederick Douglass Papers, Series One: Speeches, Debates and Interviews, 1847–54*. vol 2. New Haven, Conn.: Yale University Press, 1982.

———. *The Frederick Douglass Papers. Series One: Speeches, Debates and Interviews, 1855–63*. vol. 3. New Haven, Conn.: Yale University Press, 1986.

Blassingame, John W. and John R. McKivigan, eds. *The Frederick Douglass Papers. Series One: Speeches, Debates and Interviews, 1881–95*. vol. 5. New Haven, Conn.: Yale University Press, 1992.

Foner, Philip S. and George E. Walker, eds. *Proceedings of the Black State Conventions, 1840–1865*. vol. II. Philadelphia: Temple University Press, 1980.

McFeely, William S. *Frederick Douglass*. New York: W. W. Norton & Co., 1991.

Quarles, Benjamin. *Frederick Douglass*. New York: Atheneum, 1968.

Woodson, Carter G. *The Education of the Negro Prior to 1861*. New York: Arno Press and the New York Times, 1968.

—*Monroe Little*

J

Jim Crow Laws

Jim Crow laws designated institutional racism. The term "Jim Crow" derives from the name of a stereotypical minstrel show character created by Thomas "Daddy" Rice who performed in black face while dancing a jig and singing the lyrics to the song "Jump Jim Crow." Due to the weight of the racial, ideological, and stereotypical contamination that the term had acquired throughout the nineteenth century, the theatrical caricature eventually transformed into the name of a conceptual model describing the array of political, economic, and social ideas and practices of white supremacy that attempted to systematically govern and control the lives of African Americans in post-slavery America. After the Civil War, the emerging and systematic imposition of Jim Crow laws in many states became a unique, discernible, and multifaceted attempt to institutionalize racial segregation, economic exploitation, and African American disenfranchisement.

Jim Crow laws were not simply phenomena of Southern culture; they were also deeply rooted in the North and permeated throughout American society. Whether Jim Crow manifested in the form of overt public laws or private discriminatory practices, it was consistently contested by African Americans. Frederick Douglass had many recollections of his own personal resistance to Jim Crow in Northern communities. In September 1841, while traveling on the Eastern Railroad, which ran from Boston to Portland, Maine, Douglass was forcibly removed twice from the train because he refused to leave the first class section to be placed in the "negro car." In the second incident, Douglass resisted so forcibly that the chair that he was sitting in had to be thrown out with him in it because he held onto it so tightly. Douglass also resisted Jim Crow in Northern churches. While trying to take the sacrament, a religious act of devotion, in a Methodist church in New Bedford, **Massachusetts**, Douglass was shocked to observe "Jim Crow pews" and the pastor's discriminatory behavior, which insured that all white parishioners received the sacrament before African Americans. In **Rochester, New York**, where Douglass resided for a quarter-century, he faced the force of Jim Crow Laws in his efforts to educate his children. Due to the success attributed to the Tracy Seminary in providing young women a quality Christian education, Douglass enrolled his daughter, **Rosetta**, in the school in 1848. His daughter was relegated to "solitary confinement" inside and outside the classroom, unable to interact intellectually or socially with the white students.

Douglass removed her from the school after protest, but faced similar Jim Crow practices in the local public school system. Douglass consistently protested to the Board of Education and as a consequence of his agitation along with other local activists, Rochester eventually desegregated its public schools in 1857. In 1858, Douglass extended his support to the efforts of the Legal Rights Association in New York City, which had been established by African Americans in 1855 to dismantle Jim Crow Laws on venues of public transportation, especially the discriminatory practices of the Sixth Avenue Railroad. As Douglass lived and traveled in the North experiencing Jim Crow, Douglass continually highlighted the unifying ideology of white supremacy that transcended regional particularities between the North and South.

In the aftermath of the Civil War, Douglass was perceptive in analyzing and critiquing the emerging framework of legal strategies employed by Southern states in their reluctant attempts to accommodate changes instituted by the federal government while striving to impose the *de facto* continuity of the existing relationships of domination between blacks and whites. These Southern legal strategies can initially be seen in the form of **Black Codes**. As a genetic precursor to the more elaborate Jim Crow laws, the Black Codes were representative of a composite system of political, social, and legislative attempts to lay the foundation for the social and political reality of the post-Civil War South. Under the Reconstruction program of President Andrew Johnson which advocated for a quick restoration of the Union with limited protection for the freedmen, state after state began to pass a series of vagrancy and apprenticeship laws that severely curtailed civil rights, economic prospects, and freedom of movement of African Americans. In 1866, Douglass led a delegation to see President Johnson to persuade him to extend the right to vote to the freedmen in order to concretely translate the idea of freedom into political reality and empower African Americans to resist the Black Codes. Against the resistance of President Johnson, Congress passed the Freedman Bureau's Bill (1865), the **Civil Rights Act** of 1866, and the Fourteenth Amendment which extended basic legal protections to the ex-slaves and initially frustrated the political ability of the South to shape the future status of African Americans. In the aftermath of the Civil War, Douglass was at the forefront of active participation in various conventions and meetings advocating Negro suffrage that culminated in the passage of the **Fifteenth Amendment** (1870).

Despite these federal protections, the nation began to increasingly retreat morally and politically from addressing the growing dissatisfaction of the freedmen. The withdrawal of Federal troops from the South as an outgrowth of the Compromise of 1877 marked a diminution in the enforcement of the protections of the Fourteenth and Fifteenth Amendments and emboldened the South to produce more systematic Jim Crow Laws that played a central role in governing social and political relations. In 1875, Congress passed a Civil Rights Bill that prohibited discrimination in places of public accommodation, but in 1883 the **U.S. Supreme Court** concluded that the bill was unconstitutional because it was directed against private discrimination, not state action. Douglass critiqued the logic of the Supreme Court decision by highlighting the tragic consequences of allowing citizens of states to discriminate and deny rights to African Americans, as long as they did so as individual persons and not the state itself. For Douglass, this decision violated the liberal spirit and intent of the Fourteenth Amendment. The early 1890s witnessed the onslaught of Jim Crow laws all across the South that sought to entrench segregation in all forms of public transportation, schools, churches, hotels, theaters, restaurants, housing, and employment. One year after the death of Douglass, the Supreme Court rendered a decision in ***Plessy vs. Ferguson*** (1896) that formally inaugurated and sanctioned the Jim Crow doctrine of "separate but equal" throughout the nation.

Further Reading

Blassingame, John W. and John R. McKivigan, eds. *The Frederick Douglass Papers*. New Haven, Conn.: Yale University Press, 1992.

Douglass, Frederick. *The Life and Times of Frederick Douglass*. Hartford, Conn.: Park Publishing Co., 1892.

Martin, Waldo E. Jr. *The Mind of Frederick Douglass*. Chapel Hill: University of North Carolina Press, 1984.

—Mario H. Beatty

Joint Committee of Fifteen

The Joint Committee of Fifteen was the congressional committee called to investigate and determine Southern states' eligibility for congressional representation after the Civil War. When the Thirty-ninth Congress convened in December 1865, it faced the monumental task of opposing the Presidential reconstruction plan crafted by Andrew Johnson. After preventing Senators and Representatives from the eleven Southern ex-Confederate states from taking their seats in Congress, radical and moderate Congressmen formed the Joint Committee on Reconstruction to investigate conditions in the South and to report whether any of the ex-Confederate states should be entitled to Congressional representation. This committee of fifteen Congressmen was composed of six Senators and nine Representatives, of which 12 were **Republicans** and the remaining three were Unionist Democrats. These 15 members of Congress oversaw a massive investigation which called 144 witnesses and generated more than 700 pages of testimony. The committee concentrated its efforts primarily on the treatment of African Americans and Northern whites in Southern states, the continued necessity of the Freedman's Bureau and federal troops in the South, and the lasting hostilities of former Confederates toward the U.S. government.

On April 28, 1866, the Joint Committee submitted its findings. Their report claimed that the South was still in disarray in the aftermath of the Civil War and that the former Confederate states should not actively participate in the federal government until civil rights of all their citizens were guaranteed and high ranking Confederate officials were barred from political office. These recommendations led directly to a bill which extended the life and enlarged the functions of the Freedman's Bureau and a proposal which would grant civil rights to African Americans in the South. The two measures were vetoed by President Johnson, but Congress eventually overrode both vetoes. The extension of the Freedman's Bureau and the passage of the

Civil Rights Act in 1866 signaled the beginning of radical Republican ascension and the end of Johnson's absolute control over Reconstruction. The most lasting legacy of the Joint Committee's efforts was a set of resolutions drafted on April 30, 1866 that became the Fourteenth Amendment. Passed by Congress on June 16, 1866, this Amendment made African American citizenship a constitutional fact, but every Southern state with the exception of Tennessee refused to ratify the measure. Preparing for a protracted political fight, radical Republicans called for a convention to be held in Philadelphia of Unionists from the South to denounce the doctrine of state sovereignty and support the ratification of the Fourteenth Amendment. Among the Northern representatives at this convention was Frederick Douglass, who successfully persuaded the convention to also support granting the right to vote to Southern African American men. The Fourteenth Amendment was eventually ratified and Douglass's appeal for black suffrage became the basis for the **Fifteenth Amendment** passed by Congress on February 27, 1869.

Further Reading

Foner, Eric. *Reconstruction: America's Unfinished Revolution, 1863–1877*. New York: Harper & Row, 1988.

Franklin, John Hope. *Reconstruction: After the Civil War*. Chicago: University of Chicago Press, 1961.

—Walter Rucker

K

Kansas-Nebraska Act

Passed on May 30, 1854, the Kansas-Nebraska Act expanded slavery into the new Union states of Kansas and Nebraska. The legislation provided for the entry of Kansas and Nebraska into the Union. It also reversed the **Missouri Compromise** of 1820 by erasing the former boundary on slavery at the 36° north and 30´ west parallel lines which had formerly confined the institution to the American South. Stephen Douglas, author of the Kansas-Nebraska Bill, told his **Republican** critics that Congress had already abandoned their efforts to limit slavery through the passage of the **Fugitive Slave Act** requiring Northerners to help capture and return runaways. Southern strategy now called for "Popular Sovereignty" whereby a state would decide the issue of slavery through the vote. Abolitionists and "Free Soilers" felt that the Kansas-Nebraska Act destroyed their chance to halt slavery's expansion into the Western states and territories. In the 1850s, Kansas was home to nearly 100 free African Americans, less than a dozen of whom were enslaved. Out of a population of 28,000, fewer than 67 free African Americans lived in Nebraska during the mid-nineteenth century, along with 15 enslaved Africans. Acting against the wishes of **William Lloyd Garrison**, Frederick Douglass founded the *North Star* abolitionist newspaper in 1847, arguing that African Americans should lead the fight against slavery. Both men used their publications to argue against slavery in the territories, a victory they once thought was sealed by the Northwest Ordinance of 1787. Douglass, along with his colleague, the Reverend John Brown and other **abolitionists**, took direct action against slavery through their opposition to the **Fugitive Slave Act** of 1850. The proposed Kansas-Nebraska Act reignited the battle when Southern and Northern congressmen debated and even went to blows over the admission of Kansas into the nation as a slave state. The argument quickly spilled into the streets, earning the state its nickname "Bleeding Kansas." Rioters destroyed several abolitionist presses, and the antislavery town of Lawrence was ransacked in May of 1856. Brown responded by killing a group of five pro-slavery men at Pottawatomie Creek, an act that he would attempt again at **Harpers Ferry** in 1859. Douglass did not join in Brown's attack on the Virginia arsenal although he knew about the plan in advance. Responding to critics in the abolitionist community that he had behaved like a coward, Douglass said that he was willing to speak, write, and conspire against slavery when there was a hope of success and that each person should fight in his or her own way. Despite his lack of faith in Brown's tactics, Douglass called Brown a hero, since the antislavery faction eventually prevailed, and Kansas was admitted to the Union on January 29, 1861 as a free state. After the Civil War, African American leaders in Kansas insisted that the abolitionists' efforts not be reversed and that the state remain an outpost of liberty for freedmen and women who furthered the cause through their development of all-black towns.

Further Reading

Dann, Martin E., ed. *The Black Press 1827–1890: The Quest for National Identity*. New York: G. P. Putnam's Sons, 1971.

Du Bois, W. E. B. *American Crisis Biographies: John Brown*. Philadelphia: George W. Jacobs and Company, 1909.

Quarles, Benjamin. *Blacks on John Brown*. Urbana, Ill.: University of Illinois Press, 1972.

—*Tekla Ali Johnson*

Ku Klux Klan (KKK)

The post-Civil War period of Southern Reconstruction (1865–1877) found both formerly enslaved and free African people struggling to attain political and economical equality in the United States. While political forces debated in society about the best approach toward reunification of the former Confederate states, many Southern whites began to launch a serious counterattack to retrieve lost ground, due to the political advancement of some African Americans during Reconstruction. The theory of white supremacy was enacted by organizations founded in the years after the end of the Civil War to keep black people in a subservient position.

After the Civil War, former Confederates in Tennessee were the first to resume their suffrage (within 12 months) followed quickly by other states. Many states pardoned almost all former rebels. It was in Tennessee that returning Confederate soldiers would form the Ku Klux Klan (KKK). This organization was based initially on the college Greek fraternal system and later used as a tool to promote racial segregation through violence for protecting white Southern society from black integration. The KKK and other "terrorist societies" used violence and intimidation against African Americans who protested having their rights violated. Churches and schools were firebombed and black people were beaten and killed.

Testimonies about these events influenced Frederick Douglass to continue his advocacy for African American rights and protection. Douglass's response to the rise of the KKK occurred in two prominent ways. First, he supported the passage of the Fourteenth and **Fifteenth Amendments** of the United States Constitution by Congress and helped to illuminate the violence and injustice exhibited by the KKK in Southern states. Another response afforded Douglass was editing and publishing his second newspaper, the *New Era* (changed to the *New National Era* in 1870). Douglass believed knowledge was power which would help in the "deliverance of my people not only from the terrible bondage of slavery but from the more terrible bondage of ignorance and vice."

Frederick Douglass used his newspaper to speak out against the resistance to investigating the KKK's acts of violence against African Americans in the South, and he warned the **Republican Party** not to take the African American vote for granted. Political pressure from the Negro conventions forced President Ulysses S. Grant to take steps to subdue the Klan, both in policy and praxis of physical enforcement. Frederick Douglass supported these actions while rebuking conservative Republicans.

Douglass eventually praised Grant for enforcing laws in the South which curbed the KKK's violence against African Americans. Frederick Douglass supported President Grant and the Republican Party in spite of personal slights because he believed this was the best chance for freedom in the South. He believed the 1872 presidential election was important to prevent Democrats from coming to power. Douglass's praise drew criticism from his colleagues concerned about corruption and other issues in Grant's administration. The Democratic Party began to resume its control of the South with the election of Rutherford B. Hayes in 1876 resulting in the withdrawal of federal troops, the end of martial law, and a return to Southern self-governance in 1877. The year 1877 proved to be a watershed year, predicting upheaval for African Americans in the years ahead.

Frederick Douglass publicly warned of the KKK's growing influence behind the increasing acts of violence against Southern blacks. At the National Colored Labor Union (NCLU) meeting in January 1871, Douglass demanded that the federal government take forceful measures to fight the KKK's terrorism and maintain black suffrage. Douglass's newspaper reported the proceedings of the conference which included a speech calling for the federal government to protect the rights of African Americans from acts of violence during Reconstruction: "Shall the Ku Klux Klan rule the South? . . . Are our citizens in the south to be protected from this murderous band or are they the victims until the end that of another administration?"

After the end of Reconstruction, **lynchings** and threats of violence continued to be frequently used by the KKK and other groups to keep black people from power. The KKK's subversive actions—relocating polling stations far away from black communities, devising special requirements for suffrage such as "literacy tests" and "poll taxes" along with general acts of violence—were successful in keeping African Americans disenfranchised and economically and socially impoverished.

Douglass's response to the KKK's justification for lynching black men—to protect white women from rape by black men—was with firm denial, believing instead that lynchings were done intentionally to retard African Americans' upward mobility to a higher social status in Southern society as well as to further exacerbate racial prejudice in a society that fostered second-class citizenship for African Americans. Douglass commented that lynch mobs in effect castrated black men and opened the door for assault on black women. He, with others, vigorously attempted to stop lynchings and racism by arguing the principles of American society require letting the courts, not mobs, judge the accused. Douglass traveled extensively and advocated for land and property ownership by black people while also stating his opposition to black migration to the North and West happening in response to the climate of violence in the South in the late 1870s. He was not aware of the real conditions of

Southern blacks and when better informed, he withdrew his criticism of black migration out of the South. Douglass disagreed with these "exodusters," but asked the federal government and private donors to help black resettlement in 1886. In 1888, after he went to Georgia to investigate the conditions of black people, he pledged his support to help them in any way he could.

Further Reading

Foner, Philip S. *Frederick Douglass: A Biography*. New York: The Citadel Press, 1964.

Jin-Ping, Wu. *Frederick Douglass and The Black Liberation Movement*. New York: Garland Publishing, 2000.

Ruiz, Jim. *The Black Hood of the Ku Klux Klan*. San Francisco: Austin & Winfield, Publishers, 1998.

—Andrew Smallwood

Liberator

William Lloyd Garrison, who some refer to as one of the leading activists of the abolitionist movement in the United States, established the *Liberator* newspaper on January 1, 1831, in Boston, Massachusetts, along with his colleague, Issac Knapp (1804–1843). The objective of the *Liberator* was to educate American citizens about slavery and provide written and aesthetic documents supporting Garrison's and Knapp's position. On the other hand, Garrison used the *Liberator* to recruit and advocate for abolitionism. Indeed, the strong views concerned with ending slavery expressed by Garrison in the *Liberator* were considered especially unpopular in the Southern states. In fact, the state of Georgia offered a $5,000 award for the capture, arrest, and conviction of Garrison.

This weekly journal-newspaper was an important media outlet addressing abolitionism and human rights issues. Equally important, Garrison used the *Liberator* as a vehicle to advocate for social change as well as the abolition of enslavement. The newspaper ran consecutive issues for three decades (1831–1866) and ended with Garrison acknowledging the passage of the Thirteenth Amendment to the United States Constitution, the amendment that abolished slavery in the United States. Interestingly, this newspaper supposedly never exceeded a distribution of over 3,000, and it is estimated that most of its subscribers were African Americans, postulating a broader level of literacy among African Americans than previously thought.

Still, the posture, swagger, and language in this paper clearly established its proactive antislavery stance. As noted in the first edition of the *Liberator*, Garrison with no hesitation penned the position of this journal, "I do not wish to think, or speak, or write, with moderation... I am in earnest—I will not equivocate—I will not excuse—I will not retreat a single inch—AND I WILL BE HEARD."

Further Reading

Africans in America, http://www.pbs.org/wgbh/aia/part4/4p1561.html.

William Lloyd Garrison.: NNDB http://www.nndb.com/people/966/000049819/.

———.: NNDB http://www.nndb.com/people/966/000049819/.

———.: Ohio History Central http://www.ohiohistorycentral.org/entry.php?rec=167.
———.: Spartacus Educational http://www.spartacus.schoolnet.co.uk/USASgarrison.htm.

—*James L. Conyers*

Lincoln, Abraham (1809–1865)

The sixteenth President of the United States, Abraham Lincoln served during the Civil War. Born in Hardin County, Kentucky, Lincoln trained as a lawyer. In 1858, he made a run for the Illinois Senate seat against incumbent Democratic candidate Stephen Douglas. The two candidates participated in a number of debates around the state, known as the Lincoln-Douglas debates, in which they discussed their views on slavery and race. The focus of the debates was the expansion of slavery and the future of the Union. Douglas accused Lincoln of caring more for African Americans than white citizens. He also championed his belief in white superiority. Lincoln did not believe in racial equality, and he said that blacks should never have the right to vote, serve on juries, hold office, or intermarry with whites. He argued that his opposition to slavery did not necessarily mean that he wanted social or political equality between whites and blacks. But Lincoln also attempted to dismiss his critics who called him a racist. He argued that all workers, regardless of race, should be paid for their labor. Douglas won the Senate election, but Lincoln had established his reputation.

Four candidates ran for president in the 1860 election. The Democratic votes were split between Southern Democrat John Breckinridge and Northern Democrat Stephen Douglas. John Bell of the Constitutional Union Party nominated John Bell. The fractured Democratic Party helped to elect **Republican Party** candidate Abraham Lincoln, with 59 percent of the electoral vote and 40 percent of the popular vote.

Free blacks in the North, including Frederick Douglass, did not initially support Lincoln's presidency. They doubted his ability to help African Americans based on his political ideology that called for an end to slavery but still promoted racism. After Lincoln's election, African American leaders awaited the secession of Southern states. **South Carolina** seceded on December 20, 1860 and by February 1861, seven other Southern states followed suit (South Carolina, **Mississippi**, Alabama, Florida, **Louisiana**, Georgia, and Texas), forming the Confederate States of America. Lincoln gave his inaugural address on March 4, 1861, telling white Southerners that they should return to the Union and that he would not abolish slavery in the states where it already existed. Lincoln surmised that the only debate between the North and South was over the expansion of slavery, and he stated that the Constitution would not allow for secession. Southern whites ignored his admonitions. On April 12, 1861 Confederate leaders ordered the surrender of Fort Sumter in Charleston, South Carolina, and when the United States Army refused, Confederate soldiers fired on Fort Sumter, marking the beginning of the Civil War.

Lincoln sought to preserve the Union as his ultimate goal in the Civil War. Frederick Douglass criticized Lincoln for his insistence that the war was not about the institution of slavery. Lincoln called for state militias to put down the rebellion and four more slave states (North Carolina, Virginia, Tennessee, and Arkansas) seceded from the Union in 1861. Lincoln hoped to keep the four remaining slave states (Delaware, **Maryland**, Kentucky, and Missouri) in the Union and, as a result, made no moves toward abolishing slavery. He issued a call for 75,000 men to volunteer for a 90-day stint in the war. Thousands of black and white men responded to his call, yet Lincoln rejected the applications of black men.

As soon as the war began, many Southern slaves asserted their freedom, although there was no policy addressing the status of African American slaves. Union Commander General Benjamin Butler called three escaped Virginia slaves "contraband" and seized them as enemy property. Butler did not free the slaves or keep them enslaved. This raised questions about the status of slaves in Confederate states. On August 6, 1861, Congress passed the First Confiscation Act which stated that Confederate property that was used to aid the war effort could be seized by Federal forces. Therefore, any slaves Confederate forces used to aid in the war effort would be freed. Union General John C. Frémont ignored the Act and freed all the slaves owned by Confederates in Missouri. Lincoln reprimanded Frémont and told him that only slaves used in the war effort were freed under the law. Lincoln feared that such an action would force the remaining slave states to secede. African American leaders were dissatisfied with Lincoln's refusal to accept black troops as well as his failure to free all Southern slaves. Lincoln was steadfast in his efforts to keep the issue of slavery out of the Civil War.

Lincoln initially proposed that the war would be ended when masters were compensated for their slaves and blacks were settled outside of United States. His colonization plan called for the relocation of African Americans to the **Caribbean**, Latin America, or West **Africa**. He proposed the idea to the border states in July 1861 and threatened that, if they refused the offer, they might have to accept uncompensated emancipation. By 1862, after the border states refused the compensated emancipation proposal, Lincoln realized slavery was at the war's center. In cabinet meetings held on July 21–22, 1862, Lincoln discussed the abolition of slavery. On September 22, 1862, Lincoln issued the Preliminary Emancipation Proclamation that stated that all slaves in rebelling states on January 1, 1863 would be free. The Proclamation, therefore, failed to free slaves residing in the four border states. The **Emancipation Proclamation** also allowed black troops to join the Union Army, and Frederick Douglass began a campaign to encourage black men to enlist.

In December 1863, Lincoln proposed a 10 percent plan to reorganize the state governments of the Confederacy. The plan stipulated that a state government could be formed when 10 percent of those who had voted in 1860 accepted a loyalty oath to the Union. He proposed that high-level Confederate soldiers be denied the opportunity to take the oath, and he also suggested that a small group of African Americans be allowed to take the oath. Lincoln was assassinated by John Wilkes Booth before the end of the Civil War, on Friday, April 14, 1865, while attending a play at Ford's Theater in Washington, D.C.

Further Reading

Donald, David Herbert. *Lincoln*. London: Jonathan Cape, 1996.

McPherson, James. *Battle Cry of Freedom: The Civil War Era*. New York: Oxford University Press, 1988.

Oates, Stephen B. *With Malice toward None: A Life of Abraham Lincoln*. New York: Harper & Row, 1977.

—*Jane E. Dabel*

Lincoln, Mary Todd (1818–1882)

Mary Todd, the wife of President Abraham Lincoln, was born in Lexington, Kentucky, where both her maternal and paternal families were prosperous and influential. She was the third of seven children and had a happy nurturing life until her mother died in childbirth when Mary was six. This marked a sad turning point in young Mary's life as her stepmother proved to be critical and unsupportive, creating a physically comfortable home yet leaving Mary emotionally deprived. Robert Todd defied convention by ensuring that Mary received 12 years of exceptional education. At 17 Mary left home to live with an older sister in Springfield, Illinois. Suitors found Mary appealing with her attractive looks, blue eyes, and light chestnut hair. She was also vivacious, intelligent, lively, and a good conversationalist. Here she met the young lawyer **Abraham Lincoln**. His awkward gangly physical appearance combined with his inferior social status caused Mary's family to disapprove of the match. Despite the strong objections, Mary and Abraham were attracted to each other through their mutual love of poetry, intense interest in politics, and great ambitions. They became engaged in 1840 only to break up after several months. During this period Lincoln suffered severe depression. In 1842 the couple reconciled and were married in the home of her sister. Abraham placed a gold ring on her finger engraved with the words "Love is Eternal." She wore this ring until the day she died.

The young married couple moved to Springfield, Illinois, and boarded at the Globe Tavern where, for the first time in Mary's life, she was without slaves or servants. After the birth of their first child, whom they named after Mary's father, they purchased a home in Springfield. Eventually, the couple had three more children, Edward, William, and Thomas (Tad). Mary supported her husband's political aspirations and campaigned for him using her social and political connections. Lincoln eventually represented Illinois in the House of Representatives. After Abraham's congressional term ended in 1849, his political career stalled and the family moved back to Springfield. Upon his inauguration in 1860, the Lincolns moved to Washington under the cloud of the impending Civil War.

Mary's term as First Lady was controversial. Her activities in this time of national crisis angered many Americans. She redecorated the White House and far exceeded the congressional appropriations, often entertaining extravagantly.

Additionally, she shopped excessively, running up large bills. With the country devastated by war, the public thought her behavior was inappropriate. Perhaps the worst allegation leveled at Mary was that she had Confederate sympathies because several of her half-brothers and brothers-in-law fought for the South. While in the White House the Lincolns' second son, Willie, died.

Lincoln was shot while seated next to Mary at Ford's Theater on April 14, 1865. Her behavior following the assassination further alienated Mary from the American public when she secluded herself in her bedroom for 40 days. She then quarreled with her Springfield neighbors over the site of Lincoln's grave and decided to have him interred in Chicago instead. Forever worried about a lack of income, Mary relentlessly petitioned Congress for a pension. To raise funds, she decided to sell her old clothing, a tradition of European royalty which caused the press and public to rail against the plan. During this controversial period, Frederick Douglass offered to go on a lecture tour on her behalf to help improve her image, but Mary sent her thanks with her rejection of his offer. When Mary's health began to fail, she took her son, Tad, to Germany, hoping the water cures would improve her physical condition. She returned to Chicago in 1871 and Tad died after a long illness. Her only surviving son, Robert, successfully petitioned to have his mother declared insane in 1875, and she was placed in a private asylum in Batavia, Illinois, where she lived for four months until gaining her release with the help of friends. Mary left the United States and lived in Europe until 1880 when she returned to Springfield to live with her sister, Elizabeth. Her health deteriorated and she died in the same house in which she was married.

Further Reading

Baker, Jean H. *Mary Todd Lincoln: A Biography*. New York: Norton, 1987.

Randall, Ruth Painter. *Mary Lincoln: Biography of a Marriage*. Boston: Little, Brown, 1953.

Turner, Justin G., and Linda L. Turner. *Mary Todd Lincoln: Her Life and Letters*. New York: Knopf, 1972.

—Minoa Uffelman

Longfellow, Henry Wadsworth (1807–1882)

Henry Wadsworth Longfellow was a poet, translator, editor, and educator. Born in Portland, Maine, Longfellow attended Bowdoin College and spent three years in Europe before assuming the chair of modern languages at Bowdoin (1829 to 1835). In 1836, he became Smith Professor of Modern Languages at Harvard, a post he held until 1854.

Longfellow published poems and essays during his undergraduate years, but his first major literary effort was *Outre-Mer: A Pilgrimage Beyond the Sea* (1835), a collection of sketches and observations on European travel. His early poems, "A Psalm of Life" and "The Wreck of the Hesperus," established his popularity; the volumes, *Voices of the Night* (1839) and *Ballads and Other Poems* (1841), established his reputation as a leading American poet. Like other nineteenth-century writers in search of a national literature, Longfellow often addressed American themes in plain English. Like **Ralph Waldo Emerson**, John Greenleaf Whittier, and Henry David Thoreau, Longfellow was sympathetic to efforts to abolish slavery in the United States. In 1842, he published *Poems of Slavery*, typical **abolitionist** verse that warned of the evils of slavery and of the possibility of civil war. "The Quadroon Girl" from this collection illustrates wretchedness in the white father's selling of his daughter. A more pointedly topical example of Longfellow's poetry as ideological weapon is "On the Capture of Fugitive Slaves Near Washington" (1845), a sentimental condemnation of immorality, which emphasizes the contradictions between professed and practiced democratic principles and religion.

Other works by Longfellow reflecting the tense evolution of national identity are the narratives *Evangeline: A Tale of Acadie* (1847), dealing with forced migration, and *The Song of Hiawatha* (1855), a romantic handling of the noble savage theme. From the end of the Civil War until his death, Longfellow was venerated as the "grand old man of American letter," and his pious verities remained popular until the triumph of modernism in the 1920s. Longfellow died in Cambridge, Massachusetts.

Further Reading

Arvin, Newton. *Longfellow: His Life and Work*. Boston: Little, Brown, 1963.

Wagenknecht, Edward. *Longfellow: A Full-Length Portrait*. New York: Longmans, Green, 1955.

—*Jerry W. Ward, Jr.*

Louisiana

In the year of 1872, the Republican National Negro Convention was held in Louisiana. In April of that year, Frederick Douglass, one of the most venerable advocates of black rights in the United States, made what seemingly was his only trip to New Orleans, Louisiana. He came to the city as president-elect and the keynote speaker for the National Convention of Colored People. Delegates to this Republican Convention were to address a number of issues concerning blacks in the various states and on the national level. Of paramount concern were the presidential election and the direction of the **Republican Party** with reference to its black citizens.

Just as living in a nation constructed upon a racial ideology had not been easy for black people, neither was hosting the National Negro Convention. First, Douglass, who was elected as the president of the Convention, was delayed in his arrival to the city, and this caused great consternation among some of the delegates. Some of the delegates announced publicly that it had been a serious error electing Douglass as their leader, because they did not believe that he ever had any intention of attending the Convention. However, by the third day of the Convention a telegram arrived stating that Douglass was in **Mississippi** journeying to New Orleans, and would arrive later during the day. Second, they had to deal with the logistics of the meeting. The Convention was scheduled to take place at Mechanics' Institute beginning on April 9, 1872, but, on the second day of the gathering, the gas was turned off for the building. Mechanics' Institute was a state building, and the state had defaulted on its payments to the gas company, causing services to be interrupted. As the Republican leaders scrambled to come up with an alternative meeting site, some delegates saw the event as a ploy to disrupt their deliberations. The leaders were able to secure an alternative meeting place, but the inconvenience caused a drop in attendance for the next session. However, they did have enough delegates in attendance for a quorum and proceeded with the business of the Convention. As a result of the unexpected change in venue, no reporters were present and there is no verbatim record of the speeches. Finally, they had to deal with the reasons for calling the Convention: the election of delegates to attend the National Republican Convention to be held in Philadelphia, Pennsylvania, on June 5, 1872.

In Douglass's absence, the Honorable P. B. S. Pinchback of Louisiana officially called the Convention to order, and later power was transferred to the First Vice President, Jas. H. Ingraham. One of the first discussion items was whether Senator **Charles Sumner** of **Massachusetts** would support the national Republican Party since it had been rumored that Sumner was one of the most influential radical Republicans in Congress who dedicated himself to fighting for the rights of black people. He had fought for the abolition of slavery. Black people appreciated him; many whites excoriated him. Therefore, this Convention found itself in a peculiar position but, in the end, the delegates decided they were Republican first, and since they did not know for certain what Sumner would do, they would continue to support him and, at the same time, pledge their allegiance to the Republican Party.

The delegates came to the Convention because they wanted to help determine the direction of the government for the next four years. They were interested in such issues as whether the nation would be Republican or Democrat and support equal rights or fight against them; in favor of progress, education, and improvement for all people, black and white, or in favor of white progress only; education and improvement and opposed to equal advantage for the black people; whether blacks could retain all they had won and go forward, or whether they would lose all and go back to where they were at the end of the Civil War.

Douglass's arrival at the Convention was not only symbolic but also instructive. He delivered his widely publicized lecture to the delegates and others on "Self-made men." According to the *Semi-Weekly Louisianan*, "the hall was well occupied with an audience that fully appreciated the literary treat given them by the celebrated speaker. The lecturer alluded extensively to the principles of success and the true mode of forming and establishing character..." As the Convention was drawing to an end, Lieutenant Governor Pinchback invited Douglass and the delegates to his home for drinks and entertainment.

The most important resolution to come from the National Negro Convention was the delegates pledging to support the National Republican Party and Ulysses S. Grant's reelection for president.

Further Reading

Douglass, Frederick. *Narrative of the Life of Frederick Douglass, and American Slave*. Wortley, U.K.: J. Barker, 1846.

The Semi-Weekly Louisianian. April 14, 18, 1872.

—Dorothy V. Smith

L'Ouverture, Toussaint François Dominique (1743–1803)

The Haitian nationalist and revolutionary leader Toussaint L'Ouverture represented Frederick Douglass's archetypal Africana hero on many accounts: He was unquestionably of African ancestry, a quintessential embodiment of the passion and power of the human spirit, an ardent egalitarian and libertarian and, most like Douglass himself, a prototypical self-made man. In his essay "Toussaint L'Ouverture," Douglass averred that in addition to being the personification of the Haitian Revolution, L'Ouverture "taught slaveholders of whatever land and color, the danger of goading to madness, the energy that slumbers in the black man's arm." Similar to C. L. R. James, and especially in his classic, *The Black Jacobins,* Douglass maintained a dialectical view of L'Ouverture that enabled him to simultaneously critique the Haitian's political pitfalls and often unfounded and utopian vision of former colonized and colonizers peacefully and progressively cohabiting, and at the same time take into consideration the historical fact that L'Ouverture represented a brand of Africana radicalism and heroism that had on the one hand been ignored by the slavocracy and French colonial class, and on the other hand, had inspired and ignited that august quest for freedom to which he, Douglass, had devoted his own life and work.

Little is known of the life of L'Ouverture before the first uprising of the enslaved in 1791 in Saint Domingue (present-day Haiti). It is believed that his parents were from Dahomey, now known as Benin, where his father served as a mighty chief before his enslavement. L'Ouverture was the eldest of eight children, born in Haut du Cap on the Bréda plantation, near Saint Domingue's northern coastline. Having been exposed early on to the culture of the French colony where he was born, L'Ouverture was not considered an African, but a Creole. With the social status afforded this designation, and the plantation owner's partiality toward him, L'Ouverture was spared from ever having to toil in the infamous Caribbean sugar cane fields. Instead, he worked as a domestic servant in the plantation house.

Toussaint was manumitted in 1776 at the age of 33. In 1779 he rented a plot of land on which he harbored 13 enslaved Africans and curiously practiced the prerogatives of a colonizer. This subsequently led L'Ouverture to amass a small fortune. It is reported that in his later years he avoided making public mention of his more prosperous years, instead focusing his political energies on his time as a slave. However, in keeping with his complex and, at moments, contradictory life history, he gained the trust of the French because he had formerly owned African slaves, even though he had actively participated in the island's first slave revolts. This winning of the French colonial class' faith would prove a distinct and determining factor in the efforts of the enslaved, under L'Ouverture's leadership, to rid the island of the French slavocracy and bring revolution and ultimately independence to Saint Domingue.

On August 22, 1791, the first revolt of the enslaved was spearheaded by the Jamaican Boukman. L'Ouverture was named secretary of the movement. As L'Ouverture noted, and as historically documented by others, the enslaved revolted and were reacting against a deep divergence in the ideals on the one hand, which were popularized by the French Revolutionists of 1789—the ideals of liberty, equality, and fraternity for all—and on the other hand, their own endurance and life experiences as Africans, mulattos, and unenslaved persons of color in the jagged jaws of French colonialism. In fact, according to C. L. R. James in *A History of Pan-African Revolt*, the part played by Africans, enslaved and unenslaved, in the success of the French Revolution has never received adequate recognition, and so it is no mystery that French calls for liberty, equality, and fraternity for all resonated so deeply with L'Ouverture and the other revolting enslaved Africans. By focusing on how the Haitian Revolution and the French Revolution have a sort of symbiotic relationship, James, as Douglass had before him, is highlighting and accenting Africans as active agents—black radicals and revolutionaries—deeply entrenched in the struggle against domination and discrimination, and for human liberation and positive and progressive social transformation.

If, as the French Revolutionists would have us believe, all human beings are created equal, L'Ouverture and the Haitian Revolutionists critically queried, how could and why did the African holocaust happen and subsequent colonialism and enslavement ensue and exist? These are questions which Frederick Douglass doggedly attempted to answer throughout his life, questions he held a deep affinity and affection for, but queries to which he nonetheless—on his own terms and arising out of his own unfaltering faith in humanity—found neither sufficient nor satisfactory answers to. In L'Ouverture's day, the French addressed these issues and the revolts they impelled by abolishing enslavement in all the colonies on September 4, 1793 (or February 4, 1794 by James's account). From the perspective of the enslaved (a perspective which Douglass waxed wickedly about in his classic, **"What to the Slave is Your Fourth of July?"**), the first slave revolt was a success. However, slavery would resume in all the French colonies and would remain the established order until 1848.

With the temporary abolition of slavery by the French, and with France at war with **Great Britain** and Spain, and, most importantly, the British and Spanish attacks on the island in 1794, L'Ouverture offered the services of his guerillas to the French army, on the grounds that they would abolish slavery. He and his battalion's courage and cunning in beating back the British and the Spaniards enabled him to rise swiftly through the ranks and become Lieutenant Governor of Saint Domingue. However, L'Ouverture was not content with being second-in-command of the former colony. As commander in chief of the military, appointed by the French government, he did not obscure his intention to become leader of Saint Domingue. At this point the French initiated an intrigue against him, and under the guise of the infamous colonial tactic of "divide and conquer," they engineered a rivalry and wrangle between L'Ouverture and Rigaud, reportedly a mulatto, from whence ensued a bloody and bitter civil war. L'Ouverture was victorious and put the viciousness of the civil war behind him only to be confronted with more of the machinations and maneuverings of French and other colonial forces. The French were so threatened by his enormous clout that in 1798, French General Hédouville was sent to the former colony on a covert mission to undermine L'Ouverture's authority. But L'Ouverture outmaneuvered Hédouville and several others sent to oust him. After gaining control of the entire island of Hispaniola—present-day Haiti and the Dominican Republic—L'Ouverture formed a commission of 10 called the Central Assembly, which drafted a constitution in 1801. Though continuing to confirm that the island remained a French colony, the new constitution rendered it administratively independent and named L'Ouverture governor-general of Saint Domingue for life. From that point forward, relations with France disintegrated, swiftly breaking down and leaving L'Ouverture at loggerheads with Napoleon Bonaparte, now first consul of France.

Governor-General L'Ouverture, in less than 18 months, remarkably developed an island devastated by centuries of colonialism, years of civil war, and other forms of civil unrest, to some semblance of prosperity. However—and here is the loose thread that has always threatened to unravel L'Ouverture's heroism and the Haitian revolutionary legacy—he was, to put it honestly yet bluntly, a despot, confining laborers to plantations in the old fashion of French colonialism, and brooking no interference with his will, rule, and leadership under the severest penalties and punishments. Unlike the French colonial rulers, though, L'Ouverture saw to it that workers were paid their wages, and he also protected them from the acrimony and injustices of their former enslavers. He set up free trade and religious toleration, made every effort to abolish racial domination and discrimination, and laid the foundation for an education system by sending young islanders of African ancestry to France to study social and political philosophy so as to return and contribute constructively to Haitian social development and social policies.

Napoleon, who was a virulent racist and sought to restore African enslavement and French colonial rule, responded to L'Ouverture's leadership by sending military might to the island under the command of his brother-in-law, General Charles Leclerc. Leclerc's orders were to reclaim the former colony in the name of France. General Leclerc and his 30,000 troops outmaneuvered L'Ouverture, surrounding him in his stronghold in Crête-à-Pierrot, and on May 5, 1802, forced him to surrender. Toussaint was shipped to the Fort de Joux prison in France, where he died from malnutrition and tuberculosis. Though the Haitian Revolution had lost its controversial architect and leading light, those who had served under him continued to advocate for his cause. On January 1, 1804, Jean Jacques Dessalines, one of L'Ouverture's lieutenants, was able to declare unequivocally that the French former colony of Saint Domingue was now the independent republic of Haiti; named both because it was the original Carib name for the island and to symbolize a definite break with French colonialism and culture.

Toussaint L'Ouverture looms large in Douglass's discourse not simply because of his "wisdom and heroism," as Douglass put it, but insofar as Douglass understood him, in many senses, to personify and embody the best ideals and ultimate objectives of Africana liberation struggle specifically, and human liberation struggle generally. Douglass's host of heroes often included persons who, like himself, had been enslaved, but whose deep desire and willingness to fight for their own freedom and the freedom of other oppressed persons lead them to radical political thought and revolutionary praxis. Alongside Toussaint L'Ouverture, Douglass held Gabriel Prosser, **Denmark Vesey**, **Nat Turner**, **Harriet Tubman**, and **Sojourner Truth** in the highest esteem, and often argued that, "if these men had struck for the freedom of white men held in slavery, their act would have immortalized them as benefactors, the noblest of mankind." But it was L'Ouverture that Douglass singled out as being especially heroic and invaluable to Africana radical thought traditions because "his work was peculiar and his character unique. Both his task and the material with which he had to work were of an uncommon kind. In fact he is without example and stands alone." Toussaint L'Ouverture's most impressive achievement, in Douglass's view, was that he, perhaps more than any other single individual, articulated and inspired modern Africana freedom fighters and liberation movements: fighters and movements which in Douglass's philosophy of human freedom represent an essential aspect and an integral part of the continuing struggles for democracy and human rights. In the final analysis, L'Ouverture's life work, for Frederick Douglass and for many contemporary Africana freedom fighters, symbolizes and serves as a solemn reminder of the potentialities and possibilities of the human spirit.

Further Reading

Geggus, David Patrick, ed. *The Impact of the Haitian Revolution in the Atlantic World.* Columbia, S.C.: University of South Carolina, 2001.

James, C. L. R. *The Black Jacobins: Toussaint L'Ouverture and the San Domingo Revolution.* New York: Vintage Books, 1989.

Tabasuri, Tabiri Hasani. "A Theory of Revolution and a Case Study of the Haitian Revolution," Ph.D. dissertation, University of Oklahoma, 1981.

—*Reiland Rabaka*

Lynchings, 1882–1895

Just after Reconstruction, a civil crisis developed in the United States, but especially in the South: the problem of lynching, a terrorist tactic of the Ku Klux Klan. Blacks were attacked, hung, and burned at the stake in these savage attacks. Frederick Douglass from the 1880s to 1895, the year of his death, repeatedly and vociferously denounced these incidents, keeping the practice of lynchings in the national spotlight.

A conservative record of the lynching data is suggestive of its horror: Douglass and other black leaders were faced with a situation where at least 679 blacks were known lynching victims between 1882 and 1889, and another 724 died "at the hands of persons unknown" in the years 1890–1895.

Douglass's activism focusing on the illegal lynchings of African Americans was reflected in his public speeches and his writings about lynching during this later period in his life. In July 1892 he published an essay, "Lynch Law in the South," in *The North American Review*, which denounced lynchings of black people. Yet Douglass noted that "race hatred and persecution" would take years to overcome in the South. Nevertheless, the old warrior continued to have "hope" for the future.

Lynchings, 1882–1895

U.S. Lynching Victims 1882–1895

Year	Total	Black	White
1882	113	49	64
1883	130	53	77
1884	211	160	51
1885	184	110	74
1886	138	74	64
1887	120	70	50
1888	137	69	68
1889	170	94	76
1890	69	85	11
1891	184	113	71
1892	230	161	69
1893	152	118	34
1894	192	134	58
1895	179	113	66

During this same period, Douglass developed a major speech, "The Lessons of the Hour," in 1894, in which he was able to capture a lifetime of work and struggle, summing up the major tasks remaining before the American people in the human struggle to promote justice, equality, and freedom for all Americans, and especially to bring an end to the lynching crisis then gripping the nation. For Frederick Douglass, the issues came down to this position:

> The presence of eight millions of people in any section of this country, constituting an aggrieved class, smarting under terrible wrongs, denied the exercise of the commonest rights of humanity, and regarded by the ruling class of that section as outside of the government, outside of the law, outside of society ... the sport of mob violence and murder, is not only a disgrace and a scandal to that particular section, but a menace to the peace and security of the whole country ... The contagion is spreading, extending and overleaping geographical lines and state boundaries, and if permitted to go on, threatens to destroy all respect for law and order, not only in the South but in all parts of our common country, North as well as South. For certain it is, that crime allowed to go unpunished, unresisted and unarrested, will breed crime. (Foner, 1999: 751–752)

Douglass's stand against the lynching phenomenon is one of the major highlights of his last 25 years of public service. Along with **Ida B. Wells-Barnett** (1862–1931), Douglass stands as a significant champion of freedom at a very low point in black American history. The continuing significance of their work is reflected in one of Douglass's key letters to Barnett.

Douglass's gifts as an orator, writer, and leader eloquently reflected his powerful ability to bring public awareness to the lynching problem in America. Unfortunately it would take another 50 years of struggle for this problem to gradually disappear from the American scene. Yet, in historical perspective, it can be said that Douglass was one of the key voices in the historic freedom struggle to end American lynchings.

Further Reading

Chesebrough, David B., *Frederick Douglass: Oratory from Slavery*. Westport, Conn.: Greenwood Press, 1998.

Dray, Philip. *At the Hands of Persons Unknown: The Lynching of Black America*. New York: Random House, 2002.

Foner, Philip S., ed. *Frederick Douglass: Selected Speeches and Writings*. Chicago: Lawrence Hill Books, 1999.

Gabbidon, Shaun L., Helen Taylor Greene, and Vernette D. Young, eds. *African American Classics in Criminology and Criminal Justice*. Thousand Oaks, Calif.: Sage Publications, 2002.

Logan, Rayford. *The Betrayal of the Negro: From Rutherford B. Hayes to Woodrow Wilson*. New York: Da Capo Press, 1997.

U.S. Bureau of the Census. *Historical Statistics of the United States, Colonial Times to 1957*. Washington, D.C.: U.S. Bureau of the Census, 1960.

Work, Monroe. *Negro Year Book*. Tuskegee, Ala.: Negro Year Book Publishing Co., 1941–64, 1947–51.

—Julius E. Thompson

M

Manifest Destiny

Manifest destiny is a collection of ideas that emerged in nineteenth century America proposing it was the United States' duty to expand its ideology and its form of government and commerce on the continent and abroad, usually expressed as a general and popular idea rather than official government policy. Manifest destiny incorporated beliefs in American nationalism, Anglo-Saxon superiority, and exceptionalism.

Frederick Douglass also supported the idea that America emerged out of divine providence, had a unique place among civilizations that was unrivaled, and that African Americans had a unique role to play in that civilization. However, Douglass differed with the predominant view of manifest destiny in two crucial areas, the role of African Americans in the divine creation of the United States, and the American self-perception.

Most white Americans had a providential view of American history, incorporating the belief that the continent the United States emerged on was land given to them by God, and that the nation represented a break from European values. This European break was expressed in the Declaration of Independence, and the Constitution. The majoritarian worldview sustained a popular belief in manifest destiny, despite the facts that American Indians had been killed or driven off their land, and the importation of African slaves was justified to develop the economic base.

Conversely, Frederick Douglass believed in a providential view of the African in America. Douglass believed that the African could redeem the shortcomings of American civilization. Furthermore, Douglass believed that God would not have allowed the slaves to suffer unless a higher purpose was involved—that Americans had a higher calling to God's will in the world. Furthermore, Douglass believed the evil of slavery would bring a terrible divine retribution on the United States. Among the earliest examples related to the concept of divine retribution upon the United States appeared in Alexander Young's book, *Ethiopian Manifesto*, published in 1829. Many black religious prophets of the time believed the injustice suffered by black Americans would cause God to send a black Messiah to deliver them from bondage.

There was an alternate view among some black leaders—that slaves should fight to free themselves, emigrate from the United States and go to **Africa** or another country. This belief in black emigration was also supported by some whites, including United States presidents from Thomas Jefferson to **Abraham Lincoln**, who believed whites and blacks could never dwell together in the same country. However, Douglass and other free black leaders believed that abandoning their brethren in bondage was a cowardly act, perhaps attributed to the fact some of the leadership was mixed race and had no cultural memory of Africa.

Turning to American self-understanding, manifest destiny was important with respect to the early imperialist designs of America when the country invaded Mexico and continued to take land from the **Native American** nations. During this period of American history, the Negro convention movement was active in organizing African Americans around the country and was wrestling with the problem of defining themselves in relation to America. Initially organized by **Richard Allen**, founder of the **African Methodist Episcopal (AME) Church**, the convention leaders **Henry Garnet**, Douglass and others frequently debated the future of blacks in America and the political ideas of the day. Frederick Douglass pointed out the contradiction between how Americans understood themselves and the condition of African Americans in a speech entitled **"What to the Slave is Your Fourth of July? (The Meaning of July Fourth for the Negro)."** Douglass persuasively argued that the phony sermons, prayers, and hymns delivered that day were no substitute for justice. However, Douglass made two important points with regard to the nation's self-understanding in his speech, "The Right to Criticize American Institutions," delivered to the American Anti-slavery Society—the Constitution and slaveholding religion.

Douglass intimated the Constitution was a pro-slavery document by virtue of the three-fifths clause, the mandated return of fugitive slaves, and the extension of the slave trade. The inclusion of the pro-slavery clauses in the Constitution demonstrated the "Peculiar Institution" was a national disgrace rather than a regional problem. Douglass's critique of Christianity in the role of slavery and manifest destiny did not escape his notice. Douglass noted how the institutions of slavery and religion went hand in hand with economics and business and that priests and churches in the North were frequently in league with their Southern counterparts in the interests of national unity.

Finally, in 1875 Frederick Douglass gave a speech, "The Color Question," in which he raised the provocative statement, "If war among the Whites brought peace and liberty to the Blacks, what will peace among the Whites bring?" Douglass railed against the American tendency to socially forget. Douglass believed the nation would have a poor understanding of present events if there was no proper understanding of its past. For example, the press and other white-controlled cultural institutions did not recall the war as a struggle against slavery and racial injustice. The popular press and media began to reflect the war as an event expressing manly deeds and need for reconciliation. In conclusion, Douglass believed it was the destiny of African Americans to become full citizens within the American polity. However, with regard to manifest destiny, Douglass knew African Americans did not have a belief in American nationalism to the extent whites did. Douglass believed African Americans had a distinct cultural memory that would empower them with a different interpretation of American history.

Further Reading

Blight, David. " 'What Will Peace Among the Whites Bring?' : Reunion and Race in the Struggle Over the Memory of the Civil War in American Culture." *Massachusetts Review*, 34 (August 1993): 393–410.

Poole, Thomas G. "What Country Have I? Nineteenth-Century African-American Theological Critiques of the Nation's Birth and Destiny." *The Journal of Religion*, 72 (October 1992): 533.

—*Reynaldo Anderson*

Maryland

Frederick Douglass was born in Maryland and spent his **childhood** years there. In 1877 he stated to an audience, "I am an Eastern Shoreman, with all that name implies." He continued, "Eastern Shore corn and Eastern Shore pork gave me my muscle. I love Maryland and the Eastern Shore."

Frederick Douglass was born in **Talbot County** on the Eastern Shore of Maryland, in either 1817 or 1818. His mother was a slave woman, Harriet Bailey, and his father, an unknown white man. Separated from his mother at an early age, he was raised by his grandparents, Isaac and Betsy Bailey. Betsy was of **Native American** descent. He referred to this heritage in a speech at the Carlisle Indian Institute, "I rejoice beyond expression at what I have seen and heard at this Carlisle School for Indians. I have been known as a Negro, but I wish to be known here and now as Indian." He spent his formative years through the dark night of slavery in various regions of Maryland. He endured lack of familial attachments, poverty, and physical hardships throughout his childhood. He witnessed and suffered the oppression, cruelty, and degradation that were the common lot of slaves. However, in the midst of these challenges he developed his inner resources and capacities to act in the world.

Talbot County was a business and government hub as well as the center of population and wealth in Maryland in the early eighteenth century. The slaves in this region were imported from the English colony of Barbados and were long

Frederick Douglass, c. 1855. Library of Congress, Prints, and Photographs Division, LC-USZ62-15887.

removed from their African culture. They had developed distinctive behavioral patterns in the West Indies that prepared them for life on the Eastern Shore of Maryland. The Barbados legal codes, plantation rules, and cultural values were similar to those of the Eastern Shore. The Lloyd plantation where Douglass lived was significant for its large number of slaves in comparison to the few that most slave owners had in the area.

The close proximity in which the slaves and the masters lived on the Eastern Shore and Northern Virginia was significantly different from that of the Deep South. In the South the slaves were imported from Africa and spoke their native languages. When Douglass was taken as a boy to the Lloyd plantation, he noted that the languages spoken by the slaves there were almost impossible to understand. Throughout his life he had problems identifying with blacks whose cultural backgrounds were not similar to his.

Douglass wrote of his early life on the Eastern Shore as "for the most part of the first eight years of his life, a spirited, joyous, uproarious, and happy boy. As he grew older he came to realize that the life he lived was controlled by someone 12 miles away on the Lloyd Plantation called "Old Master." In 1824, he was six years old and was sent to the Lloyds of Wye Plantation where the wealthiest family in Maryland lived. There were 181 slaves who worked on the plantation's 9,000 acres. The Wye House, as it is still called today, was one of the nicest homes in America.

In 1825 his masters, Aaron Anthony and his associates, decided to send him to Baltimore to live with Hugh Auld, Anthony's son-in-law. Going to Baltimore laid the foundation for Douglass's future and inspired his determination to seek freedom. Shortly after his arrival in Baltimore, Mrs. Auld taught him the alphabet. When her husband forbade her to continue teaching Douglass, he educated himself, realizing that literacy was a powerful tool. He also convinced the neighborhood children to help him with his lessons.

Frederick Douglass spent seven years in Baltimore before being sent back to the Eastern Shore, where he was shipped to a farm run by a notoriously brutal "slave-breaker" named Edward Covey. Douglass's turning point in his life occurred when he resisted Covey's beating. Covey couldn't break his spirit, and, for the first time in Douglass's life, a white man backed down. After a series of confrontations, Douglass's masters were persuaded to return him to Baltimore.

In urban Baltimore, a slave's life was not as cruel as that of a field slave's. This new setting provided Frederick Douglass with a better milieu, helping him to develop his intellectual abilities and to meet enlightened people. At the shipyard where he worked, he copied the scribbles of other workers to practice writing. From newspapers, he not only improved his reading ability, but he also discovered the existence of antislavery movements in the North. During his free time, Douglass met with a group of educated free blacks and indulged in the luxury of being a student again. Some of the free blacks formed an educational association called the East Baltimore Mental Improvement Society, which welcomed him and where he honed his debating skills. At one of the society's meetings, he met his future wife, a free black woman named **Anna Murray**, with whom he fell in love and to whom he became engaged in 1838. While in Baltimore, Frederick Douglass also achieved religious awakening. His religious faith stimulated his critical thinking, moral questioning, and perseverance in his pursuit of freedom.

After he turned 20 in Baltimore, Douglass escaped from his slavery by impersonating a sailor and fled to **Massachusetts**.

Further Reading

Douglass, Frederick. *Narrative of the Life of Frederick Douglass, and American Slave.* New York: Dover Publications, 1995.

———. *My Bondage and My Freedom.* Hartford, Conn.: Park Pub., 1882.

Preston, Dickson. *Young Frederick Douglass.* Baltimore: Johns Hopkins University Press, 1980.

—*Everette B. Penn, Tracy S. Penn, Jay Bishop, and James Raymond III*

Massachusetts

After Douglass, disguised as a sailor, escaped from slavery in **Maryland,** he and his wife, **Anna Murray,** settled in Massachusetts from 1838 to 1847 where he left a rich legacy in New Bedford, Nantucket, Lynn, and Boston, among other cities. During his three years in New Bedford, a city known for its whaling port, he changed his name from Johnson to Douglass. He worked as a manual laborer, holding jobs such as a woodcutter, caulker, and chimney sweeper. He also attended a predominantly white Methodist Church service. To his dismay, colored people sat in the back of the church and the white pastor spoke to them in a condescending tone. Frustrated with the hypocrisy of white Christians, Douglass decided to become a member of New Bedford's Zion Chapel, affiliated with the **African Methodist Episcopal** Zion (AMEZ) denomination. It was in the black church where his oratorical skills flourished. He served in many roles including that of a preacher.

Later Douglass became a subscriber to the *Liberator*, edited by the distinguished abolitionist William Lloyd Garrison. In April 1839, Douglass attended one of the Anti-Slavery Society's meetings at a Methodist church; he was impressed with the zeal of the abolitionists.

Douglass was encouraged by a friend to attend another Anti-Slavery Society meeting in Nantucket, an island of southeast Massachusetts. There, he spoke eloquently about his life as a slave and the abominable conditions of slavery. William Lloyd Garrison and other renowned **abolitionists** were moved by his poignant story and by his exceptional oratorical skills. This was the beginning of Douglass's remarkable career as an inspiring lecturer and activist.

He was hired as an agent for the Anti-Slavery Society. He and his family moved from New Bedford to Lynn, a Quaker city 20 miles north of Boston. There he would write his renowned autobiography, ***The Narrative of the Life of Frederick Douglass***. While living in Lynn, Douglass traveled with members of the Anti-Slavery Society to several New England towns to speak out against slavery and **Jim Crow Laws**. In Lynn, when he boarded a first-class car, the conductor ordered him to go to the colored car. Douglass demanded an explanation. Holding on to his bolted seat, Douglass was thrown from the train. He landed on the platform with his seat in his hand. Later protest meetings were held in Lynn and the antislavery members threatened to boycott the Eastern line. Nevertheless, the Eastern line continued its Jim Crow practices.

In Boston, Douglass left an indelible mark at historical landmarks, such as Faneuil Hall, Tremont Temple, the African Meeting House, and the Twelfth Baptist Church. He delivered his memorable speeches, "The Slaves' Right to Revolt" in May 1848 and "The Colonization Revival," in May 1849 at Faneuil Hall. On January 1, 1863 at the famous Tremont Temple, Douglass and hundreds of black and white abolitionists celebrated Lincoln's issuance of the **Emancipation Proclamation**. Several years later in 1886 during the **women's suffrage** movement, Douglass returned to the Tremont Temple to present his speech "Who and What Is Woman?" to the New England Woman Suffrage Association. Another significant Boston landmark that Douglass visited was the African Meeting House on Joy Street. It was there that he recruited Negro soldiers for the **Fifty-fourth Regiment of Massachusetts Infantry**, in which his sons, **Charles** and **Lewis**, served. Undoubtedly, as a citizen of Massachusetts, Douglass made a profound impact on the abolitionist movement and civil liberties in the larger society. After Frederick Douglass's death in 1895, the City Council of Boston held memorial services to honor him at Faneuil Hall, where he was hailed as one of America's greatest men.

Further Reading

Blassingame, John W., John R McKivigan, and Peter P. Hinks, eds. *Frederick Douglass Papers*. New Haven, Conn.: Yale University Press, 1999.

Chesebrough, David B. *Frederick Douglass: Oratory from Slavery*. Westport, Conn.: Greenwood Press, 1998.

McFeely, William S. *Frederick Douglass*. New York: W. W. Norton & Co., 1991.

Williamson, Scott C. *The Moral and Religious Thought of Frederick Douglass*. Macon, Ga.: Mercer University Press, 2002.

—*Della Scott*

Massachusetts Anti-Slavery Society (MASS)

One of the leading American and international abolitionist organizations. The MASS and its female auxiliary, the Boston Female Anti-Slavery Society, were founded in 1832. The Society was comprised of many prominent abolitionists such as **William Lloyd Garrison**, Wendell Phillips, Francis Jackson, Edmund Quincy, Parker Pillsbury, Abby Kelley Foster, Stephen Foster, Maria Weston Chapman, John Telemachus Hilton, Caroline Weston, and Ann Warren Weston. In its annual and quarterly meetings, the critical antislavery issues were discussed by members.

During its 1837 quarterly meeting, Wendell Phillips addressed the body regarding the congressional gag rule, which limited antislavery discussions. Before 1837, the society's petitions to the government were important in influencing legislation leading to the emancipation of slaves throughout the British empire and in the Northern states. In 1837, the Society established a petition campaign to encourage congressional restrictions on the admission of new slave states, abolition of slavery in Washington, D.C., and the enactment of other laws unfavorable to Southern planters' interests.

As a part of the international antislavery movement, the Society sent Ann and Wendell Phillips as delegates to the 1839 World Anti-Slavery Convention in London. Wendell Phillips had been appointed a general agent of the Society in 1838. Several Society members attempted unsuccessfully to introduce resolutions at the 1839 quarterly meeting in America which would have required Society members to vote for pure political candidates, those candidates opposed to slavery. In 1839, the Massachusetts Abolition Society, a rival society, was formed by those who opposed the resolutions. It was established by conservative white clerics who broke away from the MASS and Garrison. It lasted for only one year.

In 1843, the Society voted to dissolve the union. Members believed dissolution of the union was their Christian duty to avoid the indignity of a nation which maintained slavery using the Constitution. The dissolution vote followed the outcome of the famous *Latimer* case, about a fugitive slave whose freedom was won by **abolitionists**.

The Society's meetings in the 1850s and 1860s discussed issues such as withdrawing support from the **Republican Party**; engaging in violence to overthrow slavery; opposing **Abraham Lincoln's** second presidential term; and black enfranchisement and Reconstruction.

The Society gathered converts by using lecturers such as Pillsbury and Phillips, who crisscrossed the nation. Frederick Douglass was appointed a lecture agent in 1841.

Further Reading

Blassingame, John W. *The Frederick Douglass Papers, Series One: Speeches, Debates and Interviews, Volume 1: 1841–46*. New Haven, Conn.: Yale, 1979.

Lader, Lawrence. *The Bold Brahmins—New England's War Against Slavery: 1831–1863*. New York: E. P. Dutton and Company, Inc., 1961.

Ripley, C. Peter, editor. *The Black Abolitionist Papers, Volume III, 1830–46*. Chapel Hill, N.C.: University of North Carolina Press, 1991.

Robertson, Stacey M. *Parker Pillsbury—Radical Abolitionist, Male Feminist*. Ithaca, N.Y.: Cornell University Press, 2000.

Sterling, Dorothy. *Ahead of Her Time—Abby Kelley and the Politics of Anti-Slavery*. New York: W. W. Norton and Company, 1991.

Stewart, James Brewer. *Wendell Phillips—Liberty's Hero*. Baton Rouge, La.: Louisiana State University, 1986.

—*Donald Cunnigen*

Methodism

It is widely known that Frederick Douglass was a Methodist, albeit at times only marginally so. He became influenced by the Methodists at an early age. In fact, his slave master, Hugh Auld, was converted to Methodism at a camp meeting in 1832, although Douglass came to view such ostensible religious commitments by slave owners and overseers with suspicion and contempt. One such overseer was Edward Covey, a devout Methodist who was also a "slave-breaker," one who was charged with the responsibility of bringing under control problematic slaves. In addition, Master Hugh's wife, Sophia, was Methodist, whose pastoral leader was Bishop Beverly Waugh of the Methodist Episcopal Church. Nevertheless, it was Master Hugh whom he would hear speak of the "**abolitionists**." Initially, he did not understand the term, but he later came to associate it with being antislavery.

With Douglass's religious conversion early in his teen years came his association of religious experience with abolitionism. He came to see the two as intertwined. In 1839, Douglass would subsequently become a minister of the African Methodist Episcopal Zion (AMEZ) Church, one of the earliest and oldest black religious institutions. Both **Harriet Tubman** and **Sojourner Truth** were members of this group. It was most likely here that he gained his early oratory style, utilizing humor, anecdote, conversation, and extemporaneity.

Moreover, Douglass developed some meaningful and historically significant relationships with individual Methodists, the most dynamic of them, Martin R. Delany. Reified as the "Father of Black Nationalism," Delany was one of the first African Americans to attend Harvard Medical School, but he was dismissed due to his race. Like Douglass, he, too, was a Methodist, abolitionist, orator, novelist, newspaper editor, and political and race theorist, and Douglass's friend. In 1847, Delany left his newspaper, the *Mystery*, to edit an abolitionist publication with Douglass known as the ***North Star***. For 18 months they worked together in the basement of Memorial AMEZ Church in Rochester, New York.

Perhaps it was the strength of their characters, the depth of their convictions, and the breadth of their talents that caused them eventually to part ways. Born free in Charles Town, Virginia (now Charleston, West Virginia), Delany often touted his "unadulterated" African blood, while Douglass was the son of a slave and a white slave master. On the other hand, Douglass often valorized his slave experiences, as if slavery afforded him an authority to speak on behalf of black people, an authenticity that Delany could not know, having been born free. Similarly, both Douglass and Delany saw themselves as "the representative" of the black race, although Douglass's stature and standing with whites obscured Delany's numerous accomplishments. Douglass, maybe intentionally, played no small part in causing Delany to be less lauded. He rarely mentioned Delany's work in his speeches and writing. Subsequent historians have reified the conflict as an ideological debate over the solution to racism, namely, Delany's promotion of emigrationism, or a return to **Africa**, versus Douglass's desire to work within American structures, interpreted by some as integration.

Douglass continued to be ambivalent about the Methodists throughout his life. He was well aware of the antislavery convictions of many of them, but he found it difficult, if not impossible, to reconcile conflicting ideologies among the Methodists. On one end were the Northern Methodists who vociferously opposed slavery. Even here, Douglass found issues, for though many of them openly denounced slavery, African Americans were often subjected to segregation in Northern churches. This was one of the realities that led Douglass to join the all-black AME Zion Church. On the other end of the spectrum were the Southern Methodists, many of whom were pro-slavery, which Douglass could neither reconcile ideologically nor religiously. Needless to say, Douglass sometimes found few significant differences between the Northern and Southern churches.

Methodists and Methodism left distinctive impressions on Douglass. It is likely that without the Methodists, Douglass's life may not have gone the aggressive route toward abolitionism. At the same time, individual Methodists and Methodist churches were often objects of his critiques as he tried to reconcile his understanding of an ideal Christianity with that of pro-slavery churches, including other Christian denominations such as the Baptists and Presbyterians. It is also likely that Methodists such as Martin Delany offered Douglass a means to challenge his own ideas and to learn from those of others. Finally, it should be said that Douglass did not always find the ways and ideas of Negro Methodists commensurate with his own, evidenced by the fact that he remained AME Zion for only a relatively short period of his life. Methodists played an important but dual role in his life, as an early impetus for developing ideas related to slavery and justice, and as source material for critique. Such ambivalence often characterized his conflicting ideas about the nature of the race problems and the ultimate solutions to them.

Further Reading

Douglass, Frederick. *Life and Times of Frederick Douglass*. Hartford, Conn.: Park Publishing Co., 1888.

Levine, Robert S. *Martin Delany, Frederick Douglass, and the Politics of Representative Identity*. Chapel Hill: University of North Carolina Press, 1997.

—*Stephen C. Finley*

Mississippi

The state of Mississippi, which joined the Union in 1817, remains one of the great puzzles of the nineteenth and twentieth centuries in African American history. National leaders such as Frederick Douglass viewed it, as did most blacks everywhere, as one of the worst slave states in the Deep South. This special black consciousness on the state of black life in Mississippi has moved across time—to reflect the tremendous political, social, cultural, and economic conditions—facing black people in Mississippi.

The state population in 1860 was 791,305, of which African Americans were 55.2 percent of the total, or 437,404. Such large concentrations of black people meant that they were an essential element in cotton production in Mississippi and in the state's economy as a whole. Nevertheless, for Frederick Douglass and other **abolitionists**, this reliance on slave labor was wrong and had to end. Certainly, Douglass's efforts at his paper, the ***North Star***, his lectures, and other antislavery work helped to focus attention on the slavery and oppression in Mississippi during the long decades of the nineteenth century.

As both the national mood and debate on slavery intensified in the 1850s and early 1860s, Douglass was one of the first African Americans to call for black servicemen to fight in the Civil War. In fact, 200,000 blacks served nationally, with 17,000 coming from Mississippi. One of Frederick Douglass's goals had been realized in 1865 with the end of slavery in the United States. Much yet remained to be done in the later decades as blacks in Mississippi, the South, and the nation struggled through ages of emancipation, reconstruction, segregation, and **lynchings**. Mississippi played a major role in these periods, and Douglass fought the state's general oppression of the black community by fighting in the press, lecturing, working with **Republican Party** politicians, and writing to bring public pressure to bear on the horrors facing black people in the South, and especially in states like Mississippi.

In 1879 when Southern blacks considered migration, a movement that became known as the "Kansas Exodus" or moving to the Midwest, Douglass instead supported the idea that blacks should stay and keep their population centralized in order to protect their long-term political, economic, and social interests and advancement in the South. In fact, according to scholar E. S. Redkey, Douglass's great dream had been to work "for the integration of blacks into the mainstream of American life." Such an approach suggested that back-to-Africa movements, as promoted by Bishop Henry M. Turner (1834–1915), or perhaps mass migration by blacks from Mississippi and the South, were not the best long-term solutions for black problems.

Yet, in the historical period of 1860 to the 1890s, black Mississippians, documented by Frederick Douglass and **Ida B. Wells-Barnett**, suffered through one of the worst periods of American violence, the age of lynching. It was a time when hundreds of people were lynched in this nation, and especially in Mississippi and the South, for their blackness or for their economic, social, or political outlooks. Indeed, Douglass's last years were spent focusing public outrage and working for changes in policy, nationally, regionally, and at the state level, on the issues raised by lynching in America. It would take many more decades of active protest before this problem would disappear from American life. Certainly, Frederick Douglass's body of antilynching work helped to focus attention on Mississippi, the South, and other parts of the nation during a very critical time in this struggle.

Further Reading

Dann, Martin E., ed. *The Black Press, 1827–1890: The Quest for National Identity*. New York: G. P. Putnam's Sons, 1971.

Ginzburg, Ralph. *100 Years of Lynchings*. Baltimore: Black Classic Press, 1988.

Lowen, James W. and Charles Sallis, eds. *Mississippi: Conflict and Change*. New York: Pantheon Books, 1974.

McKee, Jesse O. *Mississippi: A Portrait of an American State*. Montgomery, Ala.: Clairmont Press, 1995.

Redkey, Edwin. *Black Exodus: Black Nationalist and Back-to-Africa Movements*. New Haven: Yale University Press, 1969.

Sansing, David G. *Mississippi: Its People and Culture*. Minneapolis: T. S. Denison and Co., 1981.

Thompson, Julius E. *The Black Press in Mississippi, 1865–1985*. Gainesville: University Press of Florida, 1993.

—*Julius E. Thompson*

Missouri Compromise of 1820

The Missouri Compromise of 1820 was a legislative attempt to balance power between free and slave states. It was implemented when the admission of Missouri as a state thrust the issue of slavery to the forefront of political debate. By 1819 the Union had an equal number of eleven free states and eleven slave states. The admission of Missouri posed to upset that balance. The controversy over Missouri proved to be a catalyst in many ways of the impending sectional crises up until the Civil War. Northerners charged that the South was conspiring to extend slavery to new territory while Southerners claimed that the North was planning to destroy the Union and end slavery.

The Missouri Compromise temporarily quelled controversy over slavery by admitting Maine as a free state in 1820 and Missouri as a slave state in 1821, and by prohibiting slavery in the remainder of the Louisiana Purchase north of the parallel 36° 30´ north latitude (the southern boundary of Missouri). However, slavery would be allowed under the boundary and the compromise also reaffirmed that it was legal to capture fugitive slaves in the non-slave territories. The Compromise was well established when Frederick Douglass was a slave, and its implications for fugitives threatened his freedom when he fled. With the addition of territories after its passage, the Missouri Compromise would be contested. Legislation such as the 1854 **Kansas-Nebraska Act** forced major changes to the Missouri Compromise and its 36° 30´ boundary with the addition of new states.

Further Reading

Franklin, John Hope. *From Slavery to Freedom*. New York: A. A. Knopf, 1947.

Stewart, Jeffrey. *1001 Things Everyone Should Know about African American History*. New York: Doubleday, 1996.

—*Kelton R. Edmonds*

Murray-Douglass, Anna (1813–1882)

Anna Murray-Douglass, Frederick Douglass's wife of 44 years, is rarely remembered as his partner in abolitionist work. Historical accounts often reduce her role to ironic counterpart—a freeborn, illiterate woman who married the famously literate runaway slave. As the accomplice who helped plan and financed his escape from slavery in 1838, however, Anna Murray-Douglass can be credited with a far more pivotal role in launching her husband's career than even that of **William Lloyd Garrison**, Wendell Phillips, and many other **abolitionists** whose interactions with Douglass usually obscure her own.

Born to enslaved parents Banarra and Mary Murray in Denton, Caroline County, **Maryland** (Eastern Maryland), in 1813, remarkably Anna's seven older siblings were born enslaved, while she and her four younger brothers and sisters were born free. At the age of 17, young, industrious Anna Murray had established a self-sufficient lifestyle as a laundress and housekeeper and social ties within Baltimore's free black community. She met Douglass at the docks, where she took in extra laundry from ship captains to accumulate savings. He had been hired out as a caulker to increase his master's income. Through Anna and her place in a community of free black people, Frederick Douglass saw the possibility of his own freedom. With her encouragement, her access to sailors' clothing, and a portion of her savings, he made his way to Philadelphia and on to New York. Upon his arrival, Anna rendezvoused with Frederick, they married on September 15, 1838, and the newlywed couple adopted the last name of Johnson. It was only after moving to New Bedford, **Massachusetts**, and meeting Mr. Nathan Johnson that the couple was formally introduced as Mr. and Mrs. Frederick Douglass.

Mrs. Anna Douglass. Drawing by O. W. Brooks. Courtesy National Park Service, Museum Management Program and Frederick Douglass National Historic Site, FRDO 246. http://www.cr.nps.gov/museum.

Hope and hardship marked the Douglass' early years. Between 1839 and 1847, she gave birth to five children: **Rosetta, Lewis, Frederick Jr.**, Charles, and **Annie**. During this time, Frederick Douglass shifted from menial laborer to antislavery orator. As her husband's burgeoning career on the abolitionist circuit brought high visibility but low and sporadic pay, theirs would continue to be a marriage that demanded Anna Murray-Douglass's skill and labor. Accustomed to her own income, she supplemented Douglass's earnings and donations from local abolitionists by learning to make shoes and continuing to work as a laundress. Anna's struggle intensified in 1845, when the publication of Douglass's *Narrative* compelled his flight to England to avoid slave-catchers. She managed money adeptly. She also took her own stand as an abolitionist, making financial contributions to and participating in the work of the Boston Female Anti-Slavery Society while the family lived in New Bedford and later, Lynn, Massachusetts.

The Douglasses were drawn to **Rochester, New York**, where women's rights activism and increasing tensions regarding slavery ran high. As Frederick Douglass launched his struggling *North Star* newspaper, Anna urged him to train his young sons as typesetters. She turned her efforts to those most in need. From the rambling home that she managed meticulously, Anna established a headquarters for Underground Railroad service. Especially through the years surrounding the **Fugitive Slave Act** of 1850, Anna provided the accommodations, food, and clean linen that sped hundreds of passengers on to safety in Canada. Frequently, she played hostess to the more public faces in the antislavery movement. Her daughter, Rosetta, recalled her mother's limitless contributions at all hours of the night for what could be best termed a "hungry lot of fleeing humanity." The Douglass home, until destroyed by fire in 1872, became an actual nexus and a symbol for progressive action.

After Frederick returned from his prolonged **European lecture circuit**, he was once again distracted from familial issues and began publishing his abolitionist newspaper, the *North Star*. The Douglass children understood their mother, Anna, was the stabilizing force of the family. In response to the voluminous adulation piled upon her renowned father, Rosetta, the eldest daughter, reminded outsiders that her father's life and accomplishments "was a story made possible by the unswerving loyalty of Anna Murray."

Anna Murray-Douglass's domestic acumen should not be misread as simple conformity to the nineteenth century "cult of true womanhood." It can be argued that she understood the fragile dynamics of public image, as her husband's notoriety enlarged to include women's rights advocate and newspaper editor. The stable home life that Anna Murray-Douglass created for Douglass was vital to his public and political images. Ironically he was the one who damaged his public image by incorporating Julia Griffiths and Ottilie Assing, white women with whom he was linked professionally and romantically, into the household for extended periods which generated recurring scandals. A private person, Anna Murray-Douglass found public scrutiny painful, but nevertheless, she remained a staunch supporter of her husband's role as a voice for justice. After years of failing health, she died of a stroke at the Douglass home in Washington, D.C.

Further Reading

McFeely, William S. *Frederick Douglass*. New York: W. W. Norton & Co., 1991.

Yee, Shirley J. *Black Women Abolitionists: A Study in Activism, 1828–1860*. Knoxville: University of Tennessee Press, 1992.

—Michelle Nzadi Keita and James Jones

My Bondage and My Freedom

Published in 1855, Frederick Douglass's autobiography, *My Bondage and My Freedom*, focuses on his early life, from his enslavement to his status as a free man. Some narratives are more detailed than those in his earlier book, **Narrative of the Life of Frederick Douglass, an American Slave,** first published in 1845. The book describes the hell of slavery, its injustice, contradiction, cruelty, and abominable conditions, by transferring his speeches into narratives. Its strong storyline evokes sympathy and engenders anger and deep philosophical and moral outrage. Indeed, readers feel, whatever the time and place, anger at the inhumane slavery system, pity for the child searching for love and family, and pride for the man who stood up, said "enough is enough," and decided to fight back to free himself and his people.

Frederick Douglass became fatherless and motherless, not because of his parents' deaths, but because slavery tore his family apart. Slavery separated him from the only home he enjoyed, his grandparent's log cabin, and from the only person he had learned from and loved, his grandmother. Enslavement worked against African American family structures by reducing slaves to the level of basic child bearers and denying them the rights to raise and educate their own children.

Frederick Douglass was a freedom fighter, a humble, unselfish leader who "long entertained...a somewhat positive repugnance to writing or speaking anything for the public which could, with any degree of plausibility, make him liable to the imputation of seeking personal notoriety, for its own sake." He was a very smart leader, a great scholar who understood the law and the dominant theories of his era. He was also a great deconstructionist who adapted to fight slavery within its own parameters. Fighting slavery from within, Frederick Douglass uses the same intellectual, religious, and moral tools as those used by slavery's proponents. He states, "I have never placed my position to slavery on a basis so narrow as my own enslavement, but rather upon the indestructible and unchangeable laws of human nature, every one of which is perpetually and flagrantly violated by the slave system." Douglass believed those

Frederick Douglass. Carte-de-Viste. Courtesy National Park Service, Museum Management Program and Frederick Douglass National Historic Site, FRDO 3928. http://www.cr.nps.gov/museum.

who used laws to justify enslavement were wrong because those laws protected, everybody including the "enslaved."

His autobiography is divided into 25 chapters, which can be grouped into two major themes. The first theme, chapters one through twenty, focuses on his life as an "enslaved"; the second theme, chapters 21 through 25, focuses on his escaping from enslavement and on his life as a free person. The appendices that end the book can be included in the second general theme.

Beside narrating Frederick Douglass's experiences as an enslaved, these first chapters describe the harsh realities of enslavement—its inhumane conditions, cruelties, heartlessness, and contradictions—and the hardship under which Frederick Douglass lived during his childhood. He was born in 1818 in Tuckahoe, **Maryland**, to **Harriet Bailey**, a slave of Captain Aaron Anthony, and an unknown white father (possibly Captain Anthony himself). Captain Anthony was the chief manager of the plantation of Colonel Edward Lloyd V who served as U.S. senator and Maryland governor.

Frederick Douglass's neighborhood was poor and illiterate. Like many enslaved, Frederick Douglass knew neither his age nor his genealogy. He grew up with his grandparents, Isaac and Betsy Bailey, in their log cabin where he was much loved. His grandmother, a well-respected handcrafter and sweet potato planter, was Captain Anthony's slave; his grandfather was a free man.

Living with his loving grandparents was no longer joyful for him when Douglass learned that his grandmother was enslaved. His grandfather being free could not ease his concerns because he feared he would have to join the house of Captain Anthony, or "Old Master," and "whose name seemed ever to be mentioned with fear and shuddering."

His fear became reality when, at seven years old, he was taken from his joyous life with his grandparents to the plantation house of Captain Anthony 12 miles away. Frederick Douglass was very hurt. Leaving his grandparents meant losing love, freedom, family memories, and childhood. The heartbreaking separation happened when his grandmother asked him to play with the other children, then left. Once Douglass saw that his grandmother was gone, he realized the reason for the trip and cried.

At Captain Anthony's plantation house, Frederick Douglass lived the inhumane, degrading conditions of enslavement. He ran errands for Lucretia Auld, Captain Anthony's daughter, who sometimes showed him kindness and tenderness. Frederick Douglass only rarely saw his mother, who slaved at a farm miles away from the plantation house. Douglass also saw his brother and sisters for the first time. They had no familiar affection for each other because they had not lived together. As Douglass stated, "Brothers and sisters we were by blood, but slavery made us strangers." Enslavement destroyed family structures by separating parents from their children. In fact, the children were not even theirs; they belonged to the enslavers. Hence, the family became reduced to its reproductive function, childbearing, instead of a structure that provided love and safety and encouraged learning. As Douglass stated, "Slavery uses successful methods of obliterating from the mind and heart of the slave, all just ideas of the sacredness of the family as an institution." Understanding the present-day black family crisis should take into account the effects that slavery's anti-family policies had on black families during the enslavement era. Frederick

Douglass evidenced it well: "My poor mother, like many other slave-women, had many children, but no family."

At Captain Anthony's plantation house, Frederick Douglass witnessed many cruel incidents: Captain Anthony mercilessly whipping his Aunt Ester; "Aunt Katy" starving him; Captain Anthony refusing to protect his cousin Betsy from a drunken overseer; malnourished enslaved children often lacking appropriate clothing; Captain Anthony treating his horses and dogs better than his enslaved; Colonel Lloyd's whipping of Old Barney, the stable's keeper; and overseer Gore cruelly killing young enslaved, Denby.

After witnessing a beautiful enslaved woman's whipping by Captain Anthony for refusing to stop loving Edward, son of the favorite enslaved of Colonel Lloyd, Douglass started to inquire about enslavement: "Why am I a slave? Why are some people slaves, and others masters? Was there ever a time when this was not so? How did the relation commence?" In response to those philosophical and ontological musings, his young mind did not accept the notion that enslavement was a divine order. He refused the religious interpretation of a God that maintained him enslaved. He refused God's goodness that excluded his people. If God was goodness, he would not have allowed that horrible, monstrous system of enslavement. Color could not be a basis for enslavement because there were free blacks and non-enslaver whites. Frederick Douglass found the true response to his inquiry: "It was not color, but crime, not God, but man that afforded the true explanation of the existence of slavery."

In 1826, Frederick Douglass was sent to Baltimore to live with Hugh and Sophia Auld to care for their two-year-old son. Douglass spent almost the next seven years in Baltimore, where Sophia Auld taught him to read. But her husband forbade her to give Frederick Douglass further instruction. The interdiction to teach Frederick Douglass to read made him understand enslavement's true philosophy and the direct pathway from enslavement to freedom. Enslavement understood that knowledge is power for the enslaved, and a threat to the enslaver. Oppression and injustice feed off ignorance. To keep the enslaved Africans in their oppressive condition, the enslavers made them believe in the motto, *obscuritas mea lex* (ignorance is my *raison d'être*). The enslaved Africans were taught that suffering would lead them to redemption, making them children of Israel, God's chosen people. Frederick Douglass disagreed. He rejected the use of God to justify enslavement, leading him to later stress liberation instead of salvation. Frederick Douglass is considered the precursor of liberation theology by Reginald Davis because of his use of the same Christian God as a tool mixed with human rights principles to fight enslavement.

Following her husband's request, Sophia stopped teaching Frederick Douglass. But his intellectual awakening was already underway. Frederick Douglass found other ways to learn: using young poor white playmates as teachers by paying them bread; buying the *Columbian Orator*, a very popular schoolbook at that time; and copying words in the used copybook of Hugh and Sophia Auld's son.

In 1833 Douglass was returned to Thomas Auld, who hired him out for a year to Edward Covey, a local farmer and heartless tyrant known as a slave-breaker. Edward Covey repeatedly beat Douglass until one day in August 1834, Frederick Douglass vehemently resisted Covey's beating: "Enough is Enough!!! " Because he resisted, the beatings stopped: "This battle with Mr. Covey ... was the turning point in my *life as a slave*. It rekindled in my breast the smoldering embers of liberty; it ... revived a sense of my own manhood. I was a changed being after that. I was nothing before; I was a Man Now." Two years later, Frederick Douglass was hired out to William Freeman. Frederick Douglass attempted unsuccessfully to escape with five other enslaved. He was sent to jail where he was rescued by Thomas Auld who sent him back to Baltimore to work in the shipyards.

In 1838, Douglass escaped enslavement by dressing like a sailor and carrying a seaman's protection paper. He went to New York where he was protected by David Ruggles, then-Secretary of the New York Vigilance Committee and an important figure in the Underground Railroad. He wrote a letter to his fiancée, Anna Murray, informing her of his safe arrival. She quickly joined him; they married and moved to New Bedford, **Massachusetts**, where for precaution, he changed his name from Frederick Bailey to Frederick Douglass. He worked as a general laborer because discrimination prevented him from finding a better-paid job as a caulker. He started reading the *Liberator*, a paper edited by **William Lloyd Garrison**, which denounced oppression and called for the end of enslavement. In 1841 Frederick Douglass joined the **Massachusetts Anti-Slavery Society (MASS)**. After delivering a speech at the Massachusetts Anti-Slavery Society Convention and talking about his enslaved life, they offered him and he accepted a salaried public lecturer position. His speeches' eloquence made some question whether he was ever a slave. In 1845, in response to the doubters, Frederick Douglass wrote *Narrative of the Life of Frederick Douglass, an American Slave*. The book was a critical success, but exposed him to the possibility of being recaptured. He fled to **England** and later to Ireland. On board the *Cambria*, the ship that took him to England, he encountered discrimination and racism.

Frederick Douglass spent 20 months in England lecturing against enslavement, meeting British and Irish **abolitionists** and intellectuals. In a reception speech at the Finsbury Chapel in 1846, Douglass described the horrible conditions of the enslaved:

> The condition of the slave is simply that of the brute beast ... He is a piece of property ... He is spoken of, thought of, and treated as property. His own good, his conscience, his intellect, his affection, are all set aside by the master. The will and the wishes of the master are the law of the slave. He is as much a piece of property as a horse ... He is carefully deprived of everything that tends in the slightest degree to detract from his value as property. He is deprived of education. God has given him an intellect; the slaveholder declares it shall not be cultivated. If his moral perception leads him in a course contrary to his value as property, the slaveholder declares he shall not exercise it. The marriage institution cannot exist among slaves, and one sixth of the population of democratic America is denied its privilege by the law of the land. (Douglass, 1855: 408–409)

Speeches like this won support for him and his cause. His eloquence convinced two British Quakers, Ellen and Anna Richardson, to raise money in order to purchase his freedom.

Frederick Douglass returned to the United States in 1847. He moved to New York where, against the advice of his abolitionist friends including William Garrison, he launched his own antislavery weekly, the ***North Star***. That journal was devoted to the causes of freedom and progress for the people of African descent. According to Frederick Douglass,

> I have felt to be as part of my mission—under a gracious Providence—to impress my sable brothers in this country with the conviction that, notwithstanding the ten thousands of discouragements and the powerful hinderances, which beset their existence in this country—notwithstanding the blood-written history of Africa, and her children, from whom we have descended, or the clouds and darkness... now overshadowing them—progress is yet possible, and bright skies shall yet shine upon their pathway; and that Ethiopia shall yet reach forth her hand unto God. (Douglass, 1855: 405)

This marked another turning point in his life: Frederick Douglass as a black leader.

Further Reading

Andrews, W. L., ed. *The Oxford Frederick Douglass Reader*. Oxford: Oxford University Press, 1996.

Davis, R. F. *Frederick Douglass: The Precursor of Liberation Theology*. Macon, Ga.: Mercer University Press, 2005.

Douglass, F. *My Bondage and My Freedom*. New York: Miller, Orton, and Mulligan, 1855.

Miller, D. *Makers of America: Frederick Douglass and the Fight for Freedom*. New York: File Publications, 1988.

Preston, D. J. *Young Frederick Douglass: The Maryland Years*. Baltimore: Johns Hopkins University Press, 1980.

Sundquist, E. J., ed. *Frederick Douglass: New Literary and Historical Essays*. Cambridge: Cambridge University Press, 1980.

—*Alioune Deme*

N

NAACP (National Association for the Advancement of Colored People)

The National Association for the Advancement of Colored People is perhaps the most well-known of the American civil rights organizations. Renowned for its groundbreaking legal work during the civil rights movement, it is also one of the most lauded. Having its origins in multiple and converging movements of the early twentieth century, however, Frederick Douglass would not have been involved in its founding given that he died in 1895. While no direct relationship exists between Douglass and the NAACP, notwithstanding, one does find indirect connections and influences and thematic similarities that an exploration of the initial history and development of the NAACP will reveal.

The commonly accepted date of the founding of the NAACP is February 12, 1909, and the founders are typically described as an admixture of whites and African Americans, Jews and Protestant Christians, that generally includes Harvard- and Fisk-educated W. E. B. Du Bois, the great sociologist, philosopher, and race theorist; **Ida B. Wells-Barnett**, the anti-lynching crusader and campaigner for woman's rights and suffrage; and Mary White Ovington, a white social worker, socialist, and Unitarian. To the contrary, however, the primary impetus for the initial foundation of the movement, it seems, was a group of white professionals and activists who were meeting prior to February 1909 and in fact issued "The Call" to which many—including several African Americans—responded, forming the nascent NAACP, first called the National Negro Committee.

Dismayed by the **lynching** of black people in anti-Negro riots of Springfield, Illinois, in 1908 and disillusioned with the accommodationist ideas of the primary Negro leader of his time, **Booker T. Washington,** this group, which included primary founder Mary White Ovington, Henry Moscowitz, William English Walling, and Oswald Garrison Villard, the grandson of **William Lloyd Garrison**, met to discuss ways in which they could respond to the oppression, inequities, and racial violence committed against black citizens, and how they might form an organization that could perpetually come to the aid of Negroes. The result was this call for a meeting that came to fruition in New York on February 12, but the written statement of "The Call" was actually composed by Villard. The meeting was also meant to commemorate the one hundredth anniversary of the birth of **Abraham Lincoln**, who perhaps coincidentally had lived in Springfield, Illinois, prior to being elected President of the United States. It was at this February 12 conference that W. E. B. Du Bois, Ida B. Wells-Barnett, Mary Church Terrell, **Francis Grimke**, and other black leaders and activists endorsed the written statement and became affiliated with the burgeoning interracial group.

In 1910, Du Bois, a friend of Ovington, became the only African American member of its official leadership, as editor of the NAACP's periodical, the *Crisis*. The NAACP would remain white-dominated in its leadership for decades, but it was this strategic move to co-opt Du Bois and others that ensured Negro mass support of the movement and the support of more militant voices within the black community. To that end, Du Bois had been the founder of the short-lived Niagara Movement. Founded on July 11, 1905, this radical group of about 60 African Americans had been opposed to the policies of Booker T. Washington, which made them attractive allies to the white founders of the NAACP, especially Ovington and Villard. In fact, Du Bois had invited Ovington to become Niagara's first white member in 1908. She, Villard, and the others were vociferously opposed to 's accommodationist attitude toward those who held economic and political power and oppressed black people in America. It was here where Frederick Douglass might have objected to Washington and been a part of the voices that opposed Washington, voices that gave early ideological shape to the NAACP.

Douglass lived to see the greatest renaissance of black leadership America has ever known, particularly near the turn of the century. His contemporaries would have been W. E. B. Du Bois; Bishop Henry McNeal Turner, the militant AME minister; **Alexander Crummell**, Edward Wilmot Blyden, Francis Grimke, Bishop Alexander Walters of the AME Zion Church, Reverdy C. Ransom (later Bishop Ransom of the AME Church), and Ida B. Wells-Barnett, Sutton Griggs, and Martin R. Delany, and many others, some of whom, like Wells-Barnett and Grimke, were Niagara and NAACP members and like Frederick Douglass were Christian ministers. Yet, Douglass stood out among them, as did Bishop Turner at times, as the dominant leader of black people. But it was the year in which Frederick Douglass died that was thrust into the national spotlight with his speech at the Atlanta Exposition, which espoused accommodationism, and it was in the cacophonic convergence of responses to this accommodationism that the ideological basis of—and indeed the NAACP itself—was born.

It is in this sense that Douglass's indirect influence on the NAACP can be seen most clearly, for it was this putative opposition to the platform of Washington that would have placed Douglass squarely in the camps of Bishop Turner, Du Bois, the NAACP founders, and the Niagara Movement, who obstreperously renounced his acquiescence to oppressive social and political circumstances rather than engaging and confronting them in an effort to dismantle and destroy them, an aggressive attitude toward injustice that Douglass helped to create. It is quite obvious, then, that Douglass would have advocated political engagement and "agitation," and even violence as a means to achieving freedom and equity, even though he would have found merit in Washington's focus instead of on the **industrial education** of Negroes.

Other indirect connections existed. For instance, Oswald Garrison Dillard, one of the NAACP founders, was the grandson of Douglass's abolitionist colleague, William Lloyd Garrison. Moreover, the early NAACP leadership saw itself recapitulating the work of Douglass and other abolitionists. Many other connections were thematic. Douglass would have agreed with the NAACP's platform against forced segregation, for civil rights and equal protection under the law and equal education, and most certainly its anti-lynching stance. Finally, one of the most appalling thematic relationships between Frederick Douglass and the NAACP was the paternalistic manner in which whites related to them both, condescendingly affirming them, supporting them financially, often controlling and even exploiting them for their own sociopolitical purposes including utilizing them as instruments to be their voice on behalf of Negroes.

Further Reading

Andrews, William L. *Critical Essays on Frederick Douglass*. Boston, Mass.: G. K. Hall, 1991.

Rogers, William B. *"We Are All Together Now": Frederick Douglass, William Lloyd Garrison, and the Prophetic Tradition*. New York: Routledge, 1995.

Zangrando, Robert L. *The NAACP Crusade Against Lynching, 1909–1950*. Philadelphia: Temple University Press, 1980.

—*Stephen C. Finley*

Narrative of the Life of Frederick Douglass

Priced at 50 cents and first published in 1845, Frederick Douglass's 125-page autobiography, *Narrative of the Life of Frederick Douglass*, proved to be enormously popular. *Narrative*, Douglass's first autobiography, also provides one of the earliest examples of "black consciousness." Many Southern whites were captivated by Douglass's gift for words, while at the time wondering how a person of African descent—let alone a former slave—could write in such an eloquent and convincing manner. Therefore, Douglass had two purposes for writing the book: first, to prove that he had indeed been a slave he chronicled his experiences, including details that only a slave would know; and secondly, Douglass hoped to reach those supporters who had not yet heard him speak in order to persuade them to join the antislavery movement.

Although the term, black consciousness, came into popular usage during the 1960s' civil rights movement, the words have come to signify the historical struggles of African peoples, most notably African Americans, defining them against a white mainstream that insisted on imposing its own (negative) meanings of blackness. Black consciousness includes the beliefs that: real black people are those who can hold their heads high in defiance rather than willingly surrender their souls to the white man; simply by acknowledging one's blackness, one is on the road toward emancipation, since true freedom and equality demand that people of African descent feel good about themselves, their culture, and their history; black people recognize the need to work together with other black people in order to end racial oppression; and black people decide, by all means necessary, to be the determinant of their own fate. Douglass's *Narrative* explores his own evolution toward freedom, toward an understanding that he was a man—a black man—deserving respect.

From the *Narrative*, Douglass's black consciousness emerges in at least eight distinct life stages: at age eight after learning to read and write, he understands the power of literacy and the connection between freedom and knowledge; as a young man, he works on improving his oratory skills and his mind; as a slave when, after a fight with his white master, Edward Covey, he discovers self-respect, being transformed from a slave into a man; as a slave working for Mr. Freeland, he decides to live upon free land; as a slave in Baltimore, he shapes the consciousness of other slaves, organizing them to all work together to secure freedom; as a slave who is able to hire himself out, he learns about the inequities of slavery; as a free man, after he escapes from slavery; and as a free man, he uses his voice, both oral and written, pleading on behalf of his black brethren.

Douglass's consciousness began to take shape at age eight when he was sent to Baltimore, **Maryland**, to be a slave for Hugh and Sophia Auld. The city held much more freedom for Douglass than the plantation did, and while working as a shipyard laborer, Douglass was able to mingle with some of the city's free black population. This was really the first time Douglass became conscious that some black people did, in fact, have control over their own lives as well as their future. With the help of his white mistress, Douglass learned to read and write. However, when Mr. Auld found out about his wife's instruction, he forbade her to continue teaching Douglass, declaring "learning will spoil the best nigger in the world." "If you teach that nigger how to read," he told his wife, "there would be no keeping him. It would forever unfit him to be a slave. He would at once become unmanageable, and of no value to his master.... It would make him discontented and unhappy." For Douglass, Mr. Auld's words sank deep into his heart and forced him to think about his life in an entirely different light. He now understood that knowledge was the key to unlocking the white master's power over the black slave. Armed with this information, Douglass was on the path from slavery to freedom.

Even though physically he was still a slave, Douglass was, in many respects, at least no longer mentally a slave. He continued to find ways to improve his reading, oftentimes tricking his white school-aged "friends" into teaching him the letters of the alphabet. Later, Douglass would use his own money to buy a handbook on oratory, the *Columbian Orator*, which contained patriotic speeches. The book also contained a dialogue between a master and slave. This exchange between master and slave, in which the slave makes a compelling and eloquent case for his rebelling and running away, gave Douglass the necessary words to articulate his own thoughts and feelings about his condition. Ironically, the more Douglass read, the more he hated the white enslavers who had gone to Africa and stolen his people from their native land, and the more he hated his own condition as a slave, feeling powerless to escape from slavery to freedom. Despite these feelings of powerlessness, Douglass never lost hope. He continued to read, and he sought out ways to learn how to write. When he returned to Baltimore some years later to serve another master, Douglass, along with some free black workers, formed a Mental Improvement Society. These black men debated issues relevant to the time period and used this forum to improve their minds. It is in these variant ways that Douglass held his head high, refusing to surrender. Yet in a more meaningful way, he had taken the first tangible steps on the road to his physical freedom—psychological transformation from a slave into a man.

It was in this way that Douglass's blackness transcended his life as a slave, and his desires to become a free man became a daily part of his consciousness. This transcendence took place when he was hired out to work for a Mr. Edward Covey. At the time Douglass was sent to work for Covey, he was deemed "unmanageable," but after two weeks on Covey's farm, Covey succeeded in breaking Douglass's "body, soul, and spirit." In addition, Douglass lost his desires to continue developing his intellect, to read, to be, in general, cheerful. Covey had, Douglass writes, succeeded in making him "a brute." Yet, it was a fight with Covey that transformed Douglass from a slave to a man. With an unknown spark of defiance, Douglass grabbed Covey by the throat and choked him until Covey gave up. Never again would Covey lay a hand on Douglass for the remaining six months that Douglass spent with him. This battle with Covey was, according to Douglass, a "turning-point" in his career as a slave. Standing up to Covey, both physically and mentally, rekindled in Douglass his desire for freedom and gave him a sense of his own manhood. From that day forward, Douglass writes in his autobiography, his "long-crushed" spirit rose, his fear of white men was abated, and his bold defiance was renewed. Whether or not he spent the rest of his life as someone else's property no longer mattered to Douglass because his mind was free, and he was willing to die in order to be protect his physical being and his rights as a man. Moreover, Douglass made it known to all whites who tried to exercise control over him by whipping him that they had better be willing to kill him, because he was not willing to stand idly by as they beat him like some animal. He would fight back, even if fighting back would result in his own death.

Toward the end of 1834, Douglass began to think more concretely about gaining his physical freedom, after being hired out to work for a Mr. Freeland for the following year. Certainly not lost on the irony of his new master's name, Douglass said that he wanted to live "upon free land," in control of his own life and destiny. He resolved that sometime during 1835, he would make an attempt at securing his liberty. In line with his decision, Douglass decided to share his resolve with his fellow slaves. Because they were so dear to him, he believed that it was important to share his "life-giving" determination with them. Douglass quite prudently asked each slave's opinion about slavery, and for those who were resistant to escaping, Douglass persuasively allayed their concerns and focused on helping them think about freedom. After finding them open to discussion, Douglass continued speaking to the men about their enslavement and their desire for self-respect, and they all agreed to make one noble effort at freedom. The men spoke of their hopes and fears, the difficulties they might encounter, their thoughts about just giving up and living the rest of their lives as slaves. In the end, however, the men attempted to escape, inspired by their own understanding of Patrick Henry's speech, to give him liberty or give him death. For Douglass and the others, a doubtful liberty, and a certain death should they be caught, was preferable to a hopeless bondage. Using the master's tool, Douglass wrote a pass for himself and his fellow slaves, a pass which should allow them to go North should they be confronted by a white person. Before they were able to escape, however, they were caught, and one mistress blamed Douglass for tainting his fellow slaves with thoughts of freedom.

Douglass was sent back to Baltimore, where he worked at the shipyard alongside whites and free black carpenters. After a fight with his white coworkers who refused to work alongside black workers, Douglass realized that, in the excitement of being in Baltimore and working in the shipyard, he had forgotten about his liberty. Consequently, Douglass resolved to escape. He had again become aware that even with improved conditions, his desire to be free had not waned. For slaves to remain contented and to not seek their freedom, Douglass writes, whites must do their best at keeping slaves thoughtless, without powers of reason, and without moral or mental visions. They must be taught that slavery is right and that they are not men. This, of course, was not true for Douglass. He decided to once again take control of his fate and seek his freedom, by whatever means necessary.

In the final chapter of his *Narrative*, Douglass lays out the events and his thoughts leading up to his escape from slavery to freedom. By early 1838, Douglass felt quite restless about his life as a slave. He questioned why, at the end of each week, he was forced to turn over all of his earnings, the result of his hard work and labor, to his master, who would look at him and simply ask, "Is that all?" Even though Douglass's master tried to exhort him into accepting his life as a slave, to not prepare for the future, to not think, Douglass decided otherwise. He continued to think about his life and the injustices of his enslavement, and to prepare for his escape. When his master allowed Douglass to hire himself out, Douglass saved some of the money he made for his escape. After being forced to quit this job, Douglass resolved, for the final time, to break the chains of slavery. On September 3, 1838, Frederick Douglass reached New York; he was now a free man.

With freedom, however, came a great sense of fear. Douglass feared every white person he sees, for he knew that he could be returned to slavery. After meeting a white man named David Ruggles, Douglass sent for and married **Anna Murray**, a free woman, and moved to New Bedford, **Massachusetts**, where he continued in the caulking trade. Shortly thereafter, Douglass received a copy of **William Lloyd Garrison**'s *Liberator*, an antislavery newspaper. From the *Liberator*, Douglass learned about the principles of the abolitionist cause and later attended their meetings. At an antislavery convention in Nantucket on August 11, 1841, Douglass began what would become his lifelong quest, securing the freedom of his black brothers and sisters. For it was at this gathering that Douglass would, for the first time, tell white people about his experiences as a slave. His black consciousness now fully formed, Douglass would, for the rest of his life, use his gift of words and speech to plead on behalf of his black brethren.

For **abolitionists**, Douglass's *Narrative* served as a powerful tool for the antislavery movement. In a letter to Douglass, abolitionist Wendell Phillips explained how the veracity of Douglass's experiences as a slave would reverberate throughout the entire world as well as give more proof about the inhumanity of slavery. It would do all this, and today, more than 170 years after its publication, Frederick Douglass's *Narrative of the Life of Frederick Douglass* still offers us this lesson about undoing one of the world's most horrific institutions: "what man can make, man can unmake."

Further Reading

Douglass, Frederick. *Narrative of the Life of Frederick Douglass: An American Slave*. New York: New American Library, 1968.

Ernest, John. "The Education of Othello's Historian: The Lives and Times of Frederick Douglass." *Resistance and Reformation in Nineteenth-Century African-American Literature*. Jackson: University Press of Mississippi, 1995.

Meltzer, Milton, ed. *Frederick Douglass: In His Own Words*. San Diego: Harcourt Brace, 1995.

—Dwonna Goldstone

National American Woman Suffrage Association (NAWSA)

The National American Woman Suffrage Association (NAWSA) was formed in 1890 by the merger of two rival suffrage groups, the American Woman Suffrage Association (AWSA) and the National Woman Suffrage Association (NWSA). These two organizations had been politically divided and competitors ever since they were established in 1869. NAWSA became the primary political framework and organization of the women's suffrage movement. The NAWSA eventually became the League of Women Voters once the ratification of the Nineteenth Amendment was secured in 1920. The Nineteenth Amendment prohibited the federal and state governments from denying a citizen the right to vote on account of sex. This amendment was modeled on the **Fifteenth Amendment**.

The NAWSA was created in part to heal the schism that had splintered the women's suffrage movement in 1869 and in part to consolidate the efforts of women's rights advocates in expanding the voting franchise to include women. Elizabeth Cady Stanton was elected as the first president of NAWSA. Stanton was the pioneering organizer and leader of the nineteenth-century women's rights movement, helping to organize the historic 1848 **Seneca Falls Women's Rights Convention**. She was the force behind the political resolution adopted at this convention, calling on the women's rights movement to secure the right to vote for women.

During the antebellum years, Frederick Douglass worked alongside many of the leaders in the women's rights movement. Douglass had a long history and association with the pioneers and leading figures in this movement such as **Sojourner Truth**, Frances Ellen Watkins Harper, Lucy Stone, Elizabeth Cady Stanton, **Susan B. Anthony,** and Lucretia Mott. He not only had attended the historic 1848 Seneca Falls Women's Rights Convention, but he also had been an active participant in the deliberations. Moreover, Douglass usually attended many of the women's rights conventions, where he was often a featured speaker and honored guest on their platform. In the newspaper edited and published by Douglass, the *North Star*, he defended the women's rights movement at its embryonic stage, writing sympathetic editorials and articles highlighting the movement's issues and accomplishments. Furthermore, he published the conventions' proceedings. Douglass used his paper, advocating and promoting the fundamental ideas of this movement that he dearly cared about. Moreover, he used his pen to garner favorable public opinion on behalf of **women's**

suffrage and the women's rights movement and to inform the public about its agenda.

However, Douglass's esteem and credibility in the women's suffrage movement was unable to prevent a serious rift between various factions within the suffrage movement and the AERA after the Civil War. Despite his best efforts, Frederick Douglass found himself on the opposite side of Elizabeth Cady Stanton and Susan B. Anthony in what soon devolved into an acrimonious political stand off.

The American Equal Rights Association (AERA) was a short-lived organization founded in 1866 and disbanded in 1869. The AERA had emerged out of the first post-Civil War National Women's Rights Convention in 1866. Frederick Douglass was chosen to serve as one of the three vice presidents of the AERA. This organization had been formed primarily by white women's rights advocates who now wanted to link the enfranchisement of women to the enfranchisement of blacks, believing that doing so would increase the likelihood women would be enfranchised sooner rather than later. It was a calculated political strategy more than an expression of unconditional support for black suffrage. Stanton reasoned that if both black suffrage and women's suffrage were not pushed through Congress together, then women's suffrage would possibly be delayed for decades. She was shrewd enough to understand that the women's rights movement had been unable to achieve women's suffrage, on a wide scale, before the war. In light of this fact, Stanton reasoned that the Reconstruction period was the most opportune time to link women's suffrage to black suffrage because the country was focused on formulating different legal and political statuses for former slaves. She believed that in the process of contemplating a new status for blacks in America, new legislation would have to be passed, and Stanton correctly assumed that voting privileges would be among the issues addressed.

At the 1868 meeting of the AERA, Douglass sought to foster reconciliation between the different factions in the suffrage movement. Yet again at the 1869 meeting Douglass tried to reduce the level of disagreement and conflict. He tried to assure the movement's Stanton-Anthony faction of his unwavering support for women's suffrage. He asserted that in supporting the **Fifteenth Amendment** he was not turning his back on women's suffrage. In making the case for ratification of the Fifteenth Amendment, he pointed out that at no time had he ever argued for it on the grounds that women should be denied the right to vote, or that women did not equally deserve the right to vote. He pledged to them that he would continue to struggle for extending the franchise to women, even after successful passage of the Fifteenth Amendment. Any assessment of his record by even his harshest critics cannot deny that Douglass was faithful to this pledge.

However, despite Douglass's best attempts at resolving this conflict, disagreements and irreconcilable differences between those who supported and those who opposed the Fifteenth Amendment finally led to the demise of the AERA and the splintering of the women's suffrage movement. Frederick Douglass was in favor of the Fifteenth Amendment. Frances Ellen Watkins Harper, African American women, and the majority of the black community sided with Douglass in this conflict. Stanton, Anthony, and their allies were opposed to the Fifteenth Amendment. Sojourner Truth is said to have aligned with the Stanton-Anthony faction, but that would have been the exception rather than the rule among African Americans. The Fifteenth Amendment prohibited federal and state governments from denying or restricting the right to vote based upon race, color, or previous condition of servitude, but it did not give an affirmative right to vote. This fact was not lost on many Southern lawmakers who later placed conditions, such as poll taxes and literacy tests, on voting in their respective states, effectively nullifying the promise of the Fifteenth Amendment. In the **U.S. Supreme Court** decision of *United States vs. Reese* (1876), the Court held that the Fifteenth Amendment did not give anyone a right to vote. Hence, state governments retained the authority to set the qualifications for suffrage so long as they used standards which were apparently racially neutral.

Although Douglass personally supported extending the right to vote to women and was not against women and blacks being enfranchised at the same time, most lawmakers and white male voters felt differently. African Americans like Douglass were in no position to override white male voters' opinions on women's suffrage since political power was concentrated with white male voters. In light of this harsh political reality, a hard choice had to be made between opposing or supporting the Fifteenth Amendment, even if it was imperfect and not as strong as Douglass and others would have liked. In their opinion, the Fifteenth Amendment at least represented a defeat of racism that had explicitly used race in the past to exclude blacks from politics and from voting. Although the Fifteenth Amendment would not give blacks an affirmative right to vote, it would at least ban states from setting obvious and overtly different sets of voting qualifications for whites as opposed to African Americans. Doubtless Douglass would have preferred a much stronger suffrage amendment, but he saw the Fifteenth Amendment as a partial victory and a step in the right direction. He reasoned that a partial victory was better than the status quo.

In evaluating this dispute it is important to understand the reasoning behind Douglass's position on these issues. His arguments in favor of the Fifteenth Amendment did not rest on repudiating women's suffrage or arguing that black men were more deserving of the vote than women. Instead, Douglass expressed regret that both groups would not be enfranchised by this amendment. Douglass's arguments must not be taken out of context from the social and the political climates faced by African Americans both before and immediately following the Civil War. In this era when African Americans had little political leverage, Douglass believed that it was strategically unwise to give a political ultimatum to Congress saying, in essence, include the issue of women's suffrage explicitly or else. Unfortunately, the necessary political support, and more importantly the required number of votes, was not there to pass the amendment with this degree of change in its meaning. He believed that African Americans definitely were not in a position to insist on such changes without adversely impacting their interests. He was acutely aware that only a very fragile political coalition supported the Fifteenth Amendment. Ultimately Douglass had a well-grounded fear that insisting on such changes would not only jeopardize the Amendment's ratification but would in fact guarantee its defeat.

Douglass's position on the Fifteenth Amendment was based on the harsh realities of Reconstruction and that African Americans were only five years removed from over 200 years of chattel slavery. He feared that without some political rights soon, African Americans were vulnerable to being re-enslaved by those extremely hostile to the changes in the status of African Americans brought on by the Civil War and those in favor of white domination over blacks reminiscent of the slavery era. His position on the Fifteenth Amendment was developed within the social context of mob violence, racial atrocities, discrimination, and terrorism that far too many

African Americans were being subjected to in the South. In light of this reality, he viewed the ratification of the Fifteenth Amendment as a matter of life and death for the African American community. He said, in essence, that the vote was an urgent necessity for African Americans as protection from terrorism while for (white) women, voting privileges were merely desirable. He believed correctly that disenfranchised African Americans were far worse off and their political situation was more dire and tenuous than the one faced by disenfranchised (white) women. Douglass rested this claim on the premise that (white) women were not facing the same level of risk and grave danger as African Americans. Therefore, in his view the ramifications of the defeat of the Fifteenth Amendment would not be the same. Douglass implored his critics not to pretend that disenfranchisement holds the same meaning or significance for them as it did for African Americans. In this debate, Frederick Douglass was not indifferent to the plight of African American women, but instead he viewed the political destiny of African American women as intertwined with African American men rather than mirroring white women's political status. Likewise, the legal barriers that African American women faced, he believed, were indivisible from the body of laws and political practices aligned against African Americans collectively. Therefore, he did not separate the interests of African American women from African American men.

Frances Ellen Watkins Harper, abolitionist and writer, agreed with Douglass's position in this dispute, contending that if the nation could not accommodate both black and women's suffrage demands simultaneously, then she and other black women would not do anything to jeopardize the passage of the Fifteenth Amendment. Harper's analysis was sensitive to the fact that it was not Douglass or black men but rather lawmakers and white male voters who were the biggest obstacle to the enfranchisement of women. Harper, like Douglass, recognized that the passage of the Fifteenth Amendment would, in the end, empower allies of women's suffrage such as black men to help women achieve suffrage. In this sense she viewed the benefits of this amendment for the African American community as outweighing its cost to the women's suffrage movement. In addition, neither Harper nor Douglass conceptualized the Fifteenth Amendment as benefiting African American men alone. They understood its significance and meaning from a collective consciousness. Most African Americans were disenfranchised, therefore, if any segment of the community could gain access to the ballot box this represented a political triumph for the entire race. Moreover, they understood that African American women directly benefited from the Fifteenth Amendment because its ban on racial discrimination covered both genders. Ironically, later in the history of NAWSA when white suffragists began appeasing white supremacists in the South by calling for explicitly white-only suffrage laws in order to gain the right to vote for white women, the Fifteenth Amendment barred this strategy. While the Fifteenth Amendment did not give black women the right to vote, neither did it give black men the right to vote, according to the Supreme Court's interpretation of the Fifteenth Amendment in a number of Court decisions. However, it did circumscribe the power of the states to directly use race to disenfranchise African Americans.

Before and after the Civil War, the issues of women's suffrage and black suffrage were controversial and unpopular ideas separately, and linking them together did not change this basic fact. Those citizens already enfranchised were reluctant to expand the right of suffrage. As it became more evident that lawmakers and white male voters were not willing to enfranchise African Americans and women at the same time, the Stanton-Anthony faction of the suffrage movement began to argue that (white) women's enfranchisement must be given priority. Moreover, they began to demonstrate that they were ready to join forces with any group, even those opposed to black enfranchisement, to achieve this end.

Elizabeth Cady Stanton's and Susan B. Anthony's faction in 1867 began to work with Democrats (former slaveholders, ex-Confederates, conservatives, those committed to white supremacy) who were opposed to black suffrage, forming an alliance with George Francis Train, a Democrat who opposed the right to vote for African Americans. Train offered to finance a weekly magazine for Anthony and Stanton. Together with Train they established the *Revolution*. Douglass was highly critical of this political alliance. He was equally critical of Stanton's and Anthony's support and promotion of "educated suffrage," understanding this was favored by those who believed it to be an effective strategy for keeping most African Americans and the poor disenfranchised.

In contrast to Douglass and Harper, the Fifteenth Amendment symbolized and meant something different to Elizabeth Cady Stanton, Susan B. Anthony, and their allies. For them it symbolized a betrayal of white privilege. White suffragists argued that if black suffrage and women's suffrage could not be achieved simultaneously, then white women deserved and indeed were entitled to the right to vote, by virtue of their whiteness, before black people. More and more the Stanton-Anthony faction of the movement argued that (white) women's claim to suffrage must be given preference. Their belief in white supremacy strongly influenced and colored their perception of and reaction to the Fifteenth Amendment. Stanton argued that (white) women, as the daughters of the founders of this nation, deserved to be enfranchised first based on their race. Douglass was quite critical of the racism embedded in the premise of this line of thinking. He neither liked nor approved of the nature of the arguments that Stanton was advancing in the "name of women" and women's suffrage. In particular, Douglass came to the defense of African American women by challenging Stanton's appeal for women's suffrage on the grounds that certain women, as the daughters of Jefferson, daughters of Adams, and the daughters of Washington, in other words, the founders of the nation, were entitled to the vote more than others who were disenfranchised. Douglass challenged Stanton's premise by rhetorically querying, what is the difference between other daughters, daughters of gardeners, daughters of bootblacks, daughters of **Africa**, and the daughters of the founders of this nation?

In her editorials, Stanton would use derogatory names to slander and negatively stereotype black men in an effort to turn public opinion against black suffrage and the Fifteenth Amendment. She characterized black men as "Sambos," ignorant and degraded brutes. The language and descriptions she used to slander black people were substantially the same in both tone and content as the anti-black descriptions and racist assumptions used by those who argued that without the discipline of slavery and white supremacy, African Americans would revert back to being menacing "brutes" and "savages" who would endanger America as a white civilization. Stanton and Anthony were deeply disturbed, insulted, and infuriated by the idea that members of the so-called inferior races and foreigners, people they deemed not their equals, could potentially vote before they could. Their arguments against this amendment demonstrated contempt and hostility toward black men, even those such as

Frederick Douglass were not spared their wrath and anger. In the final analysis, this amendment reflected the complete failure of their strategy to attach women's suffrage to black suffrage and defeated the purpose—to enhance the probability of securing women's suffrage—of linking the two causes together. Because this no longer seemed likely, they joined forces with others opposed to the Fifteenth Amendment to defeat this Amendment.

The Stanton-Anthony wing of the suffrage movement, the women-first group, decided to abandon the AERA since the conflict of interest between their position and Douglass's could not be reconciled in their favor. They left the AERA and formed a new organization called the National Woman Suffrage Association (NWSA) in 1869 with the position that white women must be enfranchised before black men. This organization divorced the issue of women's suffrage completely from black suffrage. The NWSA, based in New York, officially opposed the Fifteenth Amendment and concentrated on extending the right to vote for women by securing a federal constitutional amendment. The two issues remained separate for white suffragists even after black women were disenfranchised not long after the passage of the Nineteenth Amendment. In essence, they repudiated black suffrage. Men could associate with NWSA, but they would not be permitted to hold office or an official position. From here on out, men had to accept second-class status in the women's suffrage movement if they wanted to affiliate with NWSA.

A rival suffrage organization called the American Woman Suffrage Association (AWSA) was also formed in 1869. Its organizers, Lucy Stone and Henry Ward Beecher, disagreed with the NWSA on many issues and were in favor of the Fifteenth Amendment. The AWSA concentrated on winning the vote for women at the state level rather than through a federal constitutional amendment. Men were encouraged to join the AWSA and could hold office. In fact, Henry Ward Beecher became the first president of the AWSA; Frances Ellen Watkins Harper, an African American leader, was one of the founding members of AWSA. Both the NWSA and AWSA worked to secure the right to vote for women but disagreed on how best to achieve this goal.

Despite his political differences with some suffragists, Douglass did not let this division within the ranks of the women's suffrage movement or the conflict over the Fifteenth Amendment interfere with his commitment to women's suffrage. He continued to struggle on behalf of women gaining the right to vote even after the dissolution of the AERA. In March 1870, the Fifteenth Amendment was ratified. There were major celebrations by African Americans of both sexes throughout the United States. African American women and men alike hoped that this Amendment would afford them a measure of protection and a new tool to defend themselves against the forces trying to restore white supremacy through violence and virtually re-enslave them. Unfortunately they were disappointed when, by the 1890s, the federal government completely retreated from enforcing the Fifteenth Amendment, leaving most African Americans disenfranchised until the passage of the Voting Rights Act of 1965. Frederick Douglass's commitment to the principle of equality and the belief that the disenfranchisement of women was unjustified went beyond the individual women who were at the center of the conflict over the Fifteenth Amendment. Thus, despite his personal and very public disagreement with the Stanton-Anthony wing of the women's suffrage movement, Douglass was comforted by the fact that African American women, the women of AWSA, and indeed many others, shared and supported his views of the importance of the passage of the Fifteenth Amendment. Furthermore,

Douglass saw fit to continue in his quest to enfranchise women because this meant enfranchising African American women and, by extension, further strengthening the African American community politically and legally. Over time, Douglass reconciled with the Stanton-Anthony wing of the women's suffrage movement. He affiliated with both the NWSA and the AWSA, attending their meetings as an honored guest and speaker. Additionally, Douglass continued to affiliate and participate in the movement after NAWSA was created from the merger of the two associations. Notably, Douglass participated in special events commemorating the thirtieth and fortieth anniversaries of the 1848 Seneca Falls Women's Rights Convention. In light of his staunch support and dynamic role in the women's rights movement, it seems to be no coincidence that Douglass died soon after attending a meeting of the National Council of Women earlier in the day of February 20, 1895. Frederick Douglass was remembered by the pioneering leaders of the suffrage movement and other women with great respect and admiration upon news of his death. He was even memorialized in some newspapers as a champion of women and a leading figure in the nineteenth-century women's rights movement.

Further Reading

Andolsen, Barbara Hilkert. *Daughters of Jefferson, Daughters of Bootblacks: Racism and American Feminism.* Macon, Ga.: Mercer University Press, 1986.

Foner, Philip S., ed. *Frederick Douglass on Women's Rights.* Westport, Conn.: Greenwood Press, 1976.

Terborg-Penn, Rosalyn. *African American Women and the Struggle for the Vote 1850–1920.* Bloomington: Indiana University Press, 1998.

—*Valethia Watkins*

National Anti-Slavery Standard

The *National Anti-Slavery Standard* (1840–1870) was established under the editorship of Lydia Marie Child and David Lee Child. It was the official weekly publication of the American Anti-Slavery Society (AAS), a group that openly promoted the prohibition of slavery in the United States. Frederick Douglass was a member and lecturer for this group. Included within the *National Anti-Slavery Standard* were documents such as news, debates, essays, letters, and petitions about slavery in the United States. Through the *National Anti-Slavery Standard*, the Society was able to reach out to and convince individual states and the U.S. Congress to abolish slavery in every state in the Union.

Writers for the *National Anti-Slavery Standard* engaged their readers by making "persuasive" arguments and posing rhetorical questions on slavery. Although each state determined its own stance regarding slavery, the publication wanted to inform and influence those who read it to be an organized political force working to abolish slavery, regardless whether on a state or the national level. The publication ended in 1870 after the **Fifteenth Amendment** which enfranchised former slaves was ratified. The Amendment granted the right to vote to every man in state and national elections, regardless of his race, color, or former slave status.

Further Reading

Johns, Robert L. "North Star." *Encyclopedia of African-American Culture and History* Vol. 4, 2nd ed. Detroit: Macmillan Reference USA, 2006. 1658. Gale Virtual Reference Library.

Roberts, Bette B. "Child, Lydia Maria (Frances)." *American Women Writers: A Critical Reference Guide from Colonial Times to the Present.* Vol. 1, 2nd ed. Detroit: St. James Press, 2000. 198–199. Gale Virtual Reference Library.

—*Kareem Jordan*

Native Americans

Frederick Douglass was born Frederick Augustus Washington Bailey on a farm on Lewiston Road, Tuckahoe, near Easton in **Talbot County, Maryland,** during February 1818. He was a son of an unknown white father and **Harriet Bailey,** a slave who may have been part Native American. No clue remains as to which Native tribe or nation he may have claimed ancestry from. As a boy, Douglass's owner, Aaron Anthony, referred to him as his "little Indian boy." Such mixed genealogy is not unusual. For example, Crispus Attucks, son of an African American father and a Massachusetts Indian mother, was the first casualty of the Boston Massacre of March 5, 1770, the first death in the cause of the American Revolution. Attucks's father was a black slave in a Framington, Massachusetts, household until about 1750, when he escaped and became a sailor. Crispus' mother lived in an Indian mission at Natick. Poet **Langston Hughes**, singer Tina Turner, actor James Earl Jones, and civil rights activist Jesse Jackson all have African American Indian ancestry.

Native Americans and escaped slaves found common cause in sizable groups. One such group, the Black Seminoles, sometimes called "Seminole Maroons" by ethnologists, live mainly in Oklahoma, Texas, the Bahamas, and Coahuila, Mexico. Their ancestors, runaways from South Carolinian and Georgian plantations between the late seventeenth and mid-eighteenth centuries, sought refuge in Spanish-controlled Florida. The name "Seminole," derived from the Spanish word, *cimaroon*, meaning "fugitives" or "wild ones," was incorporated into the local Native American language. The word "maroon," in English, stems from the same Spanish word.

Fugitive slaves from Charleston arrived in Spanish St. Augustine, Florida, as early as 1687, where many began new lives as free men and women in a multicultural community. Some of the men worked as cartwrights, jewelers, butchers, and innkeepers, while women were employed as cooks and laundresses. Some owned small businesses. During 1838 the Spanish authorities established a settlement for escaped slaves, Gracia Real de Santa Teresa de Mose, where roughly 100 men, women, and children came into contact with various bands of Native Americans living nearby.

The Seminoles, originally one of the five "Civilized Tribes" of the same area (the others being the Cherokee, Choctaw, Chickasaw, and Creek) were chased into Florida by armed forces under the command of General (and later United States President) Andrew Jackson. Jackson's pretext for invading Florida, over Spanish diplomatic objections, was pursuit of freed slaves, as well the Seminoles. For several decades, through the first half of Frederick Douglass's life, escaped slaves found common cause with the Seminoles, sometimes mingling and at other times establishing a separate identity and preserving their own culture and traditions. In the meantime, the Seminoles fought the United States Army to a stalemate.

To avoid capture, the Black Seminoles developed skills at guerilla warfare. They also became very adaptable, finding ways to survive in new environments that other people regarded as uninhabitable or marginal, such as the Florida Everglades.

During 1818, General Andrew Jackson's troops chased the Seminoles into Florida, which was still under Spanish jurisdiction (the area was ceded to the United States in 1821). The Seminoles, many of whom were descended from Creeks, had elected to ally themselves with Spain rather than the United States, an act of virtual treason in General Jackson's eyes.

In addition, the Seminoles were giving shelter to escaped slaves. The pretext of Jackson's raid was recovery of stolen human property. After Florida was purchased from Spain by the United States, slave-hunting vigilantes invaded the area *en masse*, killing Seminoles as well as blacks. Later, during the 1830s when President Jackson proposed to remove the Seminoles to Indian Territory, they refused. Moving deep into the swamps of southern Florida (an area that, ironically, was being used as a removal destination for other Native American peoples), the Seminoles fought the Army troops to a bloody stalemate during seven years of warfare. They were never defeated, and never moved from their new homeland.

In 1823, Seminole leaders agreed to the Treaty of Mounltrie Creek that ceded land and created reservations for the Seminoles. Later, as a result of federal removal policies, the Treaty of Payne's Landing of 1832 required all Seminoles to leave Florida for Indian Territory within three years. According to the treaty, Seminoles with African American blood were to be sold into slavery.

Escaped slaves joined the Seminoles during the Second Seminole War (1835–1842), a guerilla war in which blacks served prominently as advisers, spies, and intermediaries. At one point, General Thomas S. Jesup said it was "a Negro and not an Indian War." Jesup eventually promised the former slaves their freedom if they would emigrate to Indian Territory as part of the Seminole Nation.

The war against the Seminoles was one of the most expensive Indian campaigns that the United States Army had waged to that time. In addition to the 1,500 soldiers killed (one for every two Seminoles eventually removed to Indian Territory), the government spent an average of 6,500 dollars for each Native American person transferred to Indian Territory. At a time when the average salary was less than 1,000 dollars a year, this amount represented a small fortune.

Following the First and Second Seminole Wars (1817 to 1818 and 1835 to 1842), some of the Black Seminoles escaped to the Bahamas; others were separated from their Native American allies and transported to Indian Territory (present-day Oklahoma), where they became known as "Freedmen." Some of them moved to

Mexico where their descendants, *Indios Mascogos*, still live. After the Civil War, some Black Seminoles moved to Texas, where, during the 1870s and 1880s, they served with the U.S. Army on the Texas frontier as the Seminole Negro Indian Scouts. Today, members of the Black Seminole community in Texas refer to themselves as Seminoles to set themselves apart from other blacks, emphasizing the pride they have in their unique history of having escaped slavery.

Further Reading

Black Indians: An American Story. A documentary film directed by Chip Richie, produced by Steven R. Heape, written by Daniel Blake Smith, and narrated by James Earl Jones. January 2004.

"The Black Seminoles' Long Road to Freedom." The City College Library, 1998. [http://www.ccny.cuny.edu/library/News/seminoles2.html]. Accessed March 13, 2009.

Forbes, Jack D. *Africans and Native Americans: The Language of Race and the Evolution of Red-Black Peoples.* Urbana: University of Illinois Press, 1993.

—*Bruce E. Johansen*

Nell, William Cooper (1816–1874)

William Cooper Nell was an abolitionist, civil rights activist, historian, and journalist. The son of William Guion, a tailor formerly of Charleston, **South Carolina**, and Louisa, a native of Brookline, **Massachusetts**, he was born free in Boston. Nell's father was an associate of David Walker, whom Nell knew in his childhood. Known as an advocate of independent African organization and activism, the senior Nell was also a founding member of the Massachusetts General Colored Association in 1826, a group the younger Nell later helped to dissolve. From his teens he became a lifelong supporter of the white abolitionist **William Lloyd Garrison**, beginning his association with Garrison's newspaper, the *Liberator*, in the early 1840s. He later ran the newspaper's black employment office, wrote articles, and organized mass meetings on abolitionist and human rights issues. Although he had legal training, he refused to enter the Massachusetts bar and pledge allegiance to an American Constitution that legalized African American enslavement.

Unlike his father, Nell was a radical assimilationist who opposed all independent African organization and activism, including conventions, schools, newspapers, churches, associations, and other institutions. Chosen to represent Boston at the Buffalo, New York National Colored Convention in August 1843, Nell opposed all-African conventions, condemned independent African activism, and urged total assimilation into the white social mainstream. Four years later at the National Colored Convention at Troy, New York, he joined Frederick Douglass in opposition to independent African action, including the convention itself, as well as proposals for an independent African college and national newspaper. He held that black-led and focused efforts were anti-progressive and served only to alienate white Americans. Nell was among several delegates urging blacks to seek admission to all-white colleges, where he believed outstanding black students would prove their intellectual merit and equality and thereby win the respect of racist enemies and convert them into friends. In that winter of 1847, Nell joined Douglass in **Rochester, New York**, to publish Douglass's newspaper, the *North Star.*

A product of Boston's segregated public educational system, Nell was a leading figure in dismantling it. He orchestrated a campaign over several years in the city to abolish all segregated or "caste" schools for Africans that included a massive boycott by African parents, who removed their children and privately educated them. Finally, in 1855, the Massachusetts legislature abolished segregation in public schools, making Boston the first major American city to desegregate public education in the nineteenth century.

Nell also fought segregation in public accommodations and was active in the underground antislavery resistance. He formed with other Africans in **New England** the Freedom Association, which illegally assisted Africans escaping Southern enslavement. Nell called it an essential activity and the obligation of abolitionism. In Boston and later Rochester, he founded literary societies for the intellectual and moral uplift of African youth, whom he actively recruited into the abolitionist struggle.

In 1851 Nell split with Douglass over the latter's break with Garrison, who championed moral suasion and condemned political abolitionism. A Garrison protégé, Douglass, declaring his independence, joined the Liberty Party with white antislavery party leader, Gerrit Smith. Smith was a philanthropist who had given 40 acres of land in the Rochester area to numerous Africans, including prominent activists such as Douglass, William Wells Brown, and Nell himself. Nell broke with Douglass out of loyalty to Garrison, despite the fact Garrison had in 1850 made a failed bid for election to the Massachusetts legislature on the racist Free Soil Party ticket. The break with Douglass would be complete by 1853, the same year in which Nell founded the Garrisonian Association to annually celebrate his mentor's contribution to the abolitionist movement. At the 1853 National Free Colored People's Convention in Rochester, Nell opposed Douglass's proposals for a Colored National Council and a manual labor school. Douglass, who had reversed his position on independent action and institutions, later denounced Nell as a contemptible Garrison tool and an enemy to African people. In rebuttal, Nell insisted he consistently opposed as hindrances to equality and progress any and all measures that did not promote total assimilation into American cultural, social, and political mainstream.

Two years later Nell published a history, *The Colored Patriots of the American Revolution*, which discussed African patriotism and contributions to the formation and preservation of the American republic. In it he urged radical assimilationism, arguing against continued caste proscription and so-called African separatism in the North. *Colored Patriots* was an extensive revision and enlargement of his 22-page 1852 pamphlet titled *Services of the Colored Americans in the Wars of 1776 and 1812.*

Nell championed the establishment of a Crispus Attucks memorial for that African's role as the first person to be slain in the Boston Massacre and in the cause of the American Revolution. He unsuccessfully petitioned the state legislature to establish the memorial, which had for him enormous symbolic significance in the quest for black citizenship and absorption into white American polity. In response to the

U.S. Supreme Court's *Dred Scott* decision of 1857, he launched in March 1858 an annual Crispus Attucks celebration, the first in U.S. history, to demonstrate that blacks were American citizens and entitled to the rights and privileges enjoyed by whites in the country.

In August 1859, retreating somewhat from his absolute commitment to assimilationism, he joined with Brown in calling a convention in Boston for New England's Africans, arguing the all-African assembly was a necessary means to influence American public opinion and to protest anti-African discrimination. Two years later Nell became the first African to hold an appointment as a postal clerk and in the federal government. In 1863 Brown listed Nell as one of 53 African luminaries from across the Diaspora in his history titled *The Black Man: His Antecedents, His Genius, and His Achievements*.

On December 29, 1865, nine days after his forty-ninth birthday, Nell's journalistic career came to an end with the closing of the *Liberator*. In 1869 he married, but died five years later, leaving behind his wife and two sons.

Further Reading

Browne, Patrick T. J. " 'To Defend Mr. Garrison': William Cooper Nell and the Personal Politics of Anti-slavery." *The New England Quarterly*. LXX (September 1997): 415–442.

Smith, Robert P. "William Cooper Nell: Crusading Abolitionist." *Journal of Negro History*, 55 (July 1970): 182–199.

Wesley, Dorothy Porter. "Integration versus Separatism: William Cooper Nell's Role in the Struggle for Equality" in *Courage and Conscience: Black and White Abolitionists in Boston*, Donald M. Jacobs, ed., 207–224. Bloomington: Indiana University Press, 1993.

—*Ahati N. N. Toure*

New England

The United Colonies of New England (The Confederation, 1643–1684) was organized in 1643 by representatives from colonies of Connecticut, Massachusetts Bay, Plymouth, and New Haven with the purpose of working collectively in defense against Native Americans and French and Dutch aggressors. This union was the earliest attempt at colonial unity. The Confederation's members did not intend to be a federal state but rather a loosely-formed league based on their mutual friendship and communal needs. Meeting annually, two important national governance concepts emerged: the proceedings of any state court should be recognized by others; and the return of fugitive slaves should be guaranteed by law. In addition, the Confederation broke the power of Native Americans in southern New England colonies. The Confederation lasted until 1684. Maine and the Narragansett Bay settlement (Rhode Island) were refused admission to the Confederation for political and religious reasons.

After several early colonial disputes were resolved with **Massachusetts** regarding whether or not Maine and New Hampshire should be a part of its territory, Maine and New Hampshire became separate states in a region known as New England. This region, located in the northeastern corner of the country, included the six states of Connecticut, Maine, Massachusetts, New Hampshire, Rhode Island, and Vermont.

Further Reading

Osgood, H. L. 1904–1907 (rev. 1957). *The American Colonies in the Seventeenth Century.* New York: Columbia University Press, 1930.

—*Donald Cunnigen*

North Star

The *North Star* was published expressly to augment Frederick Douglass's campaign against slavery in the United States and named for the North Star that freedom-seeking slaves followed at night as they escaped, south to north, along the Underground Railroad. The weekly newspaper was established by Frederick Douglass in **Rochester, New York**, and published from 1847 until 1852. The *North Star*'s masthead spelled out the newspaper's purpose: "The object of the *North Star* will be to attack slavery in all its forms and aspects; advocate universal emancipation; exalt the standard of public morality; promote the moral and intellectual improvement of the colored people; and hasten the day of freedom to the three millions of our enslaved fellow countrymen." The motto of the *North Star* declared "Right is of no sex—Truth is of no color—God is the Father of us all, and we are all Brethren."

While the paper's goals and objectives were certainly tied to supporting the antislavery and abolitionist movements, its publishers viewed its role as a universal medium to express all aspects of the human experience. This position is clearly stated by Frederick Douglass in the first issue of the paper:

> We solemnly dedicate the North Star to the cause of our long oppressed and plundered fellow countrymen. May God bless the offering to your good! It shall fearlessly assert your rights, faithfully proclaim your wrongs, and earnestly demand for your instant and even-handed justice. Giving no quarter to slavery at the South, it will hold no truce with oppressors at the North. (Douglass, F., ed. December 3, 1847 [Masthead])

> While our paper shall be mainly anti-slavery, its columns shall be freely opened to the candid and decorous discussion of all measures and topics of moral and humane character, which may serve to enlighten, improve, and elevate mankind. Temperance, Peace, Capital Punishment, Education—all subjects claiming the attention of the public mind may be freely and fully discussed here.

> While advocating your rights, the North Star will strive to throw light on your duties: while it will not fail to make known your virtues, it will not fail to make known your faults. To be faithful to our foes, it must be faithful to ourselves, in all things.

Douglass believed that it was very important for a black person to publish an antislavery paper. According to historian Charles H. Wesley, Douglass was especially impressed by the fact that owning a black "newspaper that appeared regularly would serve to counteract the racist who justified the enslavement of his people." This perspective explains Douglass's lifelong commitment to black freedom and equality in America. This journalistic standard would survive for 16 years, although the paper's name was later changed to *Frederick Douglass's Paper* and later still to *Douglass's Monthly*.

The *North Star*'s staff consisted of its editor, Douglass, and its assistant editor, Martin R. Delany and later two of Douglass's five children, **Charles** and **Rosetta**, which served to disprove the pro-slavery argument that black Americans were intellectually inferior by their nature and suited only to vocations of servitude. This was indeed a small staff, but what the paper lacked in staff, it made up for in its quality of coverage of abolitionist causes, and it stayed true to its prospectus:

> To attack slavery in all of its forms and aspects; advance universal Emancipation; exact the standard of public morality; promote the moral and intellectual improvement of the colored people; and to hasten the day of freedom to our three million enslaved fellow-countrymen. (Wesley, 1969: 215)

Like many other early American papers, Douglass faced difficult financial decisions at the *North Star*. The challenge of producing roughly 3,000 copies, at a financial cost of 80 dollars a week, was a great undertaking for a small media business in the nineteenth century. Douglass, with few assets of his own, launched the paper with a $2,135 gift from his British supporters, which was quickly spent. Douglass, by his own admission, foolishly spent half of that money to purchase a printing press that proved inadequate to the task. According to the University of Rochester Frederick Douglass Project (2003), Douglass was thus forced to contract out printing of the paper at an additional 20 dollars per month. Meanwhile, subscriptions, at two dollars per year, and a minimal amount of advertising failed to cover the paper's expenses. He sent out appeals for fundraising in 1848, but not enough donations came into his office to meet expenses. Douglass was forced to mortgage his home, and by June 1851, to merge his paper with the *Liberty Party Paper* (700 subscribers), in order to survive. The new paper, *Frederick Douglass's Paper*, circulated until 1860. Douglass devoted the next three years to publishing an abolitionist magazine called *Douglass's Monthly*. In 1870, Douglass assumed control of the *New Era*, a weekly published in Washington, D.C., serving freed slaves. Renamed the *New National Era*, Douglass published this paper until 1874.

Finances aside, the *North Star* developed into the most influential black antislavery news medium in the United States with a circulation of more than 4,000 readers in the United States, Europe, and the West Indies. It increased the journalist standards of the abolitionist press for news coverage and analysis of political developments, as well as supporting and reporting on women's suffrage rights. The paper had a national and international audience, reaching readers in all parts of the United States, Europe, the West Indies, and Canada. Frederick Douglass left this model of activist journalism as his legacy for future generations of African Americans to use when facing the nation's abusive racism in the years ahead.

Further Reading

Bryan, Carter T. *Negro Journalism in America Before Emancipation*. Lexington, Ky.: The Association For Education in Journalism, University of Kentucky, Monograph #12, September 1969.

Fischel, Lislie H., Jr. and Benjamin Quarles, eds. *The Negro American: A Documentary History*. Glenview, Ill.: Scott, Foresman & Co., 1967.

Jarvis, Michael, faculty advisor. University of Rochester Frederick Douglass Project, 2003. http://www.lib.rochester.edu/index.cfm?page=2494

———.http://www.lib.rochester.edu/rbk/douglass/fassett.stm. Accessed March 10, 2009.

Martin, Waldo E., Jr. *The Mind of Frederick Douglass*. Chapel Hill: University of North Carolina Press, 1984.

Penn, Garland. *The Afro-American Press and Its Editors*. Salem, N.H.: Wiley and Sons, 1891.

The North Star, Rochester, N.Y., 1847.

Romero, Patricia W. *I Too Am America: Documents from 1619 to the Present*. Washington, D.C.: Publishers Company / The Association For the Study of African American Life and History, 1969.

Senna, Carol. *The Black Press and the Struggle for Civil Rights*. New York: Franklin Watts, 1993.

Wesley, Charles H. *In Freedom's Footsteps*. New York: Publishers Co., 1969, 215.

—*Julius E. Thompson and Bruce E. Johansen*

Notes on America

Charles Dickens, the famous novelist from **England**, visited the United States in 1842 observing its social conditions to garner support for copyright laws. When he returned to England, he wrote *Notes on America* (1842), chronicling his five-month trip around the United States. In it he records his observations of public institutions such as schools, prisons, and railroads, and public behavior between whites and blacks which he severely criticizes.

In his chapter entitled "Slavery," Dickens discusses the status of slaves in the United States, arguing that Americans' ideals of liberty are in direct opposition to slavery. Dickens describes many brutal and inhumane interactions between slaves and whites. He writes of witnessing a slaveholder with federal authorities searching for two male runaway slaves in Washington, D.C., and of observing a black mother and her children being led to the auction block to be sold. In both cases, he comments on the brutality of slavery which treats slaves as chattel and states that the institution should be abolished. He quotes from newspaper advertisements where masters list the distinguishing features, such as whipping scars and branding marks used to identify their runaways, when seeking their return. Dickens argues that slavery demonstrates the cultural crudeness and materialism of Americans.

Dickens never clearly articulated his opposition to slavery while in America, fearing the ramifications of broaching the subject. Other English **abolitionists** had faced physical attacks after voicing their antislavery views. In his *Notes on America*, however, he explicitly states his abolitionist views.

Dickens spent one month of his trip in New York City, and comments on the status of African Americans in New York City where Frederick Douglass had briefly resided. He reserves his most vehement attacks for the primarily African American neighborhood known as Five Points where Park, Baxter, and Worth Streets came together. This working-class area had a reputation for vice and crime as well as interracial mingling. Frederick Douglass notes that Five Points housed the poorest blacks alongside new European immigrants. Because of their limited financial resources, many free blacks settled there. At the same time, European immigrants poured into the area, seeking inexpensive housing as well. Dickens describes the dismal living conditions in Five Points, including the most infamous building in this neighborhood, the Old Brewery, a brewing plant that had been converted into housing in 1837. The inhabitants of the Old Brewery were evenly divided between African Americans and Irish immigrants who crowded into the rooms on the upper floors of the building as well as the cellar.

Dickens returned to England, where he wrote *American Notes* and *Martin Chuzzlewit* (1844), both of which provide scathing reviews of American culture and society. He returned to New York City in 1867 where he gave a series of lectures promising he would never again criticize America. Three years later, Dickens died in Kent, England.

Further Reading

Meckier, Jerome. *Innocent Abroad: Charles Dickens's American Engagements*. Lexington, Ky.: University Press of Kentucky, 1990.

Moss, Sidney P. *Charles Dickens' Quarrel with America*. Troy, N.Y.: Whitson Publishing Company, 1984.

—Jane E. Dabel

"Nuestra América"

References to Latin America and the Caribbean in Frederick Douglass's speeches and writings span half a century and include Haiti, the Dominican Republic, Mexico, Cuba, Jamaica, and Nicaragua (in order of frequency). This engagement with "nuestra América" began with his opposition to the United States war against Mexico in 1846. The capstone of Douglass's engagement with the Caribbean world was his residency as U.S. Minister in Haiti from 1889–1891, and his work as commissioner of the Haiti pavilion during the 1893 World's Fair in Chicago.

The concept of "nuestra América" (our America) comes from Cuban patriot José Martí. Martí was Douglass's younger contemporary: they both died in 1895, although Douglass, born in 1818, was 35 years older than Martí. Slavery was not outlawed in Cuba until almost a quarter century after the **Emancipation Proclamation** in the United States. Martí witnessed the brutality of slavery in Cuba as a youth, and this profoundly influenced his commitment to racial equality and to political self-determination in Latin America. During a 15-year exile in New York, Martí warned of the United States' threat to the sovereignty of people south of the Rio Grande (Rio Bravo in Spanish). He famously described "our America" as a cultural and political entity that "stretches from the Rio Bravo to the Straits of Magellan." Martí described this imagined "American republic" in multiethnic terms: "the indigenous, negro or criollo."

To speak of Douglass and "nuestra América" in the same breath, then, requires not only a review of Douglass's relations with and attitudes toward Latin America and the Caribbean, but also an inquiry about the degree to which Douglass was able to transcend North American myopia, and to understand something of the cultural and political realities of this other America.

Douglass's interest in "nuestra América" rose in part from a sense of kinship with Africana and indigenous peoples, based on his empathy with their suffering or exclusion. (He frequently reminded audiences that he was part Indian.) But his political perspective was almost entirely shaped by his opposition to slavery. Since **slavery** persisted in parts of "nuestra América" through the 1880s, this allowed Douglass to continue his abolitionist campaign, in some sense, long after legal slavery had been abolished in the United States.

It was while Douglass was in **Great Britain** in 1845 to 1847, promoting his ***Narrative of the Life of Frederick Douglass*** and helping to build "an antislavery wall," that he became fully aware of both the transnational nature of slavery as an institution, and the international reach of opposition to slavery. In a farewell address in London on March 30, 1847, Douglass remarked: "Slavery never sleeps or slumbers." But clearly, neither did **abolitionists**. Douglass specifically chose to mention two abolitionist ministers in Jamaica, William Knibb and Thomas Burchell, as examples of men of faith who followed the Biblical injunction to "preach deliverance to the captive."

It is appropriate that Douglass first mentioned the U.S.-Mexican War while in Great Britain in 1846. As Europeans put pressure on the U.S. South and on those in the North and in Europe who bought products produced with slave labor, the "slavocracy" began searching for offshore colonies where they could transplant their plantation system. "The Mexican War gave the South its last relief from constriction," as William McFeely has noted. Douglass roundly condemned the Mexican War, from English soil, and supported the Wilmot Proviso, an attempt to outlaw the importation of slavery into territories taken from Mexico. We see him beginning to develop a sort of cultural relativity, reminding a Bristol audience in 1847: "In 1829 Mexico, although a semi-barbarous state, had declared the entire abolition of slavery in her territories."

Having listened to the racist rhetoric being bandied about during the War with Mexico, Douglass later put this in comparative perspective, when making a case for the "semi-barbarous state" of white supremacists during the Civil War years:

> But it is said that the Negro belongs to an inferior race. Inferior race!... It is an old argument... When the United States wants to possess herself of Mexican territory, the Mexicans are an inferior race. When Russia wants a share of the Ottoman Empire, the Turks are an inferior race, the sick man of Europe. So, too, when England wishes to impose some new burden on Ireland...the Irish are denounced as an inferior race. (Foner, 355–56)

After the War, Douglass became a **Republican Party** loyalist and political appointee. As such, he was able to speak in mainstream forums such as the *New York Times*. One senses that Douglass was trying to bring new thinking into the public sphere, yet having to speak in a language intelligible to his readers. So it is not always clear how much of what Douglass has to say about "nuestra América" reflects his own opinions, and to what degree Douglass was consciously trying to work around the biases he assumes in his readers.

In 1871 Douglass published an essay called "Our Southern Sister Republic" in which he welcomed the imminent reelection of Mexican President Benito Juárez, and praised Juárez's "remarkable gifts as a statesman." Douglass clearly identified with Juárez, "originally an illiterate Indian." To a degree his attitude was progressive for its time. When assessing the predicament of a country like Mexico, Douglass wrote that people in developed countries should strive not "to commit the error of judging them from our own standpoint, making ourselves the standard." Yet he went on to speculate that "their comparatively low state of civilization" might be due not only to Spanish tyranny, but also "perhaps a deficiency inherent to the Latin races."

Waldo Martin argues that Douglass's "Americanism, assimilationism, and race consciousness tended to impede his comprehension of the perspectives of other colored peoples. Ultimately, he could [not] see beyond...the dominant Anglo-American cultural paradigm which he essentially accepted, though he rejected its racism."

Slavery, both in its physical persistence and its political and cultural legacies, continued to be central to Douglass's thinking about the Caribbean and Central America. In 1869 to 1870, Douglass had a rare difference of opinion with Senator Charles Sumner over "the Cuba question." "It has seemed to me, that our government might have conceded belligerent rights to the insurgents," he wrote. To grant belligerent rights meant to recognize that the rebels were fighting a just war, not only against Spanish imperialism, but against slavery. But the Grant administration refused this recognition, and even former abolitionists like Sumner had sided with Grant. In a letter written in 1873, Douglass recalled: "The first gleam of the sword of freedom and independence in Cuba secured my sympathy with the revolutionary cause." But he repressed his conviction that the United States should have accorded belligerent rights. "I have deemed our government, with all the facts of the situation at hand before it, a safer guide than my own feelings."

Douglass had engaged in a long antebellum campaign to sway public opinion in favor of "belligerent rights" within the United States, in other words, the right of slaves to gain their freedom by any means necessary. But trying to expand U.S.

support for revolutionary movements in America's "back yard" was an uphill battle, whether that concerned rebellion against slavery and against Spanish rule in Cuba, or resistance to North American military interference in Nicaragua.

Before the Civil War, Douglass was willing to attack U.S. imperial ambitions. His politically astute speech, "Aggressions of the Slave Power," included a fierce, historically-grounded critique of the fiasco of William Walker's invasion of Nicaragua. The recognition of Walker's government in Nicaragua in 1856, proclaimed Douglass, "is part of the foreign policy of the slave power, which now rules everything at Washington. It is the first definite step... by our Government, towards the extension of Slavery over South America, the conquest of Cuba, and the final absorption of all the Caribbean Islands. [It is] a re-enactment of that part of our history, which records the progress of events leading to the annexation of Texas."

Douglass's diagnosis was unflinching: "They purpose to plant Slavery in South America, to overthrow the Black government of Hayti; and possess themselves of the West Indian Islands, and to reduce this whole continent to the rule of Slavery." His view of international reactions to U.S. imperial delusions has a contemporary ring:

> The conservatives of Europe hate us for our loud-mouthed professions of Liberty; and the Democrats of Europe despise us for our hypocrisy, and our shameless support of Slavery." His rejection of US imperialism, when paired with slave power, was uncompromising: "No intelligent man can suppose for a moment, that the United States... can peaceably annex any part of South America to this Union." ("Aggressions of the Slave Power: An Address Delivered in Rochester, New York, on May 22, 1856," in Blassingame, 119, 129)

Yet Douglass later supported attempts by the Grant and Harrison administrations to "annex" all or part of the Dominican Republic and Haiti. His willingness at times to tow the Republican Party line, or even to convince himself that North American land grabs in "nuestra América" were a good thing, grew out of three main factors. First, Douglass was convinced that if the Republicans were driven from power, the fragile rights of African Americans would evaporate. Second, Douglass was a genuine patriot; after the war, he subscribed to some degree to the ideology of America's "civilizing mission" in the world. And third, Douglass's post-Civil War attitudes about the imperial ambitions of the United States were guided by the hope that an expansion of U.S. interests into the Caribbean would abolish slavery in the region more quickly.

In the early 1870s, Douglass's "eyes were riveted on the success of [President Ulysses Grant's] vigorous Southern policy in crushing **Ku Klux Klan** terrorism and in safeguarding the lives and civil rights of the freedmen," writes Philip Foner. In Douglass's view, Grant was "for stamping out this murderous *ku-klux* as he stamped out the [Southern] rebellion." His support for the Grant administration grew "from no spirit of hero worship or blind attachment to a mere party," he insisted, but from the conviction that "in this hour there is no middle ground." Douglass went so far as to describe Grant and the Republicans as "the only visible hope of the colored race in the United States" in 1871.

In this context Douglass became involved in Grant's efforts to annex the Dominican Republic (or Santo Domingo). This young nation had endured almost a quarter century of tribal war between two generals. In 1861 General Pedro Santana invited the Spanish to take control of the nation, although they were soon forced out. Then General Buenaventura Baez asked the United States to step in, first during the Andrew Johnson administration, and later with Grant.

Beginning in September 1869, Grant tried to line up support for a treaty of annexation between the United States and the Dominican Republic, which had been approved by President Baez. But Senator Sumner, Chairman of the Senate Committee on Foreign Relations and an abolitionist ally of Douglass's since the early 1850s, came out strongly against annexation. In June 1870, Sumner convinced the Senate to reject the treaty. Yet Grant obtained authorization from Congress to appoint three commissioners to survey conditions in Santo Domingo, and determine whether or not Dominicans desired annexation. Douglass was appointed secretary to the commission in January 1871. Before departing, Douglass visited Ottilie Assing, who reported that Douglass was "enchanted at the prospect of visiting a tropical island."

Douglass and the Santo Domingo commission spent about two months in the Dominican Republic, January 24 through March 26, 1871. Douglass also visited Jamaica briefly, writing an article about the "Coolie Trade" in which he contrasted the suffering of the "genuine Hindus" (imported after the abolition of slavery in the Anglo West Indies) with "the broad mouths, full lips, cheerful faces of the Negroes of Jamaica." Now conscious of the need not to give "offense to the rights of property," he concluded that "this new class of cheap laborers" was "a respectable commerce, in no way inconsistent with high morality and advanced civilization."

Douglass claimed to have entered Santo Domingo with an open mind. He was receptive to Senator Sumner's argument, made in private meetings, that President Baez was a despot, and that annexation "would commit the American people to a dance of blood." Reporters who talked to Douglass on ship seemed to have convinced him that the whole annexation affair was a sordid business designed to benefit "land sharks." Yet once on land, he became convinced that the people of Santo Domingo were "earnest and eager for annexation."

After Grant submitted the Commission's report to Congress in April 1871, Douglass published a series of seven essays in *New National Review*, explaining why he now supported annexation. While acknowledging that commercial interests were important to the United States, he was, as always, focused on racial equality. "The antislavery side of annexation is to me the strongest and most controlling," Douglass wrote. By annexing Santo Domingo, North Americans could "strike a blow at slavery wherever it may exist in the tropics." By acting as a "grand civilizing force," the United States could hasten the abolition of slavery in Cuba. Sidestepping the issue of self-determination for a "Negro republic," Douglass even argued that Haiti, as well Santo Domingo, could do more to raise the world's opinion of "the colored race" in association with the United States, than in isolation, should she "of her own free will" decide "to join the American Union as a state." Perhaps he thought of the "greater South" of "nuestra América" like he did the American South: "It is better to be a part of the great whole than to be the whole of a small part."

As Philip Foner observes, "Douglass's confidence in the ability of the United States to plant the seeds of liberty and equality all over Latin America must have puzzled a number of his colleagues." He had recently spoken of his sympathy for the "revolutionary cause" in Cuba, and written in 1870 about the "inhuman brutishness" of racists in New York. Yet one should not underestimate either the patriotism or the "buoyant disposition" that had always coexisted with Douglass's fiercest critiques of the United States. Even after the passage of the **Fugitive Slave Act** in 1850, when acknowledging that things did "not appear very favorable to our remaining here," Douglass still spoke firmly of the United States as "our country," as McFeely points out.

Douglass had always opposed emigration ("colonization"). But he did have a moment of doubt in faith in 1861, in the dark period after the *Dred Scott* decision, after the repeal of Personal Liberty Laws by Republican legislatures, while Northern mobs attacked innocent Afro-Americans. It is not surprising that at that moment, he looked to Haiti as a possible adopted homeland. In early April, he made plans to visit Haiti to investigate an emigration movement being advocated by James Redpath. His steamer was scheduled to sail April 25, chartered by the Haitian Bureau of Emigration in Boston. He published an announcement about his planned trip in *Frederick Douglass's Paper*. But he changed his plans at the last moment, after the Confederate attack on Fort Sumter initiated the Civil War, and **Abraham Lincoln** called for volunteers.

Haiti had always held a very special place in Douglass's heart, as it did for so many people in the African Diaspora. **Toussaint L'Ouverture** was one of the heroes in the gallery of freedom fighters he honored, along with British abolitionists like Thomas Clarkson. But Haiti was different, with the "peculiar and romantic interest" of "first things." Late in life, in an 1893 lecture at the Haiti Pavilion of the **Chicago World's Columbian Exposition**, Douglass said: "We owe much to Walker for his Appeal, to John Brown for the blow struck at **Harpers Ferry** . . . and to the abolitionists in all the countries of the world. But we owe incomparably more to Haiti than to them all. I regard her as the original pioneer emancipator of the nineteenth century."

Douglass had first been mentioned as candidate for Minister to Haiti in 1869, after Grant's first election. But he threw his support to Ebenezer Bassett, who reported after taking up office in Port-au-Prince: "Frederick Douglass is well known here." Therefore, we can probably take it at face value when, after President Benjamin Harrison appointed Douglass as Minister Resident and Consul General to the Republic of Haiti in 1889, Douglass told Haitian President Louis Mondestin Florvil Hyppolite that he had received no honor "at the hands of my Government" that he valued more highly.

Douglass's tenure in Haiti is a cautionary tale: first, about the difficulties of trying to restrain the worst impulses of empire, while serving as a representative of empire, and second, the myopia that a sense of racial allegiance can produce in the fields of politics, or human rights.

Regarding Douglass's racial affiliation with Haiti, it should be remembered that although Haiti had been independent since 1804, Congressmen from slaveholding states had blocked recognition until 1864. Considered a "Negro Republic" by supporters and detractors alike, Haiti had been isolated by European and American powers for much of its existence. So it was natural that Douglass would feel some sense of racial allegiance. Yet this clearly led Douglass and his second wife, **Helen Pitts**, to ignore or rationalize the routine executions that Hyppolite ordered.

Douglass was predisposed to look for the best in America's only "Negro republic." Douglass, who did not speak French, presented Hyppolite with a French translation of *My Bondage and My Freedom*. And Hyppolite responded by calling Douglass "the incarnation of the idea which Haiti is following." Out in the streets,

Haitian President Florvil Hyppolite, c. 1893. Hyppolite gave this portrait to Douglass at the World Columbian Exposition. The French inscription reads: "Sincere regards to F. Douglass from Hyppolite President of Haite." By Watson, Port-Au-Prince. Courtesy National Park Service, Museum Management Program, and Frederick Douglass National Historic Site, FRDO 159. http://www.cr.nps.gov/museum.

his wife, Helen, would see Hyppolite, "a man naturally humane and just," change "from a lamb to a lion" and rage through the streets of Port-au-Prince on his horse, personally leading the massacre of his political opponents. In court, Hyppolite retreated behind his gold-rimmed blue glasses and a dignified manner.

Douglass was in Haiti because the island of Hispaniola had become a stepping stone for American expansionists. The United States had backed Hyppolite's coup d'état, and now, after Douglass's arrival, President Harrison's Secretary of State James Blaine began playing hardball. Blaine insisted that there had been a quid pro quo in which, in return for U.S. military backing, Hyppolite would allow the U.S. Navy to lease Môle St. Nicolas as a coaling station. It was hoped that Douglass could soften up Hyppolite.

In fact, many U.S. businessmen had opposed Douglass's appointment, fearing that a "Negro Minister would not approve of transactions that favored American interests at the expense of Haitian interests." In a way, that proved to be true. The Douglasses returned to the United States on leave in June 1890. Their return was delayed almost half a year, as Blaine and Secretary of the Navy Benjamin Franklin Tracy tried to convince President Harrison that Douglass would hurt their chances to establish a naval base at Môle St. Nicolas. Harrison refused to fire Douglass, but assigned as his negotiating partner Rear Admiral Bancroft Gherardi, who McFeely describes as "a man of fierce, even sadistic, temper and monumental arrogance."

Appalled by the parading of Gherardi's fleet in Haitian waters during negotiations, and by the Rear Admiral's heavy-handed, condescending manner toward Haitian Secretary of State Antenor Firmin, Douglass announced bluntly that he could "not accept this as a foundation upon which I could base my diplomacy."

With Haitian sensitivity about sovereignty, in the context of a long history of European and North American nonrecognition and interference, rejection of a U.S. naval base at Môle St. Nicolas was an almost foregone conclusion. Businessmen in New York and expansionists in Washington were quick to blame Douglass, equating his blackness and friendly relations with Haitans as being equivalent to treason. In truth, Douglass's "lack of enthusiasm for a predatory move on Môle St. Nicolas" was exceeded only by that of President Harrison, as McFeely writes. But the press viciously attacked Douglass, not Harrison.

His competence and patriotism had been called into question. Douglass first responded defensively. He felt compelled to point out that he had been advocating the acquisition of Môle St. Nicolas for 20 years. "Since the abolition of slavery I have always contended that the United States should secure a freehold in the islands of the Caribbean Sea," Douglass told a *Washington Post* reporter. His response will not please contemporary anti-imperialists, but his reasoning reveals a degree of sophistication about the *realpolitik* of his era. If **Great Britain**, France, Holland, Denmark, Portugal, and Spain already had footholds in the region, then why should the United States not also maintain a presence? Douglass seemed to believe that the United States, even with its limited political participation by African Americans, would better represent the interests of Africana peoples in "nuestra América" than the European powers.

But taking the offensive, Douglass also challenged conventional wisdom on whom a Minister should serve. If Haitians viewed him as defending their independence, rather than participating in imperial landgrabs, then he would "gain for the United States the trust and allegiance of the Haitian people." Such a perspective differentiated between short-term and long-term interests, recognizing that the long-term well-being of the United States required developing the trust of its neighbors in "nuestra América."

The Haitians did remember Douglass as "a Haitian by heart and sentiment." But Leon Pamphile's view that "Douglass resisted American imperialism and tried to keep foreigners off Haitian soil" seems romanticized. In fact, Douglass was capable of seeing both the Dominican Republic and Haiti without rose-colored glasses. He was reported to have remarked privately during his stay in Santo Domingo, "If this is the outcome of self-government by my race, Heaven help us." He also came to feel that "This revolutionary spirit is [Haiti's] curse." There is little doubt that Douglass referred in part to himself as one of the "friends" who felt distressed by Haiti's continuing turmoil, and somewhat shamed by the racial conclusions that many would draw. "Many who would gladly have believed in her ability to govern herself wisely and successfully are compelled at times to bow their heads in doubt and despair."

But for the most part, Douglass played the role of "defender of Haiti." And, he had a "bully pulpit" and a degree of moral legitimacy far beyond the reach of most diplomats. His analysis of his tenure in Haiti for the *North American Review* included some biting criticisms of American arrogance and racial myopia. "White men professed to speak in the interest of black Haiti; and I could have applauded their alacrity in upholding her dignity if I could have respected their sincerity," Douglass declared. "They thought it monstrous to compel black Haiti to receive a minister as black as herself... Prejudice sets all logic at defiance."

Martin's view that Douglass could not see beyond Anglo-American culture, although he rejected its racism, seems only partly true. There are dimensions of Douglass's critique of U.S. racialism that called into question the very foundations of the dominant culture. In a speech addressed as much to African American as to Euro-American racialists, Douglass asked: "What is the thing we are fighting against, and what are we fighting for in this country? What is it, but American race pride; an assumption of superiority upon the ground of race and color?" Douglass felt kinship with people of African descent, but he also insisted that the Irish and Native American components of his background inspired in him a sense of community that transcended "race" or national borders. In that sense, Douglass was much closer to the *mestizo* version of national identity that was emerging in many Latin American nations, than to the black vs. white world view in which North America was still so deeply and tragically invested.

Further Reading

Abel, Christopher and Nissa Torrents. *José Martí: Revolutionary Democrat*. Durham, N.C.: Duke University Press, 1986.

Belknap, Jeffrey and Raul Fernandez, eds. *José Martí's "Our America": From National to Hemispheric Studies*. Durham: Duke University Press, 1998.

Blackett, R. J. M. *Building an Anti-slavery Wall: Black Americans in the Atlantic Abolitionist Movement, 1830–1860*. Ithaca, N.Y.: Cornell University Press, 1989.

Blassingame, John W., ed. *The Frederick Douglass Papers, Volume 2: 1847–54*. New Haven, Conn.: Yale University Press, 1982.

———. *The Frederick Douglass Papers, Volume 3: 1855–63*. New Haven, Conn.: Yale University Press, 1986, 117–18.

Blassingame, John W. and John R. McKivigan, eds. *The Frederick Douglass Papers, Volume 5: 1881–95*. New Haven, Conn.: Yale University Press, 1992, 400.

Brantley, Daniel. "Black Diplomacy and Frederick Douglass's Caribbean Experiences, 1871 and 1889–1991: The Untold Story." *Phylon*. 45, 3 (September 1984): 205.

Diedrich, Maria. *Love Across Color Lines: Ottilie Assing and Frederick Douglass*. New York: Hill & Wang, 1999.

Douglass, Frederick. "Haiti and the United States: Inside History of the Negotiations for the Môle St. Nicolas," Part I, *North American Review*. 153 (Sept. 1891): 338. Quoted in McFeely, 358.

———. "Haiti and the United States: Inside History of the Negotiations for the Môle St. Nicolas," Part I, *North American Review*. 153 (Sept. 1891): 344–45.

———. "Lecture on Haiti," in *Frederick Douglass Papers*. Quoted in Pamphile, Leon. *Haitians and African Americans, A Heritage of Tragedy and Hope*. Gainesville : University Press of Florida, 2001, 88.

Foner, Philip. *The Life and Writings of Frederick Douglass*. New York: International Publishers, 1950.

———. *The Life and Writings of Frederick Douglass, Volume II: Pre-Civil War Decade 1850–1860*. New York: International Publishers, 1950, 102.

———. *The Life and Writings of Frederick Douglass, Volume III: The Civil War 1861–1865*. New York: International Publishers, 1952, 355–56.

———. *Frederick Douglass: A Biography*. New York: Citadel Press, 1964, 292. Also in *The Life and Writings of Frederick Douglass Vol. IV*. New York: International Publishers, 1950, 70.

———. *Frederick Douglass: A Biography*. New York: Citadel Press, 1964, 293 and also in *The Life and Writings of Frederick Douglass Vol. IV*. New York: International Publishers, 1950, 71.

———. *Life and Writings of Frederick Douglass, Vol. IV*. New York: International Publishers, 1950, 478.

———. *The Life and Writings of Frederick Douglass, Volume IV: Reconstruction and After*. New York: International Publishers, 1955, 490.

Isaiah 61:1, *King James Bible*.

Martin, Jr., Waldo E. *The Mind of Frederick Douglass*. Chapel Hill: University of North Carolina Press, 1984, 217, 213.

McFeely, William S. *Frederick Douglass*. New York: Norton, 1991, 133–34, 156.

Pamphile, Leon D. *Haitians and African Americans: A Heritage of Tragedy and Hope*. Gainesville: University Press of Florida, 2001, 86.

Quarles, Benjamin. *Frederick Douglass*. New York: Atheneum, 1968.

"The Nation's Problem: An Address Delivered in Washington, D.C. on 16 April 1889," in Blassingame and McKivigan, *Frederick Douglass Papers, Vol. 5*. New Haven, Conn.: Yale University Press, 1979, 412.

White, Andrew D. *Autobiography*. Vol. I, p. 501, in Foner, Philip S. *Life & Writings of Frederick Douglass, Vol. IV*. New York: International Publishers, 1950, 532.

—*Gregory Stephens*

P

Pennington, James William Charles (1807-1870)

James William Charles Pennington was a blacksmith, abolitionist, educator, historian, Congregationalist, Presbyterian, African Methodist Episcopal minister, and human rights activist. Born James Pembroke on **Maryland**'s eastern shore and trained as a first-rate blacksmith, he changed his name after escaping from slavery at 21 in 1827. By 1828, after a brief sojourn among Quakers in Pennsylvania who hid him from recapture, he settled in Brooklyn, New York. Intensive studies since his escape led him to activism almost immediately upon his arrival in New York. By 1831, Brooklyn activists elected him a delegate to the first annual Free Colored Conventionin Philadelphia, founded in 1830 by AME Church Bishop **Richard Allen**.

In early 1833 he taught in a segregated school in New Town, Long Island, seven miles from his Brooklyn home. He later moved to New Haven, Connecticut, to pursue theological studies at Yale's School of Divinity in preparation for the Christian ministry. Because he was African, Yale refused to enroll him as a regular student. Officials allowed him to attend lectures, but did not permit him to participate in classes or to borrow library books. He completed his training, returned to Brooklyn in 1837, and received his ordination and license in 1838. That year, on September 15 in New York City, the 31-year-old minister married the 21-year-old refugee Frederick Douglass and his bride Anna Murray, a free woman of Baltimore, shortly after Douglass escaped with his wife's help from Maryland's eastern shore. One year later Pennington became the pastor of the newly-formed African Congregational Church in New Town. In 1840, he became the pastor of Talcott Street Colored Congregational Church in Hartford, Connecticut.

In 1841 he published *A Text Book of the Origin and History of the Colored People*. In it he asserted the African origin of the ancient Kemetic civilization and the Kushite origin of Africans in the United States. He also argued against European claims to superiority and established the African origins of western European civilization.

That same year he became the founder and president of the Union Missionary Society, an African-led organization created to evangelize in **Africa**, Jamaica, and other parts of the world. This launched him into national and international prominence and led to his nomination to the World Anti-Slavery Convention, at which in 1843 he represented Connecticut in London, **England**. That same year, he was also a delegate to the World Peace Society in London. In Europe he called for international pressure against the American enslaver system and America's practice of discriminating against non-enslaved Africans.

He left Hartford in 1848 to take up the pastorate of the First Colored Presbyterian Church in New York City. In the next year the University of Heidelberg in Germany awarded him an honorary doctorate of divinity. In 1850 he published in London his brief autobiography, *The Fugitive Blacksmith; or Events in the History of James W. C. Pennington, Pastor of a Presbyterian Church in New York, Formerly a Slave in the State of Maryland, United States.*

During that year he also attended the second Peace Congress in Paris with William Wells Brown and agreed that enslavement was a form of war against Africans, although he opposed armed struggle, insisting on the use of moral force and arbitration in international and other conflicts. He argued, however, that slavery, as a system, threatened world peace and must be eliminated. He also urged an international economic boycott of U.S. goods produced by enslaved labor. With the Rev. Henry Highland Garnet, he also attended the Peace Congress in Frankfurt, Germany, where he urged international cooperation in the struggle against enslavement in the United States and renewed the call for an international boycott of slave-produced U.S. goods.

By the time he left **Great Britain** he had become a leading figure in the international **abolition**, peace, and temperance movements. He had also become a leading figure in the United States and the pastor of the largest African Presbyterian church in the country. In 1853 he was elected president of the National Free Colored People's Convention in Rochester. He was also heavily involved in New York City's underground railroad movement.

Pennington's reputation was later damaged by accusations of misappropriation of funds, a bout with alcoholism in the 1850s, and strong opposition from Garrisonian abolitionists who, fearing competition for contributions, envied his national and international reputation in the abolitionist circuit. Frederick Douglass frequently published articles in his newspaper written by Pennington, allowing Pennington to defend himself against his opponents.

In 1855 *Frederick Douglass's Paper* reported Pennington was ejected from a public streetcar in New York City for violating segregated-seating requirements. When he complained to police, he was arrested and jailed, only to have the charges later dismissed. He formed the Legal Rights Association (LRA) in New York City with the African physician Dr. James McCune Smith, who was trained at the University of Glasgow in Scotland, and Garnet. The LRA fought to end discrimination against Africans in public accommodations, until the Civil War, representing Africans forced off public streetcars.

During the Civil War, Pennington reversed his position on nonviolence, advocating African support of and enlistment in armed struggle. After pogroms against Africans in New York City, and threats to his wife's safety from European, mostly Irish Catholic, ruffians, he urged the study of the use of weapons and the right of African self-defense.

Pennington returned to England and in 1861 edited and published the autobiography of J. H. Banks titled *A Narrative of Events in the Life of J. H. Banks, an Escaped Slave, From the Cotton State of Alabama in America.* Banks had fled the United States and was living in Liverpool, England.

After the Civil War he broke from the Presbyterians because of his impatience with their reluctance to get involved with uplift efforts for freed Africans. He joined the Missouri Conference of the AME Church serving in Mississippi, later traveling to Portland, Maine, under the Congregationalists, and to Jacksonville, Florida, under Presbyterians, where he died.

Further Reading

Blackett, R. J. M. *Beating Against the Barriers: Biographical Essays in Nineteenth-Century Afro-American History.* Baton Rouge: Louisiana State University Press, 1986.

Pennington, James W. C. *The Fugitive Blacksmith; or Events in the History of James W. C. Pennington, Pastor of a Presbyterian Church in New York, Formerly a Slave in the State of Maryland, United States.* Third edition. London: C. Gilpin, 1850.

Swift, David E. *Black Prophets of Justice: Activist Clergy Before the Civil War.* Baton Rouge: Louisiana State University Press, 1989.

—*Ahati N. N. Toure*

Plessy vs. Ferguson

Plessy vs. Ferguson was the **U.S. Supreme Court** decision setting the "separate but equal" standard. Frederick Douglass's relationship to the landmark legal case of *Plessy vs. Ferguson* is not an obvious one, but rather a thematic one based upon the ideological relationship between the issues of the case and the issues that he addressed in his lifetime. His convictions on issues of race, gender, and economic and social equality were relevant both then and now. To be sure, Douglass died in the year 1895, and the legal case in question began in 1892 and culminated in 1896. Nevertheless, the central issues that *Plessy vs. Ferguson* raised, segregation as well as "separate but equal" public accommodations, were significant for Douglass. Therefore, the elucidation of this ideological relationship necessitates a brief historical overview of the etiology of and issues that gave rise to the case.

The genesis of *Plessy vs. Ferguson* is the 1890 Louisiana Separate Car Act, previously known as Louisiana House Bill #42, which mandated "separate but equal" accommodations on passenger trains by requiring railways to provide no less than two passenger coaches for "colored" patrons, or partitioning train compartments to create colored sections, while the majority of the coaches would be restricted to white patronage. It should be noted that the one-way punishment, the punishment for black people sitting in white sections but not whites sitting in so-called "colored" sections, was 20 days in jail or a 25 dollar fine, a particularly severe monetary fine for the average black person in post-Reconstruction South. It was inevitable that someone would violate this law or challenge its constitutionality, and New Orleans citizen and activist Homer Plessy did both.

Plessy was born free in New Orleans in 1862, prior to the **Emancipation Proclamation** and only two years after the city, lead by the racist Democratic Party, enacted a segregated streetcar system in which Negroes were only allowed to ride on cars that were marked with a star in deference to the Nazi Party of Germany. The New Orleans into which he was born would be soon characterized by "**Black Codes**," which were meant to maintain white domination after slavery was outlawed and limit the rights of black "citizens," including barring them from the right to vote.

Though he was of European Creole and African ancestry, Plessy was characterized in the South as an "octoroon," since he was believed to be only one-eighth black. Nonetheless, he lived as a Negro; the law recognized him as one, and hence he faced many of the painful realities of a black person in the South during that era. Moreover, he was an activist who opposed racial segregation and discrimination. To that end, an elite group of 18 like-minded Republican men with social and professional standing, black but of lighter hues, and with French ancestry, organized in 1891 to form the Comité des Citoyens (The Committee of Citizens) in order to fight segregation based on color or race. They purposely targeted the Separate Car Act, enlisting Albion Tourgee as their lead legal counsel, who, along with cocounsel Louis Martinet, began to strategize ways to challenge the law.

They decided to force the issue by setting up test cases to publicly challenge its legality in court. First selecting Daniel F. Desdures, a Committee member and black man who could pass for white, to be the first to defy the law openly, the Committee secretly made arrangements with the Louisville & Nashville Railroad and its detectives to make the arrest. The same criteria were in place on June 7, 1892 for the second test case of Homer Plessy, selected in part because of his racially ambiguous physiognomy, his social activism, and his social standing. Tourgee and Martinet had strategically chosen this date to coincide with the National Republican Convention in Minneapolis to bring attention to their subversive work. Armed with a first-class ticket, Plessy boarded the train, sat in the white section, and was arrested and booked, initiating the legal battle that would reach the Supreme Court in 1896.

Plessy first went to court in 1892, arguing that the Separate Car Act violated the Thirteenth Amendment, which abolished slavery and guaranteed citizenship to African Americans, and the Fourteenth Amendment, which subsequently prohibited states from denying or abridging the rights of citizens. The judge, John H. Ferguson, had previously ruled that the Act was unconstitutional on trains that traveled through several states, but he ruled in favor of the state with regard to Plessy, whom he found guilty. Frederick Douglass must have been disappointed, since he was aware of this case and had previously spoken openly about its significance. Notwithstanding, Plessy appealed the ruling to the Louisiana Supreme Court, then to the U.S. Supreme Court in 1896, both of which upheld Ferguson's ruling. The U.S. Supreme Court voted eight to one in favor of the ruling, and "separate but equal" would continue to be the standard until *Brown vs. Board of Education* in 1954.

Several parallels and tenuous connections with Frederick Douglass are noteworthy. Like Douglass, Plessy and the Comité des Citoyens were Republican activists and elite men of mixed cultural heritage. Furthermore, like the Niagara Movement and the founders of the **NAACP**, the Comité des Citoyens opposed **Booker T. Washington**'s accommodationism, but, like Douglass, advocated and practiced direct confrontation or what Douglass called "agitation" in order to change oppressive laws and conditions. In fact, the Niagara Movement paid tribute to Douglass and Albion

Tourgee, the Committee's legal counsel, in 1905. Likewise, Douglass had honored Tourgee by inviting him to speak to the Howard University Alumni Association on race relations, to which Tourgee enthusiastically consented. Finally and most importantly, Douglass opposed segregation based on race, color, or gender, issues that were at the heart of the *Plessy vs. Ferguson* case. He believed wholeheartedly in Plessy's argument that Negro citizens should enjoy the same legal privileges guaranteed to them under the law as any other citizen.

Further Reading

Medley, Keith Weldon. *We as Freemen: Plessy v. Ferguson*. Gretna, La.: Pelican Pub. Co., 2003.

Olsen, Otto H. *The Thin Disguise: Turning Point in Negro History; Plessy v. Ferguson; A Documentary Presentation*. New York: Published for AIMS by Humanities Press, 1967.

—*Stephen C. Finley*

R

Recorder of Deeds

After moving to Washington, D.C. in 1870, Frederick Douglass was rewarded for loyal service to the **Republican Party** with a number of appointed government posts, including the post of Recorder of Deeds. On March 17, 1877, Republican President Rutherford B. Hayes appointed Douglass to the highly visible post of U.S. Marshal to the District of Columbia, making Douglass the first African American appointed for a position requiring **U.S. Senate** confirmation. Douglass's appointment was highly controversial; his critics maintained that the position allowed Hayes to pose as a champion of black rights while engaging in politics that bargained away their freedom. Although Douglass remained grateful for his appointment, he continued to criticize the President's policy of recognizing questionable state governments and pacifying segregationists in the South. Douglass's black critics were also insulted that Douglass's role as Marshal was reduced under the Hayes administration. During **Abraham Lincoln's** term, it had become customary for the Marshal to stand next to the President and announce guests at formal White House receptions. Douglass was relieved of this duty. This, critics charged, was a great slight against black people. Douglass, however, thought it would have been foolish to resign his position for that reason. Perhaps the most positive effect of Douglass's service as Marshal was his ability, through patronage, to distribute minor government positions to black civil servants. During the Lincoln and Grant administrations, these positions formed the cornerstone of Washington's staunchly middle-class black community. Douglass's last duty as Marshal was to escort the official procession of both the outgoing and incoming administrations through the Capitol rotunda upon the inauguration of James A. Garfield as President on March 4, 1881. The incoming administration shifted Douglass to the less-prestigious office of Recorder of Deeds for the District. The demands of the Recorder's position were less than those of the Marshal, allowing Douglass to employ three of his children, **Frederick, Jr., Lewis, Rosetta**, and finally, his future wife, **Helen Pitts**, as clerks in the office at one time or another. In January 1886, Douglass lost the post to Blanche K. Bruce, an African American and former U.S. senator under the incoming Democratic president, Grover Cleveland. Douglass objected vehemently to his critics' insistence that the federal appointments of his later years served to silence the protest that had been the focus of his life's pursuits. Douglass believed that no political office could ever quench his hatred of tyranny and violence.

Further Reading

Blassingame, John W. & John R. McKivingan. *The Frederick Douglass Papers: Series One: Speeches, Debates and Interviews ,Vol 4:1864–1880*. New Haven, Conn.: Yale University Press, 1979.

Foner, Philip S. *The Life and Writings of Frederick Douglass, Volume IV: Reconstruction and After*. New York: International Publishers, 1950.

McFeely, William S. *Frederick Douglass*. New York: W. W. Norton & Co., 1991.

—*Tanya Price*

Republican Party

Frederick Douglass was a Republican party man *par excellence*. His loyalty to that party is best summarized in one of his most famous quotes: "The Republican Party is the ship and all else the sea." This posture served as a guide to most, if not all, of his political activities from 1870–1895.

In order to better understand Douglass's position, it is necessary to take a brief look at the Reconstruction and post-Reconstruction eras—the periods during which Douglass became wedded to the "Grand Old Party." During the Reconstruction era, conditions and circumstances for blacks were different from what they had been before the Civil War. In the antebellum days, the official government view of African Americans was that of Chief Justice Roger B. Taney—blacks were not citizens and had no rights which a white man was bound to respect. During Reconstruction, with the passage of the Thirteenth, Fourteenth, and **Fifteenth Amendment**s, there could be no doubt that blacks were citizens. This new era held the promise that blacks could, and should, work within the system, rather than agitate from without, that the reunited nation would be able to enforce a standard for human rights throughout the land. This was an era in which government was expected to be an instrument working for the advancement of black people.

As time progressed, the Republican Party became both halfhearted and unfriendly in moving toward an egalitarian course. During the post-Reconstruction period (1877 to 1900), as far as blacks were concerned, governmental restraints were relaxed and the Grand Old Party turned its attention away from African Americans. As such, blacks were denied the right to vote in the South; a Republican **Supreme Court** declared the **Civil Rights Act** of 1875 unconstitutional; a Republican Congress defeated the Blair and Federal Election Bills; attempts were made to establish a Republican party in the South, without the support or participation of blacks. In other words, the party shifted its emphasis from civil rights to silver rights. While Douglass never advocated anything less than full citizenship and justice for blacks during the post-Reconstruction era, he was unwilling to lay the blame for the plight of black folks at the feet of the Republican leadership. Such a posture caused him to be used by white Republicans and to run into great difficulty with blacks of all political persuasions. It is Douglass's actions at black gatherings and his posture in the election of John Mercer Langston that brings his partisanship under close scrutiny.

Because Douglass saw his mission as keeping the Republican Party in government, at every black gathering he attended, he took the Republican Party with him. He spoke of the Party when his audience was receptive, as well as when it was not; whether it was a political rally or a labor rally; whether it was a national convention of black men or simply a small gathering of men of color. A good example of this is the formation of the National Colored Labor Union in 1869. Douglass served as guest speaker at the inaugural meeting of this group and emphasized the importance of having such an organization to fight for better working conditions for urban and rural black workers. As a friend of labor, Douglass attended the second conference of the National Colored Labor Union which was held in Washington, D.C. in January 1871. This meeting was the last attempt on the part of the black leadership to persuade black workers to make an alliance with the white unions. When this effort failed, another national black convention of black workers was held in New Orleans, **Louisiana**, in April 1872. A couple of weeks before going to New Orleans, Douglass expressed what he thought should be the objective of the convention, arguing that the purpose of the convention should be to reelect the Republican ticket in the fall of 1872. Douglass cautioned his audience to be wary of those who would come to the conference with the intent of splitting up or taking votes away from the Republican Party.

For 11 years after the New Orleans conference, the national black convention movement lay dormant. It was not until September 1883 that blacks decided to come together as they had done on so many other occasions to discuss how they could improve their condition in a period that has been described by one historian as the "nadir" for black folks. Surprisingly, the call for this convention met with opposition, not only from white Republicans, but blacks as well. Many felt this meeting would be anti-Republican. Others contended that this was not the right time. Still, others (mostly blacks from the District of Columbia) opposed it on the grounds that it was called only by the "Fred Douglass faction." Despite these negative remarks, the call for the convention went out in May 1883. This conference, originally scheduled to be held in Washington, was later rescheduled for Louisville, Kentucky. Although Douglass argued that this convention would give blacks an opportunity to discuss how they could improve their condition as a class, when he arrived in Louisville on September 23, 1883, accompanied by his daughter, he told news reporters that "I come in the interest of no political party, though I am a party man, but if my party is assailed, I will endeavor to defend it." While he chastised the Republican Party for not upholding the rights of blacks, he defended it when it was criticized. When some people accused him of leaning toward the Independent Party, he responded that "I am as independent as I want to be in the Republican Party."

But was Douglass truly independent? In the postwar years, unlike white Republican national conventions which were purely political in nature, blacks held various conferences to discuss how they would coordinate their efforts to improve their own welfare economically, socially, politically, and educationally. They also met in 1888 to discuss whether or not they were going to support a black candidate for Congress in Virginia, John Mercer Langston. Yet, despite blacks' favorable response to Langston's candidacy, the Republican Party's leadership felt that it was not the right time for a black candidate. While most blacks took offense at the Republican establishment for their choice of a white man, Douglass sided with the party.

It is worth mentioning that Douglass was used by white Republicans. Sometimes to advance the rights of blacks, but most times as a means to an end, Douglass was used to advance the candidacies of white Republicans. Perhaps recalling the role that his fervid oratory had played in the abolitionist movement, scores of politicians would descend upon Douglass before each election to solicit his support. In 1880, the chairman of the Republican National Committee wrote Douglass: "Glad to learn that your voice will be alright again. For when the *Republican Party Loses Fred Douglass's Voice*, it will meet a heavy loss." The treasurer of that same committee made similar comments in 1888: "Speeches from you this year will place the Republican Party under a new debt and obligation to you by the part that you will take in this campaign for the restoration of the party to power."

To be sure, Douglass's partisanship often placed him in an untenable position; his political guidance system gave him conflicting signals, pointing him simultaneously in opposite directions. As a dedicated black Republican, clear-cut choices were not easy to make, but more often than not it was his partisanship that won out. To the middle, Douglass was usually a practical man dealing with justice. But as a partisan politician, his deeds and words were often at odds. In some things, he was a traditionalist and in others a reformer. So it should neither surprise nor discomfort anyone to know that it was the perils of this partisanship that accounted for most of the contradictions in his behavior during the post-Civil War years.

Further Reading

Cheek, William F. *The Forgotten Prophet: Life of John M. Langston.* Unpublished doctoral dissertation, University of Virginia, 1961.

Douglass, Frederick. *The Life and Times of Frederick Douglass.* New York: MacMillan and Co., 1962.

———. *Douglass Manuscripts, 1870–1895.* Library of Congress, Washington, D.C.

Foner, Philip S. *The Life and Writings of Frederick Douglass, Volume 4.* New York: International Publishers, 1955.

Pitre, Merline. "The Partisan Politics of Frederick Douglass." *Journal of Social and Behavioral Sciences XXIV* (Fall 1980).

Louisville Courier Journal. September 24 and 26, 1883.

New National Era. March 25, 1872.

—Merline Pitre

Rhetorical Techniques

Careful examinations of Frederick Douglass's public and private communication evince a prolific writer waging a rigorous rhetorical campaign against oppressive systems which promote slavery, herald intemperance, and deny women's suffrage. Douglass uses such rhetorical techniques as humor, satire, wit, melancholy, controlled and righteous denunciation and ridicule, and satire, but the focus here will be to examine his use of narrative pathos and argumentative analysis and advocacy.

Rhetoricians use narrative pathos to appeal to the human emotions of love, anger, disgust, and repulsion. By using very graphic and emotion-grabbing narratives or stories, the skillful rhetorician sways an audience, motivating them to action. Douglass was a masterful rhetorician. In addition to narrative pathos, Douglass showed intellectual prowess by using argumentative analysis and advocacy, dismantling his opponent's arguments and then, in turn, arguing strongly for a different course of action or policy.

Douglass uses both narrative pathos and argumentation analysis and advocacy to protest two nineteenth-century discriminatory practices in his two speeches, the "Dred Scott Decision" and the "Fugitive Slave Law." In the first speech, Douglass uses graphic narrative pathos to evoke horrific images of what happens when a people are denigrated and shorn of their humanity until they become existential property like horses, sheep, and pigs—in essence, chattel. Thus, he argues cogently against the *Dred Scott* decision because it denies the humanity of four million coloreds in America. In turn, he advocates for the abolition of slavery by asking the American people to live up to the Constitution, adopt its principles, imbibe its spirit, and enforce its provisions. After presenting a brilliant argument in support of the Constitution and the Declaration of Independence, wherein Douglass insists that the principles are broad enough to encompass the humanity of the four million coloreds in America, he warns his

Frederick Douglass on a pavillion platform, 1892. Library of Congress, Prints and Photographs Division, Booker T. Washington Collection, LC-USZ62-120533.

audience that slavery will fuel a brooding civil war unless it is abolished. In addition to supporting both documents, he advocates for the survival of the Union. He calls on his fellow citizens to awaken from what he calls their "moral blindness." Because he is not convinced men will always do the right thing, the just thing, he evokes the sovereignty of a higher power, one he proclaims even greater than the **U.S. Supreme Court**'s alignment with democratic slavery. He assures his audience that one day God will abolish slavery forever. Douglass holds firm to his belief that no human decision can ever make a man the property of another man nor ever destroy a man's, even a slave's, God-given rights. Therefore, Douglass contends the *Dred Scott* decision is morally wrong and must not be allowed to stand.

Similar to his rhetorical stance in the "Dred Scott" speech, Douglass continues the theme of righteous indignation as he advocates against the **Fugitive Slave Act**. He avers that the earth is God's; therefore, it ought to be covered with righteousness, not slavery. He pledges to commit his life to circumscribe and damage slavery by every possible means available. He makes it plain: slavery has no rightful existence anywhere. Douglass uses narrative pathos to make his point. He argues the only way to make the fugitive slave law a dead letter (law) is to "make half a dozen or so dead kidnappers." He goes on to assert this position because he says in indignation, "colored men's rights are less than those of a jackass." After expounding upon the flawed Christian practices used to justify capturing slaves, Douglass argues that there can be no justification for such a law and that any such law cannot be Christianized or legalized. In both speeches Douglass used narrative pathos and argumentative analysis and advocacy to protest the oppressive system of slavery.

By advancing moral arguments, Frederick Douglass's discourses on "Southern Barbarism" and "The Church and Prejudice" provide evidence of an evolved rhetorical campaign against slavery. In his speech, "Southern Barbarism," Douglass is heartened when emancipation comes to the slaves, but he is appalled at the subsequent inhumane treatment blacks suffer in the shadows of emancipation. He argues that the emancipation and enfranchisement of the colored people of the United States is woefully incomplete because they, collectively, remain victims of merciless brutality. He calls unequivocally for protections of the persons, the property, and the ballot of the colored man. He argues cogently that the government reneged on its constitutional promise to protect all citizens. Here he speaks of the injustices of the South where colored men are forced into barbaric phenomenological experiences. He is livid because blacks are not presumed innocent—they are wholesale, without due process—convicted. Note his use of narrative pathos to make his point, "Fellow-citizens, there is no right so neglected as the Negro's right. There is no flesh so despised as the Negro's flesh. There is no blood so cheap as the Negro's blood." Douglass raises the specter of fear when he says that "a colored man's only trial is a **lynching** mob whose retaliatory tactics include hanging, shooting, stabbing, burning, or whipping... to death blacks." He is outraged that the government takes on the role of solemn mockery and sham with no intention of protecting colored people. His most masterful use of narrative pathos comes in the speech when he details a horrible massacre in Carrolton Courthouse, in **Mississippi**, where the white perpetrators were protected and the black victims were violated. Thus, he rails against the government's attitude of complacency and the lack of human decency. He is even more outraged that there is no moral outcry from the good white citizens of both North and South. Concluding, Douglass remains defiant yet optimistic. After exposing the dangers of a nation apathetic to the indignities placed upon his black brethren, Douglass advocates for a viable solution, arguing that despite the slave's bondage, time, education, and training will help to restore the slave's humanity. He implores his audience to give the slave such an opportunity. He concludes with his signatory trademark, articulating hope and confidence that ultimately justice and liberty will be the triumphant hallmarks of America.

In his 1841 speech, "The Church and Prejudice," Douglass expresses disgust at the church leaders who espouse that God is no respecter of persons while denying equal access to the Holy Sacraments. Douglass is outraged that religion serves as an instrument of slavery, using narrative pathos to create sympathy for the perils of slave life. He personalizes slavery when he laments that the system that sold his four sisters and brother into bondage compels its priests to defend slavery using Biblical justifications. Based on this belief, Douglass proclaims that humanitarianism is absent in church policy, arguing religion is a handmaiden to the institute of slavery. He states that "while you degrade us, and then ask why we are degraded—you shut our mouths, and then ask why we don't speak—you close your colleges and seminaries against us, and then ask why we don't know more." Douglass constructs powerful imagery of the unfathomable albatross of enmity endured by black individuals when he argues cogently that "the country...church...government...and its constitutions are all aligned against black humanity." Douglass's narrative pathos is revved up in his litanies of disenfranchisement. He argues he has no love for America, no patriotism, and no country, asking "What country do I have? Why aren't I recognized as a man?" Instead of being a man, a human being, Douglass argues that he and his brethren are not spoken of except as a piece of property belonging to some Christian slaveholder, in which "all the religious and political institutions in this country, alike, pronounce us as slaves and chattel."

"Oration in Memory of **Abraham Lincoln**" and "The Woman's Suffrage Movement" showcase Douglass's masterful use of narrative pathos and argumentative analysis and advocacy. Speaking of Lincoln, Douglass argues that it is fitting that he be honored as the first martyred President of United States, whose death becomes the crowning crime of slavery. Arguably, this is one of Douglass's pantheon speeches, not because of its ceremonious unveiling of the Negro race's magnificent bronze tribute to Abraham Lincoln, but because he uses a brilliant argumentative analysis to deconstruct the slave's idolized Lincoln. Indeed, while Douglass lauds Lincoln for the incidental emancipation of slaves, he makes clear Lincoln's actions were strategic and selective. What is truly profound about this speech is that Douglass, a contemporary of Lincoln, immortalizes Lincoln as a man, whose interests, associations, habits of thought, and prejudices, in the final analysis, remained that of a white man concerned with the well-being of white people. Although Lincoln opposed the expansion of slavery, he remained more than willing to defend slave states' rights to maintain slavery. The most telling moment in the speech is when Douglass laments Lincoln's willingness to comply with the Fugitive Slave Act, wherein a slave no matter how shackled and abused was returned to the Southern slave master, even during the pivotal moment when the Nation was embroiled in a bloody civil war.

Douglass meticulously uses argumentative analysis to convince Negroes that slaves were not Lincoln's heirs but his stepchildren, his adopted children, who became emancipated by forces of circumstance and necessity. Furthermore, using one of his most powerful rhetorical techniques, narrative pathos, Douglass expounds upon the duress the slaves experienced during Lincoln's moral struggle. He catalogs the flux of emotions the slaves felt as they became disheartened to discover Lincoln's focus was not on their freedom but on salvaging the nation for the prosperity of his white brethren. Douglass notes that despite the dire news, the slaves, grieved, stunned, and greatly bewildered by Lincoln's actions, clung to the belief that Lincoln would be the one to make their emancipation a reality. Armed with a more realistic assessment of Lincoln's actions during the civil upheaval in America, Douglass challenges the Negroes assembled to honor Lincoln, to remember him as a man whose fate caused him to pen the immortal emancipation paper that would, in its broadest principle, ultimately lead to the abolishment of slavery in the United States. After, and only after, a thorough analysis of the crisis, Douglass blesses the anniversary of Lincoln's assassination and proclaims that it is fitting that Lincoln's stepchildren honor his memory with a bronze statue befitting the man of the hour.

Another example of Douglass's ability to transform an epideictic ceremonial speech into a deliberative process is his oration on the "Women's Suffrage Movement." Evoking goodwill via narrative pathos he creates an image of his steadfast solidarity with the women's suffrage cause. Too, while Douglass praises the achievements of courageous women in the Suffrage Movement, namely **Susan B. Anthony** and Mrs. Elizabeth C. Stanton, he uses argumentative analysis and advocacy to chronicle their valiant efforts to gain the women's right to vote. While he is careful to respect the woman as her own best advocate, he repeatedly solidifies his allegiance to her great cause. He challenges women in the movement to press on even though their dream is yet unrealized. He advocates the use of inflexible assertion, which he contends is more powerful that mere argument, as a means to gain victory because in Douglass's view women should share equal liberty with men. He feels compelled to honor women who master the three elements of power: (1) administrative and executive ability; (2) organizational ability; and (3) the ability to discover truth. He proclaims that, certainly, the women leaders in the **Women's Suffrage Movement** evince mastery of all three elements of power.

Further Reading

Foner, Philip S. *The Life and Writings of Frederick Douglass Vols. I–IV*, New York: International Publishers, 1950.

Ganter, Granville. " '…He Made Us Laugh Some': Frederick Douglass's Humor." *African American Review*, Vol. 37, 4, 2003. 535–552.

—*Andrew Ann Lee*

Rochester, New York

Rochester is one of New York State's largest cities and is located along the Genesee River, near its outlet into Lake Ontario. Seneca Indians had lived in the area prior to white settlement. The first white settler, Ebenezer Allen, moved to the area in 1789 where he built a flour mill on the river. Nathaniel Rochester, a Maryland businessman, founded Rochester in 1812. The area's rich soil and proximity to the river enticed many settlers to move there. Incorporated as Rochersterville in 1817, the name was changed to Rochester in 1822. After the completion of the Erie Canal in 1825, trade flourished as farmers and industrialists used the waterway to transport their goods.

Frederick Douglass escaped from slavery in **Maryland** on September 3, 1838. Shortly after marrying his wife, **Anna**, in New York City that year, the Douglass family moved to New Bedford, **Massachusetts**. In the fall of 1841, they relocated to Lynn, Massachusetts, and then, in late 1847, they settled in Rochester, New York.

Frederick Douglass helped to make Rochester a center for the **abolition** movement in the antebellum period. Douglass gave a number of notable speeches in his city of Rochester. He had been a follower of **William Lloyd Garrison**, a white abolitionist, but in 1847, Douglass severed ties with Garrison, arguing that white abolitionists viewed him as nothing more than a fugitive slave. In reality, Douglass was becoming a talented speaker and African American political activist. Douglass and Martin Delany, a black abolitionist, formed their antislavery newspaper, the *North Star*, in Rochester in 1847. The *North Star* was so —named because slaves escaping at night followed the North Star in the sky to freedom. The newspaper later changed its name to *Frederick Douglass's Paper*. Douglass's newspapers published antislavery articles and were supported by both white and black abolitionists. During the 1840s, escaped slave and author Harriet Jacobs moved to Rochester to assist Douglass with his newspaper. While residing in Rochester, Douglass also worked with the Underground Railroad, harboring over 400 runaway slaves in his home, hiding them from authorities as they made their way to freedom across the border in Canada.

On July 5, 1852, Douglass delivered his famous speech, **"What to the Slave is Your Fourth of July?"** to the Rochester Ladies' Anti-Slavery Society at the Corinthian Hall. At the event held to commemorate the signing of the Declaration of Independence, he spoke about the contradiction of American principles of liberty and the institution of slavery. In his scathing indictment of slavery, he stated that only white Americans could rightfully celebrate the Declaration of Independence. He said African Americans could not celebrate because they had not yet been freed.

While residing in Rochester, Douglass also supported the movement for women's rights, arguing that both women and African Americans deserved equality. In 1852, **Susan B. Anthony**, a women's suffrage activist, visited Rochester and organized the Temperance Society of Rochester. She organized a number of women's rights conventions in Rochester and Syracuse, winning support from Frederick Douglass.

In 1853, African American leaders gathered for a national convention at Rochester, New York. In the wake of the **Fugitive Slave Act** of 1850, which required the authorities as well as citizens to apprehend suspected runaway slaves and return them to the South, blacks met in Rochester to develop a political strategy to fight the law. The convention members agreed to protest the law and to band together to block the re-enslavement of African Americans. They called for unity among all African Americans during the time of increased racial discrimination. Black leaders argued that they deserved equal rights and citizenship. They also discussed the economic competition between black and immigrant laborers in cities like New York. Frederick Douglass emphasized the importance of education for African Americans including schools to teach blacks skills. The convention also considered a proposal to found an African American museum and library.

Douglass and his family faced racial discrimination while residing in Rochester. For example, Douglass enrolled his daughter, **Annie**, at the Seward Seminary in Rochester. School officials placed her in a separate room from whites and gave her a different teacher for her lessons. Douglass objected to her treatment and removed his daughter from the school. The school principal assured Douglass that his daughter would be treated equally after a number of semesters, when the other students adjusted to the presence of an African American student.

In the late 1850s, Rochester became the center of many debates over the future of slavery. In 1858, John Brown arrived in Rochester to encourage Douglass to join him in an attack on the federal arsenal located at **Harpers Ferry**, Virginia. Brown, a radical white abolitionist, intended to lead a massive slave revolt and form a sanctuary for freed slaves. Brown wrote the constitution for his raid at a secret convention in nearby Chatham, Ontario, Canada, a major point in the Underground Railroad. Although Douglass refused to join Brown in his crusade, Brown went ahead with the raid on Harpers Ferry in 1859. The revolt failed, and Brown was captured and hanged. Douglass's connection to Brown forced him to briefly seek refuge in Canada in 1859. In 1858, U.S. Senator William H. Seward gave a speech in Rochester in which he predicted that slave states and free states could no longer exist peacefully. He correctly predicted that civil war would erupt over the issue of slavery.

The Douglass family remained in Rochester until a suspicious fire leveled their home in 1872. Frederick Douglass and his wife then moved to Washington, D.C.

Further Reading

Martin, Jr., Waldo E. *The Mind of Frederick Douglass*. Chapel Hill: University of North Carolina Press, 1984.

Quarles, Benjamin. *Frederick Douglass*. New York: Atheneum, 1968.

—Jane E. Dabel

S

Seneca Falls Convention

The Seneca Falls Convention was a women's rights convention held on July 19–20, 1848, in Seneca Falls, New York. The convention marked the beginning of the women's suffrage movement, when women first publicly demanded the franchise. By 1848 feminist ideology and societal forces were such that a few women felt the vote was the only path to full civil rights. Individuals such as Mary Wollstonecraft and Margaret Fuller wrote about various injustices women suffered. Additionally, the early nineteenth century was a period of great reform movements including temperance and abolition. Women agitated for property rights reform, educational opportunities, and admission to professions. Many of the women who devoted their lives to the fight for women's suffrage began their work in other movements and adapted the successful tactics of the abolitionists and temperance reformers.

In 1840 Lucretia Mott and Elizabeth Cady Stanton met at the World's Anti-Slavery Convention in London. Mott and her husband, James, were Quakers and had long been involved in abolition. Stanton, the well-educated daughter of a judge, had recently married Henry Stanton, an **abolitionist**. The women were indignant when, after hot debate, the convention voted to bar women from being seated. Mott and Stanton decided that when they returned to America they would organize a convention for the rights of women. It would be another eight years before they could plan one; Stanton was busy having and rearing her seven children. By 1848 the Stantons were living in Seneca Falls, New York, and Lucretia Mott was nearby visiting friends. They put an announcement in the local paper that a women's rights convention would be held five days later at a Wesleyan Chapel. Approximately 300 people attended the meeting. When none of the women felt competent to chair the two-day event, James Mott agreed to do so.

Elizabeth realized they needed some sort of manifesto and decided to use the Declaration of Independence as a model, thereby linking women's rights with the founding principles of the American republic. Titled the "Declaration of Sentiments," she listed women's grievances and proposed 12 resolutions including property ownership, educational opportunities, and divorce reform. The ninth resolution demanded the right of women to vote. It was so controversial that the attendants debated including it because it was so radical. Frederick Douglass, realizing that voting was essential to civil rights, encouraged the convention to demand the right to vote. With his support the resolution narrowly passed. 68 women and 32 men signed the "Declaration of Sentiments."

Word of the Seneca Falls demands spread quickly across the country by the newly-formed Associated Press, which disseminated the news of the meeting. Reaction was swift and ferocious from critics, saying the women and men at the convention were threatening the sanctity of the family and the entire social order. The negative public reaction was so intense that many of the signers removed their names under pressure and ridicule from family and friends. Soon after the convention, Stanton met another young reformer, **Susan B. Anthony**. They forged a friendship and partnership that lasted 50 years. Unceasingly and tirelessly they organized, campaigned, wrote, and spoke promoting women's suffrage. Of the 300 people attending the convention, only one woman, Charlotte Woodward, lived to see American women gain the right to vote in 1920.

Further Reading

Du Bois, Ellen Carol. *Feminism and Suffrage: The Emergence of an Independent Women's Movement in America, 1848–1869*. Ithaca, N.Y.: Cornell University Press, 1978.

Flexner, Eleanor. *Century of Struggle: The Woman's Rights Movement in the United States*. Cambridge, Mass.: Belknap Press of Harvard University Press, 1959.

Gurko, Miriam. *The Ladies of Seneca Falls: The Birth of the Woman's Rights Movement*. New York: Schocken Books, 1976.

—*Minoa Uffelman*

Sherman, William T. (1820–1891)

Union Army general William T. Sherman was born in Lancaster, Ohio, attended local schools, and graduated sixth in his class from the United States Military Academy in 1840. He held assignments on army posts throughout the South, and in 1854 he resigned his commission to become a banker in San Francisco. Though not of his own doing, failure dogged him there and in banking, real estate, and legal occupations in New York City and Kansas. He successfully founded the Louisiana Military Seminary, but the coming of the Civil War sent him back to Ohio into eventual Union Army leadership. After a stumbling start early in the war, he became one of the chief architects of Union victory with his Atlanta Campaign and the marches through Georgia and the Carolinas. In 1869, he became commanding general of the United States Army, a post he held until retirement in 1883.

If Sherman ever met Frederick Douglass, apparently they did not discuss their meeting. Sherman does not mention Douglass in his memoirs, and Douglass's remembrances mention Sherman only in tandem with Ulysses S. Grant as helping defeat the Confederacy so **Abraham Lincoln** could be reelected in 1864. Douglass's 1888 support of Sherman's brother, John, for the presidency, however, may have provided at least one opportunity for some kind of acquaintance.

Sherman and Douglass had completely opposite views about the place of black people in American society. Douglass was a strong advocate of political and economic rights for freed people, while Sherman remained a supporter of slavery even during the war. He opposed the **Emancipation Proclamation** and only reluctantly cooperated with the effort to include black soldiers in the Union Army. When, during the march to the sea, one of his generals, Jefferson C. Davis, pulled up a pontoon bridge which resulted in the drowning of several escaping slaves, Sherman defended his subordinate's action. He did, however, issue Special Field Order No. 15, which set aside abandoned land on the Sea Islands off **South Carolina** and Georgia for former slaves. When President Andrew Johnson later rescinded the order, Sherman accepted the decision without protest. During Reconstruction, he called himself the South's best friend, and he was indeed a leading Northern advocate for the South's postwar ideology.

Sherman treated individual black people with respect, shaking hands and speaking to anyone regardless of race, at a time when this was not common. Still, Sherman simply could not imagine blacks playing any kind of leading role in American society, quite the opposite of Frederick Douglass.

Further Reading

Marszalek, John F. *Sherman, A Soldier's Passion for Order.* Carbondale, Ill.: Southern Illinois University Press, 1933.

Sherman, William T. *Memoirs of General William T. Sherman.* 2 vols. New York: D. Appleton and Company, 1876.

———. *William T. Sherman Family Papers, 1820–1891.* Notre Dame, Ind.: University of Notre Dame Archives.

—John F. Marszalek

South Carolina

On December 20, 1860, South Carolina seceded from the Union. On February 4, 1861, South Carolina, along with **Mississippi**, Florida, Alabama, Georgia, and **Louisiana**, was admitted to the Confederate States of America (CFA). The Confederate States of America (CFA), also referred to as the "Confederacy" and "Dixie," formed a country in North America from 1861 to 1865 comprised of Southern slave states that seceded from the United States. After the confirmation of the election of **Abraham Lincoln** to the presidency of the United States on March 4, 1861, Jefferson Davis became the president of the CFA. Although Lincoln considered the secession "legally void," originally he did not plan to invade the states. He only considered using federal troops to protect and secure federal property and assist in collecting federal taxes and duties.

On April 12, 1861, South Carolina troops belonging to the Confederacy opened batteries on the Union's Federal garrisons stationed at Fort Sumter, located on an island in the Charleston, South Carolina, harbor. This was the beginning of the American Civil War, in which the Confederate military was successful in seizing and retaining the fort until 1865, the end of the Civil War. However, the initial victory and seizure of the fort by Confederate troops on April 13, 1861 prompted Lincoln to retaliate by summoning troops from all the remaining states in the Union. In response, additional Southern states seceded from the Union, joined the Confederacy and sent troops. Among these states were Texas, Virginia, Arkansas, Tennessee, and North Carolina. Later, Kentucky and Missouri joined the CFA, increasing the number of Confederate states to thirteen.

Frederick Douglass envisioned the Civil War as a means to end slavery. He believed that if former slaves and freed blacks fought in the war against the Confederacy they would become citizens in a new American Republic. In 1863, Douglass became a recruiter for the **Fifty-fourth Regiment of Massachusetts Volunteer Infantry**, the first regiment comprising African American volunteer soldiers. While two of his sons, **Lewis** and **Charles**, joined the regiment and were sent to South Carolina, a third son, **Frederick Douglass, Jr.**, became an army recruiter.

Throughout the war, Fort Sumter was intermittently fired upon by the Union troops. However, it was not until February 17, 1865, under the leadership of Major General William T. Sherman, that the Union troops advancing north from Savannah, Georgia, seized Fort Sumter. South Carolina was reinstated into the United States during Reconstruction. During the 1880s, the state became a political epicenter of racial and economic debates.

Further Reading

Blight, David W. *Frederick Douglass' Civil War: Keeping Faith in Jubilee*. Baton Rouge: Louisiana State University Press, 1991.

Risley, Ford. *The Civil War: Primary Documents on Events from 1860 to 1865*. Westport, Conn.: Greenwood Press, 2004.

—*Sharon Pruitt*

Sumner, Charles (1811–1874)

Senator and abolitionist Charles Sumner was born in Boston, **Massachusetts**. He received a B. A. from Harvard in 1830 and a L. L. B from Harvard Law School in 1833. He practiced law in Boston and briefly lectured at Harvard Law School. From 1837 to 1840, Sumner toured Europe (**England**, France, and Italy) in order to broaden his legal knowledge and enhance his teaching prospects. When Sumner returned to the United States, he resumed his law practice but ultimately became a prominent statesman advocating for human equality. As he possessed similar concerns as Frederick Douglass, they shared a mutual respect for one another. In 1854, Sumner financially supported the *Frederick Douglass's Paper*, edited by Douglass, and praised Douglass's publication efforts in proclaiming the injustices toward blacks in the United States. Likewise, Douglass admired Sumner's antislavery and equal rights speeches.

Sumner, a Whig Party member, ascended to leadership positions in the Massachusetts Free Soil Party, formed by members of the Whig, Democrat, and Liberty Parties with a platform opposing the extension of slavery into new territories. He ran unsuccessfully as a Free Soil candidate for Congress in both 1848 and 1850. In 1851, he was elected to a U.S. Senate seat by the Massachusetts state legislature. A year later, Sumner began a successful campaign to release three white men imprisoned in Washington since spring 1848 for attempting to help 77 slaves to escape from slavery on a schooner.

At the beginning of Sumner's senatorial tenure, he was unpopular. During his first five years in office, had he been scheduled for reelection, he probably would have been defeated. However after an 1855 speech which precipitated a brutal attack, Sumner's popularity as a politician increased among antislavery Northerners. In his 1855 "Crime against Kansas" speech, Sumner deliberately insulted Senator Butler from **South Carolina**. For his insults, Sumner was severely beaten with a cane by Butler's nephew, Preston Brook. These events not only spawned sympathizers for Sumner but also secured him a second term in the Senate as well as assuring his seniority and prestige within the Republican Party. By 1861, Sumner became one of the most powerful men in the United States.

Sumner's debates with President **Abraham Lincoln** reflected similar concerns as those of Douglass. Both expressed frustration with Lincoln's procrastination in issuing the **Emancipation Proclamation**. In 1865, Sumner supported Douglass and other abolitionists in a campaign to secure voting rights for black men. Sumner, like other Republicans, believed black men would naturally support the Republican Party's quest to maintain dominance in Congress during the readmission of Southern states into the Union.

In 1872, while Douglass campaigned for the reelection of President Ulysses S. Grant, Sumner chose to support the Democratic candidate, **Horace Greeley**. Grant easily won the 1872 election. Sumner's opposition to the annexation of the Dominican Republic, which he correctly assessed as a corrupt bargain, fueled bitter arguments with Grant. Because of their differences, Sumner was removed as chairman of the Senate Foreign Relations Committee. Sumner died in Washington, D.C.

Further Reading

Donald, David H. *Charles Sumner and the Rights of Man*. New York: Knopf, 1970.

Foner, Philip S. *Life and Writings of Frederick Douglass; Early Year, 1817–1849*, 2 vols. New York: International Publishers, 1950.

Palmer, Beverly W. *The Selected Letters of Charles Sumner*, 2 vols., Boston: Northeastern University Press, 1990.

—Sharon Pruitt

T

Talbot County, Maryland

For Frederick Douglass, Talbot County, on the eastern shore of **Maryland,** was a place and time of deep significance, evoking many memories and emotions, most filled with pain, others filled with joy, but all of which inevitably shaped his identity. Talbot County was established in 1662 and was named for Lady Grace Talbot, sister of the Second Lord Baltimore and wife of Sir Robert Talbot. The Talbots were one of England's wealthiest Catholic families. Although wealthy families such as the Tilghmans and Lloyds greatly influenced the political and economic development of Talbot County, the county was also a home for persecuted Quakers, Puritans, and many Irish and Scottish rebels who labored as indentured servants.

The early commercial world of Talbot County revolved around tidewater and tobacco. The relative ease of navigating the waterways along more than 600 miles of tidal shoreline attracted many early European settlers who established tobacco plantations. The early colonists vigorously traded with English merchants for manufactured goods. The beginning of the American Revolutionary War marked the waning of the so-called Tobacco Era of Talbot County.

By 1790, approximately 5,000 African Americans, both slave and free, made up 45 percent of the total population of the county. Many of the African Americans in Talbot County during Frederick Douglass's youth came from Barbados and other islands in the Caribbean West Indies. Douglass's master, Aaron Anthony, cultivated an appreciation for charting family genealogies of slaves, and the value of his effort in describing the Bailey family suggests that the enslaved ancestors of Douglass can be traced back to the beginning years of the county. Douglass was born in 1818 on Holme Hill Farm in Tapper's Corners, Talbot County, located on the western shores of the Tuckahoe River, near Cordova.

After spending 20 years in slavery, Douglass escaped in 1838 by train and boat and eventually arrived at New Bedford, **Massachusetts,** where he was inspired by **William Lloyd Garrison** and Wendell Phillips to become involved in abolitionism. Douglass did not return to Talbot County for 41 years after he initially departed. In 1877, Douglass first returned to St. Michaels to make peace with his former master, Captain Thomas Auld. On this trip, Douglass noted that the condition of the African American population had changed little since he left, with males working primarily as farm laborers and females engaging in domestic service. Douglass returned to

Talbot County on three other occasions before his death in 1895. In 1878, Douglass was brought back to Talbot County by the County Republicans to assist in registering African American voters. He took the opportunity on this occasion to visit the site of his birth on Tuckahoe Creek. In 1881, Douglass returned to visit the famous Lloyd Plantation of his youth in slavery, commonly known as Wye House. On his final trip in 1893, it was reported that Douglass visited to investigate purchasing an estate for his retirement home, but he never purchased any real estate there and never returned again to Talbot County.

Further Reading

Douglass, Frederick. *Life and Times of Frederick Douglass.* Hartford, Conn.: Park Publishing Co., 1888.

Preston, Dickson J. *Young Frederick Douglass: The Maryland Years.* Baltimore: Johns Hopkins University Press, 1980.

Wennersten, John R. *Maryland's Eastern Shore: A Journey in Time and Place.* Atglen, Pa.: Tidewater Publishers, 1992.

—*Mario H. Beatty*

Truth, Sojourner (1797–1883)

Sojourner Truth was an African American **abolitionist**, women's rights advocate, and evangelist. Living during a period when America was being transformed from an agricultural to an urban nation and from a slave culture to a pluralistic democracy, Sojourner Truth was herself the subject of profound personal changes while becoming a critical source for identifying changes in public attitudes toward the abolition of slavery and the political liberation of women. Named Isabella at birth, she was the youngest daughter of James and Elizabeth, Dutch-speaking slaves on the farm of Johannis Hardenergh in Ulster County, New York. Truth lived through the chaos of slavery by having to serve several masters in her youth before marrying at 14 the slave named Thomas from whom she gave birth to four children: Diana, Peter, Elizabeth, and Sophia, between 1815 and 1826.

One of the earliest events in her life typified the pain of separation experienced by slave parents. Isabella's oldest son, Peter, was stolen and taken by force to live in Alabama. With the help of Quakers, Truth successfully petitioned the courts for his return. From this encounter with the court system, Truth's life changed even more dramatically. Isabella had a conversion experience. She heard the voice of God telling her to go out and spread the word about the sin of slavery, the necessity of social reform, and the possibilities of salvation. At the same time, New York state laws freed her from slavery in 1827. With this new spiritual and physical emancipation, Isabella gradually moved away from her slaveholders and traveled around the state's **Methodist** community until she arrived in New York City in 1828, during a time of intense religious fervor. Established denominations conducted revivals and various personalities publicly presented themselves with divine messages on temperance, Sabbath-keeping, and antislavery. In 1843, Isabella declared that the Holy Spirit had directed her to travel and lecture under a new name, Sojourner Truth, a name that symbolically addressed her role and purpose as an itinerant preacher.

The most compelling event in 1845 from an abolitionist's perspective was the publication of Frederick Douglass's autobiography. *The Narrative of the Life of Frederick Douglass* started the long and distinguished career of the brave and articulate abolitionist voice and editor of the **North Star**, who escaped from chattel slavery in 1838. History records meetings between Truth and Douglass, but we do not know about all of them. In fact, their most celebrated and important connection is the subject of debate over the exact time and place of their meeting.

Frederick Douglass and Sojourner Truth first met in Florence, Massachusetts, in 1842, not far from historic Northampton, a utopian community and a frequent gathering place for abolitionists. Florence was a retreat for the members of the abolitionist community and a site for experimental healing using water therapy, but principally a place where the abolitionists could relax and unwind from the tensions involved in teaching, preaching, and fighting for their cause. In their respective narratives, Truth and Douglass comment on the egalitarian climate of the Florence retreat. They discussed its openness, especially the absence of class and race consciousness. Ironically, it was in his first impressions of the evangelist that Douglass revealed his attitudes toward class. There was too much of the plantation manner in Sojourner for Frederick. He described her in the *North Star* as a wise woman, but one who belittled his attempt to behave and speak as a cultivated person.

For much of history, the most celebrated meeting between Truth and Douglass placed them both in Boston's Faneuil Hall in 1850 just after the passage of the **Fugitive Slave Act**, undoubtedly the vilest part of the **Compromise of 1850**. At this antislavery rally, Truth listened as the redoubtable Douglass, frustrated by the perniciousness of the Fugitive Slave Act, spoke against nonviolence and moral suasion, encouraging slaves to rise up with violence against their oppressors. Perceiving Douglass's comments as a challenge to God's justice, Truth stood with piercing self-righteousness and asked the great orator, "Frederick, is God dead?" Revisionists confirm the meeting but question the date, location, and the exact words that Truth spoke. The meeting did indeed take place, the revisionists argue, but it happened not in Boston but in Salem, Ohio, in 1852. It did indeed feature Douglass speaking against nonviolence in the light of the 1850 Fugitive Slave Act; however, Sojourner's challenge to Douglass was different from the popularized question. Her question was, "Frederick, is God gone?"

Feminist scholars and historians have traditionally turned to the famous "Aren't I a Woman?" speech given by Truth in 1851 as one of the defining moments in gender and race history. Delivered in Akron, Ohio, the speech is one of the most widely published in American history. Yet it too, like the "Frederick, is God dead?" speech, is debated by revisionists who maintain that the words "Aren't I a Woman?" were never spoken at all.

Why the historical discrepancies between fact and belief? There are no simple answers. Part of the problem involves the judgment of chroniclers who in their own time choose to exploit the lives of the evangelist and the editor of the *North Star* for their own purposes.

Sojourner and Frederick present some striking biographical similarities and differences, comparisons that demonstrate the complexity of slave culture and the boldness required to escape it. They both use the personal narrative to describe their lives as chattel and to explain the circumstances under which they changed their names, acts which symbolized their new sense of freedom. Sojourner escaped from slavery in 1826, according to *The Narrative of Sojourner Truth*, published in 1850, a book she dictated and which was probably motivated by the success and substance of Douglass's *Narrative* of 1845. She had a vision and a conversion experience, shortly after she joins the Methodists. He was ordained as a preacher in the African Methodist Episcopal Zion Church. Truth and Douglass never ceased to influence the powerful. For example, they both met with President **Abraham Lincoln** and sought to expand the Civil War President's understanding of antislavery and the freedmen's plight. When the war ended, both maintained their commitment to social reform and to the newly freed slaves. Douglass became a Marshal for the District of Columbia before accepting diplomatic offers in Santo Domingo and later in **Haiti**. Sojourner Truth continued her fight for women's rights and reform. Her final reform act was to support a proposal for Kansas to be set aside for former slaves, many of whom moved to Kansas in 1879 and became known as "exodusters." Truth supported their cause, traveled to Kansas, and then returned home to Battle Creek , Michigan, where she died on November 26, 1883.

Further Reading

Painter, Nell. *Sojourner Truth: A Life, A Symbol*. New York: W. W. Norton, 1996.

—*C. James Trotman*

Tubman, Harriet (1820–1913)

The lives and work of Frederick Douglass and of abolitionist and women's rights activist Harriet Tubman span two of the major periods in African American and American history—enslavement and the years of Reconstruction. During these periods of history, Tubman and Douglass stood as towering figures in circles of men and women of similar stature in the struggle for freedom: Maria Stewart; William Still; **Sojourner Truth**; Charles Lenox Redmond; Frances Ellen Watkins Harper; James McCune; Sarah Parker Redmond; and William Wells-Brown. There is a paucity of information on how and where they first met, but given the emancipatory and reconstructive nature of their work, and the stature they both gained as a result of their dedication and achievements, they were destined to meet and work on common concerns, even if from different vantage points. It has been suggested that Douglass may have met Tubman in December 1851 on her way to take a group of 11 freed persons to Canada, for in his autobiography, *The Life and Times of Frederick Douglass*, Douglass wrote that "on one occasion, I had eleven fugitives at the same time under my roof."

The focus and foundation of both Tubman's and Douglass's work was in the struggle for emancipation which included abolitionism, but also involved direct rescue and freeing of enslaved Africans by various means. Also, both Douglass and Tubman had refused to accept their roles as enslaved persons and the racist rationalization given for this. They both freed themselves and, recognizing the indivisibility of African freedom, dedicated their lives to ending enslavement as state-sanctioned social policy, freeing African people, and aiding those Africans in rebuilding and pushing their lives forward. On this point it is important to note that in her biography, *Scenes from the Life of Harriet Tubman*, Tubman relates how her individual escape had first lifted her up, for her freedom had brought "such a glory over everything." In fact, she said "I felt like I was in heaven." But then a sadness came over her, because although she had obtained the freedom which she had dreamed of so long and was free, she felt alone, "a stranger in a strange land" with no one "to welcome (her) in the land of freedom." For all the people she knew and loved were still enslaved.

Thus, she said, "to this solemn resolution I came. I was free and they should be free also. I would make a home for them in the North, and the Lord helping me, I would bring them all there." In this momentous decision, she redefined freedom from its narrow meaning of "individual escape," to a more expansive definition of the "collective practice of self-determination in community." In a hazardous, hard, and heroic struggle against the most difficult odds and with the largest bounty of the times on her head, she made numerous trips into the South and rescued hundreds of enslaved Africans, helping at the same time to build and sustain that process and passage to freedom called the Underground Railroad. Her record of success and of never having lost a "passenger" or having been captured herself, in spite of extensive efforts to do so, testify to her sharp-mindedness, meticulous planning, resourcefulness, and audaciousness, for which Frederick Douglass and others would rightfully praise her.

Tubman, like Douglass, lectured and gave powerful personal testimony on the lives and aspirations for freedom of the enslaved Africans. Sought after by the abolitionist John Brown for her vast knowledge and experience in the Underground Railroad, she met and planned with him a massive armed revolt by enslaved Africans. Although illness prevented her from being a part of his failed raid on the federal arsenal at **Harpers Ferry**, she had endorsed armed struggle as a road to freedom. Douglass had disagreed with both the method and the timing of the raid, although he had earlier supported Brown's efforts.

When the Civil War broke out, Tubman, like Douglass, contributed greatly to the war effort and encouraged other Africans to join the fight for freedom. She herself served in various roles in the Union Army including advisor, organizer of revolts and defections of enslaved Africans, nurse, scout, spy, soldier, and strategist. In fact, she earned the unique distinction of being the only woman in United States military history to plan and carry out an armed mission against the enemy. Moreover, she accompanied the army in several battles, remembering and offering in her biography a powerful portrait of the great sacrifice of the black **Fifty-fourth Regiment of the Massachusetts Volunteer Infantry** in metaphors of lightning and thunder in the war. It is her statement, "And then we heard the thunder," describing this, that served as the title of John Killens' famous novel.

Furthermore, Tubman and Douglass worked diligently during Reconstruction and after to provide support and assistance for freed Africans and the families of

African veterans of the Civil War, and to win legislation and reform in the interest of Africans' and women's rights. She, like other African American women of her time, worked tirelessly and selflessly for social reform, social justice, and the strengthening of the African American family and community. An instructive example of her work was the home she established for elderly formerly-enslaved Africans on a plot of land she had originally purchased for her parents' future home.

In a letter to the Ladies Irish Anti-Slavery Association and in another to Tubman herself, Douglass paid impressive homage to this great woman who weighed so heavily in the scales of history for African and human freedom. In the first letter he praised Tubman for her "great courage and shrewdness" and for her initiative, selfless service and audaciousness, having freed herself and returning several times at great risk to herself to save others. His most extensive and laudatory letter was written to Harriet Tubman herself, in response to her request of him to write a statement of commendation for her biography written by Sarah E. Bradford.

He begins by telling her that although she has asked him for words of commendation for the book, she does not need it from him. He describes her work as superior to his own, and ends by noting the heavens bear witness to the wonder of her work. He writes:

> You ask for what you do not need when you call upon me for a word of commendation. I need such words from you far more than you can need them from me, especially where your superior labors and devotion to the cause of the lately enslaved of our land are known as I know them. The difference between us is very marked. Most that I have done and suffered in the service of our cause has been in public, and I have received much encouragement at every step of the way. You, on the other hand, have labored in a private way. I have wrought in the day—you in the night. I have had the applause of the crowd and the satisfaction that comes of being approved by the multitude, while the most that you have done has been witnessed by a few trembling, scarred, and footsore bondmen and women, whom you had led out of the house of bondage, and whose heartfelt *"God Bless you"* has been your own reward. The midnight sky and the silent stars have been the witnesses of your devotion to freedom and of your heroism. (Bradford, 1974: 7)

Harriet Ross Tubman died in March 1913, leaving a legacy of dedication, discipline, sacrifice, and achievement in the context of the most taxing and horrific times in African American and American history.

Further Reading

Bradford, Sarah E. *Scenes in the Life of Harriet Tubman*. Secaucus, N.J.: Citadel Press, 1974.

Conrad, Earl. "I Bring You General Tubman." *Black Scholar*. Vol 1, 3–4 (Jan/Feb, 1970): p. 4.

Douglass, Frederick. *Life and Times of Frederick Douglass*. Hartford, Conn.: Park Publishing Co., 1888.

Foner, Philip S. *The Life and Writings of Frederick Douglass*. 4 vols, New York: International Publishers, 1950.

Quarles, Benjamin, Litwack, Leon & Meier, August, eds. "Harriet Tubman's Unlikely Leadership." *Black Leaders of the Nineteenth Century*. Urbana: University of Illinois Press, 1988.

—*Maulana Karenga*

Turner, Nat (1800–1831)

Born in Southampton County, Virginia, on a plantation owned by Benjamin Turner, Nat Turner displayed extraordinary abilities and talents at an early age. At his birth, his parents noted that Turner was indeed intended for a great purpose after observing particular marks on his head and chest. By age three or four, Turner was overheard by his mother relating events which occurred before his birth. After others were called upon to listen to Turner retell the past, he was told by many of his fellow slaves that one day he would become a great prophet, having already demonstrated remarkable cognitive powers. According to his confession, Turner miraculously learned how to read after being shown a book, spelling the names of items to the astonishment of onlookers. Possessing a keen mind and a singularity of purpose made Turner a leader among slaves, even as a young man. His many talents in combination with his divine conviction and ascetic lifestyle gave Turner a great deal of influence on the plantation which explains his following as preacher and later as leader of the most destructive slave revolt in U.S. history.

In October 1810, Benjamin Turner died during a typhoid fever outbreak, and Nat Turner became the property of his former holder's younger brother, Samuel. At some point before Benjamin Turner's death, Nat Turner's father successfully escaped from the plantation and likely became an inhabitant of the nearby "Dismal Swamp." Extending 25 miles east of Southampton into North Carolina, this swamp was the destination and home of hundreds of slave runaways and outlyers. Sometime between 1821 and 1822, Nat Turner followed his father's lead by escaping from Samuel Turner's plantation. It was at this time that Turner came into contact with what he referred to as "the Spirit." His first contact with this Spirit came earlier in 1821 and from that point forward he was in frequent communion with this supernatural entity. After Turner's escape attempt, the Spirit informed him that he should return to his earthly master, apparently because he had a greater task to accomplish later in life. Turner returned to the plantation after being missing for 30 days and upon his arrival, his fellow slaves sharply criticized his decision to come back.

After his return, Turner would devote much of his time to prayer, fasting, and meditation, and would remain in constant contact with the Spirit from 1822 until 1828. During the course of this communication with the Spirit, Turner gained esoteric and mundane knowledge—learning how to manufacture paper and gunpowder and gaining divine insights into various astronomical phenomena.

In 1822, Turner married Cherry Turner but the two were separated soon after. The same year, Turner was sold to Thomas Moore after the untimely death of Samuel Turner and Cherry Turner was sent to a nearby farm owned by Giles Reese. The two would have as many as three children but would never again reside on the same plantation. After Thomas Moore's death in 1828, Turner became the property of Moore's nine-year-old son, Putnam. Two years later, Putnam Moore's mother, Sally Moore, would marry a local wheelwright, Joseph Travis. Though Putnam Moore remained Nat Turner's legal master, he was for all intents and purposes the property of Joseph Travis from 1830 until the time of the Southampton insurrection in 1831.

In 1825, Turner had perhaps the most important revelation in his communication with the Spirit. He received a vision of black and white spirits engaged in mortal combat. Turner would interpret this vision as a sign of a coming apocalyptic battle between slaves and their white oppressors. The visions and communion with supernatural forces would intensify as Turner would discover blood drops on stalks of corn and hieroglyphic characters and numbers on leaves while laboring in the fields. Soon after these signs began to appear, Turner states in his confession that the Holy Ghost revealed itself to him to fully explain the various images and visions. All signs pointed to an impending judgment day.

Sometime between 1827 and 1828, Turner revealed his supernatural communications to a local white man named Etheldred T. Brantley. After Brantley suffered through skin eruptions and unusual bleeding, Turner prescribed nine days of praying and fasting which ultimately cured him of his ailments. After ceasing his wickedness, Brantley, with the assistance of Turner, was baptized by the Spirit at Pearson's Mill Pond. Not only did he successfully cure Brantley of his affliction, but according to the trial records, Turner could by the imposition of his hands cure disease by laying his hands on the afflicted. During the trials which followed the insurrection, one slave testified that Turner had, on one particular occasion, effected a cure of an ailment upon one of his comrades.

By 1828, Turner would begin making concrete plans to foment a slave revolt. On May 12, the Spirit informed him that a rebellion was imminent and that he would lead this effort. After a solar eclipse appeared on February 12, 1831, Turner finally revealed the details of the plan he had been crafting for at least three years. Henry, Hark, Nelson, and Sam became his first converts and a very ironic date, July 4, 1831, was chosen as the day for the plan of rebellion would be put into effect. The five conspirators met but failed to reach a consensus regarding the particulars of the plot, and Turner's untimely illness forced the band to change the date of the revolt. They waited until August 13, 1831 for a heavenly sign to appear which came in the form of a greenish-blue sunrise which was reportedly witnessed throughout the eastern seaboard. The next week, Turner, along with Henry and Hark, decided to prepare a dinner on Sunday, August 21, for the men who joined the rebellion. Turner later confessed that the conspirators gathered for dinner near Cabin Pond, and he joined them around 3:00 p.m. After being joined by another slave named Austin sometime later that evening, this band of eight men began their destructive work during the early morning hours of Monday, August 22.

The rebels' first target was the home of Turner's latest master, Joseph Travis. After delivering a glancing blow to the head of his master, Turner's failed attempt to kill Travis was completed by Will, who managed to slay both Joseph and his wife, Sally. After the entire family of five was slain, the rebels equipped themselves with guns and additional weapons and attacked the homes of Salathiel Francis, Mrs. Reese, and several others in the immediate vicinity. Turner's main goal was the capture of the nearby town of Jerusalem—a location which reportedly contained a large quantity of guns and ammunition. On their way to Jerusalem, a number of rebels decided to raid the residence of James W. Parker in order to liberate relatives and other potential recruits. As the main body of the rebel force preceded to the Parker home, Turner and about seven or eight others posted guard at the main gate. After becoming impatient, Turner left the main gate to retrieve his forces from Parker's home. Upon their return to the main road, Turner's band was met by 18 white militiamen under the command of Captain Alexander Peete. Having already dispersed the men Turner left at the gate, the militia volunteers exchanged fire with the slave insurgents before being forced into retreat. The rebels pursued the white militia only to be met by a much larger body of reinforcements. The ensuing battle left a number of slaves injured and the rest of Turner's force dispersed and retreated.

By the morning of August 23, 1831, Nat Turner's force, which at its height numbered some 70 men, had cut a bloody swath across Southampton, leaving a total of 57 white men, women, and children dead. Ultimately, several local militia units and three companies of federal troops were called in to quell the insurrection and, by the morning of August 24, 1831, Southampton had survived the worst slave rebellion in Virginian history. With the rebellion effectively over, a mass hysteria among local whites began. More than a 100 slaves, many of whom were not involved in the insurrection, were killed in the aftermath of the revolt. The severed heads of a number of slaves were placed on signposts and poles throughout Southampton County as a warning against future acts of slave resistance and rebellion.

Nat Turner was not immediately captured. With his forces dispersed, captured, or killed, Turner unsuccessfully tried to mount another attempt to storm Jerusalem on August 23. Between August 25 and October 30, he successfully eluded local authorities by hiding in the vicinity of Joseph Travis' plantation. On October 30, Turner was captured by Benjamin Phipps, a poor farmer who stumbled upon the rebel leader on his way to a neighbor's house. Armed with only a sword, Turner surrendered and was immediately brought to Southampton County jail. While awaiting trial, Turner was interviewed in his cell by Thomas R. Gray, a white lawyer who transcribed and published *The Confessions of Nat Turner*. Though Gray's editorial comments, phrasing, and framing remarks are obvious throughout the text, this valuable document provides the only tangible insight into Turner's motivations for the revolt.

On November 5, Turner was charged with insurrection and murder, to which he pled not guilty. Turner never denied leading the revolt, but he explained to the court that he did not feel guilty for the destruction he wrought. Turner was defiant to the end. After being convicted of conspiring to rebel and making insurrection, the Southampton County Court of Oyer and Terminer sentenced him to be hanged on November 11. Turner's life and death would serve as an important model for future black activists. In a March 1863 *Douglass's Monthly* editorial entitled "Men of Color, To Arms," Frederick Douglass implored black Union Army enlistees to remember Nathaniel Turner of Southampton. **Abolitionists** of the 1850s and 1860s as well as Black Power advocates a century later would continue to be inspired by Turner's courageous efforts to break the shackles of bondage.

Further Reading

Aptheker, Herbert. *Nat Turner's Slave Rebellion*. New York: Published for A.I.M.S. by Humanities Press, 1966.

Higginson, Thomas W. "Nat Turner's Insurrection." *Atlantic Monthly*. 8 (1861): 173–86.

Oates, Stephen. *The Fires of Jubilee: Nat Turner's Fierce Rebellion*. New York: Harper & Row, 1975.

—*Walter Rucker*

U

U.S. Senate

Between 1870 and 1895 Douglass held five appointed offices and was a loyal member of the "Party of Lincoln," the Republican party. He appreciated the Party's war effort and was satisfied with several Republican initiatives, including the "Reconstruction Amendments" which included the Thirteenth, Fourteenth, and **Fifteenth Amendment**s to the United States Constitution. Perhaps most importantly, Douglass worked well with Republican Party members, including President **Abraham Lincoln**.

During Reconstruction, Douglass was arguably the most famous African American in the United States. His persuasive rhetoric and collegial manner made him an attractive choice for politicians who wanted to appoint an African American to public office. Notwithstanding the idealism of Reconstruction, black public office holders in post-Civil War America were caught in a dilemma. Although they eagerly sought public office with the intent of bettering the black community, they were often forced to settle for low-level patronage jobs that had impressive titles but little authority. Consequently, their effectiveness was impeded by their lack of real power and the subsequent inability to effect change once they were in office.

After President Lincoln's assassination, Vice President Andrew Johnson, a Democrat, assumed office. In 1867 Douglass declined President Johnson's offer to head the Freedman's Bureau. The Bureau was established for the purpose of providing medical, educational, and financial assistance to Southern blacks suffering the vestiges of slavery. Douglass refused Johnson's offer because he did not want to be publicly associated with a white leader who was overtly against black equality. During the 1868 presidential race, Douglass openly campaigned for Republican candidate Ulysses S. Grant, the former commander in chief of the Union Army. Partly because of Douglass's efforts, black voters were instrumental in helping Grant get elected. After Congress passed the **Fifteenth Amendment**, many of Douglass's supporters urged him to move to the South so that he could be appointed to a public office that had real authority and power. Douglass refused, citing the need for blacks in Congress and contending that he could do more as a member of Congress or as a public office-holder in Washington, D.C.

In 1871 President Grant appointed Douglass to the Legislative Council. Prior to 1871, whites represented blacks on the Council. Douglass was thrilled by his appointment, believing that it signaled a new day for blacks in politics. Across America there was a surge of black political gains. African Americans were elected to several seats in Congress. Hiram Revels of **Mississippi** became the first African American U.S. Senator, while Joseph Rainey of **South Carolina** became the first black member of the House of Representatives. President Grant also appointed Douglass to a panel investigating the possibility of the United States annexing the Dominican Republic. During this time Douglass was spending a considerable time abroad, and as a result he resigned his seat on the Legislative Council. Douglass's two-year term was completed by his son, **Lewis Henry Douglass** (1840–1908).

Douglass's next political assignment was Marshal of the District of Columbia, a position somewhat similar to that of a county sheriff. The Marshal's position was significantly more challenging and prestigious than the Legislative Council. Douglass was the first black to hold this position. In 1881 President Garfield appointed Douglass **Recorder of Deeds** for the District of Columbia. On July 1, 1889, Douglass became the U.S. Minister and Consul General to the Republic of Haiti. In 1890 Douglass was ordered by U.S. officials to lobby the Haitian government for the U.S. Navy to use the Haitian port town of Môle St. Nicolas as a refueling station. When Haiti rejected the Navy's proposal, U.S. newspapers claimed that Douglass was too sympathetic to Haitians. In July 1891 Douglass resigned as Minister to Haiti. From 1892–1893 Douglass was commissioner in charge of the Haitian exhibit at the **World's Columbian Exposition** in Chicago.

Douglass did not speak out when President Arthur formed a coalition with the White Independents of Virginia, a group of disgruntled Democrats who had split from their party. Arthur saw this as an opportunity to establish a Republican stronghold in the South without the aid of blacks. Arthur's support of the White Independents was both ideological and financial. The Republican Party's new emphasis resulted in a drastic reduction of blacks in federal government. In his speech, "The Return of the Democratic Party to Power," Douglass lamented that the Republican Party had lost its moral underpinnings and its thirst for justice and equality. Nonetheless, some civil rights leaders became openly critical of Douglass's actions, contending that he had tempered his commitment to civil rights and lost his political influence.

Douglass always championed working with or within the government for solutions to social problems. Though he was never elected to office, Douglass served in appointed positions under Presidents Garfield, Arthur, and Cleveland. Douglass had no constituency to satisfy but he suffered from the problems that many social reformers have when they accept government appointments. First, they suffer from dual allegiance. In Douglass's case, he felt he owed the person who appointed him because that person took a risk to appoint a black to the position. Second, they often appear to be hypocritical. Douglass could no longer talk truth about power because he was now part of that power establishment. Third, Douglass had to constantly fight the public perception that he was working for a racist government.

Many people were concerned about the Republican Party's shift toward big business and away from African American civil rights. Notwithstanding, Douglass's behavior should not be deemed hypocritical. He sincerely believed that the Republican Party was the most efficient mechanism to uplift blacks. In fact, his work as an office-holder remains the standard for ideals of equality in the Republican Party.

Further Reading

Goldstein, Leslie Friedman. "Morality and Prudence in the Statesmanship of Frederick Douglass: Radical as Reformer." *Polity*. Vol. 16, No. 4 (1984): pp. 606–623.

—Otis Grant

U.S. Supreme Court

The valiant efforts of Frederick Douglass as an abolitionist and lobbyist for black civil rights were often met with little or no support from the U.S. Supreme Court of Douglass's day. Many decisions announced by the court struck at the very heart of the abolitionist movement. In its 1857 *Dred Scott* decision, the Supreme Court made unconstitutional the **Missouri Compromise**, which prohibited the expansion of slavery above the state of Missouri. The Supreme Court, led by Chief Justice Roger Taney, declared that Congress had no power to limit the expansion of slavery by law. Three justices, including Taney, went further to declare that blacks, free and enslaved, could never become citizens of the United States. This decision was met with feverish attacks on the Court by **abolitionists**. Although accepting the *Scott* decision as a setback, Douglass was able to find a positive side by noting that it served to bring slavery to the nation's attention which, he thought, would go toward its ultimate eradication in the United States. True to his prediction, the debates spurned by the decision would last throughout the **Lincoln** presidential election and into the Civil War.

The fierce and compelling pull of the abolitionist movement set in motion the nation's eventual intolerance of slavery. After the Civil War and the emancipation of slaves, other progressive changes of the Reconstruction Era followed. The **Civil Rights Act** of 1875 was enacted, which sought to give social and economic leverage to former slaves. Getting the Thirteenth, Fourteenth, and **Fifteenth Amendment**s adopted were marked by Douglass and the abolitionists as their greatest accomplishments. These amendments banned slavery and gave citizenship to blacks and suffrage to the once disenfranchised population of the United States. Although the end of slavery and the ensuing Reconstruction engendered optimism among blacks, the South struggled to rebuild and regain its economic footing. Many rights to benefit blacks were met with increased Southern indignation and, as a result, were short-lived. In 1883, the Supreme Court declared the Civil Rights Act unconstitutional, holding that racial discrimination in public places was not contrary to the United States Constitution. **Black Codes**, designed to oppress and disenfranchise former slaves, became prevalent in the South. The overturn of the Civil Rights Act inflamed civil rights activists, and Douglass saw it as disregarding the object and intent of the Fourteenth Amendment, leaving blacks utterly defenseless against all kinds of prejudices. Other rulings held that the right of suffrage was not a necessary attribute of national citizenship, that states cannot prohibit segregation on public transportation. These decisions marked a vacillating period for black struggles. Ardent in their opposition of Supreme Court decisions, the abolitionist voices, led by Frederick Douglass, continued to demand fairness and justice. A passionate reader and writer, Douglass always viewed education as the first step toward freedom and equal rights of blacks. However, with the Court's "separate but equal" ruling in ***Plessy vs. Ferguson***, the fight for black equality would be driven well into the mid-twentieth century, and once again before the Supreme Court.

Further Reading

Douglass, Frederick. "The Civil Rights Case." Address at Lincoln Hall in Washington, D.C.: (Oct. 22, 1883). (Transcript available at the Library of Congress.)

———. Address at the American Abolition Society, New York: The Dred Scott Decision (May 1857) (transcript available at the Library of Congress).

Dykes, DeWitt S., Jr. "Major U.S. Court Decisions." Vol. II: 472. *Reference Library of Black America*, ed. Jessie C. Smith and Joseph M. Palmisano. Farmington Hills, Mich.: Gale Group, Inc., 2001.

—*Everette B. Penn*

V

Vesey, Denmark (1767-1822)

Born a slave, Denmark Vesey went on to become a minister and revolutionary. Born in St. Thomas or in West Africa, Vesey was owned by Captain Vesey but purchased his freedom in 1799. In the years following the American Revolution, Vesey sought to organize African American slaves to violently overthrow the institution that kept them in bondage. Inspired by the success of Haitian revolutionaries Dessalines and **Toussaint L'Ouverture,** he believed that blacks could free themselves only through armed struggle.

Denmark Vesey and Frederick Douglass represent two different black political ideologies, black Nationalism or separatism, and integration or liberal pluralism, but both men were committed to freedom and emancipation for African Americans. Frederick Douglass and Denmark Vesey both understood the psychological effects of slavery, but had different responses to the "peculiar institution." First, Vesey believed in armed struggled while Douglass believed in oratory and persuasion; both believed in the psychological effects of the slavery and the transformation that occurs from fighting the master. Second, both men's families were disrupted by the institution of slavery; Douglass never knew his father, and Vesey never freed his family and fathered children out of wedlock. Lastly, Vesey and Douglass pursued two different political strategies to achieve their objectives that represented two different sections of the African American community.

For most of his abolitionist career, Douglass believed in the power of moral suasion as a means to ultimate freedom for slaves. However, on the eve of the Civil War, he drifted away from the conservative opinions of Garrison abolitionists and moved politically closer to the more radical opinions of men like John Brown. Ultimately, Douglass wasn't persuaded to participate in the ill-fated **Harpers Ferry** raid and fled to Canada following Brown's subsequent capture and hanging. Although criticized for not participating in the raid, Frederick Douglass eventually came to believe that political violence could be used to gain freedom for African Americans. In contrast, Denmark Vesey's radical strain of black nationalism involved the violent overturn of slavery and an ultimate exodus from the American Republic. Denmark himself had been inspired by the Haitian slave revolution, the rhetoric surrounding the American Revolution, the support from the **African Methodist Episcopal Church,** and the congressional debates in 1819 and 1820 surrounding Missouri's admission into the Union.

Frederick Douglass and Denmark Vesey each utilized different approaches in their struggles to overthrow slavery, but both well understood the psychological transformation that occurs from fighting back. Douglass, in his autobiography, disclosed how he was transformed after he physically fought a white slave-breaker, Edward Covey, who attempted to punish him. But before Douglass fought Covey, he had learned how to read and believed that morals, suasion, and reason could triumph over slavery. Douglass, influenced by **William Lloyd Garrison**'s teachings, was a pacifist. He was assaulted by a white mob in 1843 and met with the antislavery leader, John Brown, in 1848.

Vesey, a leader of the Charleston African Methodist Episcopal Church, used its class leader system to organize some 9,000 slaves in Charleston, South Carolina, to rebel and slay all the white citizens of Charleston, burn the city to the ground, and flee to Haiti. Betrayed by other slaves, Vesey, along with 35 other conspirators, was hung on July 2, 1822.

Slavery, the "peculiar institution," disrupted many blacks' lives and adversely affected their abilities to have normal family structures. Douglass's and Vesey's family lives were both similarly impacted by slavery. Douglass never knew his father, a white man who had sexual relations with his slave mother. Douglass, a mulatto, married a former slave woman, **Anna Murray**, who never learned how to read. However, during the marriage, Douglass was openly having an affair with a white woman, Ottilie Assing, and later, following the death of Anna, married another white woman, **Helen Pitts**. Denmark Vesey, married to a black woman named Susan, fathered several children out of wedlock with several black slave women. White men played vital roles in Frederick Douglass's life: the white father he never knew; Edward Covey, the slave-breaker; William Lloyd Garrison; and John Brown. However, there is little evidence beyond being owned by Captain Vesey that Denmark Vesey was influenced by white men. Vesey, a leader in the African Methodist Episcopal Church, organized within the black community of Charleston and never believed that anything less than the destruction of its white community would create the proper conditions for black emigration to Haiti. Their different choices of women with whom they socialized, their different racial backgrounds, and their different political associations may explain their different strategies pursued in the name of black freedom. Finally, their pursuit of African American freedom was influenced by creolization, biracialization, and class division that created problems within the black community with respect to the goal of emancipation.

Douglass and Vesey lived during two distinctly different eras in black American history. Vesey was a leader at the time when many blacks still retained memories of Africa reflected by many of their institutions' names, the African Lodge or the Free African Society, and he lived in a predominantly agrarian Southern society. Conversely, Douglass emerged as a leader during the rise of the American abolitionist and Negro convention movements, which were initiated primarily by mulatto freemen, small business owners, and ministers in the North, and when America was beginning westward expansion in its early stages of becoming an industrial powerhouse.

Frederick Douglass believed that African Americans could ultimately become a part of American society, whereas Vesey wanted to violently overthrow slavery and emigrate to Haiti. Douglass, influenced by the ideas of the **German Enlightenment**,

Greek philosophy, and concepts from the American Revolution, believed that human beings could overcome social, racial, and political barriers and live together. However, Vesey, influenced by the horrible conditions of slavery in the Caribbean and the American Deep South, never believed that blacks and whites could live together in peace, but instead advocated for extreme violence to gain black freedom.

Further Reading

Huggins, Nathan Irvin. *Slave and Citizen: The Life of Frederick Douglass*. Boston: Little, Brown, 1980.

Pearson, Edward. *Designs against Charleston: The Trial Record of the Denmark Vesey Slave Conspiracy of 1822*. Chapel Hill: University of North Carolina Press, 1999.

—Reynaldo Anderson

W

Washington, Booker T. (1856–1915)

Booker T. Washington, after Frederick Douglass's death in 1895, emerged as the most powerful black leader in America until his own death in 1915. In fact, because of Washington's influence during this time, this era is known in African American history as "the Age of Washington."

Born in Virginia to a black slave mother and an unknown white father, Washington spent his first nine years working as a slave. After the Civil War, he moved to West Virginia with his mother and stepfather where he worked in the coal mines, giving the money to his parents while securing a basic education in school. Washington returned to Virginia in 1871 and enrolled in the Hampton Institute, an educational institute for blacks headed by General Samuel Armstrong (1839–1893), a former white missionary and soldier during the Civil War. General Armstrong was a great influence on Washington and a father figure to him. Graduating from Hampton in 1875, Washington accepted a teaching position in West Virginia. He continued his education at Wayland Seminary in Washington D.C. in 1878 to 1879 and later taught at Hampton. In 1881, he left for Alabama where he founded the Tuskegee Normal School (later the Tuskegee Institute), located in the Deep South. Starting with very little, by 1915 his institution grew to become the most important black school in America with 1,500 students and 180 faculty. Publicly, he was indeed the best-known black man in America.

Yet, unlike Frederick Douglass's radically divisive outlook and actions, Washington's emergence as a powerful black leader in the mid-1890s suggests that his success centered on making conciliatory and "compromising" positions with white America because he associated with many important white industrialists, government leaders, and philanthropist organizations. Washington was a very complex personality who, while befriending white political leaders often covertly took pro-black positions on such controversial issues as voting rights for blacks and better treatment of blacks by the criminal justice system. He aided select black news media and drew attention to the horrors of the lynching problem, especially in the South. In the late 1890s and early twentieth century, other national black leaders such as William E. B. Du Bois (1868–1963) and William Monroe Trotter (1872–1934) increasingly became alarmed at Washington's unchecked power and influence and became some of his harshest critics. Frederick Douglass was clearly a more active reformist of American society during his lifetime than Booker T. Washington. Although both men were born into slavery, Douglass's sharp personality and brilliant self-taught mind heledp him to become a more well-rounded individual who offered a more rational and reasoned program of action for the African American community. On the other hand, Washington's background influenced him in the opposite direction, to a more conservative approach to race relations. It is true that his greatest body of work was completed in Alabama, a challenging social climate for black leaders in the 1890s and at the turn of the century with its **Jim Crow laws** and segregation. Yet it is also very clear that Washington's conciliatory approach on too many occasions left the black community in strange untenable positions regarding their dealings with some elements of the white community.

What are the lasting legacies of Booker T. Washington and Frederick Douglass with regards to their programs, personalities, outlooks, and places in history? Both men were the most powerful and influential black leaders of their generations; Douglass from the mid-1840s to 1895 and Washington from 1895 to 1915. Each leader set a tone and mood for black America. Douglass brought the black community through the last stages of American slavery to Emancipation and Reconstruction; Washington stood guard during the nadir of African American history, the height of the "Age of **Lynching**" and the "Age of Segregation," especially in the South and boarder states. Douglass's achievements define his lasting legacy as being the leading black spokesperson against slavery for over 25 years, and that from the mid-1840s to 1895 he demanded equal rights and justice for all Americans, not just blacks, in this nation. Washington, on the other hand, is noted primarily for establishing a significant university in Alabama, the Tuskegee Institute, which has educated thousands of African Americans since 1881. His work as an educator remains his greatest legacy to the black community.

Further Reading

Franklin, John Hope and August Meier, eds. *Black Leaders of the Twentieth Century*. Urbana: University of Illinois Press, 1982.

Glasson, William H. "The Statistics of Lynching." *The South Atlantic Quarterly*. V, no 5 (October 1906): 342–348.

Harlan, Louis R. *Booker T. Washington: The Making of a Black Leader, 1856–1901*. New York: Oxford University Press, 1972.

Meier, August. *Negro Thought in America, 1880–1915*. Ann Arbor: University of Michigan Press, 1963.

Washington, Booker T. et al. (eds.). *The Booker T. Washington Papers: 15 Volumes*. Urbana: University of Illinois Press, 1972–1989.

———. *Up From Slavery: An Autobiography*. New York: Doubleday 1901; reprint ed.: New York: Bantam Pathfinder, 1970.

———. *The Wizard of Tuskegee, 1901–1915*. New York: Oxford University Press, 1983.

White, John. *Black Leadership in America: From Booker T. Washington to Jesse Jackson*. New York: Longman, 1990.

—*Julius E. Thompson*

Washington, D.C.

In 1870, Frederick Douglass moved with his first wife, Anna Murray, and most of their grown children from **Rochester, New York**, to a home on A Street in the Capitol Hill neighborhood of Washington, D.C., where he would spend the final 23 years of his life. Douglass believed that his wife would feel more at ease among her own people in the District. Douglass supported himself initially by editing a weekly newspaper, the *New National Era*; however, publication ceased in 1874. During his Washington years, Douglass was rewarded for loyal service to the Republican Party with a succession of political appointments which allowed him to relax his heavy touring and speaking schedules. Living more leisurely, Douglass would make periodic addresses to both black and white audiences in the Baltimore/Washington region. For example, Douglass was appointed president over the financially beleaguered Freedman's Savings and Trust Company from March 1874 until the institution collapsed the following July. Douglass was also appointed Assistant Secretary of a special commission to Santo Domingo (present-day Dominican Republic) to examine the feasibility of annexation to the United States in January 1871. Upon his return to the District of Columbia, he served briefly in the city's Legislative Assembly. From July 1889 to August 1891, Douglass served as U.S. Minister Resident and Consul General to the Republic of Haiti. On March 17, 1877, Republican President Rutherford B. Hayes appointed Douglass to the highly visible position of U.S. Marshal to the District of Columbia, making Douglass the first African American appointed to a federal position requiring Senate confirmation. In 1881, incoming Democratic President James A. Garfield removed Douglass from the Marshal position and installed him as Recorder of Deeds for the District. In September 1877, when Douglass was nearly 60 years old, he moved his wife, Anna, into an 1850s 20-room Victorian estate at 316 A Street N.E. In purchasing the estate that Douglass named "Cedar Hill," he broke a "Whites Only" covenant, making his family the first black homeowners in Anacostia, then a predominantly white suburb located across the Anacostia branch of the Potomac River. His grown children and grandchildren were a constant presence at Cedar Hill. Following the death of his beloved first wife on August 4, 1882, after a long illness, Douglass married his friend and former secretary, Helen Pitts, on January 24, 1884. Their union ignited an intense public debate on interracial marriage that Douglass deflected by pointing out the unity of the human race. Despite his many appointed offices, Douglass continued to reject segregation in the District and elsewhere in the country. In May 1877, he delivered a virulent speech denouncing Jim Crow segregation and "taxation without representation" in the nation's capital and declaring the District a disgraceful contradiction to civilization compared to other areas of the country. The speech ignited an unsuccessful drive to remove him from public office. In 1894 Douglass delivered his last great speech, the "Lesson of the Hour," wherein he denounced the evils of lynching as a pernicious device for controlling Southern blacks. Douglass continued to speak against injustice until his death by heart attack on February 20, 1895 at Cedar Hill, shortly after attending a women's rights meeting. Upon his death, Douglass was mourned nationally and publicly acclaimed as a gifted orator and champion of the oppressed. Douglass's widow, Helen Pitts, worked vigorously toward the preservation of Cedar Hill, which today is maintained by the National Park Service as a memorial to Douglass's life and legacy.

Further Reading

Blassingame, John W. and John R. McKivigan, eds. *The Frederick Douglass Papers, Volume 5:1881–1895*. New Haven, Conn.: Yale University Press, 1992.

Douglass, Frederick. *The Life and Times of Frederick Douglass, Written by Himself*. Hartford, Conn.: Park Publishing Co., 1888.

Foner, Philip S. *The Life and Writings of Frederick Douglass, Volume IV*. New York: International Publishers, 1950.

—*Tanya Price*

Webster, Daniel (1782–1852)

Daniel Webster was born in Salisbury, New Hampshire, and graduated from Dartmouth College. He studied and practiced law before being elected to the U.S. Congress as a Federalist representative from New Hampshire (1812–1816). After several years in Washington, he moved to Boston and worked as a successful lawyer and a prominent speaker. In 1823 he was elected to the House as a representative from Massachusetts, and he served until elected to the Senate in 1827. As a senator, his career was defined by his lauded oratorical skills used in support of the national union, and his passionate pleas were quoted by Frederick Douglass and **Abraham Lincoln**, even as Webster's later politics betrayed abolitionist activists. In the early 1830s, Webster rallied against states' rights and led the northern attack on South Carolinian nullification in the Senate. As secretary of state in 1842, Webster, now a Whig, cowrote the Webster-Ashburton Treaty with Britain to resolve the Canada-Maine border and to initiate a joint Anglo-American plan to patrol Africa's Atlantic coast in order to suppress the illegal slave trade. In 1845, he returned to the Senate. After the Mexican War, which he opposed, Webster worked with Henry Clay on compromises over slavery and expansion, and defended them against abolitionist critics. As secretary of state in 1851–1852, he enraged **abolitionists** by enforcing the **Fugitive Slave Act** and by arresting not only fugitives but also those who aided them. After failing to win the Whig nomination for the presidential election of 1852, Webster retired to Marshfield, Massachusetts, and died there before the election.

Further Reading

Collison, Gary. " 'This Flagitious Offensive': Daniel Webster and the Shadrach Rescue Cases, 1851–1852." *New England Quarterly*. 68 (1995): 609–625.

Dalzell Jr., Robert, F. *Daniel Webster and the Trial of American Nationalism*. Boston: Houghton Mifflin, 1973.

Kenny, Gale. "1852." *New England Quarterly*. 68 (1995): 609–625.

Remini, Robert V. *Daniel Webster: The Man and His Time*. New York: W. W. Norton, 1997.

—*Gale Kenny*

Wells-Barnett, Ida B. (1862–1931)

While Ida B. Wells-Barnett was active in many social reforms, like Frederick Douglass she concentrated her efforts in two to three. First, and foremost, she was a teacher and journalist, becoming one of the best-known journalists of her day. During the 1880s and 1890s, she was the leading African American advocate in the campaign seeking an end to the Age of Lynching, as well as a leader in African America's centuries-long struggle to overcome radical oppression, economic exploitation, sexual discrimination, and classism.

Wells was born in Holly Springs, **Mississippi**, in the extreme northern part of the state. She attended Rust College (earlier known as Shaw), and taught in both Mississippi and Tennessee in the 1880s. In May 1884, Wells became a national symbol of transportation discrimination against blacks when she refused to relocate from the ladies' coach to the segregated car for blacks. She was forcibly removed from the train and subsequently sued the Chesapeake and Ohio Railroad, winning a judgment of 500 dollars in the lower courts. However, upon appeal to the state supreme court, her case was reversed.

Like her good friend Frederick Douglass, Wells spent most of her active years as a journalist. In 1887 she owned a one-third interest in the *Memphis Free Speech and Headlight*. Later, she wrote for the *New York Age* and the *Chicago Conservator*, a newspaper owned by lawyer Ferdinand Barnett, who she married in 1895. Together they raised a successful family in Chicago.

Wells wrote for other organs throughout the United States, yet her central contribution as a journalist came with her studies, articles, and lectures on the horrors of the lynching crisis facing the United States in the late nineteenth and early twentieth centuries. She documented that perhaps as many as 10,000 **lynchings** took place in America between the 1880s and the early twentieth century. Much of the data, of course, remains hidden or unknown. One of her most noted books on this topic was published in 1895, *A Red Record: Tabulated Statistics and Alleged Causes of Lynchings in the United States, 1892–94*. It remains a classic text in the field today.

Wells-Barnett's collective body of work in the United States and her travels in Europe were essential elements in the anti-lynching crusade in this country. Her body of work, like Frederick Douglass's efforts against slavery, stands as a major testament to her lifelong efforts to advance social justice. Perhaps scholar William S. McFeely best sums up the total impact of Ida B. Wells-Barnett's and Frederick Douglass's careers when he notes that: "Ida Wells was remarkably like her friend. Both were editors, both orators, both began their careers passionately committed to righting the worst from of injustice that, in their respective times, was inflicted on their people."

Further Reading

Duster, Alfreda, ed. *Crusade for Justice: The Autobiography of Ida B. Wells*. Chicago: University of Chicago Press, 1970.

Hendricks, Wanda. "Ida B. Wells-Barnett." in Darlene Clark Hine, ed. *Black Women in America*. vol. 3. New York: Oxford University Press, 2005.

McFeely, William S. *Frederick Douglass*. New York: W. W. Norton & Co., 1991.

Sewell, George A. and Margaret L. Dwight. *Mississippi Black History Makers*. Jackson: University Press of Mississippi, 1984.

—*Julius E. Thompson*

West Point

The United States Military Academy (USMA), located in West Point, New York, was founded in 1802 as a school for the U.S. Corps of Engineers. American soldiers had occupied the site since 1778, and Congress officially purchased the land in 1790. During the War of 1812, West Point was transformed by an Act of Congress to allow for a larger corps of cadets and to institute a four-year curriculum. Blacks were excluded from being candidates for admission until granted citizenship rights after the Civil War. During the Reconstruction Era, the first African Americans became candidates for admission to West Point. Before **Jim Crow laws** severely restricted black rights in the 1890s, as many as 27 black men were nominated as USMA candidates, and 12 passed the necessary academic and medical exams required for admission. The black students who matriculated at West Point faced racism and complete social exclusion during the 1870s and 1880s, yet despite this opposition, three black men graduated. In 1877, Henry O. Flipper, a former slave from Georgia, was the first black man to graduate from West Point. In 1887 and in 1889, two other black men, John Alexander from Arkansas and Ohioan Charles Young, graduated. Flipper wrote an account of his years at West Point in addition to an autobiography of his military service, and in the former he noted that **Charles Redmond Douglass**, Frederick Douglass's third son, attended his graduation party in New York City.

Further Reading

Buckley, Gail. *American Patriots: The Story of Blacks in the Military from the Revolution to Desert Storm*. New York: Random House, 2001.

Flipper, Henry Ossian. *The Colored Cadet at West Point: Autobiography of Henry Ossian Flipper*. Lincoln, Neb.: University of Nebraska Press, 1998.

Vaughn, William P. "West Point and the First Negro Cadet." *Military Affairs*. 35 (1971): 100–102.

—*Gale Kenny*

"What to the Slave is Your Fourth of July? (The Meaning of July Fourth for the Negro)"

While most critics characterize Frederick Douglass as a one dimensional, ceremonial speaker, his oratory clearly reveals a man of learned wisdom capable of holding his own in the arena of classical argumentation and debate. Notably, Douglass's famous speech, "What To The Slave Is Your Fourth of July?," given in **Rochester, New York** on July 5, 1852, captures his mastery of Aristotelian oratory. First, Douglass utilizes

Frederick Douglass in his study at Cedar Hill, where he wrote many speeches, as well as his third autobiography.

epideictic oratory (demonstrative oratory) to both praise and blame; he uses the occasion to praise the founding fathers for their courage in forging a new nation and to blame the nation for its failure to grant justice to its three million slaves. Second, Douglass utilizes deliberative oratory to speak boldly against what he calls democratic slavery, which he decries as a destructive law that will both harm the well being of the slave and the nation. Third, Douglass employs judicial (forensic) oratory to advance moral arguments that asserts the evil of reducing human beings to nothing more than brutes and chattel.

Historically speaking, Douglass's Fourth of July oration pinpoints a significant time in his life because it marks his very public and controversial rejection of William Lloyd Garrison's philosophical claims that the Declaration of Independence and the United States Constitution are pro-slavery documents. Although Douglass shunned political agency and affiliations in support of Garrison's position for nearly seven years, circumstances moved him to change his mind. Despite the vigorous antislavery campaigns the Garrisons waged, none had been effective in the abolition of slavery. Douglass came to believe after intense deliberations that every means available must be utilized in the fight against slavery, including political agency and affiliations. So, after digesting voluminous legal and political treatises, debating the pros and cons of issues with learned contemporaries, and sharpening the logic and reasoning of his own intellect, Douglass reached the conclusion that both the Declaration of Independence and the Constitution were antislavery documents.

Furthermore, he believed both documents provided the political clout—the political agency in alignments with powerful political affiliations—needed to dismantle the formidable system of slavery. Even in the midst of significant criticism, Douglass remained steadfast in his belief that to part ways with the Garrison abolition movement was correct. In fact, his private correspondences with friends and acquaintances reveal his adamant thoughts on the matter: that no man, including himself, should be obliged to remain devoted to any position which he can no longer, in good conscience, defend.

Douglass waxes eloquent as he lavishes commemorative praises on the founding fathers. He admires their love of country, their reputation as men of peace, and their enviable decisiveness. He builds common ground with his audience when he articulates a historical moment where the founding fathers found it necessary to distance themselves and the colonies from England's demands, which they believed were "unjust," "unreasonable" and oppressive. He asks his audience to put themselves in the slaves' place because slaves also suffer similar unreasonable demands. Douglass argues that it is not enough for privileged citizens to rest on the laurels of their forefathers, because they must wrestle with the issues of their own day. They must be compelled to do their own work—and Douglass argues that this work should be a commitment to abolish slavery. Thus, Douglass uses the July Fourth oration to turn the cacophonous celebration on its head as he challenges the nation to confront its own epistemological hypocrisy. Douglass is plainspoken: "There can be no celebratory democracy until America destroys Democratic Slavery."

Douglass implores his audience to see that their beliefs, traditions, and customs rest upon an epistemological impulse that acquiesces to dominant racial paradigms and ideological scripts of Southern mores. He argues cogently that the Fourth of July celebration exposes a nation unable or unwilling to confront a difficult truth: it cannot admit its inhumanity to African Americans and neither can it recognize them as fully-functioning human beings. Consequently, Douglass insists that this national tragedy gets silenced within shameless exhibitions of patriotism. Douglass confronts the nation's hypocritical stance with three thought-provoking philosophical questions. Rhetorically, he asks his audience to explain why, if indeed all men are created equal, blacks and whites live a different reality, a white life is more valued than a black one, and why blacks are considered "brutes" and not men.

Douglass uses his **rhetorical techniques** to counter blatant "disparity" between blacks and whites. He goes to the heart of the causes that make men discriminate against other men and shackle them as chattel, simply because of racial markers and political differences. Douglass speaks in solidarity with his black brethren when he tells his primarily white audience that July Fourth is the birth of their independence and their political freedom, and that the legacy of American culture celebrates their achievements, not those of the Negro. Douglass asks why the slave should celebrate, given this reality. He asks his audience to help him understand how any slave could celebrate independence when he has never been free.

Douglass contrasts the jovial festivities of the Independence Day celebration with the shameful lives of the slaves. He describes two Americas: one black and one white. Douglass contends that while the nation enjoys the clashing cymbals, he cringes in horror as he hears the mournful wail of millions of slaves. Douglass contends that human mockery and sacrilegious irony make it almost impossible for the white race to sympathize with or empathize with the plight of enslaved people. Douglass finds fault also in what he characterizes as the blasphemous arrogance of church leaders who support the institution of slavery. Douglass decries a nation willing to boast of its love of liberty, of its status as a superior civilization, and of its so-called pure Christianity, while every political element in the nation is obliged to support and perpetuate the enslavement of three million people. This irony reaches its pinnacle when the Nation pledges allegiance to the democratic principles, while at the same time it promotes democratic slavery. Douglass is adamant that such blatant hypocrisy should not stand.

Douglass poses one of his most famous axiological questions: "What to the American slave is your Fourth of July? . . . This Fourth of July is yours, not mine." He asks: "Why am *I* called upon to speak here today? What have I, or those I represent, to do with your independence?" He questions the value of such a pompous celebration to him and his slave brethren since freedom does not exist for slaves, primarily because of the color of their skin. Most poignantly, Douglass declares emphatically that slavery is a man-made construct, and not a divinely ordained condition. He mourns the fact that his kindred brethren have nowhere to turn, not even to the church.

Douglass presses the value issue when he inquires whether the great principles of political freedom and natural justice, embodied in that Declaration of Independence, are extended to slaves. He sees folly in a request that seeks his support of the Fourth of July celebration. He presses the value question still further when he asks whether the slave should be asked to express gratitude for the blessings of freedom neither he nor his fellow-bondmen have ever tasted. Douglass is certain he can find no value in the celebration of the Fourth of July, when the slave remains in bondage without any recognition of his personhood or his manhood.

Arguably, the most powerful part of Douglass's July Fourth speech is when he expresses sheer outrage that the black man would be diminished of his human qualities not by God but by his fellow men. He challenges his audience to explain why it is acceptable for the black man to live without dignity in the chains of servitude while his brethren boast loudly of their freedom. He pressures his audience to contemplate this profound ontological question, "What is man?" Clothing himself in religious persona, Douglass hurls righteous indignation at the audience's (and by extension the nation's) apathetic response to the black race's cry for freedom and need to be counted as fully-functioning human beings. Douglass declares that all men want to free and to actualize their inalienable rights. He asks his audience a litany of questions, including, "Must I undertake to prove that the slave is a man?" Taking on the burden of his enslaved brethren, Douglass lays out a brilliant argument that advances the proposition and conclusion: the slave is a moral, intellectual, and responsible being. Professing to take the moral high ground, Douglass insists every man is entitled to liberty because he is entitled to it by virtue of the Creator. He implores his audience to see that it is morally wrong to make men brutes.

Douglass concludes that there can be no legitimacy in the celebration of the Fourth of July until independence, freedom, and justice abide for all. And until such time, Douglass holds out with his signature eternal optimism—that with the maturity of the nation the citizens will not walk in mental darkness but will work toward the downfall of slavery. He believes two incontrovertible forces will command it: spiritual providence and the eternal bridge of brotherhood. Douglass proclaims a hope in the transformative power of the nation's ability to aspire to its highest ideals. He is certain that through providential interventions and human understanding, the nation will realize its true greatness; it will abandon its hypocritical allegiance to slavery and will ultimately work diligently to embrace the true democratic principle of equality for all men.

Further Reading

Deacon, Andrea. "Navigating 'The Storm, the Whirlwind, and the Earthquake': Re-Assessing Frederick Douglass, the Orator." *The Rocky Mountain Review of Language and Literature* 57, no. 1 (2003): 65–83.

Foner, Philip S. *The Life and Writings of Frederick Douglass*, Vol. II. New York: International Publishers, 1950, 181–204.

McClure, Kevin R. "Frederick Douglass's Use of Comparison in His Fourth of July Oration: A Textual Criticism." *Western Journal of Communication*, 64, 4 (September 1, 2000): 1057–0314.

—*Delores P. Aldridge*

Women's Suffrage

The fight for women's suffrage began in 1848 when the **Seneca Falls Convention** issued the "Declaration of Sentiments" demanding female franchise. The ideological and social background began earlier when individuals such as Mary Wollstonecraft and Margaret Fuller explored various ways culture exploited women. As the founding fathers gathered to write the new Constitution, Abigail Adams unsuccessfully lobbied her husband to include rights for women. Antebellum America was rife with vibrant and varied reform movements including antislavery, improvement in education, and temperance movements. Women were involved in all these movements and some became frustrated by the way the men treated them. Eventually women began to feel a common awareness of grievances based on gender and became frustrated with their isolation from political and economic life. At the World's Anti-Slavery Convention in London in 1840, Lucretia Mott and Elizabeth Cady Stanton were not seated because they were women. The two women resolved to have a convention to discuss ways in which women were discriminated against.

Frederick Douglass was known as a "woman's rights man" because of his long-term commitment to and strong involvement in the nineteenth-century women's suffrage movement. He took great pride and satisfaction that his dedication to this political cause had earned him this label. From the earliest days of the movement up to the end of his life, Douglass played a dynamic role in this fight for justice on behalf of women. Many other African American women and men were involved in the struggle to enfranchise women. Abolitionists such as Frances Ellen Watkins Harper, Charles Remond Douglass, **Sojourner Truth**, Robert Purvis, Sarah Remond, George T. Downing, and James Forten, Sr., joined Douglass in advancing the idea that women were entitled to vote as citizens. The participation, thoughts, and activities of many African Americans are often overshadowed by a focus on the political activities, organizations, and views of elite white women such as Elizabeth Cady Stanton and **Susan B. Anthony**, two pioneering leaders and organizers of the women's suffrage movement. Nonetheless, African American men and women made significant contributions to the cause of securing the right to vote for women.

In 1848 at a Wesleyan Chapel in Seneca Falls, New York, the first Woman's Rights Convention met with 300 women and men attending, including Frederick Douglass. Lucretia Mott and Elizabeth Cady Stanton helped to organize this meeting. The convention produced 12 resolutions including property and divorce reform and improved educational opportunities. The most radical proposal was the ninth, the demand for women's suffrage. This was so controversial that the women debated among themselves whether to include it. When Elizabeth Cady Stanton needed an ally to support her resolution calling on women to demand the right to vote, she turned to Frederick Douglass, and he did not disappoint her. It was soon clear that Lucretia Mott and others were initially uneasy with the women's suffrage resolution. After Stanton made a motion for the adoption of her women's suffrage resolution, Douglass used his considerable oratorical talent to argue in favor of the resolution when it appeared vulnerable to being defeated. Additionally, he is on record as having seconded Stanton's motion. Douglass argued that only through suffrage could women have full equality. His passionate encouragement swayed the debate and the resolution narrowly passed. It is interesting to note that all of the other resolutions introduced at this convention were passed unanimously; the women's suffrage resolution passed only by a small margin. Public reaction to the convention was furiously negative. People accused the women of wanting to destroy the family and American society.

Frederick Douglass supported women's rights well before the Seneca Falls Convention. In 1847, a year before the convention, the masthead of his newspaper, the *North Star*, contained a declaration that a person's entitlement to rights is not determined by either sex or color. In a variety of ways, Douglass used his paper, the *North Star*, in his effort to promote women's rights. The *North Star* became a forum for the new movement. He wrote favorable and sympathetic accounts of the annual women's rights conventions, published the proceedings of these conventions, and wrote supportive editorials. In many respects, the *North Star* served as an important means of communication for the women's rights movement. In addition to writing about the movement, Frederick Douglass rarely missed the annual women's rights conventions. He was a featured speaker at many of these meetings throughout the 1850s up until they were interrupted by the Civil War.

In the decade leading to the Civil War, there was a great deal of overlap between members and leaders of different reform movements. During the war, leaders for female suffrage suspended agitation and concentrated on winning the war and on antislavery activity. The end of the Civil War and the debate over black and female suffrage created a great schism between former friends and allies, and for two decades the United States had two rival national women's suffrage groups. Prior to the schism in 1866, Douglass was selected to serve as one of three vice presidents of the American Equal Rights Association (AERA), whose goal was securing the right of suffrage for all blacks and white women (universal suffrage). This organization was short-lived because of disagreement over whether or not to support the Fifteenth Amendment, and it eventually collapsed in 1869. Ensuring the vote for African American men was the lynchpin of Reconstruction.

When **Republicans** wrote the Fourteenth and **Fifteenth Amendment**s, it included black male suffrage but not the franchise for female suffrage. The Fifteenth Amendment disallowed federal and state governments from denying or abridging the right to vote on account of race, color, or previous condition of servitude. This amendment did not, however, affirmatively confer the right to vote to anyone as interpreted in 1876 by the United States Supreme Court in *United States vs. Reese*. Frederick Douglass was in favor of the ratification of the Fifteenth Amendment, despite its limitations. Like many others, he would have preferred that Congress would have been willing to go much further in expanding, affirming, and protecting the right to vote.

Frederick Douglass, Lucy Stone, and Henry Blackwell, among others supported the strategy of securing black male suffrage first and women's suffrage later. Douglass argued that black suffrage must be given priority to ensure black equality not only in politics, but in all aspects of American life.

One faction of the women's suffrage movement led by Elizabeth Cady Stanton and Susan B. Anthony was unequivocal in its opposition to the Fifteenth Amendment because the Amendment did not prohibit sex discrimination along with racial discrimination in the area of voting. They argued that if the nation could not accommodate women's suffrage and black suffrage at the same time, then the enfranchisement of (white) women must be given priority. Eventually, the Stanton-Anthony faction of the women's suffrage movement left the AERA and created a new suffrage association called the National Woman's Rights Association (NWSA) in 1869. The NWSA opposed the Fifteenth Amendment and worked to defeat it. This move represented the end of white suffragists linking women's suffrage and black suffrage.

Another faction of the women's suffrage movement formed the American Woman's Suffrage Association (AWSA), also in 1869. Lucy Stone and Henry Ward Beecher were behind this organization which favored the ratification of the Fifteenth Amendment. These two rival associations (the NWSA and the AWSA) remained separate and apart for over 20 years before they were able to put aside their differences and merge together to form the **National American Woman Suffrage Association (NAWSA)** in 1890. By the mid-1890s four states had franchised women, Wyoming, Colorado, Idaho, and Utah. Several states had granted partial suffrage. Still resistance was strong to female suffrage. Many Americans believed that women's proper place was in the domestic sphere. Suffragists developed a new strategy using the concept of moral and welfare reform based on a woman's proper role as wife, mother, and nurturer. Instead of arguing for suffrage based on equality, they articulated the moralizing influence women voters would have on American society. This strategy caused the powerful liquor industry to oppose female suffrage, as they feared women would vote for prohibition. Business and factory owners resisted women voting because they feared losing their profitable child and female labor. Southerners had a whole different set of reasons to oppose women's suffrage.

Southern states had successfully disfranchised African American men by rewriting their state constitutions and implementing tactics such as grandfather clauses, poll taxes, and residency requirements. Southerners did not want black women voting. When most African American men were disenfranchised by the 1890s, the women's suffrage movement was silent. Its leaders did virtually nothing as a movement to show either solidarity with disenfranchised African American voters or to challenge this political situation. This indifference to or disregard for black suffrage was not limited to black male disenfranchisement. They were equally as silent when African American women were disenfranchised after the 1920s.

Most black women sided with Frederick Douglass and his views of the meaning and significance of the Fifteenth Amendment for the African American community. Douglass argued that even though the Fifteenth Amendment did not go far enough in expanding the franchise, it nonetheless was a step in the right direction. It represented a defeat to those who wanted to continue to restrict suffrage to a select few white men, and it was an important symbolic victory that would set a vital precedent for the eventual establishment of universal suffrage. Moreover, Douglass conceptualized the Fifteenth Amendment as a necessary tool to be used to protect and defend African Americans from the reign of terrorism that they were confronting throughout the South. In the final analysis, Frederick Douglass saw the Fifteenth Amendment as a defeat for those who wanted to keep African Americans out of the political arena.

Despite the conflict between the various factions within the women's suffrage movement, Douglass remained devoted to the struggle and to the idea of securing the right to vote for women. He continued his advocacy on behalf of this cause in a number of different ways: He attended and participated in their national meetings; he affiliated with their organizations such as NWSA, AWSA, and eventually the NAWSA; and he continued to use his formidable public speaking talents on behalf of women's suffrage. His commitment to equal suffrage rights was not, however, reciprocated by many in the women's suffrage movement.

For the rest of his life, Frederick Douglass remained a leading figure in the struggle to expand suffrage rights. Frederick Douglass was remembered with great appreciation by many of the advocates of women's suffrage because of his long-term dedication to this goal. He remained a women's rights man to the end of his life.

Further Reading

Du Bois, Ellen Carol. *Feminism and Suffrage: The Emergence of an Independent Women's Movement in America, 1848–1869.* Ithaca, N.Y.: Cornell University Press, 1978.

Flexner, Eleanor. *Century of Struggle: The Woman's Rights Movement in the United States.* Cambridge, Mass.: Belknap Press of Harvard University Press, 1959.

Foner, Philip S., ed. *Frederick Douglass on Women's Rights.* Westport, Conn.: Greenwood Press, 1976.

Gurko, Miriam. *The Ladies of Seneca Falls: The Birth of the Woman's Rights Movement.* New York: Schocken Books, 1976.

Quarles, Benjamin. "Frederick Douglass and the Woman's Rights Movement." *Journal of Negro History.* 25 (January 1940): 35–44.

Terborg-Penn, Rosalyn. *African American Women and the Struggle for the Vote, 1850–1920.* Bloomington: Indiana University Press, 1998.

—*Minoa Uffelman and Valethia Watkins*

World's Columbian Exposition (Chicago, 1893)

President Harrison appointed Frederick Douglass to the post of Minister Resident and General Consul to Haiti in 1889, where he was to represent the United States' efforts to secure a naval station in Haiti. He faced opposition from many Americans; many felt he did not heartily support the government's attempts at **imperialism in the Caribbean** through its propositions for leasing Môle St. Nicolas. Douglass resigned after holding the office for two years.

On January 2, 1893, now-ex-Minister of Haiti Frederick Douglass traveled to the World's Columbian Exposition in Chicago. The Haitian government had appointed Douglass to represent the Haitian Republic in Chicago at the World's Fair. It was there, in Jackson Park, that Douglass delivered a rousing lecture arguing for the humanity of Haitian people and confirming their willingness to make concessions that did not conflict with their country's constitution. During his lecture, Douglass drew parallels between the Haitian struggle for independence and that of the original promoters of American independence. In doing so, he emphasized Haiti's position as the only self-made black republic in the world, as well as the history, character, and the importance of Haiti's struggle from slavery to freedom and statehood. Douglass also reflected upon Haiti's potential influence on the destiny of black Americans, using Haiti as an example of a free and independent republic. Haiti's leadership did not escape criticism, being characterized as educated and overly ambitious politicians who created civil war, hindering the country's potential development.

Further Reading

Douglass, Frederick. *Lecture on Haiti*. Chicago, Ill.: Violet Agents Supply Company, 1893.

———. *Frederick Douglass: Selections From His Writings*. Foner, Philip S., ed. New York: International Publishers, 1945, pp. 41–44.

Gregory, James, M. *Frederick Douglass, The Orator*. Springfield, Mass.: Willey Company, 1893.

Foner, Philip S. *The Life Writings of Frederick Douglass, Volume IV: Reconstruction and After*. New York: International Publishers, 1955.

—Thabiti Lewis

Bibliography

Primary Sources

Douglass, Frederick. *Life and Times of Frederick Douglass, Written by Himself: His Early Life as a Slave, His Escape from Bondage, and his Complete History*. New York: MacMillan Publishing Company, 1982.

Douglass, Frederick. *My Bondage and My Freedom*. New York: Dover, 1969.

Douglass, Frederick. *Narrative of the Life of Frederick Douglass an American Slave*. New York: Kessinger, 2004.

Secondary Sources

Adler, David A., and Samuel.Byrd. *A Picture Book of Frederick Douglass*. New York: Scholastic, 2001. Original edition, 1993.

Anderson, Douglas. "The Textual Reproductions of Frederick Douglass." *CLIO: A Journal of Literature, History, and the Philosophy of History* 27.1 (1997): 57–87.

Andrews, William L, ed. *My Bondage and My Freedom*. Urbana: University of Illinois Press, 1987.

Andrews, William L. "Frederick Douglass, Preacher." *American* 54.4 (Dec.1982): 592–597.

———. "Reunion in the Postbellum Slave Narrative: Frederick Douglass and Elizabeth Keckley." *Black American Literature Forum* 23.1 (Spring 1989): 5–16.

———. "The 1850s: The First Afro-American Literary Renaissance." *Literary Romanticism in America*. William L. Andrews, ed. Baton Rouge: Louisiana State University Press, 1981. 38–60.

Archer, Jermaine O. "A Breathing of the Common Wind: Cultural and Political Expressions of African in Antebellum Slave Narratives: Frederick Douglass, William Wells Brown, Harriet Tubman, Harriet Jacobs." Diss., University of California, Riverside, 2004.

Awkward, Michael. "Negotiations of Power: White Critics, Black Texts, and the Self-Referential Impulse." *American Literary History* 2.4 (Winter 1990): 581–606.

Aymer, Margaret Patricia. "First Pure, Then Peaceable: Frederick Douglass Reads James." Diss., Union Theological Seminary, 2004.

Baxter, Geneva Hampton. "Narrative of the Life of Frederick Douglass: Its Context, Rhetoric, and Reception." Diss., Georgia State University, 2001.

Baxter, Terry Douglas. "Frederick Douglass' Curious Audiences: Ethos in the Age of the Consumable Subject." Diss., University of Iowa, 1998.

Becker, Helaine. 2001. *Frederick Douglass*. Woodbridge, Conn.: Blackbirch Press.

Bennett, Evelyn. *Frederick Douglass and the War against Slavery*. Brookfield, Conn.: The Millbrook Press, 1993.

Blassingame, John W., ed. *The Frederick Douglass Papers, Series One: Speeches, Debates, and Interviews*. 5 vol. New Haven, Conn.: Yale University Press, 1979–1992.

———. *The Frederick Douglass Papers, Series Two: Autobiographical Writings, Narrative of the Life of Frederick Douglass, An American Slave, Written by Himself*. New Haven, Conn.: Yale University Press, 1999 and 2001.

Blassingame, John W. and John R. McKivigan, eds. 2001. *Narrative of the Life of Frederick Douglass*. 3 vols. Vol. 1, *Frederick Douglass Papers: Autobiographical Writings*. New Haven, Conn.: Yale University Press. Original edition, 1845.

Blight, David W. .*Frederick Douglass and Abraham Lincoln: A Relationship in Language, Politics, and Memory*. Milwaukee: Marquette University Press, 2001.

———. *Frederick Douglass's Civil War: Keeping the Faith in Jubilee*. Baton Rouge: Louisiana State University Press, 1989.

———. "Keeping Faith in Jubilee: Frederick Douglass and the Meaning of the Civil War." Diss., University of Wisconsin, Madison, 1985.

———, ed. *Narrative of the Life of Frederick Douglass, an American Slave*. 2nd ed. Boston: Bedford Books of St. Martin's Press, 2003. Original edition, 1845.

Bloom, Harold, ed. *Frederick Douglass's Narrative of the Life of Frederick Douglass*. New York: Chelsea, 1988.

Borgstrom, Michael Kenneth. "Passing Fictions: Reading Identity in Nineteenth-Century America." (Frederick Douglass, Harriet E. Wilson, Harriet Beecher Stowe, Frances Ellen Watkins Harper, Nathaniel Hawthorne)." Diss., University of California, Davis, 2002.

Brawley, Lisa. "Frederick Douglass's *My Bondage and My Freedom* and the Fugitive Tourist Industry." *Novel: A Forum on Fiction* 30.1 (Fall 1996): 98–128.

Burchard, Peter. *Frederick Douglass: For the Great Family of Man*. New York: Atheneum Books for Young Readers, 2003.

Burt, John. "Learning To Write: The Narrative of Frederick Douglass." *Western Humanities Review* 42.4 (Winter 1988): 330–344.

Carson, Sharon. "Shaking the Foundation: Liberation Theology in Narrative of the Life of Frederick Douglass."*Religion and Literature* 24.2 (Summer 1992).

Cassuto, Leonard. "Frederick Douglass and the Work of Freedom: Hegel's Master-Slave Dialectic in the Fugitive Slave Narrative." *Prospects: An Annual Journal of American Cultural Studies* 21 (1996): 229–59.

Castellanos, Maria Susana. "Sentiment, Manhood, and the Legitimation of American Expansion, 1820–1860 (James Fenimore Cooper, Ned Buntiline, Harriet Beecher Stowe, Frederick Douglass, Maria S. Cummins)." Diss., Brown University, 2000.

Castronovo, Russ. " 'As to Nation, I Belong to None': Ambivalence, Disapora, and Frederick Douglass." *American Transcendental Quarterly* 9.3 (Sept. 1995): 245–60.

Chesebrough, David B. *Frederick Douglass : Oratory from slavery*. Great American Orators no. 26. Westport, Conn.: Greenwood Press, 1998.

Chesnutt, Charles Waddell. *Frederick Douglass*. Mineola, N.Y.: Dover Publications, 2002. Original edition, 1899.

Coleman, Beth. "The Art of Disappearance: Autobiography, Race, and Technology (Jean-Jacques Rousseau, Frederick Douglass, Norbert Wiener, Flippo Tommaso Marinetti, Italy)." Diss., New York University, 2004.

Collier, James Lincoln and Greg Copeland. *The Frederick Douglass You Never Knew*. New York: Children's Press, 2003.

Davis, Matthew Reid. "Nineteenth-Century Rhetorics of American Brotherhood (Frederick Douglass, Martin Delany, Louisa May Alcott, Thomas Dixon, William Dean Howells, Edward Bellamy)." Diss., University of Washington, 2000.

Davis, Reginald Fitzgerald. "A Critical Analysis of Selected Theories of the Philosophical and Theological Development of Frederick Douglass." Diss., Florida State University, 1997.

DeLombard, Jeannine Marie. "Eye-Witness to the Cruelty: Literary Abolitionism and the Antebellum Culture of Testimony (Harriet Beecher Stowe, Frederick Douglass, Harriet Jacobs)." Diss., University of Pennsylvania, 1998.

———. " 'Eye-Witness to the Cruelty': Southern Violence and Northern Testimony in Frederick Douglass's 1845 Narrative." *American Literature* 73.2 (2001): 245–75.

De Pietro, Thomas. "Vision and Revision in the Autobiographies of Frederick Douglass." *College Language Association Journal* 26.4 (June 1983): 384–396.

Diedrich, Maria. *Love Across the Color Lines: Ottilie Assing and Frederick Douglass.* New York: Hill and Wang, 2000.

Diller, Christopher Glen. "Aesthetic Gymnastics (Ralph Waldo Emerson, Henry Noble Day, Harriet Beecher Stowe, Frederick Douglass, William Dean Howells)." Diss., University of Utah, 1999.

Dorsey, Peter A. "Becoming the Other: The Mimesis of Metaphor in Douglass's *My Bondage and My Freedom.*"*PMLA: Publications of the Modern Language Association of America* 111.3 (May 1996): 435–50.

Dudley, David L. "Teaching Douglass's Narrative in the World Literature Survey." *Approaches to Teaching Narrative of the Life of Frederick Douglass.* James C. Hall, ed. New York: Modern Language Association, 1999. 133–38.

Dunbar-Odom, Donna. " 'Mastering' Representation: Rhetorical Constructions of the Life of Frederick Douglass." *Conference of College Teachers of English Studies* (CCTEP) 55 (1995): 26–32.

Dupuy, Edward J. "Linguistic Mastery and the Garden of the Chattel in Frederick Douglass' *Narrative.*" *Mississippi Quarterly* 44.1 (Winter 1990–1991): 23–33.

Ernest, John. "Qualified Knowledge: Douglass and Harriet Jacobs." *Approaches to Teaching Narrative of the Life of Frederick Douglass.* James C. Hall, ed. New York: Modern Language Association, 1999. 110–16.

Fichtelberg, Joseph. "The Writer against Himself: Child and Man in the Autobiographies of Frederick Douglass." *Mid-Hudson Language Studies* 12.1 (1989): 72–80.

Fishkin, Shelley Fisher, and Carla L. Peterson. " 'We Hold These Truths to Be Self-Evident': The Rhetoric of Frederick Douglass's Journalism." *Frederick Douglass: New Literary and Historical Essays.* Eric J. Sundquist, ed. Cambridge: Cambridge University Press, 1991. 189–204.

Fleming, Alice Mulcahey. *Frederick Douglass: From Slave to Statesman.* New York: PowerKids Press, 2004.

Folsom, Ed. "Portrait of the Artist as a Young Slave: Douglass's Frontispiece Engravings." In *Approaches to Teaching Narrative of the Life of Frederick Douglass.* James C. Hall, ed. New York: Modern Language Association, 1999. 55–65.

Foner, Philip S., ed.*Frederick Douglass on Slavery and the Civil War: Selections from His Writings.* New York: Dover Publications, 2003. Original edition, 1945.

———, ed. *Frederick Douglass on Women's Rights.* Westport, Conn.: Greenwood Press, 1976.

Foner, Philip S. *Frederick Douglass.* New York: Citadel Press, 1950.

———. *The Life and Writings of Frederick Douglass: Early Years 1817–1849*. New York: International Publishers, 1950.

———. *The Life and Writings of Frederick Douglass: Pre-Civil War Decade 1850–1860*. New York: International Publishers, 1950.

———. *The Life and Writings of Frederick Douglass: The Civil War 1861–1865*. New York: International Publishers, 1952.

———. *The Life and Writings of Frederick Douglass: Reconstruction and After*. New York: International Publishers, 1955.

Franchot, Jenny. "The Punishment of Esther: Frederick Douglass and the Constitution of the Feminine." *Frederick Douglass: New Literary and Historical Essays*. Eric J. Sundquist, ed. Cambridge: Cambridge University Press, 1991. 41–65.

Gates, Henry-Louis, Jr. "Binary Oppositions in Chapter One of *Narrative of the Life of Frederick Douglass an American Slave Written by Himself*." *Afro-American Literature: The Reconstruction of Instruction*. Dexter Fisher and Robert B. Stepto, eds. New York: Modern Language Association of America, 1979. 212–32.

Gibson, Donald B. "Christianity and Individualism: (Re)-Creation and Reality in Frederick Doulgass's Representation of Self." *African American Review* 26.4 (Winter 1992): 591–603.

———. "Faith, Doubt, and Apostasy: Evidence of Things Unseen in Frederick Douglass's *Narrative*." *Frederick Douglass: New Literary and Historical Essays*. Eric J. Sundquist, ed. Cambridge: Cambridge University Press, 1991. 84–98.

Goddu, Teresa A., and Craig V. Smith. "Scenes of Writing in Frederick Douglass's *Narrative*: Autobiography and the Creation of Self." *The Southern Review* 25.4 (Autumn 1989): 822–840.

Grandt, Jurgen Ernst. "Writing the Blackness of Blackness: African American Narrative and the Problem of Cultural Authenticity (Frederick Douglass, Jean Toomer, Jessie Fauset, James Baldwin, Toni Morrison)." Diss., University of Georgia, 2000.

Gregory, James M. *Frederick Douglass, the Orator*. New York: Apollo Editions, 1971.

Hakutani, Yoshinobu, and Robert Butler, eds. *The City in African-American Literature*. Madison, N.J.: Fairleigh Dickinson UP, 1995.

Hall, James C. *Approaches to Teaching Narrative of the Life of Frederick Douglass*. New York: Modern Language Association of America, 1999.

Hapke, Laura. "A Labor Studies Approach to Douglass's Narrative." *Approaches to Teaching Narrative of the Life of Frederick Douglass*. James C. Hall, ed. New York: Modern Language Association, 1999. 88–94.

Harder, Joseph A. "The Lincoln-Douglass 'Debate': Abraham Lincoln, Frederick Douglass and the Rediscovery of America." Diss., University of Virginia, 2004.

Henry, Peaches Marion. "Reference and Truth in Autobiography (Harriet Jacobs, John Henry Newman, Frederick Douglass)." Diss., Columbia University, 1997.

Hubbard, Dolan. " 'Ain't Gonna Let Nobody Turn Me Around': Reading the Narrative of Frederick Douglass." *The Intimate Critique: Autobiographical Literary Criticism*. Diane P. Freedman, Olivia Frey, and Frances Murphy Zauhar, eds. Durham, N.C.: Duke University Press, 1993. 265–71.

Huggins, Nathan Irvin. *Slave and Citizen: The Life of Frederick Douglass*. Boston: Little, Brown, 1980.

Jay, Gregory S. "American Literature and the New Historicism: The Example of Frederick Douglass." *Boundary 2: An International Journal of Literature and Culture* 17.1 (Spring 1990): 211–242.

Jehlen, Myra. "Literature and Authority." *Conversations: Contemporary Critical Theory and the Teaching of Literature*. Charles Moran and Elizabeth Penfield, eds. . Urbana, Ill.: Nat. Council of Teachers of English, 1990. 7–18.

Jenkins, Lee. " 'The Black O'Connell': Frederick Douglass and Ireland." *Nineteenth Century Studies* 13 (1999): 22–46.

Keenan, Sheila. *Frederick Douglass: Portrait of a Freedom Fighter*. New York: Scholastic Inc., 1995.

Kemerait, Judith Louise. "Routes of Freedom: Slave resistance and the politics of literary geography (Nat Turner, Harriet Beecher Stowe, Martin R. Delany, Frederick Douglass, Herman Melville)." Diss., Louisiana State University and Agricultural & Mechanical College, 2004.

Kibbey, Ann. "Language in Slavery: Frederick Douglass' Narrative." *Prospects: An Annual Journal of American Cultural Studies* 8 (1983): 163–182.

King, Jeannine Marie. "A new Millennium: Memory and Apocalypse in African-American Literature (Frederick Douglass)." Diss., University of California, Berkeley, 1999.

Klammer, Martin. "Teaching Douglass's Narrative in an Introductory Humanities Course." *Approaches to Teaching Narrative of the Life of Frederick Douglass*. James C. Hall, ed. New York: Modern Language Association, 1999. 123–32.

Lampe, Gregory Paul. "Frederick Douglass: Freedom's Voice, 1818–1845." Diss., University of Wisconsin-Madison, 1995.

Lee, Lisa Yun. "The Politics of Language in Frederick Douglass's *Narrative of the Life of an American Slave*." *MELUS: The Journal of the Society for the Study of the Multi-Ethnic Literature of the United States* 17.2 (Summer 1991–1992): 51–59.

Leverenz, David Frederick. "Douglass's Self-Refashioning." *Criticism: A Quarterly for Literature and the Arts* 29.3 (Summer 1987).

Levine, Robert S. "Uncle Tom's Cabin in Frederick Douglass' Paper: An Analysis of Reception." *American Literature* 64.1 (Mar 1992): 71–93.

Lewis, Richard O. "Romanticism in the Fiction of Charles W. Chesnutt: The Influence of Dickens, Scott, Tourgee, and Douglass." *College Language Association Journal* 26.2 (Dec. 1982): 145–171.

Lutz, Norma Jean. 2001. *Frederick Douglass: Abolitionist and Orator*. Philadelphia: Chelsea House Publishers.

McCaskill, Barbara. " 'Trust No Man!' But What About a Woman? Ellen Craft and the Genealogical Model for Teaching Douglass's Narrative." *Approaches to Teaching Narrative of the Life of Frederick Douglass*. James C. Hall, ed. New York: Modern Language Association, 1999. 95–101.

McCurdy, Michael, ed. *Escape from Slavery: The Boyhood of Frederick Douglass in His Own Words*. New York: Alfred A. Knopf, 1994.

McFeely, William S. *Frederick Douglass*. New York: W. W. Norton & Company, 1991.

McGregor-Scissum, Rachelle D. "The Positive Nature of Pain in Critical Reflection: Frederick Douglass's Understanding as Expansion of the Form of His Life in 'My Bondage and My Freedom' and 'Life and Times of Frederick Douglass.' " Diss., University of Alabama, 1996.

MacKethan, Lucinda H. "Huck Finn and the Slave Narratives: Lighting Out as Design." *The Southern Review* (Spring 1984) 20.2: 247–264.

———. "Metaphors of Mastery in the Slave Narratives." *The Art of the Slave Narrative: Original Essays in Criticism and Theory*. John Sekora and Darwin T. Turner, eds. Macomb: Western Illinois University Press, 1982. 55–69.

Mackey, William Jr., ed. *Narrative of the Life of Frederick Douglass, an American Slave.* New York: Barnes & Noble, 2002. Original edition, 1845.

Mailloux, Steven. "Misreading as a Historical Act: Cultural Rhetoric, Bible Politics, and Fuller's 1845 Review of Douglass's Narrative." *Readers in History: Nineteenth-Century American Literature and the Contexts of Response.* James L. Machor, ed. Baltimore: Johns Hopkins University Press, 1993. 3–31.

Martin, Waldo E. *The Mind of Frederick Douglass.* Chapel Hill, N.C.: University of North Carolina Press, 1984.

Matterson, Stephen. "Shaped by Readers: The Slave Narratives of Frederick Douglas and Harriet Jacobs." Karen L. Kilcup, ed. and introd.. *Soft Canons: American Women Writers and Masculine Tradition.* Iowa City, IA: U of Iowa Press, 1999. 82–96.

Maxwell, Barry Frederick. "Douglass's Haven-Finding Art." *Arizona Quarterly* 48.4 (Winter 1992): 47–73.

Meehan, Sean Ross. "Mirrors With a Memory: Nineteenth-Century American Autobiography and the Photographic Imagination (Ralph Waldo Emerson, Henry David Thoreau, Frederick Douglass, Walt Whitman)." Diss., University of Iowa, 2002.

Meer, Sarah. "Sentimentality and the Slave Narrative: Frederick Douglass' *My Bondage and My Freedom.*" *The Uses of Autobiography.* Julia Swindells, ed. London: Taylor & Francis, 1995. 89–97.

Meltzer, Milton, ed. *Frederick Douglass, in His Own Words.* San Diego: Harcourt Brace, 1995.

Miller, Keith D., and Ruth Ellen Kocher. "Shattering Kidnapper's Heavenly Union: Interargumentation in Douglass's Oratory and Narrative." *Approaches to Teaching Narrative of the Life of Frederick Douglass.* James C. Hall, ed. New York: Modern Language Association, 1999. 81–87.

Miller, Douglas T. *Frederick Douglass and the Fight for Freedom.* New York: Facts On File, 1988.

Mills, Bruce. "Teaching Douglass's Narrative in the United States Literature Survey." In *Approaches to Teaching Narrative of the Life of Frederick Douglass.* James C. Hall, ed. New York: Modern Language Association, 1999. 139–50.

Mixon, Wayne. "The Shadow of Slavery: Frederick Douglass, the Savage South, and the Next Generation." *Frederick Douglass: New Literary and Historical Essays.* Eric J. Sundquist, ed. Cambridge: Cambridge University Press, 1991. 233–52.

Montas, Roosevelt. "Rethinking America: Abolitionism and the Antebellum Transformation of the Discourse of National Identity (Ralph Waldo Emerson, Frederick Douglass, Charles Sumner, Hannah Crafts)." Diss., Columbia University, 2004.

Moses, Wilson J. "Dark Forests and Barbarian Vigor: Paradox, Conflict, and Africanity in Black Writing before 1914." *American Literary History* 1.3 (Fall 1989): 637–655.

———. "Writing Freely? Frederick Douglass and the Constraints of Racialized Writing." *Frederick Douglass: New Literary and Historical Essays.* Eric J. Sundquist, ed. Cambridge: Cambridge University Press, 1991. 66–83.

Nichols, William W. "Individualism and Autobiographical Art: Frederick Douglass and Henry Thoreau." *College Language Association Journal* 16 (1972): 145–58.

Nwankwo, Ifeoma Chinwe Kiddoe. "Cosmopolitan Consciousness: Inter-American Engagements in the Scripting of African-American and Caribbean Identities (Frederick Douglass, Mary Prince, Juan Francisco Manzano, Louise Bennett, Zora Neale Hurston, Paule Marshall, Barbados, Antigua, Bermauda, Cuba, Jamaica)." Diss., Duke University, 1999.

Olney, James. "The Founding Fathers—Frederick Douglass and Booker T. Washington." *Slavery and the Literary Imagination*. Deborah E. McDowell and Deborah and Arnold Rampersad, eds. Baltimore: Johns Hopkins University Press, 1989.1–24.

Passaro, John. *Frederick Douglass*. Chanhassen, Minn.: Child's World, 2000.

Patterson, Anita. "Doing More Than Patrick Henry: Douglass's Narrative and Nineteenth-Century American Protest Writing." *Approaches to Teaching Narrative of the Life of Frederick Douglass*. James C. Hall, ed. New York: Modern Language Association, 1999. 117–22.

Piper, Henry Dan. "The Place of Frederick Douglass's *Narrative of the Life of an American Slave* in the Development of a Native American Prose Style." *Journal of Afro-American Issues* 5 (1977): 183–91.

Phillips, Rachael. *Frederick Douglass: Abolitionist and Reformer*. Uhrichsville, Oh.: Barbour Publications, 2000.

Preston, Dickson J. *Young Frederick Douglass: The Maryland Years*. Baltimore: Johns Hopkins University Press, 1980.

Prioleau, Rachelle Charisse. "Combining Abolitionism and Women's Suffrage: The Agenda-Building Process and Discursive Strategies of Frederick Douglass." Diss., University of South Carolina, 2000.

Quarles, Benjamin. *Frederick Douglass*. New York: Atheneum, 1968.

Russell, Sharman Apt. *Frederick Douglass*. New York: Chelsea House Publishers, 1988.

Sale, Maggie. "Critiques from Within: Antebellum Projects of Resistance." *American Literature* 64.4 (Dec 1992): 695–718.

———. "To Make the Past Useful: Frederick Douglass' Politics of Solidarity." *Arizona Quarterly* 51.3 (Autumn 1995): 25–60.

Schultz, Elizabeth. "Incidents in the Life of Frederick Douglass." *Approaches to Teaching Narrative of the Life of Frederick Douglass*. James C. Hall, ed. New York: Modern Language Association, 1999. 102–09.

Sekora, John. "Comprehending Slavery; Language and Personal History in Douglass' Narrative of 1845." *College Language Association Journal* 29.2 (Dec 1985): 157–170.

———. "The Dilemma of Frederick Douglass: The Slave Narrative as Literary Institution." *Essays in Literature* 10.2 (Fall 1983): 219–226.

Shearer, Laura Baker. "The Work Force: Labor and Identity in American Lifewriting (Henry David Thoreau, Harriet Jacobs, Frederick Douglass, Lucy Larcom, Lizzie Wilson Goodenough)." Diss., University of North Carolina at Greensboro, 2003.

Sisco, Lisa. " 'Writing in the Spaces Left': Literacy as a Process of Becoming in the Narratives of Frederick Douglass." *American Transcendental Quarterly* 9.3 (Sept. 1995):195–227.

Steele, Jeffrey. "Douglass and Sentimental Rhetoric." *Approaches to Teaching Narrative of the Life of Frederick Douglass*. James C. Hall, ed. New York: Modern Language Association, 1999. 66–72.

Stepto, Robert B. "Narration, Authentication, and Authorial Control in Frederick Douglass' Narrative of 1845." *African American Autobiography: A Collection of Critical Essays*. William L. Andrews, ed. and introd. Englewood Cliffs, N.J.: Prentice Hall, 1993. 26–35.

———. "Narration, Authentication, and Authorial Control in Frederick Douglass' Narrative of 1845." *Afro-American Literature: The Reconstruction of Instruction*. Dexter Fisher and Robert B. Stepto, eds. . New York: Modern Language Association of America, 1979. 178–91.

———. "Sharing the Thunder: The Literary Exchanges of Harriet Beecher Stowe, Henry Bibb, and Frederick Douglass." *New Essays on Uncle Tom's Cabin*. Eric J. Sundquist, ed.. Cambridge: Cambridge University Press, 1986. 135–53.

———. "Storytelling in Early Afro-American Fiction: Frederick Douglass' 'The Heroic Slave.' " *The Georgia Review* 36.2 (Summer 1982): 355–368.

Stuckey, Sterling. " 'Ironic Tenacity': Frederick Douglass's Seizure of the Dialect." *Frederick Douglass: New Literary and Historical Essays*.Eric J. Sundquist, ed. Cambridge: Cambridge University Press, 1991. 23–46.

Sundquist, Eric J., ed. *Frederick Douglass: New Literary and Historical Essays*. Cambridge: Cambridge University Press, 1991.

Talbot County, Historical Society of. *Frederick Douglass Driving Tour of Talbot County, Maryland*. Easton, Md.: Historical Society of Talbot County, 2002.

Van Leer, David. "Reading Slavery: The Anxiety of Ethnicity in Douglass's *Narrative*." *Frederick Douglass: New Literary and Historical Essays*. Eric J. Sundquist, ed. Cambridge: Cambridge University Press, 1991. 118–40.

Voss, Frederick S. *Majestic in His Wrath: A Pictorial Life of Frederick Douglass*. Washington, D.C.: Smithsonian Institution Press, 1995.

Wald, Priscilla. *Constituting Americans: Cultural Anxiety and Narrative Form. New Americanists*. Durham, N.C.: Duke UP, 1995. Discusses *My Bondage and My Freedom* and its reception history.

Walker, Peter F. *Moral Choices: Memory, Desire, and Imagination in Nineteenth-Century American Abolition*. Baton Rouge: Louisiana State UP, 1978.

Wallace, Maurice. "Constructing the Black Masculine: Frederick Douglass, Booker T. Washington, and the Sublimits of African American Autobiography." *Subjects and Citizens: Nation, Race, and Gender from Oroonoko to Anita Hill*.Michael Moon and Cathy N. Davidson, ed. Durham, NC: Duke University Press, 1995.

Wardrop, Daneen. " 'While I Am Writing': Webster's 1825 Spelling Book, the Ell, and Frederick Douglass's Positioning of Language." *African American Review* 32.4 (1998): 649–60.

Warren, Kenneth W. "Frederick Douglass's Life and Times: Progressive Rhetoric and the Problem of Constituency." *Frederick Douglass: New Literary and Historical Essays*. Eric J. Sundquist, ed. Cambridge: Cambridge University Press, 1991. 253–70.

Washington, Booker T. *Frederick Douglass*. Philadelphia: George W. Jacobs & Company, 1906.

Waters, Carver Wendell. 2002. *Voice in the Slave Narratives of Olaudah Equiano, Frederick Douglass, and Solomon Northrup*. Lewiston, N.Y.: Edwin Mellen Press.

Weidt, Maryann N. and Jeni Reeves. *Voice of Freedom: A Story About Frederick Douglass*. Minneapolis: Carolrhoda Books, 2001.

Welch, Catherine A. 2003. *Frederick Douglass*. Minneapolis: Lerner Publications Co.

Wohlpart, A. James " Privatized Sentiment and the Institution of Christianity: Douglass's Ethical Stance in the Narrative." *American Transcendental Quarterly* 9.3 (Sept. 1995): 181–94.

Wortham, Thomas. "Did Emerson Blackball Frederick Douglass from Membership in the Town and Country Club?" *New England Quarterly* 65.2 (June 1992): 294–98.

Zeitz, Lisa. "Biblical Allusion and Imagery in Frederick Douglass' Narrative." *College Language Association Journal* 25.1 (Sept. 1981): 56–64.

Zilversmit, Arthur. "Douglass's 'Perplexing Difficulty.' " *Approaches to Teaching Narrative of the Life of Frederick Douglass*. James C. Hall, ed. New York: Modern Language Association, 1999. 49–54.

Repositories

Library of Congress

Frederick Douglass Papers

The Library of Congress holds the bulk of Douglass's personal papers.

Boston Public Library

Anti-Slavery Manuscripts

The Boston Public Library holds the papers of many antislavery activists based in Boston, including letters by William Lloyd Garrison and Maria Weston Chapman.

Rush Rhees Library, University of Rochester

Frederick Douglass Papers

Isaac and Amy Post Family Papers

Porter Family Papers

The Rush Rhees Library contains the papers of antislavery activists based in Rochester, New York, and includes some documents relevant to the Underground Railroad.

Bird Special Collections, Syracuse University

Gerrit Smith Papers

Library of Maryland History, Maryland Historical Society

Lloyd Papers

The Lloyd Papers contain information about Douglass's life as a slave, including the closest approximation of his birthdate and lists of his siblings.

Web sources

Frederick Douglass

Thomas, Sandra. A biography of the life of Frederick Douglass. January 2007. http://www.history.rochester.edu/class/douglass/home.html. Accessed March 4, 2009.

WGHB Educational Foundation. Africans in America: People and Events—Frederick Douglass. http://www.pbs.org/wgbh/aia/part4/4p1539.html. Accessed March 4, 2009.

Berkeley Digital Library SunSITE. The Library, UC Berkeley. December 2004. http://sunsite.berkeley.edu/Literature/Douglass/Autobiography/. Accessed March 4, 2009.

A Short Biography of Frederick Douglass. Fremarjo Enterprises, Inc. February 2004. http://www.frederickdouglass.org/douglass_bio.html. Accessed March 4, 2009.

Frederick Douglass National Historic Site—Douglass' Life. http://www.nps.gov/archive/frdo/fdlife.htm. Accessed March 4, 2009.

Frederick Douglass Comes to Life. Fremarjo Enterprises, Inc. December 2004. http://www.frederickdouglass.org/. Accessed March 4, 2009.

America's Story from America's Library: Frederick Douglass. The Library of Congress. http://www.americaslibrary.gov/cgi-bin/page.cgi/aa/activists/douglass. Accessed March 4, 2009.

Frederick Douglass: Talbot County's Native Son. The Historical Society of Talbot County. May 2004. http://www.hstc.org/frederickdouglass.htm. Accessed March 4, 2009.

Frederick Douglass Family Foundation. http://fdff.org. Accessed March 4, 2009.

Western New York Suffragists: Biographies and Images—Frederick Douglass. Rochester Regional Library Council (RRLC). http://winningthevote.org/FDouglass.html. Accessed March 4, 2009.

Brooks, Amanda. Frederick Douglass. December 2008. http://www.geocities.com/genebrooks/frederick-douglass.html. Accessed March 4, 2009.

Frederick Douglass Biography Summary: Bookrags. http://www.bookrags.com/Frederick_Douglass. Accessed March 4, 2009.

Berkeley Digital Library SunSITE. The Library, UC Berkeley December 2004. http://sunsite3.berkeley.edu/Literature/Douglass/. Accessed March 4, 2009.

Definition of Douglass, Frederick in the Free Online Encyclopedia. Farlex, Inc. February 2009. http://encyclopedia2.thefreedictionary.com/Douglass%2c+Frederick. Accessed March 4, 2009.

Thomas, Sandra. The Slave Years. A Biography of the Life of Frederick Douglass. January 2007. http://www.history.rochester.edu/class/douglass/part1.html. Accessed March 4, 2009.

Rowser, Shirley A. Frederick Douglass. March 2001. http://www-distance.syr.edu/pvitafd.html. Accessed March 4, 2009.

Documenting the American South: Frederick Douglass. The University of North Carolina Library. The University of North Carolina Press. March 2009. http://docsouth.unc.edu/neh/douglass/bio.html. Accessed March 4, 2009.

Merriman, C. D. Frederick Douglass—Biography and Works. Jalic, Inc. 2008. http://www.online-literature.com/frederick_douglass/. Accessed March 4, 2009.

Today in History: September 3. The Library of Congress: American Memory. July 2008. http://memory.loc.gov/ammem/today/sep03.html. Accessed March 4, 2009.

Frederick Douglass. Africa Within Digital Library. http://www.africawithin.com/bios/frederick_douglass.htm. Accessed March 4, 2009.

Frederick Douglass, The Accurate "Without Struggle / No Freedom" Quote. January 2009. http://www.buildingequality.us/Quotes/Frederick_Douglass.htm. Accessed March 4, 2009.

Frederick Douglass: A Powerful Voice for Abolition and Equal Rights. Louisville Free Public Library. http://www.lfpl.org/western/htms/douglass.htm. Accessed March 4, 2009.

Frederick Douglass. The Free Online Encyclopedia. Farlex, Inc. February 2009. http://encyclopedia.farlex.com/Frederick+Douglass. Accessed March 4, 2009.

Frederick Douglass American Abolitionist. http://www.americancivilwar.com/colored/frederick_douglass.html. Accessed March 4, 2009.

Frederick Douglass: Historical Preservation Foundation. http://www.frederickdouglasshpf.org/. Accessed March 4, 2009.

Frederick Douglass Papers Edition. The Institute for American Thought: Indiana University-Purdue University Indianapolis. May 2008. http://www.iupui.edu/%7Edouglass/correspondence.html. Accessed March 4, 2009.

Frederick Douglass. http://library.thinkquest.org/3337/fdoug1.html. Accessed March 4, 2009.

Frederick Douglass. The Columbia Electronic Encyclopedia. Pearson Education, publishing as Infoplease. http://www.infoplease.com/ce6/people/A0815988.html. Accessed March 4, 2009.

Abraham Lincoln's White House: Frederick Douglass. The Lincoln Institute. http://www.mrlincolnswhitehouse.org/inside.asp?ID=38&subjectID=2. Accessed March 6, 2009.

Frederick Douglass: Online Resources. The Library of Congress. February 2009. http://www.loc.gov/rr/program/bib/douglass/. Accessed March 6, 2009.

Yahoo! Education Facts from the Encyclopedia: Frederick Douglass. The Columbia Encyclopedia, Sixth Edition. Columbia University Press, 2006. http://education.yahoo.com/reference/encyclopedia/entry/Douglass. Accessed March 6, 2009.

The Frederick Douglass Republicans. http://frederickdouglassgop.com/. Accessed March 6, 2009.

Frederick Douglass Teaching Scholars Program. Lock Haven University of Pennsylvania. http://www.lhup.edu/equity/frederickdouglass.htm. Accessed March 6, 2009.

Reuban, Paul. Chapter 3: Early Nineteenth Century- Frederick Douglass. PAL: Perspectives in American Literature—A Research and Reference Guide. http://www.csustan.edu/english/reuben/pal/chap3/douglass.html. Accessed March 6, 2009.

Frederick Douglass National History Site: Virtual Museum Exhibit. http://www.nps.gov/history/museum/exhibits/douglass/. Accessed March 6, 2009.

About the Editors and Contributors

The Editors

James L. Conyers, Jr., Ph.D., is the Director of the African American Studies Program, Director of the Center for the Study of African American Culture, and University Professor of African American Studies at the University of Houston. He is author or editor of more than 20 books and has recently co-edited the *Malcolm X Reader* with Carolina Academic Press.

Nancy J. Dawson is an independent scholar of Africana Studies residing in Tennessee. She has a Doctorate of Arts in Africana Studies from the University of Albany.

Julius E. Thompson was Professor of History and Black Studies at the University of Missouri at Columbia. He wrote or edited over 15 books with a research emphasis on African American life and history in Mississippi. Thompson received a doctorate of philosophy in history from Princeton University.

The Contributors

Najjar Abdul-Musawwir is an Associate Professor in the School of Art and Design at Southern Illinois University, Carbondale. He is also Vice President of the African-American Museum of Southern Illinois

Delores P. Aldridge is Grace Towns Hamilton Distinguished Professor of Sociology and African American Studies at Emory University, where she founded the first B.A. degree-granting program in Black/Africana Studies in the South in 1971.

Reynaldo Anderson is an Assistant Professor of Education at Harris-Stowe State University. His research and teaching interests are in Rhetorical Criticism, African American Studies, World Systems Theory, and Social Studies.

Stephen Andrews is an Associate Professor in the English Department at Grinnell College, where he teaches American Literature.

Lia Bascomb is a Ph.D. candidate in the African Diaspora program at the University of California–Berkeley. She holds an M.A. in African American Studies from UC–Berkeley and a B.A. in African American Studies from Yale University

About the Editors and Contributors

Mario H. Beatty is an Associate Professor and Chair of African American Studies at Chicago State University.

Russell Benjamin is an Associate Professor in political science at Northeastern Illinois University.

Jay Bishop is an Associate Professor and Chair of the History Department at the University of MarylandEastern Shore.

Beatrice Burton is a doctoral student in History at the University of Georgia. She studies race relations in the American South with an emphasis on the early grassroots modern civil rights movement.

Orville Vernon Burton is an officer of the Congressional National Abraham Lincoln Bicentennial Commission Foundation. He was the founding director of the Institute for Computing in Humanities, Arts, and Social Science (ICHASS) at the University of Illinois, where he is emeritus University Distinguished Teacher/Scholar and Professor of History in African American Studies and Sociology. He is also serves as a Senior Research Scholar and Associate Director for Humanities and Social Sciences at the National Center for Supercomputing.

Matthew Cheney lives in San Francisco, where he serves as managing partner of Chapter Three, an open source strategy and development company. He received his Masters of Science in Library and Information Science degree in 2005 at the University of Illinois at Urbana-Champaign, where he studied southern history with Dr. Orville Vernon Burton.

Malachi Crawford is a doctoral candidate in History at the University of Missouri, Columbia. He is also Assistant Director of the African American Studies Program at the University of Houston.

Donald Cunnigen is an Associate Professor of Sociology/Anthropology at the University of Rhode Island

Jane E. Dabel is an Associate Professor in the Department of History at California State University, Long Beach.

Alioune Deme holds a Ph.D. in Anthropology from Rice University and currently teaches African History at Texas Southern University in Houston, Texas.

Paul Easterling is program manager and adjunct faculty member of the African American Studies Program at the University of Houston. He is currently a doctoral candidate in Religious Studies at Rice University.

Kelton R. Edmonds is an Associate Professor of History at California University of Pennsylvania.

About the Editors and Contributors

Tyre Fante is an independent researcher residing in Omaha, Nebraska. She holds a Master's degree in African American Studies from the University of Iowa.

Stephen C. Finley is an Assistant Professor of Religious Studies and African American Studies at Louisiana State University, where he teaches courses in African American Religious Cultures, Theory, and Method in the Study of Religion.

Marisa J. Fuentes is a postdoctoral research associate in Women's Studies at the University of North Carolina at Chapel Hill. She received her Ph.D in African American Studies at the University of California–Berkeley.

Dwonna Goldstone is an Associate Professor of English at Austin Peay State University.

Lewis Gordon is a Professor in the department of Philosophy at Temple University.

Otis Grant is an Associate Professor in the Anthropology and Sociology departments at Indiana University at South Bend.

Bruce E. Johansen is Frederick W. Kayser Professor of Communication and Native American Studies at the University of Nebraska, Omaha.

Tekla Ali Johnson is an Assistant Professor of History at Johnson C. Smith University.

James Jones is an Assistant Professor of History and serves as coordinator of the history program at Prairie View A&M University.

Kareem Jordan is an Assistant Professor of Criminal Justice at the University of North Florida. He received his Ph.D. from Indiana University of Pennsylvania.

Maulana Karenga is a professor of Africana Studies at California State University, Long Beach.

Michelle Nzadi Keita is Poet-in-Residence and Assistant Professor of Creative Writing and English at Ursinus College. She holds an M.A. in Creative Writing from Vermont College and is A.B.D. in American Literature at Indiana University of Pennsylvania.

Gale Kenny is a Lecturer in the History Department at Rice University and holds a Ph.D. in History from Rice University.

Wilma King serves as Interim Director of the Black Studies Program at the University of Missouri, where she is Arvarh E. Strickland Professor of African American History and Culture in the Department of History and also has a joint appointment in Black Studies.

Theodore Koditschek is an Associate Professor of History at the University of Missouri, Columbia. He received his Ph.D. from Princeton University.

Gregory P. Lampe is a Professor of Communication at The University if Wisconsin, Rock County.

Andrew Ann Lee is an Associate Professor of Speech at Fort Valley State University.

Thabiti Lewis is an Assistant Professor of English at Willamette University

Monroe Little is an Associate Professor of History at Indiana University, Indianapolis.

Marilyn D. Lovett is an Associate Professor in Psychology at South Carolina State University. Her research is in cultural identity, dating violence, and substance abuse prevention.

John F. Marszalek is William L. Giles Distinguished Professor of History at Mississippi State University. He also serves as Director and Mentor of the Distinguished Scholars Program.

Emerson Mungin, Jr., is the Alfonza W. Davis Chapter Historian, Tuskegee Airmen, Inc., located in Omaha, Nebraska.

Everette B. Penn is an Associate Professor of Criminology in the School of Human Sciences and Humanities at the University of Houston, Clear Lake. He was a founding faculty for the doctoral program in Juvenile Justice at Prairie View A&M University.

Tracy S. Penn is an Associate Lawyer with Gardere Wynne Sewell, LLP. She earned a jurisprudence degree from the Thurgood Marshall School of Law.

Ivory Phillips is an Associate Professor of Social and Cultural Studies at Jackson State University.

Merline Pitre is a Professor and Dean of the College of Liberal Arts and Behavioral Sciences at Texas Southern University.

Tanya Price is an Associate Professor of Anthropology at the University of Missouri, Kansas City.

Oleta Prinsloo is an Assistant Professor in the History Department at West Virginia State University.

Sharon Pruitt is an Associate Professor of Art History at East Carolina University.

Reiland Rabaka is an Associate Professor of Africana Studies in the Department of Ethnic Studies at the University of Colorado at Boulder, where he is also an Affiliate

Professor in the Department of Women and Gender Studies and a Research Fellow at the Center for Studies of Ethnicity and Race in America (CSERA).

James Raymond III is an Assistant Professor of History at the University of Maryland–Eastern Shore.

Larry Ross is an Associate Professor of Sociology and Anthropology at Lincoln University.

Walter Rucker is an Associate Professor of African American and African Studies at Ohio State University.

Della Scott is an independent scholar whose research interests are African American literature, contemporary American literature, Women's Studies, and cultural and political history. She received a Master's degree in English from Simmons College and has taught African American literature at Boston University, Simmons College, and the University of Massachusetts at Boston.

Andrew Smallwood is Director of African American Studies and Assistant Professor of History at Austin Peay State University.

Dorothy V. Smith is the Conrad Hilton Endowed Professor of History at Dillard University. She has also served as Director of the Daniel C. Thompson–Samuel DuBois Cook Honors Program and as Outreach Coordinator at the National Endowment for the Humanities in Washington, D.C.

Gregory Stephens is a Lecturer in the Department of Literature in English at the University of West Indies at Mona.

Ronald J. Stephens is a Professor and Chair of the Department of African and African American Studies at the Metropolitan State College of Denver.

Christel Temple is Associate Professor of Africana Studies at the University of Maryland at Baltimore, an Honors College.

Ahati N. N. Toure is an Assistant Professor of Africana History and Black Studies in the Department of History, Political Science, and Philosophy at Delaware State University.

C. James Trotman is a Professor of English and Founding Director of the Frederick Douglass Institute at West Chester University. He is Convener for the Douglass Institutes on all 14 campuses of the Pennsylvania State System of Higher Education.

Minoa Uffelman is an Assistant Professor of History at Austin Peay State University.

Aswad Walker is a lecturer in the University of Houston's African American Studies Program. He is also Senior Writer/Editor at Texas Southern University, and serves as a pastor of the Pan African Orthodox Christian Church's southwest regional church in Houston, Texas.

Jerry W. Ward, Jr., is a professor of English and African American World Studies at Dillard University.

Valethia Watkins is an Assistant Professor in the department of African American Studies at Olive-Harvey College-City College of Chicago.

Robert E. Weems, Jr., is a Professor of History at the University of Missouri, Columbia. He received his Ph.D. from the University of Wisconsin, Madison.

Ronald Williams II Ronald Williams II is a doctoral candidate in the Department of African American Studies at the University of California–Berkeley. He holds a B.A. in political science from San Diego State University, an M.A. in Political Science from Howard University, and an M.A. in African American Studies from the University of California–Berkeley.

Index

Bold font indicates pages of main articles.

abolitionism:
    Abolition of Slavery Act, 52;
    British Antislavery Movement, **24–27**;
    Christianity, **34–35**;
    Civil Rights Acts, **35–36**;
    Crummell, Alexander, **39–41**;
    Fugitive Slave Act, **68–69**;
    in Germany, 74–75;
    in Great Britain, 78;
    in Haiti, 52;
    international, 164;
    newspapers, 150;
    North Star, **149–51**;
    Rochester, New York, **176–78**;
    supported by African American Presses, 8–9;
    works with Garrison, 1–2
abolitionists, **1–4**;
    African American, 213;
    black leaders as recruiters for Civil War, 65;
    Brown, John, 83–85;
    Clarkson, Thomas, 59, 78;
    Dickens, Charles, 151–52;
    Emerson, Ralph Waldo, **57–58**;
    Garrison, William Lloyd, **73–74**,73;
    Grimke, Angelina Emily, **81–82**;
    Industrial Education, **89–90**;
    in Jamaica, 153;
    in Massachusetts Anti-Slavery Society (MASS), **118–19**;
    Murray-Douglass, Anna, **124–25**;
    Nell, William Cooper, **146–48**;
    Pennington, James William Charles, **163–65**;
    Phillips, Wendell, 119, 136;
    Stanton, Elizabeth Cady, 16, 137, 141–42, 179, 212–16;
    Truth, Sojourner, **186–88**
Abolition of Slavery Act, 52
accommodationism, 132;
    opposed by Comité des Citoyens, 166;
    Washington, Booker T., **203–4**
advocacy, 172–76
Africa, **4–5**;
    Douglass's genealogy, 53;
    emigration to, 14–16, 39, 113–14;
    German Enlightenment, 75;
    Lincoln's relocation plan, 101;
    migration to, 5;
    misuse of anthropology, 52;
    trade with, 6
African Aid Society (AAS), **6–8**;
    arguments against African Civilization Society (ACS), 7;
    Garnet, Henry Highland, 72
African American Presses, **8–10**;
    North Star, **149–51**;
    reporting on lynchings, 9–10
Africana radicalism, 106, 108–9
Africana thought, 20–21
African Civilization Society (ACS), arguments against, 7
African diasporic thought, 20–21, 40, 148
African Methodist Episcopal (AME) Church, **11–12**, 13, 117;
    Douglass as minister, 120;
    newspaper of, 8
"Afro-Americans," 39
Afrocentricity, 23
agency, 23
Alexander, John, 208
Allen, Richard, **12–14**;
    founded AME Church, 11–12;
    Negro convention movement organizer, 114
American Colonization Society (ACS), **14–16**, 73;
    opposed by the AMEZ Church, 12
American Equal Rights Association (AERA), 138, 214
American Woman's Suffrage Association (AWSA), 137, 142, 215
Andrew, John, 65
annexation of Santo Domingo, 53, 87–89, 154–59, 183, 196, 205;
    supported by Douglass, 156–57

Anthony, Susan B., **16–17**, 137. *See also* women's suffrage; Fifteenth Amendment, 141; in Rochester, 177
anthropology, misuse of, 52
Anthropology from a Pragmatic Point of View, 74
Antilles. *See* Emancipation of the West Indies
"Aren't I a Woman?", 187
argumentation analysis, 173–76
artistic representations (of Douglass), 18
Asante, Molefi K., 23
assimilationism, 154; William Cooper Nell, **146–48**
Assing, Ottilie, 74, 125, 156
Attucks, Crispus, 144; memorial for, 147–48
Auld, Hugh, 116; Douglass's "black consciousness," 134; Douglass purchased from, 61
Auld, Lucretia, 127
Auld, Thomas, 32, 185–86

Baez, Buenaventura, 156
Bailey, Harriet, **19**
Bassett, Ebenezer, 157
Beecher, Henry Ward, 142, 215
Bernasconi, Robert, 74
Black Codes, **20**, 36, 166; U.S. Supreme Court, 197
"Black consciousness," 133–34
Black Existentialism, **20–24**
black invisibility, 23
Black Jacobins, The, 106
black leadership, 132
black male suffrage. *See* Fifteenth Amendment
Black Seminoles, 144–46
Black Skin, White Masks, 23
black suffrage. *See* Fifteenth Amendment
Blackwell, Henry, 214
Blaine, James, 158, 159
Blassingame, John W., 155
Blight, David, 2
Blumenbach, Johann Friedrich, 75

Bonaparte, Napoleon, 108
Booth, John Wilkes, 101
Boston Female Anti-Slavery Society, 118–19, 125
Bradford, Sarah E., 190
Brantley, Etheldred T., 192
Bright, John, 59
British antislavery movement, **24–27**; Abolition of Slavery Act, 52; other movements, 24
Brown, John, 3–4, 60, 95; in Rochester, 178; Tubman, Harriet, 189. *See also* Harpers Ferry
Brown vs. Board of Education, 166
Bruce, Blanche K., 169
Buchanan, James, 84
Buck-Morss, Susan, 75
Burchell, Thomas, 153
Butler, Benjamin, 101
"by any means necessary," 85

Caribbean: Lincoln's relocation plan, 101; "nuestra América," **152–61**; source of New England slaves, 185
Carmichael, Stokely, 85
Catholicism, **29**; Talbot family, 185
Chalmers, Thomas, 78
Chase, Salmon P., 2
Chicago World's Columbian Exposition, **216–17**
Child, David Lee, 143
Child, Lydia Marie, 143
childhood, **30–34**, 126–28; in Maryland, **115–17**; Methodism, 120
Christianity, **34–35**
"Church and Prejudice," 174
civil rights: after Civil War, 92; NAACP (National Association for the Advancement of Colored People), 131–33; and silver rights, 170; U.S. Supreme Court, **197–98**

Civil Rights Acts, **35–36**, 76, 92, 94; to assist former slaves, 197; Republican Party, **170–72**
Civil War: abolitionists, **1–4**; as abolitionist war, 4; black leadership in military, 66; black Seminoles, 146; black soldiers and Freedman's Bank, 67; British antislavery movement, 26; civil rights after, 92; Davis, Jefferson, **43–44**; Douglass on, 53; Emancipation Proclamation, **55–57**; Frederick Douglass, Jr. in, 45; Fugitive Slave Act, **68–69**; Harpers Ferry, **83–85**; Lincoln, Abraham, **100–102**; Lincoln, Mary Todd, **102–3**; Pennington, James William Charles, 164; problems for blacks in, 65; recruiting black servicemen for, 122; Sherman, William T., **180–81**; South Carolina, **181–82**; Tubman, Harriet, 189; women's and black suffrage, 140–41; women's suffrage, 17, 138
Clark, Pete Humphries, 12
Clarke, John Henrik, 5
Clarkson, Thomas, 59; in Great Britain, 78
Clay, Henry, 38
clergy: Allen, Richard, **12–14**; Garnet, Henry Highland, **71–72**; Grimke, Francis J., **82**; Pennington, James William Charles, **163–65**; Tubman, Harriet, **188–90**

Cleveland, Stephen Grover, 37–38, 169
Cobden, Richard, 59
Colored Patriots of the American Revolution, The, 147
Comité des Citoyens (Committee of Citizens), 166–67
Compromise of 1850, **38**
Compromise of 1877, 92
Confederacy:
  Davis, Jefferson, **43–44**, 181;
  South Carolina, **181–82**
Confessions of Nat Turner, The, 193
Constitution:
  maintains slavery, 119;
  pro-slavery document, 114, 210;
  state and federal rights, 77
"Coolie Trade," 156
Cornish, Samuel, 89
Corn Laws, 59
Covey, Edward, 13–14, 34, 116;
  battle with, 33–34, 128–29;
  Douglass's "black consciousness," 135;
  Methodist "slave-breaker," 120
Crummell, Alexander, **39–41**
Cuba:
  abolishing slavery in, 156;
  José Martí, 153;
  Sumner, Charles, 154
Cuffe, Paul, 15

Davis, Angela Y., 23
Davis, David Brion, 24, 75
Davis, Jefferson, **43–44**, 181
Davis, Reginald, 128
Declaration of Independence: as pro-slavery document, 210
"Declaration of Sentiments," 179–80, 212
Delaney, Martin R., 6, 7, 120, 177
Democratic Party:
  Johnson, Andrew, 195;
  supporting Stanton and Anthony, 141

Desdures, Daniel F., 166
Dickens, Charles, 151–52
Discrimination:
  aboard *Cambria*, 129;
  against Catholics, 29;
  Annie Douglass's education, 49–50, 178;
  Crummell on, 40;
  ending, on steamship line, 61;
  ending as theme of press, 8;
  Grandfather Clause, **76–77**;
  Interstate Commerce Act, 37;
  Jim Crow laws, **91–93**;
  Legal Rights Association (LRA), 164;
  public transportation, 164, 207;
  railroads, 117–18;
  religious, 117
disenfranchisement. *See* voting rights
Dominican Republic, annexation of, 53, 87–89, 155–57, 183, 196, 205
Douglas, Stephen, 95, 100
Douglass, Anna Murray. *See* Murray-Douglass, Anna
Douglass, Annie, **44**, 60
Douglass, Charles, 182, 208;
  portrait of, 65;
  worked on *North Star*, 150
Douglass, Frederick:
  Artistic Representations, **18**;
  childhood, **30–34**;
  My Bondage and My Freedom, **126–30**;
  portrait of, 18, 30, 47, 54, 115, 126, 173; 209,
  as "woman's rights man," 213–16
Douglass, Frederick, Jr., **45–46**, 182;
  portrait of, 45
Douglass, Helen Pitts, **46–48**, 60;
  portrait of, 46, 47
Douglass, Lewis Henry, **48–49**, 182;
  in Civil War, 65;

  in politics, 49, 196;
  portrait of, 49
Douglass Sprague, Rosetta, **49–50**;
  discrimination in school, 49–50;
  portrait of, 50;
  worked on *North Star*, 150
Dred Scott, decision, 157, 197;
  speech on, 173–74
Du Bois, W. E. B., 131, 132, 203;
  philosophy of, 22

Economics:
  Britain's interests in Africa, 7–8;
  Freedman's Savings and Trust Company, **67–68**;
  of slavery, 2, 78, 113;
  of slavery, in Mississippi, 121–22;
  of slavery and religion, 114;
  trade with Africa, 6;
  undermined by African Aid Society, 6–7
Eddy, Sarah J., 18
Education. *See also* Industrial Education:
  discrimination against daughter in school, 49–50, 91–92;
  importance of literacy, 21, 32–33;
  of Emerson, Ralph Waldo, 57;
  of Garnet, Henry Highland, 71;
  of Greener, Richard T., 80;
  manual and liberal arts, 39, 40;
  of Pennington, James William Charles, 163;
  of Washington, Booker T., 203–4
emancipation, 122, 199;
  in speech, 174;
  Tubman's work, 188–90
emancipation of the West Indies, 51–55
Emancipation Proclamation, 55–57, 118;

and black troops in military, 101;
opposed by Sherman, William T., 181
Emerson, Ralph Waldo, 57–58, 104
emigration, 6;
American Colonization Society (ACS), **14–16**;
"colonization," 157;
Delaney, Martin R., 120;
Douglass on, 15, 53;
and Greeley, Horace, **79**
Engels, Friedrich, 75
England, 59–60;
Crummell, Alexander, 39;
Dickens, Charles, 151–52;
lecture tours, 59–61;
World Anti-Slavery Convention, 119
equal pay, for serving in Civil War, 65–66
Estlin, John, 25
Ethiopian Manifesto, 113
European lecture circuit, 60–61;
discrimination on ship, 60;
in Great Britain, 78–79;
travels in England, 59–60
Evangeline: A Tale of Acadie, 104
Existentia Africana, 23
"Exodusters," 98;
"Kansas Exodus," 122
expansion. *See* imperialism
Eze, Emmanuel, 74

family:
daughter, Annie, **44**
daughter, Rosetta, **49–50**;
mother, Harriet Bailey, **19**;
portrait of daughter, Rosetta, 50;
portrait of grandson, 30;
portrait of son, Charles, 65;
portrait of son, Frederick, Jr., 45;
portrait of son, Lewis, 49;
portrait of wife, Anna Murray Douglass, 124;
portrait of wife, Helen Pitts Douglass, 46;
slavery's effects on, 200;
son, Frederick, Jr., **45–46**;
son, Lewis, **48–49**;
wife, Anna Murray Douglass, 116;
wife, Helen Pitts Douglass, **46–48**
Fanon, Frantz, 23
feminism. *See* women's suffrage
Ferguson, John H., 166
Feuerbach, Ludwig, 75
field slave, 116
Fifteenth Amendment, 37, **63–64**, 195, 197;
black men's versus white women's suffrage, 214–16;
Grandfather Clause, **76–77**;
Ku Klux Klan (KKK), 96;
Republican Party, 170;
women's suffrage, 138, 139
Fifty-fourth Regiment of Massachusetts Volunteer Infantry, 45, **64–66**, 118;
Charles Douglass serving in, 65;
South Carolina, 182
Finely, Robert, 14
Firearms manufacture, 83–84
First Confiscation Act, 101
Five Points, New York City, 152
Flipper, Henry O., 208
Florida, Native Americans in, 144–45
Foner, Eric, 68, 110, 154
Foner, Philip, 155, 156
founding fathers, 2, 210–11
Fourteenth Amendment, 35–36, 92;
and state sovereignty, 94
France: and L'Ouverture, Toussaint François Dominique, 107;
Napoleon Bonaparte, 108
Frederick Douglass's Paper, 150, 182
Free African Society (FAS), 11
Freedman's Bank. *See* Freedman's Savings and Trust Company
Freedman's Bureau, 195
Freedman's Savings and Trust Company (Freedman's Bank), 67–68, 92, 205;
Douglass as president of, 67;
Joint Committee of Fifteen, 93–94
Freedmen, Philanthropy, and Fraud, 68
Freedom, theory of, 21;
Black Codes, 92;
Fanon, Frantz, 23;
Grandfather Clause, **76**;
Latimer case, 119;
liberty and, 22, 30, 52;
Vesey and Douglass, 199;
"What to the Slave is Your Fourth of July?", **209–12**
Freedom Association, 147
Freedom's Journal, 89
Free Produce Movement, 6
Free Soil Party, 3, 147, 183;
Kansas-Nebraska Act, **95–96**
Fremont, John C., 101
Fugitive Slave Act, 6, 38, **68–69**, 95, 125, 173, 187;
Compromise of 1850, **38**;
Douglass flees from, 69
Fugitive Slave Law, 38;
speech, "Fugitive Slave Law," 173
Fuller, Margaret, 179, 213

Garfield, James A., 169, 205
Garnet, Henry Highland, **71–72**;
abolitionist, 71–72;
Brown, John, 84;
president of AAS, 6–7
Garrison, William Lloyd, 21, 35, **73–74**, 78, 117, 177, 185;
in England, 59;
grandson, Oswald Garrison Villard, 131–33;
Grimke, Angelina Emily, 81;
ideology of, 9;
Liberator, 99–100;
portrait of, 73
Garvey, Marcus, 41
gender:
and race, Fifteenth Amendment, **63–64**
German Enlightenment, 74–75
Gilroy, Paul, 21
Gordon, Lewis R., 23
Grandfather Clause, **76–77**

grandparents, life with, 31
grandson, portrait of, with Douglass, 30
  Grant, Ulysses S., 97, 180, 195;
  Ku Klux Klan (KKK), 155;
  on voting rights, 63
Great Britain, 78–79. *See also* England;
  and AAS, 6–7;
  and antislavery lectures, 2;
  British Antislavery Movement, 24–27;
  Douglass in, 25;
  World Anti-Slavery Convention, 119
Greeley, Horace, 79, 183
Greener, Richard T., 80–81
Griffiths, Julia, 25, 125
Grimke, Angelina Emily, 81–82
Grimke, Francis J., 82
Guinn vs. United States, 77

Haiti, 52–53;
  ambassadors to, 53;
  defender of, 160;
  Douglass in, 196;
  Douglass represents, 216;
  German Enlightenment, 75;
  imperialism in the Caribbean, 87–89;
  L'Ouverture, Toussaint François Dominique, 106–9;
  "nuestra América," 155, 157–58;
  portrait, Douglass in, 54;
  portrait, Haitian President Hyppolite, 158;
  racial affiliation with, 157–58;
  slave revolt inspires Vesey, 199–200
Harlem Renaissance, 85–86
Harper, Frances Ellen Watkins, 137, 138, 140, 142, 188
Harpers Ferry, 4, 60, 83–85
Harrison, Benjamin, 37;
  imperialism in the Caribbean, 88–89
Hayes, Rutherford B., 97, 169
Hegel, Georg, 75

History of Pan-African Revolt, A, 107
History of Woman Suffrage, The, 17
Howard University, 80
Hughes, Langston, **85–86**, 120
Hyppolite, Louis Mondestin Florvil, 157–58;
  portrait of, 158

imperialism:
  British Antislavery Movement, 26;
  in the Caribbean, **87–89**, 216;
  invasion of Nicaragua, 155;
  Manifest Destiny, **113–15**;
  used to abolish slavery, 155;
  war with Mexico, 153–54
imperialism in the Caribbean, **87–89**
Indians, and Manifest Destiny, **113–14**;
  Native Americans, **144–46**
Indios Mascogos, 146
Industrial Education, **89–90**, 132. *See also* education;
  Crummell, Alexander, 40
international diplomats:
  Greener, Richard T., 80–81
interstate commerce:
  discrimination by railroad, 117–18;
  Jim Crow laws, **91–92**
Interstate Commerce Act, 37

Jackson, Andrew:
  invaded Florida, 145–46
James, C. L. R., 106, 107
Jim Crow laws, **91–93**, 117, 204;
  and lynchings, 9–10
Johnson, Andrew, 181, 195;
  Reconstruction, 92, 93–94;
  views on voting rights, 63
Joint Committee of Fifteen, **93–94**
Jones, Absalom, 11–13
journalism:
  African American Presses, **8–10**;

Garrison, William Lloyd, 73–74;
  Greener, Richard T., 80;
  Liberator, **99–100**;
  National Anti-Slavery Standard, **143–44**;
  Nell, William Cooper, **146–48**;
  North Star, **149–51**;
  Stanton and Anthony's articles on suffrage, 141;
  Wells-Barnett, Ida B., 207–8
Juárez, Benito, 154

"Kansas Exodus," 122
Kansas-Nebraska Act, 79, **95–96**;
  Missouri Compromise of 1820, **123**
Kant, Immanuel, 75
KKK. *See* Ku Klux Klan (KKK)
Knapp, Issac, 99
Knibb, William, 153
Ku Klux Klan (KKK), **96–98**, 155;
  illegal lynchings by, 109–11

Langston, John Mercer, 171–172
Latin America, Douglass's relationship with, 153–54
Lawrence, Jacob, 18
Lawson, Charles, 34
lawyers:
  Greener, Richard T., 80–81
League of Women Voters. *See* National American Woman Suffrage Association (NAWSA)
lectures. *See* speeches
Legal Rights Association (LRA), 164
legislation:
  Civil Rights Acts, **35–36**;
  Compromise of 1850, **38**;
  Fugitive Slave Act, **68–69**;
  Kansas-Nebraska Act, **95–96**;
  Louisiana Separate Car Act, 165;
  Missouri Compromise of 1820, **123**;

"personal-liberty" laws, 69, 157
Legislative Council, 195
liberation theology, 128
Liberator, 9, **99–100**, 136;
    Grimke, Angelina Emily, 81
Liberia, 39;
    migration of freed slaves to, 15–16
liberty, and Emancipation Proclamation, **56–57**;
    freedom, 22, 30
"Liberty, Equality, and Fraternity," 52
Liberty Party, 3, 147
Life and Times of Frederick Douglass, The, 90
Lincoln, Abraham, **100–102**, 131, 180, 195;
    black migration to Africa, 114;
    Emancipation Proclamation, **55–57**;
    Fifty-fourth Regiment of Massachusetts Volunteer Infantry, 65;
    Lincoln, Mary Todd, **102–3**;
    "Oration in Memory of Abraham Lincoln," 175
Lincoln, Mary Todd, **102–3**;
    wife of Lincoln, Abraham, **100–102**
literacy, importance of, 32–33, 128–29;
    "black consciousness," 134
literacy tests, 139
literature:
    My Bondage and My Freedom, **126–30**;
    Narrative of the Life of Frederick Douglass, **133–37**;
    Notes on America, **151–52**
Longfellow, Henry Wadsworth, **103–4**
Louisiana, **104–6**;
    Grandfather Clause, 77
Louisiana Separate Car Act, 165
L'Ouverture, Toussaint François Dominique, **106–9**;
    as Africana liberation symbol, 108–9;
    frees Haiti, 51;
    "nuestra América," 157–58
lynchings, **109–11**, 203;
    by Ku Klux Klan (KKK), **96–98**;
    in Mississippi, 122;
    in speech, 174;
    U.S. lynching victims, 110;
    Wells-Barnett, Ida B., **207–8**

Manifest Destiny, **113–15**
Marshal, District of Columbia, 49, 64, 188, 196, 205
Martí, José, 153
Martin, Waldo E., 154, 160
Martinique. *See* Emancipation of the West Indies
Marx, Karl, 75
Maryland, **115–17**;
    Talbot County, **185–86**
MASS. *See* Massachusetts Anti-Slavery Society (MASS)
Massachusetts, **117–18**;
    Fifty-fourth Regiment of Massachusetts Volunteer Infantry, **64–66**
Massachusetts Anti-Slavery Society (MASS), 1, **118–19**;
    Garrison, William Lloyd, **73–74**
McFeely, William S., 159, 207–8
Methodism, 11, **120–21**;
    Allen, Richard, **12–14**;
    Truth, Sojourner, 186
Midgely, Clare, 25
migration:
    "exodusters," 98;
    from Mississippi, 122
military, 64–66;
    Black Seminoles, 145–46;
    Emancipation Proclamation, 101;
    French, in Haiti, 107–8;
    Harpers Ferry raid, 84;
    Sherman, William T., **180–81**;
    Tubman, Harriet, 189;
    West Point, **208**
ministers:
    Allen, Richard, **12–14**;
    Garnet, Henry Highland, **71–72**;
    Grimke, Francis J., **82**;
    Pennington, James William Charles, **163–65**
    Tubman, Harriet, **188–90**
Mississippi, **121–23**;
    Black Codes, **20**
Missouri Compromise of 1820, 95, **123**
Mohamed, Abdul Jan, 22
Môle St. Nicolas, 54, 88–89, 158–59
Monroe Doctrine, 88
Mott, Lucretia, 137, 179, 213
movements:
    abolitionist, 197;
    Douglass during time of, 200;
    national black convention, 171
Muhammad, Elijah, 41
Murray-Douglass, Anna, 45, 116, **124–25**, 136;
    family life, 125;
    in Massachusetts, 117;
    portrait of, 124
My Bondage and My Freedom, **126–30**;
    translated into German, 74–75

NAACP (National Association for the Advancement of Colored People), **131–33**;
    contemporary black leadership, 132
Narrative of Sojourner Truth, The, 188
Narrative of the Life of Frederick Douglass, **133–37**
narrative pathos, 173–76
National American Woman Suffrage Association (NAWSA), 17, **137–43**;
    women's suffrage, **212–16**
National Anti-Slavery Standard, **143–44**
National Association for the Advancement of Colored People (NAACP). *See* NAACP (National Association for the

Advancement of Colored People)
National Colored Labor Union (NCLU), 97, 171
National Convention of Colored People, supported Republican Party, 104–5
nationalism, 114;
    Delaney as "Father of Black Nationalism," 120;
    radical, 199–200
National Republican Convention, 166
National Woman's Suffrage Association (NWSA), 137, 142, 214
Native Americans, **144–46**;
    in New England, 148
Native Son, 22
NAWSA. *See* National American Woman Suffrage Association (NAWSA)
Nell, William Cooper, **146–48**
New England, **148–49**;
    colonial, 185;
    Rochester, New York, **176–78**;
    Talbot County, Maryland, **185–86**;
    Truth, Sojourner, 187–88
New York:
    New York City, 152;
    Rochester, **176–78**
Niagara Movement, 132
Nicaragua, 155
nonextensionism, 3
North Star, 129, **149–51**;
    as influence on antislavery movement, 2;
    against Kansas-Nebraska Act, **95–96**;
    Nell, William Cooper, 147;
    supports women's rights, 214
Notes on America, **151–52**
"Nuestra América," **152–61**

Observations on the Feeling of the Beautiful and Sublime, 75
"octoroon," 166
On the Natural Variety of Mankind, 75

oratory: Rhetorical Techniques, **172–76**;
    "What to the Slave is Your Fourth of July?", **209–12**
Osthaus, Carl R., 68
"Our Southern Sister Republic," 154
Outre-Mer: A Pilgrimage Beyond the Sea, 103
Outsider, The, 22–23
Ovington, Mary White, 131–32

Pamphile, Leon, 159
Panther and the Lash, The, 85
Patterson, Orlando, 75
Pennington, James William Charles, **163–65**
Personal Liberty Laws, 157
Phenomenology of Spirit, 75
Phillips, Wendell, 119, 136
philosophy:
    Africana radicalism, 108–9;
    agency, 23;
    antislavery, 2;
    Black Existentialism, **20–23**;
    black invisibility, 23;
    Crummell, Alexander, **39–40**;
    of Du Bois, 22;
    in *Frederick Douglass's Paper*, 3;
    German Enlightenment, **74–75**;
    nonextensionism, 3;
    phobogenic object, 23;
    of slavery, 107, 128;
    transcendentalism, 58
Philosophy of History, 75
phobogenic objects, 23
Pillsbury, Parker, 119
Pinchback, P. B. S., 105
Plessy v. Ferguson, 36, 93, **165–67**, 198
poetry, 85–86;
    Africa as iconic symbol, 4–5;
    Emerson, Ralph Waldo, 57–58;
    Longfellow, Henry Wadsworth, **103–4**
politics:
    "Bible politics," 3;

black men in, 64, 196;
colonial, New England, 148–49;
and Davis, Jefferson, **43–44**;
Democratic Party, 141, 195;
Douglass's dual allegiance, 196–97;
and Emancipation Proclamation, **55–57**;
Fifteenth Amendment as access, 215–16;
Free Produce movement, 6;
Free Soil Party, 3, 147, 183;
of imperialism in "nuestra América," 159;
Joint Committee of Fifteen, **93–94**;
Liberty Party, 3, 74;
Marshal, District of Columbia, 49, 64, 188, 205;
Radical Abolitionist Party, 3–4;
Recorder of Deeds, **169–70**;
Republican Party, **170–72**;
Sumner, Charles, **182–83**;
supporters of ACS, 15;
U.S. Senate, **195–97**;
of voting, 137–43;
Webster, Daniel, **206–7**;
Whig Party, 183
poll taxes, 20, 77, 97, 139
Presbyterians, 78;
    Pennington, James, **163–65**
presidents:
    Buchanan, James, 84;
    Cleveland, Stephen Grover, **37–38**;
    Davis, Jefferson, **43–44**, 181;
    Garfield, James A., 169;
    Grant, Ulysses S., 97, 155, 180;
    Harrison, Benjamin, 37, 88–89;
    Hayes, Rutherford B., 97, 169;
    Jackson, Andrew, 145–46;
    Johnson, Andrew, 63, 92, 93–94, 181, 195;
    Lincoln, Abraham, **100–102**, 169, 180, 195

public transportation:
discrimination in, 164, 207;
discrimination, Legal Rights Association (LRA), 164;
Jim Crow laws, 92;
segregation in, 147;
U.S. Supreme Court, **197–98**

Quakers:
assisted Sojourner Truth, 186;
in England, 179;
Grimke, Angelina Emily, **81–82**;
Lundy, Benjamin, 73;
Richardson, Ellen, 129

racism:
Black Codes, **20**;
and Black Existentialism, 21;
in editorials by Stanton, Elizabeth Cody, 141–42;
Emerson, Ralph Waldo against, 58;
Fifteenth Amendment defeats, 139;
and gender, voting rights, 63–64;
German Enlightenment, 74–75;
Jim Crow laws, **91–93**;
Ku Klux Klan, **96–98**;
Victorian, in Britain, 26;
voting rights based on race, 141
Rainey, Joseph, 196
Reconstruction:
Black Codes, 20, 36, 92;
Fifteenth Amendment and women's suffrage, 139–40;
Grandfather Clause, **76–77**;
Ku Klux Klan (KKK), **96–98**;
lynchings, **109–11**;
in Mississippi, 122;
Republican Party, 170;
Sherman, William T., 181;
Tubman, Harriet, **188–90**;
voting rights for black men, 214

Reconstruction Acts. *See* Civil Rights Acts
Recorder of Deeds, **169–70**;
Cleveland, Stephen Clover, 37
Redkey, Edwin S., 122
Redpath, James, 157
Red Record, A: Tabulated Statistics and Alleged Causes of Lynchings in the United States, 1892–94, 207
religion:
abolitionist Quakers, 73;
among slaves, 13;
Catholicism, **29**, 185;
Christianity, **34–35**, 114;
discrimination by, 117;
Jim Crow laws, 91;
to justify slavery, 128;
liberation theology, 128;
Methodism, **120–21**;
Society of Friends, 78;
speeches against, 175;
supporting slavery in England, 61;
"the Spirit," 191–93
Republican Party, **170–72**, 195;
and African American votes, 97;
civil rights, 196–97;
doctrine of nonextensionism, 3;
and Emancipation Proclamation, **56–57**;
Fifteenth Amendment and, 64;
Grandfather Clause, 76;
Joint Committee of Fifteen, **93–94**;
Lincoln, Abraham, 100–102;
and Massachusetts Anti-Slavery Society (MASS), 119;
"nuestra América," 154;
supported by National Convention of Colored People, 104–5;
supported Fifteenth Amendment, 63;
uses Douglass, 172
Revels, Joseph, 196
Rhetorical Techniques, **172–76**;

"What to the Slave is Your Fourth of July?", **209–12**
Richardson, Ellen, 129
Rigsby, Gregory, 40
Rochester, New York, 125, **176–78**
Ruggles, David, 8, 129, 136

Santo Domingo, annexation of, 53, 87–89, 154–59, 183, 196, 205;
supported by Douglass, 156–57
Scenes from the Life of Harriet Tubman, 189
segregation, 204;
Jim Crow laws, **91–93**;
in Mississippi, 122;
Plessy vs. Ferguson, **165–67**;
in public accommodations, 147, 164;
racial, and Ku Klux Klan (KKK), 96–98;
U.S. Supreme Court, **197–98**
"Seminole Maroons," 144
Seminole Wars, 145–46
Seneca Falls Convention, 143, **179–80**;
and NAWSA, 137;
women's suffrage, **212–16**
"separate but equal," 36, 93, 165–67, 198
Seward, William H., 178
Sheperd, Hayward, 84
Sherman, William T., 180–81
slave revolts:
Turner, Nat, **191–93**;
Vesey, Denmark, **199–201**
slavery, 1–2;
abolitionist theme of presses, 8–9;
Abolition of Slavery Act, 52;
affects on family life, 200;
argument against by Founding Fathers, 2;
asiento, 78;
"black consciousness," 133–34;
in Caribbean, 154–55;
childhood, 126–28;

Constitution as pro-slavery document, 114, 210;
"Coolie Trade," 156;
Crummell's opinion on, 40;
debated in England, 59;
economics of, 2;
Emancipation Proclamation, **55–57**;
escape attempt, 34;
escape from, 129, 135–36;
as field slave, 33–34, 116;
Fugitive Slave Act, **68–69**;
Harpers Ferry raid, **83–85**;
history of, and German Enlightenment, 75;
importance of literacy, 21;
and Kansas-Nebraska Act, **95–96**;
Latimer case, 119;
Lincoln, Abraham, **100–102**;
Lincoln-Douglas debates on, 100;
in Mississippi, **121–23**;
Missouri Compromise of 1820, **123**;
National Convention of Colored People, 105;
and Native Americans, **144–46**;
in the North, 116;
and "nuestra América," 153;
philosophy of, 107;
slaves as phobogenic objects, 23;
politics of, 2–3;
and Presbyterians, 78;
religion among slaves, 13;
"Slavery," chapter in *Notes on America*, 151–52;
in Spain, 78;
in speech, "Church and Prejudice," 174;
Thirteenth Amendment, 99;
Turner, Nat, **191–93**;
as war against Africans, 164;
working slave child, 31
Smith, Gerrit, 2;
Nell, William Cooper, 147
Society of Friends, 78
Song of Hiawatha, The, 104

South Carolina, **181–82**;
and Black Codes, **20**;
and Fifty-fourth Regiment of Massachusetts Volunteer Infantry, 66;
Grandfather Clause, 77;
Greener, Richard T., 80;
Rainey, Joseph, 196;
secession of, 100
"Southern Barbarism," 174
sovereignty, Haitian, 159
Spain:
slavery in, 78
Speeches:
"Aren't I a Woman?", 187;
"Church and Prejudice," 174;
"Crime Against Kansas," 183;
"Dred Scott Decision," 173;
"Fugitive Slave law," 173;
"Lesson of the Hour," 205;
"Oration in Memory of Abraham Lincoln," 175;
portrait of Douglass writing, 209;
rhetorical techniques, **172–76**;
"Southern Barbarism," 174;
"What to the Slave is Your Fourth of July?", 177, **209–12**;
"Woman's Suffrage Movement," 175–76;
at World's Columbian Exposition, **216–17**
Stanton, Elizabeth Cady, 16, 137, 179, 213;
Anthony, Susan B., 141–42;
Fifteenth Amendment, 141;
racism in editorials by, 141–42;
women's suffrage, **212–16**
states' rights, 76, 123;
Webster, Daniel against, 206
Stauffer, John, 3
Stearns, George L., 65
Stone, Lucy, 137, 142, 214;
women's suffrage, 215
suffrage. *See also* voting rights:

Douglass, Helen Pitts, 48;
and privileged whiteness, 2
suffragettes, 137
Sumner, Charles, 87, 105, 154, 156, **182–83**
Supreme Court. *See* U.S. Supreme Court

Talbot County, Maryland, **115–17, 185–86**
Taney, Roger, 197
Tariff Act of 1842, 79
temperance, 16–17;
Pennington, James William Charles, 164;
women's suffrage, 215
Text Book of the Origin and History of the Colored People, The, 163
Thirteenth Amendment, 35, 99
Tougee, Albion, 166
Tracy, Benjamin Franklin, 159
Train, George Francis, 141
Transcendentalism, 58
Travis, Joseph, 192–93
Treaty of Guadalupe Hidalgo, 38
Treaty of Mounltrie Creek, 145
Treaty of Payne's Landing, 145
Treaty of Utecht, 78
Trotter, William Monroe, 203
Truth, Sojourner, **186–88**, 213;
as suffragette, 137, 138
Tubman, Harriet, **188–90**
Turner, Henry M., 122
Turner, Nat, **191–93**
Tuskegee Institute, 203

Unconstitutionality of Slavery, The, 9
Underground Railroad, 125, 129, 177;
Nell, William Cooper, 147;
Tubman, Harriet, **188–90**
Union Mission Society, 163
United Colonies of New England, 148–49
United States vs. Reese, 76, 139, 214
universal emancipation,

championed by *North Star*, 149
U.S. Senate, **195–97**
U.S. Supreme Court, **197–98**;
and Civil Rights Acts, 36;
Dred Scott decision, 148, 157, 173, 197;
Jim Crow laws, 92;
Latimer case, 119;
Plessy vs. Ferguson, **165–67**;
United States vs. Reese, 76, 139, 214

Varick, James:
founded AMEZ Church, 11
Vesey, Denmark, **199–201**
Villard, Oswald Garrison, 131–33
vocational education. *See* Industrial Education
voting rights:
African American leaders, 213;
black male and white female suffrage, 138–43, 214;
Douglass on, 77;
Fifteenth Amendment, **63–64**;
formation of NAWSA to expand, 137–38;
Grandfather Clause, **76–77**;
and Ku Klux Klan, **96–98**;
reporting on, by *North Star*, **149–51**;
Seneca Falls Convention, **179–80**;

Voting Rights Act of 1965, 142

wage slavery, 59
Walker, David, 72
Walker, William, 155
Washington, Booker T., 90, 131, **203–4**;
accommodationism, 132;
opposed by Comité des Citoyens, 166
Washington, D.C., **205–6**
Webster, Daniel, 15, **206–7**
Wells-Barnett, Ida B., 110, 131, **207–8**
Wesley, Charles H., 150
West Indies:
emancipation of, **51–54**;
imperialism in the Caribbean, **87–89**;
Lincoln's relocation plan, 101
West Point, 43, **208–9**
"What to the Slave is Your Fourth of July? (The Meaning of July Fourth for the Negro)", **209–12**
Whig Party, 183
White, Charles, 18
white male supremacy:
Jim Crow laws, **91–93**;
Ku Klux Klan (KKK), **96–98**;
philosophy of, 75;
and voting rights, 35, 48, 141
white privilege, 141;

Jim Crow laws, **91–93**;
Ku Klux Klan (KKK), **96–98**
Wilson, J. Moses, 40
Wollstonecraft, Mary, 179, 213
Woman's Rights Convention, 213
women-first suffrage movement, 141–42, **214–15**
women's rights movement. *See* women's suffrage
women's suffrage, 118, **212–16**;
Fifteenth Amendment, **63–64**;
Garrison, William Lloyd, 74;
Grimke, Angelina Emily, **81–82**;
Seneca Falls Convention, **179–80**;
threatens family, 180;
Truth, Sojourner, **186–88**;
"Woman's Suffrage Movement," 175–76
Woodward, Charlotte, 180
World Anti-Slavery Convention, 119, 179, 213
World's Columbian Exposition, **216–17**;
Anthony, Susan B., 17;
"nuestra América," 157
Wright, Richard, 22

Young, Alexander, 113
Young, Charles, 208

Discarded
University of Cincinnati
Blue Ash College Library